£12

WATERLOO LETTERS

Waterloo Letters
is the twenty-fifth volume in the
Napoleonic Library

Eminent Napoleonic historians celebrate the publication of the twenty-fifth volume in the Napoleonic Library

The excellent work that Greenhill Books is doing by re-publishing so many long out-of-print classics on the Napoleonic Wars deserves the gratitude of every person fascinated by perhaps the most colourful period of all military history.

May the twenty-five re-published works (already probably a record for a series of this kind) become fifty in as short a time as possible and perhaps we may hope the series will reach one hundred volumes by the anniversary of Napoleon's death in 2021!

David Chandler

An excellent series – stories told by men who were there, who tramped the broken roads, went into the fire, and endured whatever Fortune sent – the raw beginnings of that era's military history.

John R. Elting

A most remarkable series that has made available a series of valuable primary sources at reasonable prices: Greenhill Books is to be highly commended.

Dr Charles Esdaile

The appearance of the twenty-fifth title in the *Napoleonic Library* is indeed a just cause for celebration. No matter how many new volumes of history are produced, the importance of the 'classics' remains: memoirs by participants in the Napoleonic Wars as well as seminal later histories. Every volume in the *Napoleonic Library* may be regarded in this light: not only the most famous memoirs like those of Coignet, Grattan, Marbot and Mercer, but some less well-known but just as valuable, from Barres, Blakeney and de Rocca; essential histories by the luminaries of the subject, from Clausewitz and Siborne to Fortescue, Oman, Petre and Weller; and even one memoir published for the first time, Webber's *With the Guns in the Peninsula*. It is not the content or existence of such works which is most significant, but the fact of their availability, for original editions are difficult and expensive to obtain, as will be testified by anyone who has searched long and hard for an elusive yet vital reference. By making readily available works which are truly essential reading, Greenhill Books deserves the gratitude of every Napoleonic enthusiast; and we await the next landmark in the series, hopefully the fiftieth volume.

Philip Haythornthwaite

Greenhill Books has performed an invaluable service for both the academic community and for those interested in the Napoleonic period by publishing a long list of extremely rare and valuable volumes. To my knowledge, there has never been such a concerted effort to produce a collection of this magnitude on the period. The efforts have been monumental, but the results have been equally monumental for all those interested in the Napoleonic era. Congratulations on publishing volume twenty-five in the *Napoleonic Library*; may we see another twenty-five titles in the next decade.

Donald D. Horward

The most frustrating thing to the modern student of the Napoleonic Wars is the scarcity of works in the English language. Greenhill Books has picked up this challenge and brought back twenty-five works, ranging from old war horses with long reputations (and equally long out of print) to less well-known, but fascinating period works. My hat is off to Greenhill for its sterling efforts. As I tried to fill out my Napoleonic library and found myself faced with a fruitless hunt of 'out of print' bookshops or simply contacting Greenhill, the choice was simple. ### *George F. Nafziger*

I congratulate Greenhill on the *Napoleonic Library*. I believe that the whole corpus of historical knowledge is better for the *Napoleonic Library*.

Jac Weller

WATERLOO LETTERS

Edited by
Major-General
H.T. Siborne

Greenhill Books, London
Stackpole Books, Pennsylvania

This edition of *Waterloo Letters* first published 1993 by
Greenhill Books, Lionel Leventhal Limited, Park House
1 Russell Gardens, London NW11 9NN
and
Stackpole Books
5067 Ritter Road, Mechanicsburg, PA 17055, USA

British Library Cataloguing in Publication Data
Waterloo Letters - New ed
I. Siborne, H.T.
940.27

ISBN 1-85367-156-8

Library of Congress Cataloging-in-Publication Data
available

Publishing History
*Waterloo Letters: A Selection from Original and Hitherto
Unpublished Letters Bearing on the Operations of the
16th, 17th, and 18th June, 1815, By Officers who served
in the Campaign* was first published in 1891 (Cassell)
and is reproduced now exactly as the original edition,
complete and unabridged. For this 1993 edition a new
Introduction by Albert A. Nofi has been added.

In reprinting in facsimile the maps from the original, any
imperfections are inevitably reproduced and the quality
may fall short of modern cartographic standards.

Printed and bound in Great Britain
by Biddles Limited, Guildford, Surrey

INTRODUCTION

Over 175 years after it ran its bloody course, the Campaign of Waterloo still manages to stir the imagination and emotions of many. And surprisingly, even after some two thousand books and numerous articles on the campaign and battle,[1] it remains remarkably controversial. It is not that the outcome of the great battle is in doubt, for that can hardly be questioned. Rather the arguments revolve around the question of responsibility – who must bear the blame or the credit – for that outcome, and over the details: which commander did or did not do what when; what regiment broke or did not break at a particular juncture; what contingent – British or Dutch or Belgian or Brunswicker or Prussian or any of the others – contributed most to Allied victory; even the colours a particular regiment wore during the battle has sometimes become a source of controversy. Some of this controversy has been useful in helping to elucidate obscure events in the greater whole, much of it has been at least intellectually stimulating, and not a little of it has been extremely amusing.

Recently there has been some renewed debate about one of the oldest and most well-regarded treatments of Waterloo, that of Captain William Siborne (1797–1849). Siborne, a young British officer with a bent for topography,[2] prepared two terrain models of the Waterloo battlefield for historical purposes, fearing that plans for various monuments and the inevitable march of progress would eventually obscure or destroy many of the contours, buildings, and roads which formed the court on which the destiny of Europe was decided. What was most interesting about his methodology was that in addition to conducting a survey of the battlefield and perusing various official documents, Siborne solicited the views of a large number of officers who had been at the battle, making use of a lengthy questionnaire, perhaps the first time this technique had ever been used in the preparation of an historical work. The response was voluminous, ultimately totalling over 700 letters, memoranda, and comments about the battle.

In 1844 Siborne published *History of the War in France and Belgium in 1815*,[3] a narrative account of the campaign based upon the materials which he had accumulated. The book provoked some controversy from the start, as officers and historians protested various real or imagined sins of omission or commission. In the Third Edition[4] of his work, Siborne incorporated corrections which he deemed legitimate. There were three of these:

1) A revision of his treatment of the performance of Halkett's Brigade, based on a series of letters which had raised questions as to his sources.[5]

2) A revision of his treatment of the operations of the Prussian Army based on materials which had been supplied to him by the Prussian General Staff.

3) Some corrections to his account of the dispositions and movements of certain Dutch–Belgian units based on a Dutch account of the battle previously unavailable to him.

On the other hand, Siborne noted that some objections to his account of the battle could not be sustained, and gave lengthy reasons for rejecting them.[6] Unfortunately, his tone towards some of his critics was sometimes strident and occasionally rude. As he was terminally ill at the time this is understandable.

Nearly half a century after Siborne's death, his son, Major-General Herbert T. Siborne, published *Waterloo Letters*,[7] a selection of excerpts from about 200 of the 700-odd letters which he had accumulated, a work which has proven a useful supplement to *History of the War in France and Belgium in 1815*. In his preface to this volume, the younger Siborne observes that he attempted to make a representative selection of the hundreds of items available. He admitted that the selection consisted entirely of items by British officers, but noted that his father's account was essentially a British account of the campaign.[8] He also indicated that he had tried to include some of the items which were 'at variance' with his father's final published account, and certainly did so, as there are a number of items which do not seem to have influenced Siborne's treatment of the battle.[9]

Siborne's work has been of immense value to students of the campaign, despite indubitable flaws. Certainly it would be wrong to rely entirely on his treatment of the events, not only because of the obvious limitations of the work, but because in the nearly 150 years since its publication considerable additional material has come to light. For example, we are told that the Duke of Wellington 'arranged to see plans of the proposed model, liked not what he saw, and said so privately',[10] and that in the opinion of the Duke, 'the model was wrong'.[11] Damning words indeed. Or are they? Actually, what the Duke said was 'the Model would not give an accurate representation of the position of the troops of either or both armies at any particular period of the day .. But this model tends to represent the whole action ..' So Wellington was objecting to the fact that Siborne's model represented the armies as they were disposed during the various notable events of the day, much like the cycloramas at Atlanta or Gettysburg, rather than their dispositions at one specific moment. In fact, Waterloo lends itself to such a presentation because none of the famous incidents of the battle – the classic 'five acts' as it were – occurred over the same ground as any of the others. The Duke had a point, but it was not necessarily that the model was inaccurate. In addition, it is worth recalling that Wellington did not believe it possible to give a coherent account of a battle, having once said 'The history of a battle is like the history of a ball. Some individuals may recollect all the little events of which the great result is the battle won or lost; but no individual can recollect the order in which, or the exact moment at which, they occurred'.[12]

A good deal of the discussion about the value of Siborne's work revolves around those of the Waterloo letters which did not get into the younger Siborne's 1891 collection. In effect, did the younger man only publish materials which would support his father's views? 'There remains a great wealth of material in the originals that has been excluded. Whether this was omitted to conform with the original history or not is pure conjecture.'[13] Among the items in question is an 'unpublished report from Saxe-Weimar's brigade, which gives an account of its actions and uniforms' contrary to Siborne's, the author of which is identified only by the handwritten comment, 'From an unknown K.G.L. Officer'.[14] Yet this seems hardly a source upon which much reliance can be placed: not only is it unsigned, but to what extent would an officer of the King's German Legion be in a position to know much about the movements of the Nassauers? Moreover, the younger Siborne admits his collection concentrates on the British Army, in his introduction to *Waterloo Letters*.[15]

A good deal of discussion has revolved around the numbers which Siborne gives for various contingents in the army. For example, in the discussion of Halkett's brigade which prompted Siborne to make some changes in his account, an officer of the 30th Foot argued that Siborne's figure, 615, is in error, for '460 bayonets was the outside of what the 30th marched into the field at Quatre Bras'.[16] Yet it is clear from Siborne's text that the 615 figure is that attributed to the battalion at the opening of the campaign. In any case, it is impossible to know the exact strength of an army at the moment it enters battle, despite often heroic efforts to ascertain such information.[17] Siborne's figure is plausible, once one deducts stragglers, casualties, and details.[18]

Siborne's critics have some useful points to make. But these hardly can be said to overturn the basic utility of his work. The undersigned's own recent work[19] on this campaign relies upon Siborne for much geographic and operational detail, recognising its shortcomings. Siborne's critics are undoubtedly correct in a number of ways, but his innovative, seminal study remains essential for students of the Waterloo Campaign.

NOTES

1. See Donald D. Horward (ed.), *Napoleonic Military History: A Bibliography* (New York and London, 1986).

2. See William Siborne, *A Practical Treatise on Topographical Surveying and Drawing* (London, 1827) for some notion of his interest and methods.

3. William Siborne, *History of the War in France and Belgium in 1815* (London, 1844).

4. William Siborne, *History of the War in France and Belgiumin 1815*, third edition (London, 1848), pp.iv-v. The Second Edition was published very soon after the first, and is identical with it, so it is the Third Edition which is the standard, incorporating Siborne's final corrections. It has frequently been reissued, most recently in 1990 by Greenhill Books in London, entitled *History of the Waterloo Campaign*.

5. See *United Service Institute Journal*, March–June 1845. It is interesting that Siborne did not identify his original informant for the actions of this brigade.

6. See, for example, his lengthy footnotes on p.58 and p.152 of the Third Edition, dealing specifically with criticisms raised in the article 'Marmont, Siborne, and Alesion', *Quarterly Review*, No. 151.

7. *Waterloo Letters: A Selection from Original and Hitherto Unpublished Letters Bearing on the Operations of the 16th, 17th, and 18th June, 1815, by Officers Who served in the Campaign*, edited, with explanatory notes by Major-General H.T. Siborne (London, 1891).

8. See *Waterloo Letters*, pp.v, viii.

9. *Ibid*, p.v.

10. See, for example, D.C. Hamilton-Williams, 'Captain William Siborne', *Journal of the Society for Army Historical Research*, Vol.66 (1988), p.74.

11. *Ibid*, p.78.

12. Wellington, letter, 8 August 1815, cited in Robert Debs Heinl, Jr., *Dictionary of Military and Naval Quotations* (Annapolis: United States Naval Institute, 1966), p.147.

13. Hamilton-Williams, p.78.

14. Cited in Hamilton-Williams, p.78. Note the concern for uniforms, a matter of antiquarian interest at best.

15. *Waterloo Letters*, p.viii.

16. *United Services Institute Journal*, March 1845, p.403.

17. Elucidating the exact number of men brought into action during a particular battle is a minor cult among military historians, and a most frustrating one. The most detailed published Waterloo order of battle, Scott Bowden's *Armies at Waterloo* (Arlington, Texas, 1982), gives the 30th 649 officers and men for the campaign, a figure which is probably too high, but defensible based on primary sources.

18. In the *United Services Institute Journal* critique we are told, 'It is not for me to say what portion ... went to guards, hospitals, commissariat, provost, stores or what not, but I know that near fifty effective soldiers were away from the battle as servants and batmen'. As an aside, it is worth noting that in his defence of his regiment, this officer has little good to say about its brigade-mate, the 33rd, which probably put in the worst performance of any British battalion during the campaign, probably because it was commanded by Lieutenant-Colonel William Elphinstone, perhaps the most inept officer of all time, who some thirty years after Waterloo would dither away an entire British Army in Afghanistan, a tale most effectively and entertainingly told in George MacDonald Fraser's novel *Flashman*.

19. Albert A. Nofi, *The Waterloo Campaign: June 1815* (Conshohocken, Pennsylvania, Combined Books/London, Greenhill Books: 1993).

Albert A. Nofi
1993

PREFACE.

WHEN my father, the late Captain William Siborne, Unattached, was engaged in the construction of his Model of the Battle of Waterloo, he was authorised by the General Commanding-in-Chief—Lord Hill—to issue 'a Circular Letter to the several surviving Officers of the Battle who might be in a position to afford him the information necessary for the completion of his undertaking. Copies of this letter, and of the plan which accompanied it (on one half the original scale), are annexed.

A great number of letters were sent to him in reply, and subsequently, when writing his History of the Campaign, he received many additional letters and memoranda relating, not only to the precise period of the Battle represented on the Model, but also to the operations and incidents of the Campaign generally.

These letters were written to Captain Siborne with the knowledge that the information contained in them would be conveyed to the public.

The greater number of the letters, amounting to several hundreds, are still in my possession, and as the 75th anniversary of the Battle occurred last year, and general attention has been redirected to that great event, I have thought that the publication of a selected portion of them might be of interest, not only to the Army, particularly to those Regiments or Corps which took part in the Campaign, but also to the public generally.

Many families and individuals will here find recorded the original accounts given by relatives who served in the Waterloo Campaign of what they experienced and of the parts which they played in it.

In some few cases the letters were not sent direct to Captain Siborne, but were forwarded to him for his information by those to whom they were addressed.

A great number of the letters or memoranda refer to more than one of the Actions or operations of the Campaign, but as the dividing them into detached portions for the purpose of strictly adhering to the sequence of events would lead to great confusion, I have found it preferable to leave the letters as they stand, and by marginal notes or other references assist the reader in recognising the situation described in the text. Where practicable also, portions of the plan on which the writers laid down the positions of their Regiments or Corps are reproduced, or else the latter are otherwise indicated.

The publication of some information at the moment intended to be private cannot, so far as it relates to the incidents of the war, be looked upon, after the lapse of half a century, as a breach of confidence.

As a rule, however, statements of a purely private or irrelevant nature, repetitions in subsequent letters by the same writer, and information regarding the state of the crops on the Field of Waterloo (necessary for the construction of the Model), are omitted.

Where single or isolated statements may seem to be at variance with the descriptions of events given in Captain Siborne's History of the War, it should be remembered that those descriptions were only finally decided on, either after further correspondence with the same writers, or from the careful comparison of a number of various and often conflicting accounts.

The following may be considered as the order of the different operations of the Campaign, and principal phases of the Battle of Waterloo, to which the letters chiefly refer:—

 The receipt of intelligence from the Allied outposts (or rather want of it, previous to the 15th of June), and consequent hasty concentration of the troops towards the line of advance of the French Army.

The Action at Quatre Bras on the 16th June.

The Retreat from Quatre Bras on the 17th to the position of Waterloo, and Cavalry engagements at Genappe.

At the Battle of Waterloo on the 18th.

The defence of Hougoumont from the commencement of the Battle till near its close.

The repulse of the first French attack on Picton's Division in the left centre of the Allied Army.

The Cavalry charges connected therewith.

The repulse of subsequent French Cavalry attacks.

The gradual co-operation of the Prussians.

The capture of La Haye Sainte by the French.

The repulse of the first attacking Column of the Imperial Guard.

The repulse of the second Column of the Guard, and advance of Adam's Infantry Brigade.

The advance of the Light Cavalry.

The General Advance of the Army and Rout of the French.

The letters are placed in the following order :—

1.—Letters from the General Staff (and that of Divisions).

2.—Letters from the six Brigades of Cavalry.

3.—Letters from the eight Batteries of Horse and five of Field Artillery.

4.—Letters from the eight Brigades of Infantry.

A short sketch of the operations in which each Brigade was engaged precedes the letters from it, and the letters from the Staff of the Brigade precede those from the Regiments composing it.

Owing to the principle I have adopted of endeavouring to make each Corps contribute its share of the correspondence, some of the letters may be thought to have little interest; but this will generally be found to be compensated for by the fuller accounts of other writers, which represent the operations, not only of their own particular Regiments, but of their Brigades, and even of the Army in general.

The only three Corps engaged in the Battle from which there are no letters of any interest in the collection are the 1st Life Guards, the Royal Engineers, and the 14th Regiment.

I may add that the collection consists of letters from British Officers only, and does not include any from our Allies in the Campaign.

Unless otherwise expressed, the letters are to be considered as addressed to Captain Siborne, and where two ranks are assigned to a writer, the latter is that which he held at Waterloo.

H. T. Siborne,
Major-General.

CIRCULAR LETTER TO SURVIVING
WATERLOO OFFICERS.

—◆◆—

Dublin.

SIR,—Having for some time past been occupied in
constructing a Model of the Field and Battle of Waterloo,
upon a scale sufficiently large to admit of the most faithful representation of that memorable Action; and the
General Commanding-in-Chief having, with the utmost
kindness, and with a view to insure to the undertaking the
greatest possible accuracy, granted me permission to apply
for such information as I may conceive desirable and necessary, to the several Officers who, from the commands
which they held, or from the circumstances in which they
were placed on that occasion, may be considered likely to
afford it;—I have accordingly the honour to request you
will have the goodness to reply to the following queries, as
far as your recollection and the circumstances of your
position at the time will admit.

What was the particular formation of the
at the moment (about 7 p.m.) when the
French Imperial Guards, advancing to attack the right
of the British Forces, reached the crest of our position? *

What was the formation of that part of the Enemy's
Forces immediately in front of the

Would you have the goodness to trace these formations, according to the best of your recollection, upon the
accompanying Plan? †

---

* The period of the Battle selected for representation on the Model.

† According to the scale of the Plan, ‡ the following lines show the
extent of front occupied respectively by a Battalion in line (700 strong),
and by a Squadron (130 strong): ———————————— ▬▬

‡ The original Plan.—ED.

Upon examining the Plan you will find that I have marked with a pencil, on the different fields in and near which the   was generally posted throughout the 18th of June, the nature of the crops which, it is presumed, from the information afforded me by the Farmers residing on the spot, they respectively contained on that day. Have you any doubts as to the correctness of such information, and if so, in what particular? Considering the extremely devastated and trodden-down appearance of all kinds of vegetation at the period of the crisis of the battle, it is more with reference to the existence of ploughed or fallow land that I ask this question.

I shall feel very much obliged by your affording me, in addition to the information already solicited, any remarks which you may consider likely to conduce to the accuracy and fidelity of the Model, as regards the positions, movements, and formations of the contending armies, not only at the precise moment of action selected for representation, but also during the day. Hints concerning the tracks of the French columns which passed near the   either in advancing or retreating; details of the different attacks made or sustained by the   , as also remarks upon the general appearance presented by that part of the Field of Battle nearest to the   , with the addition of any little circumstances which, in your opinion, ought not to be overlooked in a work of this kind, will be most acceptable. It is only by such means as these that I shall be enabled to ensure the accuracy of the Model in every particular, and, with the aid of an explanatory memoir, to lay before the public a complete and satisfactory exposition of this ever memorable Battle.

In concluding, I take the liberty of earnestly entreating that you will not allow yourself to be deterred from giving the requested information by any fear of committing mistakes; which, indeed, considering the period that has elapsed since the Battle took place, are not only most excusable, but almost unavoidable. If Officers will, however, but favour me with their remarks and opinions, freely and without reserve, I trust that, by fairly weighing and comparing the data thus afforded me, I shall be enabled to deduce a most faithful and authentic record of the Battle, the surest means of imparting to the Model that extreme accuracy which, in a work of this nature, not dependent, like a pictorial representation, on *effect* for its excellence, must always constitute its real value.

I have the honour to be, Sir,

Your most obedient, humble Servant,

W. SIBORNE,

Lieut.-Assist. Mil. Sec.

To

TABLE OF CONTENTS.

WATERLOO LETTERS.

LIST OF MAPS AND PLANS

Continued

MAPS AT BACK OF VOLUME

WATERLOO LETTERS

WATERLOO LETTERS.

GENERAL STAFF.

AMONGST the Letters from the General Staff (and that of Divisions) are two which refer to the tardy intelligence received by the Duke of Wellington from the Allied Outposts of the Advance of the French Army. One from General W. Napier (No. 1) communicating an interesting statement on this point by the Duke himself, the other from Lord Fitzroy Somerset (No. 2).

The principal remaining Letters are from Lord Anglesey (Nos. 3, 4, 5, 6), giving an account of the general movements and operations of the Cavalry, and particularly as regards the Retreat from Quatre Bras on the 17th June, and the Battle of Waterloo on the 18th up to the period when he was wounded; from Sir William Gomm (Nos. 12, 13), relating to the marching of Picton's Division and other troops on Quatre Bras, and of its share in the Battles on the 16th and 18th; and from General Freemantle (No. 11), respecting the arrival of the Prussians at Waterloo.

MAJOR-GENERAL W. NAPIER, C.B.

(NOT AT WATERLOO.)

No. 1.

November 28th, 1842.

I should not like to give my information to anybody but you, but your fairness about your Model makes me feel that I do not throw away what I am going to tell you, and it is from the Duke's mouth.

The Duke of Wellington finding the Prince of Orange at the Duchess of Richmond's Ball.

News of the advance of the French across the Sambre.

He found the Prince of Orange at the Duchess of Richmond's Ball on the evening of the 15th. He was surprised to see him because he had placed him at Binche, an important outpost, for the purpose of observing and giving notice of the movements of the Enemy. He went up to him and asked if there was any news? "No! nothing but that the French have crossed the Sambre and had a brush with the Prussians. Have you heard of it?"

This was news. So he told him quietly that he had better go back to his post, and then by degrees he got the principal Officers away from the ball and sent them to their troops. This was done, I think he said, about 11 o'clock.

Arrival of Genl. Müffling from Blucher's Army. Genl. Müffling was Prussian Commissioner to the British Army.

He then went to his quarters and found Müffling there, coming from Blucher with the news; he ought to have arrived long before, but, said the Duke to me, "I cannot tell the world that Blucher picked the fattest man in his army to ride with an express to me, and that he took thirty hours to go thirty miles."

I am in a state of great debility from sickness and pain, being carried about and held up to write this, or I would give more details, but the substance you have.

There is, however, a very curious story about the Espionage, which I believe no man knows but myself now. My authority (Grant, the Chief of the Espionage) is dead. General Dornberg was the real cause of the Duke's being surprised in his cantonments.

Yours, &c.,

W. NAPIER.

LIEUT.-GENERAL LORD FITZROY SOMERSET, K.C.B.

LIEUT.-COLONEL 1ST FOOT GUARDS, AND MILITARY SECRETARY TO THE DUKE OF WELLINGTON.

Horse Guards, November 26th, 1842.   No. 2.

I am sorry to have to say, in reply to your letter of the 22nd inst., that I do not recollect the time at which in the course of the 15th June the Prince of Orange came into Brussels, nor the circumstances which induced His Royal Highness to leave the advanced posts and repair in person to the Headquarters of the Army.

The Duke of Wellington did not stir out of Brussels on the 15th. On the 16th he left the city about 8 o'clock, and after having remained some time with the troops some distance in front of Quatre Bras, His Grace proceeded to visit Marshal Blucher, who was then preparing to receive the attack of the French Army, and after staying with him a little while, he returned to his own Army, which he reached very shortly before it was engaged with the Enemy.

The Duke leaves Brussels on the morning of the 16th. Proceeds to Quatre Bras and on to visit Blucher at Ligny. Returns to Quatre Bras before the Battle commenced.

Yours, &c.,

FITZROY SOMERSET.

GENERAL THE MARQUESS OF ANGLESEY, K.G., G.C.B., G.C.H.

LIEUT.-GENERAL THE EARL OF UXBRIDGE, G.C.B., COMMANDING THE CAVALRY.   No. 3.

Malvern, October 18th, 1842.

I have not the least objection to answer your question. I received no order from the Duke of Wellington to make the first charge or any other during the day.

I will in a moment explain to you the footing upon which he placed me upon my arrival at Brussels.

The Duke said, "I place the *whole* of the Cavalry and Light Artillery of the United Army under your command."

His instructions from the Duke of Wellington. The whole of the Cavalry and its Horse

LORD ANGLESEY.

Artillery placed under his orders.

The Prince of Orange wished his own Cavalry to remain under his own orders.

On the 17th the Duke orders Lord Uxbridge to cover the Retreat with the Cavalry.

On the morning of the 18th, the Prince of Orange requested that his Cavalry should be under Lord Uxbridge.

These *all* the orders received from the Duke by Lord Uxbridge.

A few days after this the Duke said, "The Prince of Orange has begged that the Cavalry of H.R.H.'s nation should remain under his immediate command. I hope you have no objection to this." I replied, "Not the slightest. I am quite ready to act in any way you please."

On the 17th, the Duke having decided to retire to the position of Waterloo in consequence of the Battle which had taken place on the previous day between the French and the Prussians being made known to him, ordered me " to remain in the position of Quatre Bras as long as I conveniently could, in order to cover the movement of the Army." The Army moved at 10 a.m. I remained until 1 o'clock p.m.

On the morning of the 18th, just as the Battle commenced, the Duke said, "The Prince of Orange requests that you will take charge of all his Cavalry." I replied, "I will do my best with them, but it is unfortunate that I should not have had an opportunity of making myself acquainted with any of his Officers or their Regiments."

These are *all* the orders I ever received from the Duke during this short campaign.

I felt that he had given me *carte blanche,* and I never bothered him with a single question respecting the movements it might be necessary to make.

I will only add that throughout he was invariably conciliatory and confiding.

I remain, &c.,

ANGLESEY.

MEMO. BY THE SAME.

No. 4.

See No. 56, p. 111.

Quatre Bras and Genappe.

The report from an Officer of the 11th Light Dragoons induces me to go into some detail relative to the affairs at Quatre Bras on the 16th, and at Genappe on the 17th.

The Cavalry being in cantonments at Ninove and environs, had to march between thirty and forty miles to reach the former place.

I had galloped on and reached it between 2 and

3 p.m. I found the Prince of Orange's Corps heavily engaged, and being deficient in Cavalry, I went to hasten the march of the first Light Regiments that headed the Column. About eight o'clock p.m. the 11th arrived, and a part of the Regiment was thrown out in front of the position.

At 10 a.m. on the 17th the Duke of Wellington decided upon withdrawing into the position of Waterloo, and ordered me to cover the retreat with all the Cavalry and Horse Artillery, and about two Battalions of Light Troops. There was a small river in the rear, with a bridge over it at Genappe, and my Staff had discovered two fords at half-a-mile distance on the right and left of it. The centre Column, which was to pass by the bridge along the *chaussée*, consisted of the Artillery and two Brigades of Heavy Cavalry, with the 7th Hussars and 23rd Light Dragoons as a Rear-guard. Two Brigades of Light Cavalry retired by the ford on the left, and (I think) three by that on the right. We had Ney's Corps, which had fought the Battle of Quatre Bras, still in our front, but making no signs of moving. About 1 o'clock p.m., however, very large masses of Cavalry began to show upon our left, and upon the road from Namur. It was obvious they were coming on, and I therefore withdrew, and sent back the Infantry and the 11th Light Dragoons that had been in front; and, shortly after this, the Enemy's Artillery and Cavalry advanced with rapidity and opened a smart fire. Every disposition having been previously made, the retreat was commenced, and although the attack was rapid and vigorous, the three Columns passed the river with very slight loss.

The Enemy did not pass the fords after the flank Columns, but concentrated their efforts against the centre Column. Having passed the bridge, Lord E. Somerset's Brigade and the Artillery kept the *chaussée*, and halted about 600 or 700 yards from the entrance of Genappe. Sir William Ponsonby's Brigade was deployed upon the plain to the right (as fronting the Enemy) of the

Marginal notes:

16th June. Late arrival of the British Cavalry at Quatre Bras.

17th June.

Retreat to the position of Waterloo covered by the Cavalry.

Fords discovered on each side of Genappe.

The Centre Cavalry Column to move by the *Chaussée* through Genappe.

2 Brigades of Light Cavalry retired by the Ford on the left, and 3 by that on the right.

About 1 p.m. appearance of Cavalry on the Namur road.

Advance of the French Cavalry. Their Artillery opens fire.

The Retreat commenced, and the 3 Columns cross the river with slight loss.

The Enemy only followed up the Centre Column.

Somerset's Brigade kept the *Chaussée*.

LORD ANGLESEY.

Ponsonby's
deployed on
the right.

chaussée. I placed the 7th Hussars, 200 or 300 yards from
the town, and upon the *chaussée*, and the 23rd Light
Dragoons in support. The *chaussée* is wide, but for some
distance has ditches on either side ; these filled with water,
the rain having come down in torrents from the moment
the retreat commenced.

In this position I awaited the further movements of
the Enemy. Presently their Lancers were pushed through
the town, and as I saw they were preparing to advance, I
immediately ordered the 7th to attack.

This they did most gallantly, but they could not penetrate the Lancers. In their turn these now advanced, and
drove the 7th upon their reserve. Here the 7th rallied,
and again drove the Lancers to the town.

Again the Lancers being reinforced rallied, and drove
the 7th, and again tbe 7th rallied, and thus a determined
see-saw was kept up for a considerable time. At length,
after the 7th had lost several excellent Officers and men, I
withdrew them, and, riding up to the 23rd Light Dragoons,
ordered them to advance. It is *possible* that the part of
the 11th which had been in advance during the previous
night, and which I had withdrawn previously to the commencement of the retreat, may have been joined with the
23rd, to whom I addressed myself. It is *possible*, but I do
not think it was so. Be that as it may, the sequel will
show that the 11th did *not* charge at Genappe after the
7th had been withdrawn, or at all.

My address to these Light Dragoons not having been
received with all the enthusiasm that I expected, I ordered
them to clear the *chaussée*, and said, "The Life Guards
shall have this honour," and instantly sending for them,
two squadrons of the 1st Regiment, gallantly led by
Major Kelly, came on *with right good will*, and I sent
them in to finish the Lancers. They at once overthrew
them, and pursued into the town, where they punished
them severely.

Thus ended the affair immediately at the gates of
Genappe, by which it will be seen that the *only* regiments

Cavalry
Action at
Genappe.

The 7th Hus-
sars attack
the French
Lancers.

Alternate suc-
cesses of 7th
Hussars and
French
Lancers.

See No. 65,
p. 135.

1st Life
Guards repel
the French
Lancers.

that charged there were the 7th Hussars first, and then the 1st Life Guards.

Having thus checked the ardour of the Enemy's advanced guard, the retreat was continued at a slow pace, and with the most perfect regularity. Assuredly this *coup de collier* had the very best effect, for although there was much cannonading, and a constant appearance of a disposition to charge, they continued at a respectful distance.

The Enemy being checked the Retreat is continued at a slow pace.

The Royals, Inniskillings, and Greys manœuvred beautifully, retiring by alternate squadrons, and skirmished in the very best style; but finding that all the efforts of the Enemy to get upon our right flank were vain, and that by manœuvring upon the plain, which was amazingly deep and heavy from the violent storm of rain, it only uselessly exhausted the horses, I drew these Regiments in upon the *chaussée* in one column, the Guns falling back from position to position, and from these Batteries, checking the advance of the Enemy.

Manœuvring of the Greys, Inniskillings, and Royals.

Heavy storm of rain.

We were received by the Duke of Wellington upon entering the position of Waterloo, having effected the retreat with very trifling loss.

Retreat effected with very trifling loss.

Thus ended the prettiest Field Day of Cavalry and Horse Artillery that I ever witnessed.

A.

FROM THE SAME.

TO GENERAL SIR FREDERIC STOVIN.

B. D., November 8th, 1839.

No. 5.

Waterloo.

MY DEAR STOVIN,—It is rather hard to have to fight the Battle o'er again, and at so great a distance of time; however, I will try to give you a rough and hasty sketch.

I had been visiting the extreme right of the Cavalry, and those placed in support of the attack on [? defence of] Hougoumont, when, on returning towards the centre of the position, I observed very large masses of the Enemy, both

D'Erlon's Attack on the Allied Left Centre at about 1.30 p.m., and that of the French Cavalry.

The Heavy Cavalry was formed on either side of the road. Lord E. Somerset's Brigade (1st & 2nd Life Guards, Blues and King's Dragoon Guards) on the right, Sir Wm. Ponsonby's (Royals, Greys, and Inniskillings) on the left of it.

1st Charge of these Brigades.

See plan, p. 38.

3,000 French and 2 Eagles taken.

40 French Guns put *hors de combat.*

Cavalry and Infantry (supported, too, by a tremendous discharge of Artillery from all parts of their line), moving upon our left, but principally on La Haye Sainte, the road from Genappe to Brussels appearing to be nearly the centre of their advance.

I immediately galloped to the Heavy Cavalry, and ordered the Household Brigade to prepare to form line, passed on to Sir William Ponsonby's, and having told him to wheel into line when the other Brigade did, I instantly returned to the Household Brigade, and put the whole in motion.

I led the advance, and am inclined to think that the line I took was pretty much what is in the plan, stated to be that of the Officer leading the left squadron of the 2nd Life Guards (perhaps a little more to the right) ; but this I remember, that the ground was dreadfully broken, and upon a very active horse I was much put to it to descend it.

Towards the bottom of the slope I found our Infantry mostly in line, but getting into squares to receive the Enemy's Cavalry, and making intervals for us as our Squadrons presented themselves. Thus we passed through the Infantry as fast and as well as we could (but necessarily not with exact regularity), when, again forming, we instantly charged and fell upon large masses of Cavalry and of Infantry ; but these gave way in a moment, and of the latter arm 3,000 men were taken, and two Eagles sent to the rear.

The pursuit was continued until a vast number of Guns were in our possession, or rather passed, and I have been assured by Lord Lauderdale that a French General Officer at Paris, whom he named, but whose name I have forgotten (I think, however, he was of the Artillery), told him that they had more than forty Guns put *hors de combat* by that charge. Unfortunately they could not be brought off, for the pursuit had been continued without order and too far, and the second line (excepting only a small part of Sir J. Vandeleur's Brigade—in fact, I believe, only two Squadrons of the 12th, under Sir F. Ponsonby) had not

LORD ANGLESEY.

See statement of Sir John Vandeleur, No. 51, p. 105.

followed the movements of the Heavy Cavalry, whose horses were now exhausted, and had to receive the shocks of fresh troops.

After the overthrow of the Cuirassiers I had in vain attempted to stop my people by sounding the Rally, but neither voice nor trumpet availed; so I went back to seek the support of the 2nd Line, which unhappily had not followed the movements of the Heavy Cavalry.

After the overthrow of the Cuirassiers, tried in vain to stop the pursuit.

Had I, when I sounded the Rally, found only four well-formed Squadrons coming steadily along at an easy trot, I feel certain that the loss the first line suffered when they were finally forced back would have been avoided, and most of these 'Guns might have been secured, for it was obvious the effect of that charge had been prodigious, and for the rest of the day, although the Cuirassiers frequently attempted to break into our Lines, they always did it *mollement* and as if they expected something more behind the curtain.

Effects of the 1st Charge.

My impression is that the French were completely surprised by the first Cavalry attack. It (our Cavalry) had been rather hidden by rising ground immediately before their position. I think the left wing of our Infantry was partially retiring, when I determined upon the movement, and then these 19 Squadrons pouncing down hill upon them so astonished them that no very great resistance was made, and surely such havoc was rarely made in so few minutes.

Thinks the French were surprised by the 1st Cavalry Attack.

When I was returning to our position I met the Duke of Wellington, surrounded by all the *Corps diplomatique militaire*, who had from the high ground witnessed the whole affair. The plain appeared to be swept clean, and I never saw so joyous a group as was this *Troupe dorée*. They thought the Battle was over. It is certain that our Squadrons went into and over several Squares of Infantry, and it is not possible to conceive greater confusion and panic than was exhibited at this moment.

On returning to the Position met the Duke of Wellington.

This forces from me the remark that I committed a great mistake in having myself led the attack. The

Mistake in leading the Cavalry himself.

carrière once begun, the leader is no better than any other
man ; whereas, if I had placed myself at the head of the 2nd
line, there is no saying what great advantages might not
have accrued from it.   I am the less pardonable in having
deviated from a principle I had laid down for myself, that
I had already suffered from a similar error in an affair at
Irtragau [?], where my reserve, instead of steadily following as I had ordered, chose to join in the attack, and at the
end of it I had no formed body to take advantage with.

. . . .

Truly yours,
ANGLESEY.

No. 6.

Cavalry at
Waterloo.

French
Cavalry.

MEMO. BY THE SAME.

They (the French) very frequently attacked our
Squares, but never in overwhelming masses, and with that
vigour and *speed*, which would have given them some
chance of penetrating.   No heavy mass having a well-
formed front actually came *collectively* against our
bayonets.   Constantly a few *devoted* fellows did clash with
them, and some pierced between the Squares, and when I
had not Cavalry at hand I frequently entered the Squares
for protection.   . . . . .

In the afternoon a very heavy attack was made upon
the whole of our line to the right of the road, and con-
necting itself with the troops attacking Hougoumont.
It was chiefly made and frequently repeated by masses of
Cuirassiers, but never in one connected line, and after the
first grand attack of the morning they never came on with
the degree of vigour which could give them a hope of
penetrating into our immovable Squares of Infantry.

The Infantry never fired till the Cavalry were very
close, and then they (the Cavalry) dispersed, some coming
through the intervals where they were either killed by the
fire of the Squares, or repulsed by the Cavalry in 2nd
line.   For several minutes some few Cuirassiers were in
possession of several of our Guns about the centre of our
line, at the time the British Cavalry was in pursuit else-

After the 1st
Attack the
Cuirassiers
did not charge
with so much
vigour.

The Infantry
only fired
when the
French
Cavalry were
close, and the
latter dis-
persed.

A few passed
through the
Squares, and

LORD ANGLESEY.

where, and these desperate men remained there to be picked off. . . . .
were repulsed by the Cavalry in 2nd Line.

Our right Flank being much annoyed by a Battery of (I think) 12 Guns supported by Lancers, which were over the Ravine and Stream beyond Hougoumont, and which enfiladed our Line, I caused Sir Colquhoun Grant and a part of General Dornberg's Brigade to cross the bridge there, and to manœuvre upon their flanks and rear, and to attack them.
Grant's move against French Lancers. *See* No. 62, p. 126.

In the meantime a heavy attack was made upon our centre, which I went to repel, with such of the Heavy Cavalry as remained. Sir C. Grant's movement had the fullest effect. It removed the Guns, and the Lancers did not wait to be attacked, but Sir C. Grant perceiving the attack above related, instead of pursuing, returned to support the Heavy Cavalry with which I was, and it is, I apprehend, at that moment that the collision described by Major Mercer took place. I did not see it, or it may relate to what follows.
Repels a heavy attack on the centre with the remains of the Heavy Cavalry.

See No. 89, p. 216.

Seeing a Corps formed for attack and advancing, I brought forward a Brigade of Dutch Heavy Cavalry, and they promised to follow me. I led them beyond the ridge of the hill, a little to the left of Hougoumont. There they halted, and finding the impossibility of making them charge, I left them and retired.
Dutch Cavalry.

See No. 9, p. 18.

Here Major Mercer must, from the position described, have lost sight of them, and he may have supposed that a collision had taken place. . . . . .

In covering the retreat of the 17th I found the Lance had some advantage over the Sword.

. . . .

I think the Cuirass protects, but it also encumbers, and in a *mêlée* I am sure the Cuirass causes the loss of many a life. . . . . . .
In the Retreat of the 17th found the Lance had some advantage over the Sword.

The Cuirass encumbers more than it protects.

They (the French) never risked themselves in line. They were always in column, and they never charged at speed. . . . . .
The French always charged in Column.

It is asked, "Did the British Cavalry in every

LORD GREENOCK.

British
Cavalry.

The British
always *advanced* to
resist the
Enemy. The
Light Cavalry
not always
successful.

German
Legion
Cavalry entirely of the
same worth
as the British.

instance withstand *de pied ferme* the onset of the French ? "

It did *not* stand *de pied ferme*. It invariably advanced, but the Light Cavalry was not always successful.

I have the strongest reason to be excessively dissatisfied with the General commanding a Brigade of Dutch Heavy Cavalry, and with a Colonel commanding a young Regiment of Hanoverian Hussars.

I class the German Legion entirely with the British Cavalry. Than we [are] ! there cannot be better troops.

LIEUT.-GENERAL LORD GREENOCK, K.C.B.

ASSISTANT QUARTER-MASTER-GENERAL TO THE CAVALRY.

No. 7.

5, Carlton Place, Edinburgh, Jan. 21st, 1835.

I have the honour to acknowledge your letter of the 29th ult. with its enclosures, which, however, did not reach me until the 16th inst. ; and in reply I can only express the very great regret that I feel that after the lapse of nearly twenty years, and having no memoranda at present with me by which my recollection of the positions occupied

Waterloo.

by the different Corps during the Battle of Waterloo might be assisted, I find myself to be quite incompetent to undertake the task you have assigned me of marking upon the plan transmitted for that purpose even the situations of those troops with which I was the most immediately concerned on that occasion.

I was at that period attached as Assistant Quartermaster-General to the Cavalry, and my post on the 18th of June was therefore with the Marquess of Anglesey, except when employed in conveying his orders.

At the commencement of the Battle, the several Brigades of Cavalry were formed nearly upon the ground upon which they had respectively bivouacked on the preceding night; this had been taken up without any attention to order, it having been almost dark before they arrived in the position, owing to their having all been more or less sharply engaged with the Enemy in covering the retreat of the Infantry from Quatre Bras on the 17th, and this movement having been executed by them by three different routes, the situations of their respective bivouacks had been determined more by this circumstance than by any regular disposition.

To the left of the Great Road from Brussels to Charleroi, by Genappe, the positions of three Brigades of British Cavalry from left to right were as follows, viz. :—

Sir Hussey Vivian's—Major-General Vandeleur's—Sir William Ponsonby's.

The former had communicated by patrols with the Prussians. Some Belgian Light Cavalry, to the best of my recollection, were also on that flank of the army.

To the right of that road, and of the Haye Sainte, in the same order, were :—

Lord E. Somerset's—Major-General Dornberg's—Major-General Sir Colquhoun Grant's Brigades. The greater part of the Belgian and Hanoverian Cavalry were in positions intermediate to those of Lord Edward Somerset's and Sir Colquhoun Grant's Brigades.

Of the Cavalry thus posted at the commencement of the day, on the left during the progress of the Battle previous to the hour to which you more particularly refer, Sir W. Ponsonby's Brigade had lost its General, and the greater part of its Officers and men, in consequence of having pursued the Enemy too far, after a most brilliant and successful charge; with the exception of the 12th Lancers (Light Dragoons), which had made a very gallant charge, General Vandeleur's Brigade had sustained no loss, and Sir Hussey Vivian's Brigade had not been at all engaged.

On the right of the Haye Sainte, the Household Brigade had charged at the same time with the other heavy Brigade, when one of its Regiments, the King's Dragoon Guards, having likewise been too eager in the pursuit, had been almost annihilated; the Life Guards and Blues, having been kept better in hand, had then suffered

Marginal notes:

Distribution of Cavalry at Waterloo.

See General Plan, No. 1.

Vivian's, Vandeleur's, and Ponsonby's Brigades left of Brussels-Genappe Road, and some Light Belgian Cavalry.

Somerset's, Dornberg's, and Grant's to the right of the road, with Hanoverian and Belgian Cavalry in intermediate positions.

Repulse of D'Erlon's 1st Attack, and that of the French Cavalry.

1st Charge of Ponsonby's Brigade.

1st Charge of Somerset's Brigade.

All the Cavalry engaged throughout the day in repelling the French Cavalry when it penetrated between the Squares.

(comparatively speaking) but little loss. All the Cavalry, however, both British and Foreign, on this side of the position were constantly engaged throughout the day in endeavouring to repel the masses of French Cavalry when they had penetrated between the Squares of Infantry, or had formed upon the crest of the position.

In consequence of the suddenness of the order to advance to meet the Enemy, on the 16th of June, the measure of forming the Cavalry into Divisions, which I know to have been Lord Anglesey's intention, had not taken effect. The different Brigades, therefore, having been scattered as before shown along the whole extent of the Line, without any view to such an arrangement, their operations were unfortunately never combined during any part of the day, whilst the French Cavalry acted in Corps or Divisions; consequently in these desultory attacks small bodies of the former were constantly opposed to large masses of the latter, and although the first efforts of the British were generally successful, the superiority of the Enemy's numbers in the end always turned the scale in their favour.

Disadvantages of the Cavalry not being formed into Divisions, in consequence of the sudden order to advance on 16th June.

Lord Anglesey, being sensible of this disadvantage, gave orders for the better concentration of his Corps by removing the Brigades from the left of the Haye Sainte towards the right of the position, as soon as their presence in that quarter became no longer necessary in consequence of the arrival of the Prussians on that flank. For the position and movements of the Cavalry subsequent to that period, you cannot have a better guide than Sir Hussey Vivian's letter to Major Gawler, published in the *United Service Journal*.

LordAnglesey moved the Cavalry on the left of the main road to the right of it after the arrival of the Prussians.

A short time before the Enemy's last advance, Lord Anglesey had made a very gallant but ineffectual charge against the French Cavalry at the head of Lord Edward Somerset's Brigade, which he had wished to renew with the Belgian Cavalry; but abandoning this intention, after communicating personally with the Commanding Officer, in consequence of perceiving that the Belgians appeared to

Lord Anglesey, a short time before the Enemy's last attack, charges the French Cavalry with Somerset's Brigade, but ineffectually.

be too much dispirited by having just witnessed the failure of the Household Brigade, to afford any hope of a more favourable result, his Lordship proceeded to that part of the field on which, by that time, Sir Hussey Vivian's Brigade had been formed, and as I accompanied Lord Anglesey on that occasion, I am able to vouch for the fidelity and accuracy with which all the circumstances relative to this visit of his Lordship's are described by Sir Hussey in that letter.

On quitting Sir Hussey Vivian, Lord Anglesey joined the Duke of Wellington, and it was about this time that the last attack by the Enemy took place. The Infantry had then formed into line four deep. We rode towards the left along the rear of the Infantry, crossing the Genappe Road in rear of the Haye Sainte, but immediately returned to the right of the line. It was then that Lord Anglesey sent me to bring up Vivian's Brigade, which I did as he has stated, directing him to make a flank movement to his right in order to clear the flank of the Infantry, and afterwards bring up his right shoulders. His Lordship was struck by a ball in the knee just as I came up to him, according to his desire, to report the arrival of this Brigade, it having been his intention to have directed its further movements in person. Sir Hussey Vivian, however, continued to advance, and the affair was decided in the way he has so well described.

General Vandeleur's Brigade followed this movement.

At that time the remains of the Heavy Brigade, and Ponsonby's, and a Squadron of the 23rd Lancers (Light Dragoons), under the command of Major Lautour, which, having by some accident been separated from the remainder of that Regiment, had joined the Heavy Brigade, had also been moved to the right of the position, and were formed not far from the place where Lord Anglesey received his wound.

The above facts having come more immediately under my own observation are fresh in my memory. With regard to the precise situations or movements of the rest

Marginal notes:

Last attack of the French. Advance of the British Light Cavalry.

Lord Anglesey wounded.

Vivian's advance.

Followed by Vandeleur.

See No. 49, p. 100.

of the Cavalry at the Crisis of the Battle I cannot speak with so much certainty. I shall therefore conclude, with many apologies for sending you so imperfect a sketch, by subscribing myself,

Your most, &c. &c.,

Greenock.

COLONEL W. THORNHILL.
Major 7th Hussars, and A.D.C. to Lord Uxbridge.
TO GENERAL SIR FREDERIC STOVIN.

No. 8.

New Park, July 16th, 1839.

Waterloo.

My dear Stovin,—To be cool and clear in the perilous adventures of a fight is a characteristic I might well be proud of when applied to me by so good a soldier as Sir Hussey, if I could but persuade myself to believe that I deserved it. I have been in many a hard-fought day, as you well know, but of all the *General Engagements* (some sixteen or more) in which it has been my lot as a subordinate Officer to be engaged, Waterloo is that of which I retain the least vivid impression of the details.

First A.D.C. to Lord Anglesey.

The important post I then filled as first A.D.C. to the Marquis of Anglesey, which necessitated the prompt and direct transmission of his orders, gave me but little time to contemplate passing events irrelevant thereto.

He carries Lord Anglesey's instructions to Commanders of Cavalry Brigades.

Lord Anglesey's gallant conduct.

Lord Anglesey had taken me with him at daybreak to visit the Cavalry outposts, and soon after our return the Enemy put himself in motion for an attack. It was now that Lord Anglesey directed me to go with verbal instructions to General Officers commanding Cavalry Brigades, authorising them to act discretionally under certain limitations it were needless to mention here. When I got back I found him in the thick of the fight giving orders with his accustomed clearness, and ever after, as it seemed to me, seeking to place himself *con amore* in the torrent of attack wherever he felt that his encouraging example was most needed. Thus at one time perceiving that a gallant Regiment of Infantry (which shall be nameless), pressed by the onset of superior numbers, was wavering, he galloped to the rally—reminded this regiment of its distinguished name, and that of its no less gallant Colonel, told them who he was, and led them to the charge. They followed him to a man, drove back the Enemy, and maintained their post.

It was about this time (before or after, I forget which) that I was sent with orders to the Blues to advance. Sir Robert Hill most kindly and courteously invited me to join them in the charge. In this charge I think it was that Major Pack was killed. My horse was shot, and I was so stunned by the fall that I have even now an indistinct recollection of the circumstances immediately preceding it. All that I remember was we went our best pace in the charge, and Hill told me a day or two after the fight " that the most amusing part of that scene was the uncommon *ugly face* I made at a bold Cuirassier on close quarters with me." Now this was no time to make pretty faces, but it strikes me that it might have been the charge Captain Siborne alludes to, when " a Division of Cuirassiers was cut off on one side of La Haye Sainte," or rather driven back ; but Sir Robert Hill could answer that question.

Colonel Thornhill joins in a charge of the Blues.

I have never visited the field since the Battle. If I ever possessed the clearness so extolled by my kind and partial friend, Sir Hussey, I lost it very early in the day, and in the after part of it I got into *mighty bad company* on the crest of the hill, being close to the Duke of Wellington and Lord Anglesey, when I was knocked off the perch by a cannon-shot which carried off a portion of my neck, paralysed my right ear and right nostril, and you will say the right side of my memory also.

He is wounded when close to the Duke and Lord Anglesey.

Truly yours,
W. THORNHILL.

COLONEL SIR HORACE SEYMOUR, K.C.H.

Captain 60th Rifles, and A.D.C. to Lord Uxbridge.

No. 9.   *Stoke Chichester, November 21st, 1842.*

Waterloo.

I shall be glad to give you all the information my memory retains of the circumstances to which your note refers.

Conduct of the Dutch Cavalry,

In reply to the first question, as to the conduct of the Dutch Brigade of Heavy Cavalry, the impression still on my mind is that they did show a lamentable want of spirit, and that Lord Anglesey tried all in his power to lead them on, and while *he* was advancing, I believe I called his attention to the fact of his not being followed. The Household Brigade at this time were very much reduced.

and of the Cumberland Hanoverian Hussars.

To your second query, I should prefer referring you to the minutes of the General Court-martial, which took place on Colonel ——, of the Cumberland Hussars, near Paris, about the month of August, 1815. My evidence went to the effect that Lord Anglesey, seeing that Regiment moving to the rear (about five o'clock), desired me immediately to halt it. On delivering the order to the Colonel, he told me that he had no confidence in his men, that they were Volunteers, and the horses their own property. All this time the Regiment continued moving to the rear, in spite of my repeating the order to halt, and asking the Second in command to save the character of the Regiment by taking the command and fronting them. I was unsuccessful, and in the exigence of the moment I laid hold of the bridle of the Colonel's horse, and remarked what I thought of his conduct; but all to no purpose.

I then returned to Lord Anglesey, and reported what had passed. I was again ordered to deliver the message to the Commanding Officer of the Regiment, that if they would not resume their position in the Line, that he was to form them across the high road *out* of fire. They did not even obey this order, but went, as was reported, altogether to the rear.

I have endeavoured to simplify this statement as much as possible, and should you wish for any further explanation, I shall be happy to give it.

I add two or three anecdotes connected with the three days which fell under my own observation which may assist the work on which you are engaged, and which, it appears to me, no one has ever undertaken the subject with such prospect of success.

On the 16th, as A.D.C. to Lord Anglesey, with his Lordship I joined, and found the troops engaged. Very shortly afterwards we found the Duke of Wellington, with the Headquarter Staff, in front of the Farm House of Quatre Bras. The French were in force formed on the road, the service of their Artillery beautiful, supported by Cuirassiers, who frequently charged up the road, discomforting the Duke and the Staff on each occasion, until Lord Fitzroy Somerset lined a ditch parallel with the road with some Infantry, unseen to the Enemy, who the next time they moved forward were received with such a volley that scarcely a man of the Squadron escaped, after which there was no forward movement on their part on that part of the position.

Quatre Bras.

The charges of the Cuirassiers discomposing the Duke and his Staff.

The Cuirassiers repelled by the fire of the 92nd Highlanders.

At the moment Sir Thomas Picton received the shot in his forehead which killed him, he was calling to me to rally the Highlanders, who were for the instant overpowered by the masses of French Infantry, who were moving up to their right of the high road.

Waterloo.

Death of Picton.

Late in the day of the 18th, I was called to by some Officers of the 3rd Guards defending Hougoumont, to use my best endeavours to send them musket ammunition. Soon afterwards I fell in with a private of the Waggon Train in charge of a tumbril on the crest of the position. I merely pointed out to him where he was wanted, when

Gallant conduct of a Private of the Waggon Train.

he gallantly started his horses, and drove straight down the hill to the Farm, to the gate of which I saw him arrive. He must have lost his horses, as there was a severe fire kept on him. I feel convinced to that man's service the Guards owe their ammunition.

Advance of the Prussians.

Still later in the day, when delivering the order for Sir Hussey Vivian's Brigade to move towards the centre, we saw the advance of the Prussians. Sir H. Vivian sent me with an Officer and a patrol to assure myself that it was the Prussians who were advancing on our left, which, on proving, I made the best of my way to Lord Anglesey, whom I found with the Duke of Wellington, to whom I reported what I had seen. Sir Alexander Gordon questioned me as to my certainty of it being the Prussians with whom I had communicated, I assuring him that it was so.

Reports to the Duke the Advance of the Prussians.

The Duke orders him to tell General Bulow that he wished him to send some Prussian Infantry up to supply his losses.

I was desired by the Duke of Wellington to tell General Bulow that the Duke wished him immediately to send him Prussian Infantry to fill up the loss that had taken place in his Lines. On starting to deliver this message my horse was killed, and I believe Colonel Freemantle delivered it to the Prussian General.

On starting, his horse is killed, and Colonel Freemantle takes the message.

In a work such as yours promises to be, trifling anecdotes may assist, and with that feeling I transmit them to you.

See No. 11, p. 21.

Yours, &c.,
Horace B. Seymour.

.   .   .   .

ONE MORE ANECDOTE.

Somerset recommended by Lord Anglesey to withdraw his Brigade from under heavy fire. His reasons for continuing there.

I was desired by my General to recommend to Lord Edward Somerset to withdraw his Brigade (who were extended in single file to make a show) from the heavy fire that was kept on them by the Enemy's Artillery. Lord Edward's remark was that should he move, the Dutch Cavalry, who were in support, would move off immediately. The Household Brigade retained their position until the end of the Action.

FROM THE SAME.

Stoke Chichester, November 30th, 1842.   No. 10.

I still feel positive as to the details I gave you of Sir   Waterloo.
Thomas Picton's death, and the immediate scene of it was,   Death of
Picton.
as you say, on the crest of the position, near the hedge,
and immediately over an excavation of either gravel or
stone. It may have been when our skirmishers were
driven in, in which case it was they whom he called upon
me to rally. A little circumstance strengthens me in the
idea that it was Kempt's Brigade we were in front of.
When Sir Thomas fell, my horse also came down, and in
extricating myself I found I was close to the General,
from whose trousers' pocket a Grenadier of the 28th was
endeavouring to take his spectacles and purse, which I
gave to his A.D.C., I *believe*, Colonel Tucker (the stoutest
of the A.D.C.'s.).

Sir Thomas fell from his horse the moment he was
struck, and I called the A.D.C.'s attention to the fact.
I give all this detail to show how positive I feel. Others
may be equally so of their recollections.

.   .   .   .

Yours, &c.,

HORACE B. SEYMOUR.

MAJOR-GENERAL J. FREEMANTLE, C.B.

LIEUT.-COLONEL 2ND FOOT GUARDS, AND A.D.C. TO THE DUKE OF
WELLINGTON.

November 20th, 1842.   No. 11.

I am very glad to state to you the occurrence which   Waterloo.
took place with the Prussian Army on the 18th June.   Arrival of the
Prussians.
Many Officers were sent in the morning in search of the   *See* No. 9,
Army. Towards six o'clock Sir Horace Seymour came   p. 20.
and reported to the Duke of Wellington that he had seen
the Prussian Column.

The Duke called upon me to go to the head of their   Ordered to
go to the
Column, and ask for the 3,000 men to supply our losses.   Prussians and

SIR W. GOMM.
ask for 3,000
men.
They said
they would
make no
detachments,
but that the
whole Army
was coming
up.
Found a
Prussian
Battery firing
between our
lines.

The last attack
in progress.

Meeting of
Wellington
and Blucher.

Blucher had not arrived, but Generals Ziethen and Bulow were at the head of the Column, who gave me for answer—that the whole Army was coming up, and that they could not make a detachment. I said I could [? would] return to the Duke with such a message. On my way back I found a Prussian Battery of eight Guns firing between our first and second lines, and desired the Officer to cease firing. I returned to the knoll so well described in your Model, and begged the Generals to send orders for the Battery to cease fire.

The last attack was now in full force, and when the dense smoke cleared off, we saw that the French were in full retreat.

Blucher, who had arrived, met in the village of Belle Alliance the Duke of Wellington, when it was agreed that he should follow them during the night; he did so.

Believe me, &c.,

JOHN FREEMANTLE.

LIEUT.-GENERAL SIR WILLIAM GOMM, K.C.B.

LIEUT.-COLONEL 2ND FOOT GUARDS, AND ASSISTANT QUARTER-MASTER GENERAL TO THE 5TH DIVISION.

No. 12.   6, *Upper Grosvenor Street, 7th December,* 1836.

I now send you a copy of my journal, according to your wish, as far as it regards Quatre Bras, more for the purpose of satisfying you that all which was to be gleaned from it I had already put you in possession of, than with the hopes of adding one item of importance to your already acquired stock of information.

This journal, you will see, bears evident marks of having been scratched down at the moment; meagre, therefore, and not returned to for the purpose of correcting or enlarging upon, after more ample information had been acquired.

It is, therefore, not to be looked upon as authority with respect to minute details affecting individual Corps, where you have the report direct from individuals in command of, or serving in, those Corps at the time. I put down what I *thought I saw*, as well as what I was *sure I took a part in*.

.   .   .   .   .   .

Believe, &c.,

WILLIAM GOMM.

Copy of the Journal of the operations of the Army under the Duke of Wellington from the 15th of June.

During the night of the 15th, the four Divisions of the Army covering the frontier from Mons to Ypres, and beyond these fortresses, receive orders to concentrate about their respective head-quarters at Oudenarde, Grammont, Enghien, Hal, and the Cavalry at Ninove; but the whole wait further orders for moving. Information of the French Army having forced the passage of the Sambre at Charleroi, on the 14th, reached the British Head Quarters at Brussels only on the evening of the 15th. *Concentration of Troops.* *Passage of the Sambre by the French on the 14th, only known to the Duke on evening of 15th.*

The garrison of Brussels, consisting of two British Brigades of the 5th Division—the 81st Regiment—Brigade of Hanoverian Militia of the 6th Division—Duke of Brunswick's Corps—Nassau troops—assemble during the night, and march at five o'clock next morning on the Charleroi road, halting for two hours in the Bois de Soignies, at Waterloo. *16th.*

At one o'clock p.m. move on through Genappe to Quatre Bras, a post at which the roads from Brussels to Namur and Charleroi divide. The road from Namur to Nivelles also strikes off from the Brussels road at this point, which the Enemy had gained possession of the preceding day, but which had been re-occupied by the troops of Orange-Nassau in the course of the morning, and by a Belgic Brigade under the Prince of Saxe-Weimar. *March on Quatre Bras.* *See Plans of Quatre Bras.*

The Enemy is in force about the village of Frasne, a quarter of a league in advance on the Charleroi road. In the meantime the 1st and 2nd Corps of the Army and Cavalry are marching upon Quatre Bras, it being *It is ascertained that the Enemy is making his principal attack along the*

Sir W. Gomm.

Charleroi
Road instead
of by Mons,
as was first
apprehended.

Three
Brigades of
Infantry
posted at Hal
to guard our
right flank.

Quatre Bras.

Arrival of
first Troops
at.

Distribution
of the Troops.

See Plan No.
1 of Quatre
Bras.

Attack by the
French.

The French
gain posses-
sion of the
Farm House
of Gemion-
court, owing
to the small
force of
British at
hand.

The 28th too
late in getting
to Gemion-
court.

Advantages
of its posses-
sion to the
French.

sufficiently ascertained that the Enemy is making his principal attack in this direction, and not on the side of Mons, as was at first apprehended.

Two Brigades of the 4th Division and one Brigade of Hanoverians are posted at Hal to counteract the movements of a body of Cavalry the Enemy had detached in that direction, threatening our right flank.

The troops from Brussels arrive at Quatre Bras about half-past three p.m. The Enemy immediately makes a disposition for attack with the 1st and 2nd Corps under Ney, and a numerous Cavalry under Kellerman. The British and Hanoverian Brigades drew up in two lines along the *chaussée* leading from Quatre Bras to Namur. The Brunswick Infantry to the right of Quatre Bras, a small portion of Light Troops occupying the head of the Bois de Bossu in their front. This wood was in some parts intricate, but passable everywhere for Light Infantry.

The Enemy cannonades the Light Troops and Belgic Cavalry covering our front, and advances a body of Infantry to take possession of the Farm House of Gemioncourt and enclosures, on the great road half-way between Les Quatre Bras and the village of Frasne. This post was defended by some of the troops of Orange-Nassau, which were soon driven from it by the Enemy.

The Duke of Wellington had directed, when the Enemy was making his first disposition for attack, that this house and the enclosures about it should be immediately occupied by a British Regiment, judging it of great importance to the position that it should be held. The Regiment destined for this service was otherwise disposed of, and the 28th Regiment (marched down too late to establish itself there) was withdrawn, and formed [on] the right of our position at Quatre Bras. The relinquishing of this house and enclosures forms a principal feature in the detail of this day's operations, since, without the entire possession of it, and of the Bois de Bossu, of which the Enemy possessed himself at the same time, and with equal facility, his Cavalry would have been held in check the whole of the day, and his Infantry have been prevented from assuming the offensive so securely as it did, but our force was, during several hours, very inferior to that of the Enemy—ill-composed and inadequate to the proper occupation of the whole position.

The Enemy having established himself in the post of Gemioncourt, advances his Infantry under favour of the copse and enclosures to attack our position upon the Namur road, between Les Quatre Bras and a wood on our extreme left occupied by the 95th Regiment. His attacks are vigorous and repeated—carried on by Columns of Infantry, covered by a numerous body of Light Troops, but they are sustained with firmness by the two British Brigades under Generals Kempt and Pack. A heavy cannonade is kept up by both parties during those operations, which continue for about an hour and a half, when the Enemy, who had hitherto made no impression on our post, availing himself of his great superiority in Cavalry (his Light Troops having possessed themselves of the Bois de Bossu), pushes a strong Column of Cuirassiers and Lancers with rapidity up the great road, disperses the Brunswick and Belgic Cavalry, gets possession of the post of Quatre Bras, and turns the right of the British position. But the Enemy's Cavalry at this moment [are] assailed with so galling and destructive a fire from the 92nd and Hanoverian Regiments, posted behind a bank on the left of Quatre Bras, that they are driven back in great confusion, and with considerable loss. It was in the early part of this charge made by the Enemy that the Duke of Brunswick fell.

About six o'clock the 1st Corps, composed of the 1st and 2nd [3rd] Divisions, reinforce the line. The 1st Division occupied in regaining possession of the Bois de Bossu; the 3rd strengthening our left, and relieving in their post several of our Battalions which had suffered considerably, or exhausted their ammunition. This was the situation of many Regiments on the arrival of the

Attack on Kempt's and Pack's Brigades (Picton's Division).

French Light Troops take possession of the Bois de Bossu, and their Cavalry of the post of Quatre Bras.

The latter driven back by the 92nd and Hanoverian Regiments.

About 6 o'clock arrival of Maitland's and Alten's Divisions.

reinforcement, and the Enemy was observed preparing for a fresh attack, which was again repulsed, with the assistance of the troops newly arrived.

The Enemy's Cavalry, repulsed from Quatre Bras by the heavy fire of musketry directed against it, reforms his Columns, is supported by fresh reserves, and, finding no Cavalry on our side capable of holding him in check, renews his attack upon the great road, and threatens the Infantry formed in line to the left of it. The Infantry immediately forms squares by Battalions. The 42nd Regiment being much advanced, suffers greatly from the fire of the Enemy's sharpshooters in the enclosures of Gemioncourt, but repulses the charge of the Cuirassiers.*

Continued attacks of French Cavalry on British Infantry.

The attack on the 42nd (and 44th) Regiments.

The advance of the Royals and 28th. *See* Kempt's Brigade.

The 28th Regiment, and a wing of the Royals, formed in square upon the causeway, and inaccessible (except by one front) to the approach of Cavalry, are ordered by Sir Thomas Picton to march down into the plain, and take the flank of the Enemy's Cavalry, which was making an impression on the great road. This Square advances with shouts into the middle of the plain, halts within short musket range of the Cavalry, and opens a fire upon it— charged repeatedly by the Enemy's Cuirassiers and Lancers, who are repulsed in every onset. The Lancers wound the men in the ranks, but are every time driven back with confusion and great loss.

See Halkett's Brigade.

The 30th Regiment also moves down under the same form, flanks the Square above mentioned, and receives with equal firmness the charge of the French Cavalry.

Withdrawal of the French, and occupation by the British of the advance posts.

The attacks of Cavalry upon the Infantry are continued till dark, as well as the contest in the Bois de Bossu. At length the Enemy withdraws from all his points of attack, and resumes his position in front of Frasne. The Bois de Bossu and the post of Gemioncourt are strongly occupied

---

* *Note* (in Journal).—The 42nd Regiment was charged by the Cuirassiers while in the act of forming in square ; but such was the firmness of the troops that even in an irregular mass they repulsed the charge, and, by the time the second attack was made upon them, order was re-established.

by British troops. The cannonade continues till after dark.

A heavy cannonade heard on our left the whole afternoon. The Prussians warmly engaged till long after dark.

The British Cavalry arrives upon the ground at nightfall, having made a long and very rapid march. The two British Brigades of the 5th Division lose on this day 120 Officers and 1,400 men. The brunt of the Action fell upon them.

Arrival of British Cavalry at nightfall.

The Enemy attacked with the 1st and 2nd Corps under Ney and D'Erlon, and the Cavalry under Kellerman. Bonaparte directed the attack upon the Prussians, who held their ground with obstinacy, but are at length obliged to retire upon Wavre.

The Battle of Ligny.

The whole of the British force engaged for nearly two hours did not exceed 4,000 men.

The two Armies remain in presence till two o'clock p.m., but the British commences retiring its stores, &c. &c., upon the Brussels road earlier. By two the whole Army is in movement, covered by the Cavalry; the Enemy shows no disposition to advance till the whole have moved off. In the course of the retreat the Enemy makes several charges upon our Cavalry with various success. Our Cavalry is pressed by that of the Enemy towards the close of the day.

17th.

Retreat upon the position of Waterloo.

The Army takes up a position across the great road [? roads] leading from Charleroi and Nivelles to Brussels. No baggage, stores, or wounded fall into the Enemy's hands during this retreat. A violent storm comes on while the Army is taking up its position, and heavy rain continues the whole of the night and following morning till near midday.

FROM THE SAME.

6, *Upper Grosvenor Street, 5th January*, 1837.

No. 13.

Quatre Bras.

With regard to the 28th, I may not have been correct in my statement to you. I believe I have already told you that I was leading the 28th down the road to occupy

The 28th Regiment.

Gemioncourt, but it was ascertained that the French had already driven out the Nassau or Dutch troops from it, and were in full possession. I was then ordered to withdraw the 28th, and on returning to Quatre Bras they certainly must have turned to the right, and rejoined their own Brigade. I had taken them at the moment of their reaching the point of Quatre Bras, having myself just returned from riding through the Bois de Bossu by direction of Sir Thomas Picton.

The 95th ought to have been moved down in the *first instance* to Gemioncourt. They were, however, sent to occupy the strip of wood on the left of the Namur road, opposite Piermont.

The position of the 28th upon your plan corresponds, also, with the statement in my journal respecting the Squares formed by the wing of the Royals and 28th.

The right of the 92nd upon the Charleroi Road.

The 92nd *were certainly* upon the road, and so the French Cuirassiers found to their cost when they charged up it, even beyond Quatre Bras. When I say *upon* the road, I mean with their flank resting upon it—or nearly so.

You are aware that late in the day we were reinforced by the 3rd Division, and our Regiments replaced in the advanced positions in great measure by it, Halkett's Brigade I think chiefly, to which I believe the 30th belonged.

Latterly, we were principally upon the *chaussée* leading to Namur, the Hanoverian Brigade of Landwehr, I think, always behind it, and in column; but of this I have no certain recollection.

I cannot give you any detailed information respecting the disposal of the 3rd Division, otherwise than that it took up ground to our left, and partly to our front, on its arrival about six o'clock.

And now respecting Waterloo.

Waterloo.

You are aware that at Quatre Bras our 8th Brigade was posted on the left (arriving first on the ground), and the 9th Brigade on the right. At Waterloo this was reversed, the 8th had its *appui* upon the road to the right, and the 9th upon the wooded knoll to the left, or thereabouts.

I think the order of the Regiments is correctly noted in your enclosed sketch, No. 1; there was no reason why they should not stand as in parade order.

The 95th then (as Light Troops) would be on the right of the 8th Brigade (and so they were, in advance of it), and the 28th on its left. This agrees with my report of the Enemy's right and centre Columns,* excepting as regards the position of the 44th.

Posting of the 5th Division (Picton's). *See* Plan, p. 38.

From the very circumstantial account you have received from an Officer of this Battalion, as well as for the reason I have assigned above, it is clear that the 44th *must* have been on the extreme left, notwithstanding that I have noted it otherwise in my journal. My placing it so, hastily, in my journal was most probably an *inference* of the *moment*. To my eye, the 92nd with its left flank brought up, formed our extreme left when dealing with the Enemy's right Column of attack; the 44th must have been beyond, but not so prominently engaged at the moment.

I see the 92nd now, lining a gentle ascent, opposed to the Enemy's right flank; but I recollect nothing to its left. Have you it *clearly substantiated* that the Enemy sent *three* Columns of attack against our front to the left of the Great Road? My *decided impression* is that they did. The extract you give me from the report of the Officer of the 79th would seem to favour the opinion of there having been only *two*.

And now with respect to Ponsonby's Cavalry. I can no more pretend to stand against the body of Cavalry evidence you bring forward to prove the incorrectness of one of my statements, than the French did against their charge. Undoubtedly it *must* have been with the leading Officer on the right of the *Greys* that I had the short colloquy I have already reported to you.*

Ponsonby's Cavalry. *See* Letters from Ponsonby's Brigade.

---

* These statements refer to a previous letter which, unfortunately, I cannot trace. —Ed.

Sir W. Gomm.

I have always thought it was the right of the *Brigade,* and by inference of the *Royals;* and I have no recollection of *either* Regiment passing to the front over the ground I had *myself just* traversed, yet I am convinced this *must have been the case* from the statements you forward to me. My attention was so riveted upon the French Column, and its efforts for rendering itself more effective, that it is not surprising I should have been inattentive at the moment to what was passing behind; and the same with respect to the Cavalry at hand. I have since regretted that I did not endeavour to find out who the Officer was with whom I conversed—the opportunity did not offer readily—and so the matter went to rest. Perhaps, poor fellow! he never left the field.

Pray, therefore, do not let what I have said with such apparent confidence about the Royals weigh with you for a moment.

Now, with respect to your detached queries.

The Horse Artillery driven in by the advance of the French left Column was certainly British. I cannot help thinking they had two Guns posted upon the knoll held by the 95th—at *least* two Guns, so I have noted it in my journal—and from this point they answered the French cannonade while taking up our ground on the evening of the 17th. I recollect, too, considerable bustle in getting the Guns away while the Column was approaching, against which they had done heavy execution. In all this I can hardly be mistaken. Sir Andrew Barnard, perhaps, could satisfy you on this point. I am surprised that your Artillery reports make no mention of it.

Netherland Infantry in front of Picton's Division.

The Brigade of Netherlanders were certainly in line before the French Columns advanced, and considerably down the slope, so that Rogers' Guns fired over them, first in reply to the French cannonade, and afterwards at the advancing Columns as they broke from the wood [?], and till they reached the bottom, and began to ascend our own hill.

Their exposed position.

These Netherlanders were undoubtedly much exposed—

eighty pieces of cannon opening upon them at horse-pistol range, or little more.

I did not place them there, nor have I really any distinct recollection of the order in which they stood.

.   .   .   .

Yours, &c.,
Wm. Gomm.

FROM THE SAME.

6, Upper Grosvenor Street, 9th April, 1838.   No. 14.

.   .   .   .   .   .

With respect to the position of the 30th Regiment, and of the third Division generally, on this occasion, I am not surprised that you should find some difficulty in determining matters. The main object the 3rd Division had in view, on their arrival upon the ground of Quatre Bras, was to reinforce our left (of the 5th Division), but they also relieved (upon their own ground) several of our Regiments, whose ammunition was *totally exhausted* at the moment of this arrival, which Regiments in their turn fell back towards the Causeway (the Namur one). *[Quatre Bras. 30th Regiment.]*

With respect to what I say about the 30th Regiment, such was my impression at the time; but I would not pertinaciously defend my statement against odds; nor would I wish you to abide by it, if you find it conflicting with others that hang well together in opposition to if, for this did not pass immediately under my own eye. *See* pp. 26 & 28.

.   .   .   .   .   .

Very truly yours,
Wm. Gomm.

LIEUT.-COLONEL THE HON. GEORGE CATHCART,
8th REGIMENT.

Lieutenant 6th Dragoon Guards, and Extra A.D.C. to the Duke
of Wellington.

No. 15.   *Spanish Town, Jamaica, 13th April,* 1835.

. . . .

With regard to any light I can throw on the subject
I fear this letter will be of little use, for as I was a very
young soldier at the time, and excepting one year's service
in a Cavalry Regiment, my knowledge and observation of
details of regimental formation was very imperfect, and
never having till those eventful days seen a British Army
assembled in the field, I took little note of the names or
numbers of particular Infantry Regiments or Brigades.
I had, however, had the good fortune to have been an
Had witnessed eye-witness of eight General Actions, in which Napoleon
eight General had commanded, and therefore my attention was directed
Actions in which Napoleon had commanded, and therefore my attention was directed
which Napoleon to the movements " *en grand,*" and of these you are no doubt
leon had commanded fully aware and have ample testimony.   I will, however,
manded. name two or three points relating to the ground about
which my recollection, refreshed by your accurate plan, is
pretty clear.

Waterloo. With regard to the *retiring* of the two Brigades you
mention, I have no recollection of it.   I remember on one
occasion, earlier in the day, the Duke caused two or three
Battalions about that part of the line to move a hundred
yards or so further back, in order to be behind the crest of
the hill till wanted, and in order to be less exposed, and
there they remained in column, but sitting down and some
even asleep as if nothing was going on, though sometimes
a shot or shell found its way in amongst them.

See Plan, p.38. With regard to the hollow road near our right centre,
The hollow that is the part nearest to the tree, I have a distinct re-
road leads into collection of it.
the main road
on the same For about 100 yards, more or less, it was very hollow.
side as is La At the end going down into the high road it might have
Haye Sainte, been 10 or even 15 feet deep.   I have reason to know it,
and about 270
yards in rear
of it.—Ed.

Lt. Col. Cathcart.

for there was but one way of going down into it from the field at the back of La Haye Sainte, which was very slippery, would admit not more than two horses at a time, and might have been at an angle of 45.

The so-called "Wellington tree" was in the angle formed by the main road and hollow way and in front of the latter.-Ed.

When the Duke had been looking on at the attack of La Haye Sainte at that moment of intense interest, when the ammunition began to fail the defenders, and no means of getting either reinforcements or ammunition to them for want of any postern was discovered, the Duke, who was much vexed, had remained till the Enemy's tirailleurs had actually shown themselves round the side of the house, and then had to retire by that gap into the hollow road and up again on the other side. Finding that it would be some time before it would come to my turn to get through this gap, I turned my horse round, and was looking at the affair, when he was shot in the breast and fell with me unable to rise again; I consequently left him to die, and followed the horsemen through the gap on foot. This hollow road must have been an obstacle of considerable extent, or some of us would have crossed it in another place, but at about three or four hundred yards, and perhaps less distance from the main road, it was little or no obstacle, and was frequently passed by Cavalry. The circumstance of my horse being killed by a shot at about 200 yards distance from the corner of the house, which took effect in his breast, also makes me *positive* there was no high sharp ridge there like a parapet parallel to the road in the line of that shot, though there may have been further to the right; but certainly none to impede the advance of Cavalry. What is odd, I forget the far-famed tree altogether; it would be only a small one.

At La Haye Sainte ammunition failing.

Vexation of the Duke at this.

Lieutenant Cathcart's horse shot while looking at the contest at La Haye Sainte.

.   .   .   .

I do not remember the orchard or garden at the back of the Haye Sainte, but as it had been a bivouac the night before it may very likely have been so trodden down and covered with wet straw, &c., as to have lost all trace. The *abatis* had been laid open long before the period of the

Lt. Col. Cathcart.

The *abatis* was placed across the main road, about 150 yards in rear of La Haye Sainte.—Ed.

Battle you have seized for the purpose of allowing Cavalry to pass, but the trees still lay about the road.   If I recollect right it was not much of a one at any time.

. . . .

Yours, &c.,

G. W. Cathcart.

FROM THE SAME.

No. 16.

Waterloo.

2, Lewes Crescent, Brighton, 24th December, 1835.

I regret I cannot attempt to give any information on the points you mention in your letter of the 21st November, as not sufficiently established to your satisfaction by the testimonies already in your possession, which might pretend to sufficient accuracy to be of any use.

I certainly saw the black looking Columns assembled and advancing to the attack, and should say that their appearance was more considerable as they loomed through smoke and fog than that represented in the sketch you sent

Again dismounted.

me.   I was dismounted by a cannon shot from some of the Batteries, which were, I suppose, meant to cover this attack, and therefore had not a good opportunity of minutely observing their formation or numbers.

Strength of attacking Columns of Imperial Guard.

It is, of course, the interest of the defeated party to make their numbers appear to have been as small and inadequate as possible.   I should think you could not be wrong in adopting Colonel Batty's numbers; he makes two Columns, together consisting of 12 Battalions.   Gourgaud, who whether by dictation of Napoleon or not, is certain to have written the approved version of Longwood on a subject very often discussed, also admits that there were two Columns, together amounting to 12 Battalions, and the story of eight being called off and kept in reserve and only four engaged is *" beau à dire "* and excusable enough for a beaten party—and strictly speaking in such considerable Columns, not more than four Battalions can well come in contact, although when such a flank movement as that of General Adam's Brigade is able to take effect, the whole concern, reserve and all, must be involved in one general rout and confusion, which was the result on the occasion in point.

I think you should allow for a little opening out of files as well as ranks in a large advancing column, for of course, even with better drilled people than Napoleon's troops ever had time to be, that is unavoidable, and 23 inches per man I should think in such wet and slippery ground for troops in motion not at all too much, but the troops formed four deep to receive them have no business with more than 21 inches. I long to see your work completed.

Believe, &c.,

GEORGE CATHCART.

LORD WILLIAM PITT LENNOX.

CORNET ROYAL HORSE GUARDS, EXTRA A.D.C. TO MAJOR-GENERAL MAITLAND.

1, *Berkeley Square, London, February 22nd,* 1843.   No. 17.

MEMO.   .   .   .   .   .   .

Shortly before the battle of Waterloo, I (having arrived at Brussels from Vienna with the Duke of Wellington, was appointed Extra A.D.C. to General Maitland) met with a violent accident by a fall from my horse in the Park of Enghien, where the Guards were quartered. My right arm was severely fractured, the sight of my right eye completely destroyed, and my life despaired of. While on the sick list at Brussels, the battle of the 16th took place, and the death of poor Hay of the Guards, my brother A.D.C., made me anxious to join my Chief.

Early on the morning of the 18th, my father, the late Duke of Richmond, left Brussels on horseback, accompanied by myself, with, as you mention, "my arm in a sling." Upon reaching the village of Waterloo, we saw Lord Anglesey, who was just mounting his horse. "We

The Duke of Richmond at Waterloo.

shall have sharp work to-day," said his Lordship, greeting
us, or words to that effect. At that moment we heard
some firing, and lost no time in galloping on to the plain.
Our first visit was to Maitland, who would not permit me
to remain with him. A boy of fifteen, with a maimed
arm and weak frame of body, would not have proved a
very available A.D.C.

We then rode up to the hero of the day, and remained
some time with him. During this period the musketry
was so sharp that one of the Duke's Staff urged him to
retire a little. My father and myself then proceeded to
the left of our line, accompanied part of the way by the
late Sir J. Elley. We reached Picton's Division, and after
some little time, while my father was talking to that or
some other distinguished Officer, the right of the French
Line advanced. We were then urged to retire, but my
father remained, and, turning to me, said, "I'm glad to
see you stand fire so well." This was more than my
horse did, for I expected every moment to be run away
with, probably into the French fire.

After a certain period, there were several charges of
Heavy Dragoons, and I have no doubt whatever but that
my father was the person alluded to by you as addressing
the Inniskilling Dragoons, for no one else in plain clothes
was near the spot. The whole of the morning he talked
to his friends, and made his remarks as if he was on
service, not an amateur. I perfectly remember a very
heavy Officer of some Heavy Dragoon Regiment being dismounted, and being carried to the rear, which must have
been after Ponsonby's charge.

We then again proceeded to the right, but at this time
the firing was so heavy, and the ground so strewed with
the slain, that we retired, and returned leisurely to
Brussels. Two days after the battle, my father and
myself rode over the field.

I have now given you the details in, I fear, an
egotistical manner; but they are correct. I can readily
believe my father was the individual alluded to, not only

from the interest he took in the Battle, but from the circumstance of no other person in plain clothes being with or near us.　.　.　.　.　.　.

WILLIAM PITT LENNOX.

SOMERSET'S CAVALRY BRIGADE.

The 1st (Heavy) Cavalry, or Household Brigade, was composed of the 1st and 2nd Life Guards, the Royal Horse Guards Blue, and the 1st or King's Dragoon Guards, and was commanded by Major-General Lord Edward Somerset, K.C.B.

The Brigade formed part of the centre Column of the Cavalry which covered the retreat of the Army from Quatre Bras on the 17th June. After passing through Genappe it was drawn up about 600 or 700 yards to the rear of the town, with its right on the main road.

Lord Uxbridge, having withdrawn the 7th Hussars from the contest with the French Lancers, ordered the 1st Life Guards to advance, and charge the latter. This they performed so effectually as to drive back the Lancers right through the town of Genappe.

At Waterloo, the Brigade was posted with its left near to the Brussels-Charleroi *chaussée*, about 250 yards in front of the farm of Mont-St.-Jean. *See* General Plan, No. 1

The French first attack on the Allied left centre was simultaneous with the advance of a large body of Cuirassiers, which ascended the British position to the right of La Haye Sainte. The Household Brigade moved forward to the charge, and overthrew the Cuirassiers, driving them down the slope,

across, and along the *chaussée* towards La Belle
Alliance, where the 1st Life Guards suffered
severely from the fire of the French Infantry lining
the high banks of a cutting through which the
road passed.

The 2nd Life Guards, on the left of the
Brigade, drove a portion of the Cuirassiers across
the *chaussée* to the rear of La Haye Sainte, and
down the slope in front of the right of Kempt's
Infantry Brigade. Here they were joined by the
King's Dragoon Guards, who had crossed the road
in front of the farm, and the two Regiments becoming mingled with Ponsonby's Cavalry, lost all
regularity in the eagerness of the pursuit.

The Blues had been originally in support, but
had joined the front line during the charge. They
were, however, kept well in hand, and being comparatively in good order, facilitated the drawing off
of the remainder of the Brigade from further
pursuit.

Later in the day, during one of the attacks
on the Infantry Squares by the French Cavalry, a
large body of the latter passed between the Squares
to assail the Allied Cavalry in second line. It was
charged by the Brigade, though with greatly
diminished numbers, and by other Corps, and,
after a sanguinary conflict, driven back through
the Squares, and down the slope of the position.

The Brigade was next employed by Lord Uxbridge in repelling a strong Column of French
Infantry, which was advancing against the centre
of the Allied right wing. The Column was attacked, and its advance stopped, but the Brigade,

Repulse of D'Erlon's First Attack on Picton's Division

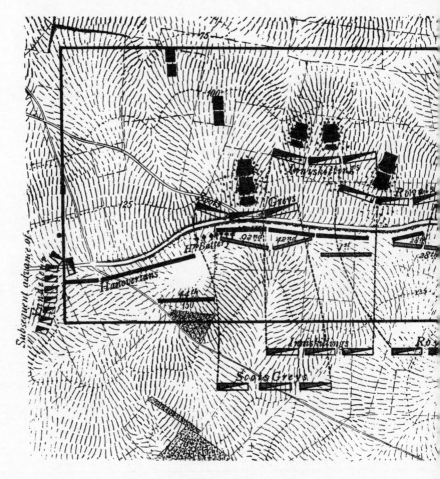

N.B.—The parallelogram shows the extent of ground rep

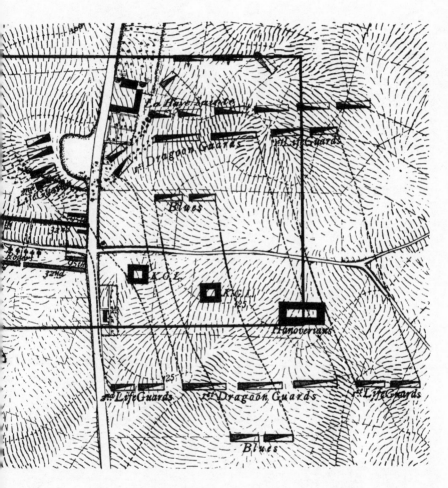

Captain Siborne's second and smaller Model of Waterloo.

in its reduced state, was unable to penetrate it, and suffered much from its fire.

Towards evening the remains of Somerset's and Ponsonby's Brigades were united, and drawn up in single file to make a *show* of force; but although they suffered much from the French cannonade in this position, they were unable to quit it, as it was feared that a backward movement for the purpose of obtaining cover would be followed by the Dutch-Belgian Cavalry, who were in support, retiring from the field altogether.

At the close of the Battle, the two Brigades were so reduced in numbers as to form only one Squadron, but they nevertheless joined in the General Advance.

All the letters refer to Waterloo.

LIEUT.-GENERAL LORD EDWARD SOMERSET, G.C.B.

MAJOR-GENERAL, K.C.B., AND COMMANDING HOUSEHOLD BRIGADE.

Office of Ordnance, Pall Mall, April 4th, 1835. No. 18.

. . . .

I now beg to send you the enclosed Report in reply to your several Queries, accompanied by as correct a statement of the general operations of the 1st Brigade of Cavalry throughout the day, as my recollection will enable me to give at this distance of time. I hope it will reach you in sufficient time to prevent any inconvenience, and that it will assist you in completing your Model of the Battle.

I remain, &c.,

R. ED. H. SOMERSET,

Lieut-Genl.

Movements of the 1st (Household) Brigade of Cavalry at the Battle of Waterloo.

Query 1.—What was the particular formation of the 1st Cavalry Brigade at the moment (about 7 p.m.) when the French Imperial Guards, advancing to attack the right of the British forces, reached the crest of the position?

Formation of the Brigade when the Imperial Guard advanced to attack the British right.

Answer.—The 1st Cavalry Brigade and the remains of the 2nd Brigade (which had been ordered to join the former about three or four in the afternoon, after the death of Sir William Ponsonby, and at that time commanded by Colonel, now Major-General, Sir A. Clifton) were so much reduced from the severe losses they had sustained in men and horses, and from various casualties, that at the period mentioned they formed, *together*, *only* *one* squadron of about 50 *File*. Their formation was in line about 300 yards under the crest of the hill, and nearly the same distance from the right of the high road leading from Mont-St.-Jean to La Haye Sainte.

See No. 49, p. 100.

After the repulse of the Enemy's attack, they advanced to the front, and continued in pursuit until dark. Previous to the above, a small detachment of the 23rd Light Dragoons, under Major Lautour, had joined the 1st Brigade, and moved with it in the advance.

Query 2.—What was the formation of that part of the Enemy's forces immediately in front of the 1st Cavalry Brigade?

Formation of the French in front of the Brigade.

Answer.—The advance of the Enemy upon this part of the position was in heavy Columns of Infantry, with crowds of Tirailleurs in their front, and supported by Columns of Cavalry, covered by a tremendous fire of Artillery.   .   .   .   .   .   .

In addition to the above information, and in compliance with the request of Lieutenant Siborne, the following remarks respecting the positions and movements of the 1st Cavalry Brigade are submitted.

Post of the Brigade at the

At the commencement of the Battle, the position assigned to the Brigade was on the right of the high road, and in support of the Infantry posted on the height near La Haye Sainte, and extending further to the right.

About 1 p.m., simultaneously with the attack on the left of the high road, information having been received that a large body of the Enemy's Cavalry (Cuirassiers and Carabineers) was moving towards the crest of the position near La Haye Sainte, the 1st Cavalry Brigade was immediately put in motion (the British Infantry forming squares or columns in order that it might pass through the intervals), and advanced in line (the Blues supporting) to the attack of the Enemy's Cavalry, which was met on the ridge of the hill, and was completely defeated and driven back with considerable loss. In the first instance, the 1st Life Guards had a severe conflict with the Enemy near La Haye Sainte, where they did great execution, and succeeded in forcing them back to the opposite height, pursuing them to the foot of the French position.

The other Regiments of the Brigade were equally successful, and followed that part of the Enemy to which they were opposed to a still greater distance, especially the 2nd Life Guards and 1st Dragoon Guards, who, ascending the position occupied by the Enemy's Infantry on the left of the high road, encountered a heavy fire, and sustained a very severe loss in their retreat. Colonel Fuller, commanding the 1st Dragoon Guards, and several Officers and men of that Regiment fell in this attack.

The 2nd Life Guards likewise suffered severely.

By this attack, that part of the British position was completely cleared of the Enemy's Cavalry.

The Household Brigade having been rallied and formed nearly on their original post, continued in support of the Infantry, until a fresh opportunity offered of their acting offensively against a considerable force of the Enemy's Cavalry assembled on the reverse of the hill, and threatening our position, when after a severe and bloody conflict the Enemy was checked, and the 1st Brigade retired and re-formed under the cover of the hill.

On this occasion the Enemy suffered severely.   Colonel

Side notes:

commencement of the Battle.

Charge of the Brigade against the French Cavalry at the time of D'Erlon's first attack.

See Plan, p. 38.

The Brigade charges a body of Cavalry.

2ND LIFE GUARDS.

Ferrier, commanding 1st Life Guards, and Major Packe, of the Blues, were killed, besides several other Officers and men.

Next charges a Column of Infantry.

The next movement of the Household Brigade was to a part of the position towards the right, where it was summoned by Lord Anglesey to attack a formidable Column of the Enemy's Infantry, supported by Cavalry, which threatened the British troops in that quarter. The attack was made with great gallantry, and succeeded in checking the advance of the Enemy; but the Brigade being very much reduced in numbers, was unable to penetrate the Column, which received it with a heavy fire.

Somerset's Brigade joined by Ponsonby's.

After this attack the Brigade rallied and formed upon its original ground, where it was joined by the 2nd Brigade, also much diminished.

About this time there was a considerable space on the right of the Haye Sainte void of British Infantry, and as it was threatened by a strong force of the Enemy assembled under the brow of the hill, the 1st and 2nd Brigades continued to occupy the interval, exposed to a destructive fire both of musketry and artillery, from which they sustained such severe loss that they were at length reduced to one Squadron, as stated in the beginning of this Report.

1st and 2nd Brigades *together* reduced to one Squadron at the end of the day.

The Brigade joined in the General Advance.

Upon the Enemy being finally defeated, the two Brigades advanced with the rest of the troops till about 9 o'clock, when they halted and bivouacked for the night.

2ND LIFE GUARDS.

MAJOR S. WAYMOUTH, UNATTACHED.
LIEUTENANT 2ND LIFE GUARDS.

No. 19.
Waterloo.

Wounded and taken prisoner in the 1st Charge.

65, *Marine Parade, Brighton, Nov.* 18*th,* 1834.

I have the honour of acknowledging the receipt of your letter of Oct. 29th, and regret extremely that I am unable to afford any useful aid towards the interesting work you are engaged in, for as I had the misfortune to be wounded and taken prisoner in the first charge made by the Household Brigade, I can say nothing from personal knowledge of what took place at 7 o'clock.

·   ·   ·   ·   ·   ·   ·

Whether I am now going to occupy your attention with what is utterly useless, I do not know; but the last paragraph but one of your letter induces me to mark upon the plan (as nearly as I can at this distance of time) the spot where the Household Brigade was stationed at the beginning of the Action; and to this ground, as I am informed, it continually returned after every attack made by it throughout the day. The 2nd Life Guards was the left Regiment of the Brigade, and, for better understanding, allow me to say that my post was commanding its left half Squadron.

Commanded left half Squadron.

In making the charge to which I have alluded, the right of the Brigade was thrown forward in order to sweep the high road, along which the Enemy's Columns were advancing against La Haye Sainte, and by my dotted lines I wish to give some notion of the direction it took. As I was posted on the left, I can speak to that dotted line with more confidence than the other, both as to its direction and length. In our rear I saw posted for our support the Duke of Cumberland's Hanoverian Hussars. According to the printed accounts, this Regiment ran away into Brussels as we advanced to the charge. I saw Ponsonby's Heavy Brigade also charging along with us, in a nearly parallel line on the other side of the road. Soon after our left had crossed the high road, it became mingled with Ponsonby's right. In the course of their charge, every description of the Enemy's Cavalry, both heavy and light, were overthrown, and even deep Columns of Infantry passed through.

See Plan, p. 38.

Line of direction of first charge of 2nd Life Guards across the road in rear of La Haye Sainte.

When they became mingled with Ponsonby's Cavalry.

As I was taken prisoner in this charge, I am unable to add anything more of my own knowledge, except the position in which I saw some Cuirassiers and the Red Lancers; but even in this I may not be *precisely accurate.*

Taken prisoner.

My friend, Major Edward Kelly, who distinguished

Conflict
between the
Brigade
and the
Cuirassiers.

himself very much amongst the 1st Life Guards, and who afterwards died on Lord Combermere's Staff in India, told me that as far as he could see down our line to his left, the Brigade, and the Cuirassiers too, came to the shock like two walls, in the most perfect lines he ever saw; and I believe this line was maintained throughout. A short struggle enabled us to break through them, notwithstanding the great disadvantage arising from our swords, which were full six inches shorter than those of the Cuirassiers, besides its being the custom of our Service to carry the swords in a very bad position whilst charging, the French carrying theirs in a manner much less fatiguing, and also much better for either attack or defence. Having once penetrated their line, we rode over everything opposed to us. Major Kelly also told me that the 1st Life Guards made great slaughter amongst the flying Cuirassiers who had choked the hollow way, marked +—that its banks were then crowned by Chasseurs, who fired down upon the Life Guards in return, killing great numbers of them, and that this road was quite blocked up by dead.

The swords of
the Brigade
six inches
shorter than
those of the
Cuirassiers,
and not so
well carried.

The 1st
Life Guards
amongst the
Cuirassiers.

The cutting
on the
Chaussée.

Their great
loss from the
fire of French
Chasseurs.

My ignorance of the tracks of French Columns, and the little I know of the formations of our own Army, are chiefly owing to the circumstance of our being posted in such low ground that the view of the Enemy was intercepted by the high ridge of La Haye Sainte.   .   .

.   .   .   .   .

I have, &c.,

S. WAYMOUTH.

FROM THE SAME.

TO MAJOR MARTEN, ROYAL DRAGOONS.

No. 20.
Waterloo.

London, March 16th, 1837.

In the first
charge part of
the Brigade
passed to the

MY DEAR MARTEN,—I believe you are perfectly correct in saying that in the first charge one portion of our Brigade passed by the right and another by the left of La Haye Sainte. In as far as the *extreme left* of the Brigade was concerned, I can speak without the slightest hesitation, for you may remember that I commanded the left half Squadron of our Regiment and of the Brigade, and *my recollection is distinct that I crossed the road in rear, and to the left of* La Haye Sainte. And I remember seeing there—*i.e.*, on the left of the road and near its edge, a little cottage or hovel occupied by, I believe, a party of the 2nd Light Battalion, King's German Legion, for it was unroofed, and on one of the remaining rafters I saw an Officer of that Battalion (named Græme) sitting, whose name and person were familiar to me although not acquainted with him. I mention this to show how clear my recollection still is to that point.

right of La Haye Sainte and part to the left.

2nd Life Guards crossed the main road to the rear of La Haye Sainte.

Immediately after this I found men of the Royals and Inniskilling Dragoons from Ponsonby's Brigade mingled with ours. Now I cannot pretend to say how many of our Regiment, whether a Squadron, or less or more, passed by the left of the farm of La Haye Sainte; but if Captain Siborne's Model has that hovel marked upon it (which it probably has not, for it was so small and so pulled to pieces, that it was not perhaps restored after the Action), the distance from it to the corner of La Haye Sainte may give a pretty good notion of how many rank and file passed through that interval.

It could not have been Græme, as he was at La Haye Sainte. See No. 179, p. 406.—ED.

2nd Life Guards mingled with Ponsonby's Brigade.

That the Brigade was divided by La Haye Sainte I have little doubt from my recollection of conversations I afterwards had with Kelly whilst he lay wounded in Brussels, in which he spoke of going down the slope of the position, and afterwards pressing the rear of the Cuirassiers whilst they choked a part of the road bounded by high banks, which spot I perfectly remember about half-way down the hill. The 1st Regiment suffered severely there, for whilst they were occupied with the Cuirassiers, the banks were lined by French Chasseurs, who killed a great many of them by firing down upon them. My belief is that the 1st Regiment passed by the right of La Haye Sainte, and skirted round the fence of its orchard, which I think would bring them into the road a little before this

The 1st Life Guards on the high road.

hollow way. Moreover, I always understood that it was down the slope of the position to the right of La Haye Sainte that Major Packe of the Blues was killed.

As I said before, I cannot determine what portion of the Brigade, nor even of our Regiment, passed to the left of La Haye Sainte, but the circumstance of my more than once, during that advance, finding myself near Major Naylor, of the King's Dragoon Guards, and to whom I spoke, leads me to suppose that some part of his Regiment may also have passed to the left. He must have commanded a Squadron, probably the left Squadron of the King's.

Whilst writing the preceding, it occurs to me that in crossing the road I had to get my horse down a bank of perhaps some three feet or so, and then to go along the road some yards before I could find a place to mount the opposite bank, and that I did so near the aforesaid hovel.

Some of the 1st Dragoon Guards may also have crossed the road to the rear of La Haye Sainte.

. . . .

Very truly yours,
S. WAYMOUTH.

FROM THE SAME.

Grosvenor Street, May 9th, 1837.

No. 21.
Waterloo.

I very much regret that many circumstances have combined to prevent my meeting with Major Naylor at home until yesterday.

1st Charge.

I find him very oblivious of all the circumstances connected with the Brigade on the 18th excepting one, which I think is satisfactory—viz., the advance of the Brigade to the first charge. He distinctly remembers that he commanded the centre Squadron of the King's, which, as the Blues were in second line for support, there being two Squadrons of each Regiment of Life Guards, and three of the King's, was consequently the centre Squadron of the Brigade. He remembers that on advancing, Colonel Fuller placed himself by him, and that the first obstacle they encountered was the road which runs along the top of the ridge, that it was too wide to leap, and the banks too deep to be easily passed, and that having crossed it, the next obstacle was the enclosure of the farm of La Haye Sainte.

Now this seems to agree perfectly with the appearance of that road as laid down upon the plan you sent me.

He then made towards his left "along with the current of our men, which was setting that way." He cannot tell how or where he crossed the high road, but you will observe that this brings him to that part of the ground where I called to him, but he forgets that circumstance. He then went down the hill still bearing to his left, till he arrived at an enclosure,* a large field in which were Lancers. Turning from that he made his way home again round the left of our line. Meantime Colonel Fuller must, on arriving at the farm of La Haye Sainte, have turned *to his right,* for I believe there is no doubt of his having been killed down the slope of our position, to the *right* of La Haye Sainte. From all this I think we may safely infer that the farm of La Haye Sainte broke the Brigade at its centre, and that about one-half passed on each side of it.

The King's Dragoon Guards, or a portion of them, also cross the main road to the rear of La Haye Sainte.

Believe, &c.,

S. WAYMOUTH.

FROM THE SAME.

19, *Upper Grosvenor Street, April 8th,* 1841.

No. 22.

.   .   .   .

Again, I believe Capt. Kincaid's recollection perfectly correct, of Cuirassiers pouring down that hollow way into the *chaussée* pursued by Life Guards, for remember I always described to you, and I learnt it from Capt. Kelly, 1st Life Guards, that the right and centre of the House-hold Brigade met the Cuirassiers in perfect line, and this

Waterloo.

1st Charge. The right and centre of the Brigade met the Cuirassiers in perfect line before the extreme left could get into the line.

---

* Note by *writer.*—By Major Naylor's description of its distance and direction, this must be one of the inclosures in rear of the French line, in the direction of the village (I believe Planchenoit) lying to the rear and considerably to the left of La Belle Alliance.

appears to have been before the extreme left *could* get into line. I therefore think it very probable that, when the struggle immediately following the shock of the two lines began to turn in our favour, the Cuirassiers in front line, finding their escape to the rear obstructed by the dense crowd of their comrades, they should endeavour to get away by their right, which must have still been comparatively open, our left Squadron being not yet in line; and this will account for their rushing down that hollow way as described by Capt. Kincaid. For you will observe that after returning from the movement to the left by Threes, which took a part of our Brigade across the *chaussée*, the right and centre Regiments formed line by wheeling up Threes to the left, and immediately advanced to the attack. There being no time to be lost they were not allowed to wait till the whole was in line, consequently our extreme left being still moving by Threes to its right after the preceding portion of the Brigade had formed its line and commenced a forward movement, the left was obliged to scramble into line as it could, whilst that Line was every moment getting away from it towards the front, so that our right and centre may have met the Cuirassiers, and the latter begun to fly along the hollow way, whilst the left Squadron, 2nd Life Guards, was getting into the still advancing Line. You will understand by this what I mean by the Cuirassiers finding an escape open to them by their right, as well as the possibility of their having been just before that moment fired upon from the hollow way by the Germans, without the circumstance having been noted (in the hurry and bustle) by our Brigade or any one else.

Marginal note: Some of the Cuirassiers escaped by the hollow way in rear of La Haye Sainte, as seen by Captain Kincaid, 95th Rifles, stationed on the other side of the main road.

Very truly, &c.,

S. WAYMOUTH.

FROM THE SAME.

19, *Upper Grosvenor Street, April 26th*, 1841.   No. 23.

Colonel Marten has at last flown through London,   Waterloo.
and I have talked to him of your Model.

.   .   .   .

He says that having gained the plain on the left of the
chaussée, he perceived that we were in front of the Rifles
about 100 yards or more, and then he found himself in the
midst of broken bodies of Cuirassiers, engaged in sharp   1st Charge.
conflict with our men, amongst whom our famed Corporal
Shaw was very conspicuous, dealing deadly blows all round
him, and Marten is of opinion that he was killed, probably shot
down, near that spot, by a Cuirassier who stood rather   Death of Cor-
clear of our left, and occupied himself by shooting our   poral Shaw.
people with his carbine, taking very deliberate aim.

.   .   .   .

Very truly, &c.,
S. WAYMOUTH.

FROM THE SAME.

19, *Upper Grosvenor Street, July 2nd*, 1841.   No. 24.

As your letter found me confined to my room, in the   Waterloo.
fear of General Hill leaving town without my seeing him,   1st Charge.
I.wrote to him on the subject, and he has just called upon
me to talk it over.   His impression still is that the Blues
were in first line, but his recollection is not sufficiently
strong for you to rely upon it.   .   .   .

He said, " Why does not Siborne apply to Lord Edward,
that would be the best authority?"   I merely replied,
" Lord Edward is abroad."   I would not say any more, as
I considered what you wrote me of his information to you
was imparted to me " confidentially."

General Hill says he was close to Major Packe when he   Major Packe,
was killed, leading on a Squadron of the Blues.   He was   of the Blues,
run through the body by the Officer leading the French   killed by a
FrenchOfficer.

Squadron and fell dead immediately, but that was much later in the afternoon.

. . . .

The Blues in support at first, afterwards joining the front line.

Upon thinking the matter over I very much incline to adopt your opinion of the Blues having been placed in support on the primary arrangement of the first charge, and then finding themselves in front line before they almost knew where they were. The impetuosity with which the front line swept over the Enemy must have left behind quite a sufficient number for the Blues to deal with when they came up, and even to lead them to imagine themselves quite in front.

On the other hand, I do not think your argument of Lord Anglesey's general tactics, nor what he wanted to do

Lord Anglesey blamed for not providing adequate support to the Brigade in the charge.

with the Greys in Ponsonby's Brigade, a conclusive argument. For I remember that, at the time, I often heard him blamed for having thrown away our Brigade, by making it charge without an adequate support. You may also remember that I told you in my *first* letter that before the first charge, when we were all lying on the ground, by order of Lord Edward, in order to avoid as much as possible the effect of the Enemy's cannonade, I saw a certain Hanoverian Regiment, which we knew as "The Duke of Cumberland's Hussars," in line in our rear. They were in rear of the 2nd Life Guards, their left not far from the *chaussée*, and immediately in front of the hedge or skirt of the forest that was between the field of battle and the village of Waterloo. My thoughts at the time were what could possess them to sit upon their horses to be knocked over by cannon balls when they saw our Brigade upon the ground. I always have understood that this Regiment was ordered to charge in our support, but that when we attacked they ran away. I remember seeing the

Punishment of Cumberland Hussars.

Regiment afterwards doing duty in Paris as Waggon Train, assisting the Commissariat, and understood that to be their punishment, whilst their Colonel was cashiered. So here you see was a Regiment in support, although it failed, and would have proved inadequate even with its best efforts. The first time I can get hold of Sir Horace Seymour, who was said to have collared the Colonel, I will ask him.

Believe me, &c.,
S. WAYMOUTH.

FROM THE SAME.

19, *Upper Grosvenor St., May* 31*st*, 1842.

No. 25.

Waterloo.

I have at last succeeded in getting an interview with Lord Fitzroy Somerset, but I am sorry to say I have not been able to learn much from him. I was with him a long time, and he talked the whole thing over most freely, and seemed anxious to afford you all the assistance in his power, but he has only slight recollections of the points in question.

I first asked him whether the charge of the two Heavy Brigades was a *combined* attack, having the same object, viz., to repulse the French onset upon both sides of the *chaussée* at the same time? He answered he thought not, and then told me what you had previously, of his watching the attack upon Kempt, &c. &c.; but when I came to discuss the matter with him, he very soon entirely abandoned it, and said he supposed he must be confounding it with a *second* attack upon Kempt, "*i.e., if there was a second and similar attack made upon him.*" He did not at all maintain the account you mention of the two Staff Officers, but seemed convinced that his memory had failed him.

Lord Fitzroy Somerset's recollections of first charge.

He has no recollection at all of the 1st Lt. Batt., K.G.L.; indeed he says he does not remember to have seen it *at all, throughout the day*, and said he was surprised that he does not, for it was a Battalion that he was particularly well acquainted with.

He spoke of the *abatis* on the *chaussée* near La Haye Sainte, and which I think you mentioned to me. He saw Lord Edward Somerset returning from that charge on the other side of the *chaussée*, *i.e.*, in front of Picton; he had lost his hat, and was coming back bareheaded. He has

Lord F. Somerset saw Lord Edward returning from the charge bareheaded.

He doubts the

Duke's ordering a German Battalion to cross the main road to join Picton's Division.

doubts of its being the Duke who ordered the Germans across the *chaussée*, because it is perfectly unlike him to wave his hat, and shout *hurrah !* His great object always was not to do anything calculated to shake the steadiness of the men—he can scarcely believe it of the Duke. I hinted that the Duke himself could best set that question at rest. He replied, "Oh, certainly : but it would be impossible to ask him, or that he should answer any such questions." After all, he said he was very sorry not to be able to give you any more effectual aid, but that whenever he has to talk over that Battle, he finds himself so much deceived in his recollections, that he cannot rely with any confidence upon himself, and cannot conceive the possibility of your being able to attain to accuracy, considering how conflicting are the statements one continually hears from persons, all whose testimonies one considers undeniable. If you succeed in giving a tolerably correct representation, it is all you can expect.

When I had finished, I told him what I had written to you as my supposition that the contradictory statements respecting the Germans may be reconciled, and he said he thought it a very reasonable supposition.

Sir Andrew Barnard, 95th Rifles. *See* No. 158, p. 363.

However, I have since seen Sir Andrew Barnard, who came to me yesterday, and was also very ready to give me all the information in his power. He says pretty much the same as Kincaid, and gives nearly the same account of the advance of the Enemy against that point, and the withdrawal of the 95th skirmishers. He says *there was a second attack* upon Kempt about an hour later ; that it was not so formidable, but that their skirmishers (not a Column) in *considerable bodies* came up to Kempt's Brigade ; that he, Sir A., was wounded at that time, and carried off the field ; and that he thinks it very probable the Germans might *then* have come across the *chaussée* as they describe, for *he saw Baron Busche there*, who commanded that Battalion. Now, if that second attack was preceded by a heavy cannonade, and accompanied by a charge of their cuirassiers, it would seem likely to be the occasion alluded

Says there was a second attack on Kempt (who succeeded Picton) about an hour later.

to by Heisse and Leonhardt, if we could tell how to dispose of that Battalion during the first attack.

Sir Andrew says the *abatis* on the *chaussée* was made by his people the night before. On another point he was very satisfactory *to me.* I asked if he saw and remembered my hovel? His answer was, "I think I ought to remember it, for I saved it from being entirely pulled down, when the men had already taken off the thatch from the roof to burn; but the frame of the roof still remained. I slept in that hovel, and Lord Anglesey came and drank some of my tea in it during the night of the 17th." . . . .

His men (95th Rifles) made the *abatis* on the road the night before.

Believe me,

S. WAYMOUTH.

MAJOR MARTEN, ROYAL DRAGOONS.

SUB.-LIEUTENANT 2ND LIFE GUARDS.

Brighton, December 5th, 1834.　No. 26.

. . . .

I have, however, great pleasure now in sending you what little information relating to the 2nd Life Guards at Waterloo, that my memory (after so long a period) will bear me out in; but when I tell you I was then one of the youngest Cornets, and only seventeen years of age, and the greater part of the day, too, a Serrefile, you will readily conclude my observations will be chiefly confined to the immediate movements and situations of my own Regiment.

Waterloo.

. . . .

After the Brigade had taken up the ground, viz., *in rear of the right centre of the Army,* which it was destined throughout the day to support, we remained some time in close column, then deployed, and were suddenly ordered to advance to the charge, the 2nd Life Guards, as I have before observed, being on the left of the Brigade, with the King's Dragoon Guards on our right.

In descending into the plain from our Infantry position, we met a line of Cuirassiers which we charged through, but

1st Charge.

2nd Life Guards met the Cuirassiers after crossing the main road.

I think not till we had crossed the great road near La Haye Sainte (of course, I am writing now of my own Regiment *only*). After passing through the Cuirassiers (the greater part of whom were killed and wounded in this charge), we found ourselves in the midst of a routed body of French Infantry, who, many of them, threw themselves on the ground till we had gone over, and then rose and fired. This circumstance I distinctly remember, and I am equally confident that all this took place *with us* on the *left* of the Genappe road, from our having to jump over trees on that road, which I afterwards learned had been placed there by the 95th Rifles. Whether the whole Brigade brought up their right shoulders I know not, but I am sure we did ; but to continue. After this charge (from which we suffered so much, particularly in the loss of horses) we were completely broken, and as many as remained mounted of the four Troops returned by the left centre of our position, and reformed in front of a small orchard (I think) just out of Mont-St.-Jean, and in rear of our original ground, where we continued a short time, and then were marched up to the support of the right centre again on the slope of the hill.

After some little time had elapsed we were ordered to advance again to the charge, but the French Cavalry retreated on seeing us approach, and we fell back to our former ground, where we remained the whole of the rest of the day until the advance of the Line, when, after marching some distance over the fields in our front, halted to the right of a village which was set fire to by either the French or Prussians, and this, I think, could not have been far from La Belle Alliance.

.   .   .   .

I remain, &c.,

THOMAS MARTEN,

Major Royal Dragoons.

They found themselves amongst the French Infantry, routed by Kempt's Infantry Brigade.

The 2nd Life Guards suffered, particularly from the loss of horses.

Ordered again to charge, but the French Cavalry fell back.

Joined in the General Advance.

FROM THE SAME (LIEUT.-COLONEL).

Beverley, February 23rd, 1843.

No. 27.

Waterloo.

In reply to your note of this morning, I can only assure you that, *although I did not certainly see Shaw killed,* I am perfectly satisfied that he met his death in the first charge alluded to. It was told me shortly after, and I firmly believe it.

Death of Corporal Shaw.

It was said he did not die at the moment, but received in that charge several wounds of which he lingered till night. He could not have been alive the next morning, because I was ordered, in company with the Assistant-Surgeon, to collect our wounded, and see them safely conveyed to Brussels, which I did, and Shaw was certainly not one.

As there was a mistake made in our Returns of the Battle, I wish you would correct it in your new Book. Neither the Hon. Captain Irby nor Waymouth were returned as Prisoners, which they both were, and *the latter wounded,* but, of course, not known at the time.

Mistake in the Returns of the Regiment after the Battle.

Captain Irby I found myself in the town of Nivelles on my return from Brussels on the 20th, and he told me he had escaped from the French by hiding himself in a cellar in which the prisoners had been confined. Waymouth did not join for some weeks.

.   .   .   .

Yours, &c.,

THOMAS MARTEN.

ROYAL HORSE GUARDS, BLUE.

GENERAL CLEMENT HILL.

CAPTAIN AND LIEUT.-COLONEL ROYAL HORSE GUARDS.

TO MAJOR WAYMOUTH.

Hawkstone, July 14*th,* 1841.

No. 28.

Waterloo. 1st Charge.

MY DEAR WAYMOUTH,—I fear you will think me long in replying to your letter and enquiries about the *first* charge of the Household Brigade at Waterloo .   .   .   .

and had only yesterday an opportunity of asking my brother Robert his opinion. You know he commanded the

Blues in front line.

Regiment, and is *quite* sure we were in the *front* line, and not placed in a *second* to support on that occasion. He says he distinctly saw the Commanding Officer of the 1st Life Guards fall (from a shot) on his *right* as the Brigade was advancing to the charge, which may corroborate our being in the *same* line, and also be an incident for Captain Siborne to represent in a figure on his Model.

I do not recollect, nor does my brother, what may have been in a second line to support us, and regret I cannot send you or Captain Siborne any other information that might be of use in completing his new Model.

. . . . . .

Yours, &c.,

CLEM. HILL.

1ST OR KING'S DRAGOON GUARDS.

LIEUT.-COLONEL ROBERT WALLACE, UNATTACHED.

CAPTAIN KING'S DRAGOON GUARDS.

No. 29.

York, Nov. 19th, 1834.

. . . . . .

Waterloo.

We certainly passed through a great deal of standing corn a short time previous to the first charge made by the Household Brigade of Cavalry, to which the 1st Dragoon Guards belonged, which Corps at the hour of seven o'clock in the evening were so much cut up, both as to Officers and men, as to form but a small portion of a Regiment, but how formed *at that particular moment* I cannot with perfect accuracy state.

King's Dragoon Guards more in contact with the French Heavy Cavalry than

With regard to general remarks, as far as my recollection goes, we were more in contact with the French Heavy Cavalry than with other troops, and many, I am sure, suffered severely from the men of the 1st Dragoon Guards, as did ours also from them, many of our men having severe sabre wounds, particularly about the face ; with other troops ; both but there has been so much written upon the subject, and sides suffered so many anecdotes related that you can be at no loss on severely. this head, and I only regret that I had not the same re- The men having re- flection at that period that after years bring to us all, so ceived many severe face as to be enabled to give you a more detailed account of wounds. the occurrences of that eventful day, as far as we were concerned, with correctness and fidelity. . .

I have, &c.,

ROBERT WALLACE,

Lieut.-Col. Unattached.

PONSONBY'S CAVALRY BRIGADE.

The 2nd (Heavy) Cavalry Brigade was composed of the 1st or Royal Dragoons, the 2nd or Royal North British Dragoons, Scots Greys, and the 6th or Inniskilling Dragoons, hence also known as the " Union Brigade," and was commanded by Major-General Sir William Ponsonby, K.C.B., who was killed in the first charge at Waterloo.

The Brigade, together with the Household Brigade, formed the main portion of the Centre Cavalry Column in the Retreat on the 17th June. After passing through the town of Genappe, it was deployed on the right of the Brussels-Charleroi Road, and engaged for some time in skirmishing with the Enemy's Cavalry, and checking their advances, until gradually withdrawn by the road to the Position at Waterloo.

On the morning of the 18th the Brigade was See General posted on the left of the Brussels road in support of Plan, No. 1. Picton's Division, and when D'Erlon attacked the

latter, it was brought forward through the intervals
of the Infantry to charge the French Columns.

See Plan, p. 38.

The Royals on the right charged and broke
one of the Columns, Captain A. K. Clarke capturing the Eagle of the 105th French Regiment.
The left wing of the 28th Regiment fired into the
Column at the moment the Royals charged it, and
afterwards assisted them in securing great numbers
of Prisoners.

The Inniskillings in the centre advanced further
so as to charge two Columns which were moving
up in support of the others, and similarly overthrew them, and captured an immense number of
Prisoners.

The Greys had been ordered to support the
other two Regiments, but had previously been
moved to the left rear of the Brigade, for the
purpose of obtaining more cover from the French
cannonade, so that, on advancing, they found in
their direct front the head of a French Column
establishing itself on the Wavre Road. The Greys
therefore, after passing through the intervals of
the Infantry, at once charged this Column, and
dispersed it, Sergeant Ewart capturing the Eagle
of the 45th French Regiment. The 92nd Highlanders joined in the Charge, both Regiments
mutually cheering each other, and shouting, "Scotland for ever!" They also secured great numbers
of Prisoners.

The Brigade, after overthrowing the French
Infantry, lost nearly all regularity, and galloped
madly up to the French Position, notwithstanding
all the efforts of the Officers to prevent it, and began

sabreing the Gunners and stabbing the horses of the Enemy's Batteries. But they were now attacked by a body of French Lancers, and their horses being blown and exhausted, they suffered severely in their confused retreat to the British Position.

In this Charge, 3,000 Prisoners were taken, 2 Eagles captured, and from 30 to 40 Guns put *hors de combat* for the greater part of the day.

Subsequently, the Brigade was moved to the right of the road, where it was employed in giving support to the Infantry stationed there, and occasionally in making a forward movement to check the advancing French troops.

Towards evening it was united with Somerset's Brigade, and the two were employed as described in page 39.

No. 34 refers to the March on Quatre Bras.

Nos. 30 and 34 to the Retreat on the 17th June, and the remaining Letters to Waterloo.

COLONEL SIR DE LACY EVANS, K.C.B.

MAJOR 5TH W. I. REGIMENT, AND EXTRA A.D.C. TO SIR WILLIAM PONSONBY.

Oct. 14th.

On the 17th, after the Infantry, &c., had retired, or were retiring, and when the time arrived for the Cavalry to commence their retrograde movement, I was ordered to accompany Sir John Elley, the Adjt. General of the Cavalry, to Genappe to examine and report on that defile, but chiefly to select a position on the open high ground above it towards the Waterloo side, for the whole of the Heavy Cavalry and some Horse Artillery to form on immediately

No. 30.
Retreat from
Quatre Bras.

Sir De Lacy Evans.

Genappe.

as they should clear Genappe.   This was under the orders
of Lord Anglesey, and Sir J. Elley and myself remained
between that high ground and Genappe directing the heads
of the Regiments to the ground they were to form on, as
they successively debouched from Genappe.

Formation of
Household
and Ponson-
by's Brigades

The Household Brigade formed up with their right on
the main road facing the Enemy—the Heavy Brigade with
their left towards the road, but extending considerably
towards their right.

Charges of
7th Hussars
and 1st Life
Guards.

You are aware that the 7th Hussars attempted un-
successfully to check the head of the French Column of
Cavalry as it debouched from Genappe.   Lord Anglesey
then detached to their support a Squadron of the Household Brigade, which was more successful.

But our retreat was continued at short intervals, in
good order—slight skirmishing—and without being pressed,
except in the instance I have mentioned.   Such is my impression.   I remained with the Household Brigade till we
got near the Waterloo position.

I therefore do not know so well as others who were
closer to them what Sir Wm. Ponsonby's Brigade had to
do.   But I do not think they [had] much to do.

In haste, &c.,

D. L. Evans.

FROM THE SAME.

No. 31.

Bryanstone Square, Sept. 1st, 1839.

Waterloo.
See Plan, p.38.

You have placed the Inniskillings in your plan *in
advance* of the Royals and Greys.   I incline to think the
three Regiments charged nearly in line.   I myself was
with the right of the line, and I should think the Greys
and Royals were rather more engaged than the other
Regiment.   These two last Regiments took an Eagle each,
and you will see that their loss of men and Officers was
much greater, especially the Greys.

SIR DE LACY EVANS.
1st Charge.

The Brigade was in a hollow in order to screen them from cannon fire before the charge. As the Enemy advanced up to the crest of the position on their side, the Heavy Brigade was also moved up on ours. Our Brigade came up to one hundred yards in rear of the little sunken road and hedge. I communicated the order for this movement myself. We waited there for a few minutes till the head of the Enemy's Column had just crossed the sunken road—as I understood—to allow our Infantry to pass round the flanks of Squadrons, and also that the Enemy should be a little deranged in passing the road, instead of our being so, had we charged across the road.

The Enemy's Column, near which I was, on arriving at the crest of the position seemed very helpless, had very little fire to give from its front or flanks, was incapable of deploying, must have already lost many of its Officers in coming up, was fired into, close, with impunity, by stragglers of our Infantry who remained behind. As we approached at a moderate pace the front and flanks began to turn their backs inwards; the rear of the Columns had already begun to run away. The Brigade [? Division] you speak of under Sir T. Picton (and afterwards Sir J. Kempt) were successful, as your letter states, but the Infantry in our front had, I think, been obliged to yield. At all events it passed round our flanks.

Disordered state of French attacking Column.

In going down the hill the Brigade secured about 2,000 Prisoners, which were successfully conducted to the rear by parties of the Inniskillings, as far as I recollect. The Enemy fled as a flock of sheep across the valley—quite at the mercy of the Dragoons. In fact, our men were *out of hand*. The General of the Brigade, his Staff, and every Officer within hearing, exerted themselves to the utmost to re-form the men; but the helplessness of the Enemy offered too great a temptation to the Dragoons, and our efforts were abortive.

2,000 Prisoners taken.

Disordered state of the Brigade. Exertions of the Officers to remedy it.

It was evident that the Enemy's reserves of Cavalry towards [? Planchenoit] would soon take advantage of our disorder. Anticipating this, I went back for a moment to

where Sir James Kempt was, to ask him to advance to
cover our retreat, which appeared inevitable. He told
me he would advance a couple of hundred yards, but
that he could not quit the position altogether without
orders. Besides, it was evident Infantry could not
do it.

See p. 103.

It was Vandeleur's Light Cavalry Brigade on the left
which perhaps could have been useful at the moment by a
more forward movement. But I did not see it. I
galloped back to Sir William Ponsonby. The Dragoons
were still in the same disorder, cutting up the remnant of
the dispersed Infantry. We ascended the first ridge occupied by the Enemy, and passed several French cannon, on
our right hand towards the road, abandoned [on] our
approach by their gunners, and there were some French
Squares of Infantry in rear.

Brigade
attacked by
French
Lancers.

The French Lancers continued to advance on our left in
good order. If we could have formed a hundred men we
could have made a respectable retreat, and saved many ;
but we could effect no formation, and were as helpless
against their attack as their Infantry had been against

Retreat of the
Brigade.

ours. Everyone saw what must happen. Those whose
horses were best or least blown, got away. Some

Sir W. Pon-
sonby and
others tried to
escape by
going round
the left of the
Lancers, but
all fell into
the hands of
the Enemy.

attempted to escape back to our position by going round
the left of the French Lancers. Sir William Ponsonby
was of that number. All these fell into the hands of the
Enemy. Others went back straight—among whom myself
—receiving a little fire from some French Infantry towards
the road on our left as we retired.

It was in this part of the transaction that almost the
whole of the loss of the Brigade took place. But this last
occurrence took place about three hundred yards at least in
advance of the farthest line of the square or parallelogram
marked on the map you have sent me, and accordingly the

Where Sir W.
Ponsonby's
body was
found next
morning.

spot where Sir William Ponsonby fell, and his body was
found by us next morning, was about five hundred yards in
front of the centre of the Brigade as marked in the square
of your plan, on the ridge to which I have before alluded,

and on which the Enemy had, I think, occasionally their advanced Batteries in the early part of the Battle.

This is the notion or recollection that I have of the affair.

.   .   .   .

I saw nothing of the Belgian Light Dragoons in the *mêlée.* The Dutch Belgian Infantry yielded with slight or no resistance to the advancing Columns, and got quickly to the rear; and not in the stubborn, reluctant, deliberate way of our Infantry. I don't recollect anything of the Dutch Artillery at that moment. Our Artillerymen, as well as Infantry, kept firing into the Columns as long as possible. I think at the moment of the collision between the Heavy Cavalry and the French Columns there was a pause of everything else, and I think our Artillery Officers and men were standing near and about, but not close to, or serving their Guns. The 32nd and 79th had *regained their position* as we charged past their left, but I am certain their position was some fifty or a hundred yards in front of the hedge, and not in rear of it.

The Guns as well as Infantry kept firing into the Columns till the last moment before the Charge.

I remain, &c.,

D. L. Evans.

FROM THE SAME.

(No date.)   No. 32.

.   .   .   .

As to the Inniskillings being in front, I dare say you are right. I only offered you my impressions, and I confess I think I saw as much of what was going on on that occasion as most other individuals.

Waterloo. 1st Charge.

As to the person who took off his hat as a signal from the crest of the hill for the Brigade to advance, I venture to think I was myself the individual who did so. It occurred thus: I accompanied Sir William Ponsonby to the crest to ascertain the proper time for the Brigade to come up. At the moment when he appeared of opinion this should be done, he himself met with a trifling interference. The Enemy just then redoubled their cannon fire

Signal to advance made by Major Evans.

Sir Wm. Ponsonby indifferently mounted.

against the crest. The General was mounted on a secondary untrained horse, and some round shot frightened the horse, and his cloak, being loose, flew off. He dismounted for a moment to get his cloak restored to its place. It was in that interval that he instructed me to make the signal alluded to.

But I think it signifies nothing which Regiment is in front. You speak of the difficulties you have in reconciling different accounts of eye-witnesses. This is only what invariably occurs. There is scarcely an instance, I think, of two persons, even though only fifty yards distant from each other, who give of such events a concurring account.

Strength of Brigade.

As to Colonel Gurwood's account of 1,123 sabres, I dare say it is all very right as a Return, but the 1,123 sabres were not on the field according to my humble recollection and belief.

Sir William Ponsonby and all Officers of discretion did their best to prevent the advance up to the French Lines.

You are rightly informed that Sir William Ponsonby did his best to prevent the further advance up the opposite ridge and towards the left of the French cannon, and so did all the Officers of any discretion about him; but finding that we were not successful in stopping the troops, we were forced to continue on with them in order to continue our exclamations to halt, as we all, except I suppose the Cornets, saw what would happen.

Faithfully, &c.,

D. L. Evans.

FROM THE SAME.

No. 33.

Harrogate, August 23rd, 1842.

.   .   .   .   .   .

Waterloo.

D'Erlon's first attack.

The Columns became paralysed by the

I don't think the Enemy advanced more than five or ten yards on our side of the road. By the sudden appearance and closing of our Cavalry upon them (added to their previous suffering from musketry and grape), they became quite paralysed and incapable of resistance, except

occasionally, individually a little.   What followed I think
I touched on before.

.   .   .   .

I am unable to inform you as to Picton's horse.

Poor Sir William Ponsonby might perhaps have been
spared to his country had he been better mounted.   He
rode a small bay hack.   He had a handsome chestnut
charger, which he meant to mount when real business
began, but the groom or Orderly who had charge of the
chestnut was not forthcoming or within call at the moment
the General wanted his horse.

As to myself, I was well mounted on a powerful, nearly
thoroughbred bay gelding.   He received a considerable
sabre wound from near the eye to the mouth, but his action
was not impaired by it.   I, however, changed him on
getting back to the position for a brown mare, which, however, was very soon after shot by a musket ball, and I lost
her.   The bay soon recovered; but for this gossiping I
have only to plead the excuse of your inquiry.

.   .   .   .

Very, &c.,

D. L. EVANS.

THE 1st ROYAL DRAGOONS.

COLONEL A. K. CLARK KENNEDY, C.B., K.H.,
7TH DRAGOON GUARDS.

CAPTAIN A. K. CLARK KENNEDY, ROYAL DRAGOONS.

Rough Memorandum of the Movements of the Royal
Dragoons on June 16th and 17th, 1815.

The Royal Dragoons, who had been quartered for about
three weeks at Ninove and the immediate neighbourhood,
were aroused on the morning of June 16th by the trumpets
sounding to turn out about four o'clock.   The Troops
were got together as quickly as possible, and three days'
biscuits, &c., having been issued to the men, the Regiment

Royal Dragoons.

was immediately put in motion (if I mistake not), in the first instance in the direction of Ath (by way of Grammont), near which the Brigade, 1st, 2nd, and 6th Dragoons, united under the command of Major-General Sir William Ponsonby.

After the direction of our march had been three or four times changed, and there had been several halts in the course of the day, the Brigade moved towards evening

Arrival at dusk.

upon Quatre Bras, where it arrived about dusk, having marched somewhere about fifty miles.

All firing, except a little skirmishing (in the wood which had been retaken by the Guards), having ceased, the Royals bivouacked for the night in an open field a little in rear of the houses of Quatre Bras, the horses being linked in column, saddled and bridled, the Officers and men lying or standing by them. The night proved a fine one.

It having been ascertained next morning that the Prussian Army had retired during the night from Ligny, &c., the British Army commenced a similar movement on

Retreat on 17th.

the morning of the 17th, the Cavalry being drawn out and advanced a little to mask the retreat of the Infantry.

My Squadron was ordered to the Inn of Quatre Bras to

Conveyance of the wounded.

assist in conveying as many of the wounded men to the rear as were able to bear the motion of a horse, and a considerable number were removed in this manner to the rear of the position at Waterloo, though several that were severely wounded were necessarily left behind.

The other two Squadrons, under the command of Lieut.-Colonel Dorville and Major (afterwards Lieut.-Colonel) Radclyffe, remaining and retiring shortly afterwards towards the position, where they arrived a little before dusk along with the other Cavalry, which had been covering a slow and orderly retreat, during the greater portion of which, from Genappe to Waterloo, the left Squadron

Skirmishing with the Cuirassiers.

under Colonel Radclyffe was warmly engaged skirmishing with the Enemy's advanced guard of Cuirassiers who pressed them hotly, frequently collecting with the apparent intention of charging, but never venturing to do so during the regular and orderly retreat of about five miles.

Having given up the wounded men, my Squadron rejoined the Regiment on its arrival on the crest of the position, and the firing having ceased, the Cavalry was withdrawn behind the Infantry, and we bivouacked for the night without any shelter whatever; and a miserable one enough we passed, the rain having descended in torrents from about two or three o'clock on the 17th.

We remained quiet until about half past eleven or eleven o'clock, when the Brigade moved and formed line in the hollow about a quarter of a mile in rear of the crest of Sir Thomas Picton's Division, where it remained until brought forward, about twelve or half-past twelve, shortly before the charge of the Count D'Erlon's Corps took place, and that, I think, must have been somewhere about one o'clock or a little sooner, but I cannot be certain as to time.

> A. K. C. KENNEDY,
> Lieut.-Colonel 7th Dragoon Guards.

FROM THE SAME.

Cahir, April 13th, 1835. No. 35.

. . . .

I fear I have little to communicate on the subject of the 1st Dragoons at Waterloo that will prove useful to your interesting work, as I cannot of my own knowledge speak to the position of the Royal Dragoons after a quarter past six p.m., or a little later, about which hour I was obliged to leave the field, having been a second time wounded, and had two horses killed under me.

At this time, as nearly as I can judge, the Regiment, reduced to *one* Squadron, stood where I have drawn the line No. 1, with the remains of the Inniskillings and Greys in line on its left. The troops opposed to them (as far as the nature of the ground allowed me to see) was a very heavy Column of Infantry, the head of which only

ROYAL DRAGOONS.

and seventy yards in front of the cross road or hollow way.

was fully in sight, with a weak body of Cavalry. Both Columns were covered by skirmishers, and supported by Guns firing grape or canister shot, from which, as the range was short, we suffered very severely, being necessarily greatly exposed, the Brigade being drawn up in line in front of the crest of the rising ground for the purpose, as was generally thought, of giving confidence to

In support of Infantry.

a large body of Belgic* Infantry formed in square under the command of, and where, I believe, the Prince of Orange was wounded. The fire upon this Square, which stood about two hundred yards in advance, and about one hundred to the right of the Royals, was very severe, and it suffered greatly, chiefly from shells which now and then shook it a good deal, but they always re-formed on the Cavalry making an advance in their support, and, I believe, maintained its ground until the General Advance of the Allied Army took place about seven o'clock, by which time, I have been informed by Captain Phipps (now Lieut.-Colonel Unattached) that the Brigade which had remained on nearly the same position since about four p.m., was reduced to *one Squadron only.*

See General Plan, No. 1. Position of Brigade until 1st Charge.

See Plan, p. 38.

As far as my memory will serve me—but at this distance of time I may fall into error—I have marked the different operations of the Royals on the 18th of June. No. 2 is the position of the Regiment (Right of Major-General Ponsonby's Brigade) from about eleven o'clock until twelve or half-past twelve, when it advanced by Threes from the flanks of half-Squadrons to No. 3, where it wheeled into line by command of the Marquis of Anglesey, and, together with the Inniskillings on its left, and Greys supporting in second line, charged and drove back the Count D'Erlon's Corps, the head of whose Column had crossed the double hedge and road, and had passed several of the British Guns placed behind the hedge, and which for the moment had been abandoned by the gunners.

---

* An error. No Belgians were on the spot indicated. They were Germans, probably Nassauers or Brunswickers.—ED.

No. 4 is the extent of the successful charge made by about *nine hundred* swords, which cost the Enemy, independent of killed, nearly 2,000 prisoners and two Eagles, the bearer of one of which, the 105th, was run through the body by me somewhere about the letter E. I commanded the centre Squadron. The other Eagle was taken by Sergeant Ewart, of the Greys.

Extent of charge. Eagle of 105th French Regt. taken about 300 yards left of garden of La Haye Sainte, and 270 yards in front of Wavre Road.

No. 5 is the small wood to which the Brigade retired to re-form, and where it continued until about half-past three p.m., where it was ordered to move to the left [? right] of the Brussels road to No. 6, from where it advanced to No. 1, within fifty or a hundred yards of which it remained until the General Advance at seven o'clock.

·   ·   ·   ·   ·   ·   ·

I have, &c.,
A. K. CLARK KENNEDY,
Lieutenant-Colonel 7th Dragoon Guards,
Late Captain Royal Dragoons.

FROM THE SAME.

Leeds Barracks, June 18th, 1839.

In reply to yours of the 9th, received a few days ago I have endeavoured to give as correct answers as I possibly can to your questions, though I am afraid any information I can give will be of little service to you.

No. 36, With Memorandum Waterloo.

·   ·   ·   ·   ·   ·   ·

Do not consider it conceit on my part, but I cannot, as an individual concerned, think that justice has been done to that charge, and I ask you as an Officer of experience how long the British Army could have held its position if the Count D'Erlon's Corps had been able to occupy the ridge that the head of their Columns had *gained?*

Importance of 1st Charge

I may be in error, but I cannot help thinking it the most critical moment of the day. But we had lost our General, there was no one to speak for us, and the Duke

Thinks it the most critical moment of the day.

did not see the charge himself, his hands being at that time quite full enough, I believe, on the right centre.

.   .   .   .

Yours truly,

A. K. CLARK KENNEDY,

Lieutenant-Colonel 7th Dragoon Guards.

1st Charge.

Memorandum—Royal Dragoons at Waterloo.

Until within about a quarter of an hour of the charge of General Ponsonby's Brigade on the Count D'Erlon's Corps, the Brigade had been standing in line in the hollow behind La Haye Sainte, with their right about 250 yards on the left of the Brussels road.

The cannon shot that passed over the crest of the ridge beginning to fall pretty fast, the Brigade was advanced slowly towards the ridge by the Troops wheeling to the left, and taking ground to the right by the flank march of Threes.

On arriving very near the top of the ridge the Column fronted, and halted for perhaps four or five minutes.

Lord Anglesey orders the Royals and Inniskillings to charge.

Royals and Inniskillings in front line, Greys in support.

The Marquis of Anglesey came up at speed (apparently from the Household Brigade on the right), wheeled the Royals and Inniskillings into line, and ordered them to charge, the Greys forming a second line in support.

At this moment many of the Artillery (I believe all) were ordered to leave, or did leave, their Guns, which were stationed behind the hedges, and they passed through the intervals of our Squadrons. The Infantry that, I presume, had previously lined the hedges, were wheeled by

The left wing of the 28th fired on the Column, the head of which had passed both hedges of the Wavre road.

Sections to their left, and were firing on the *left flank* of the French Column, the head of which had at this time *passed both hedges unchecked*, as far as I could perceive, and were advancing rapidly. From the nature of the ground we did not see each other until we were very close, perhaps eighty or ninety yards. The head of the Column appeared to be seized with a panic, gave us a fire which brought down about twenty men, went instantly about and endeavoured to regain the opposite side of the hedges; but we were upon and amongst them before this could be effected, the whole Column getting into one dense mass, the men between the advancing and retiring parts getting so jammed together that the men could not bring down their arms, or use them effectively, and we had nothing to do but to continue to press them down the slope, the right Squadron of the Royals naturally outflanking them, as the centre one (which I commanded) also did to a certain degree.

The Royals charge, and the Column is thrown into confusion.

We continued to press on, and went a little further than we ought to have done, perhaps, getting under the fire of fresh troops stationed on the opposite height, and losing a good many men.

Carried too far.

About half-way between the two positions we endeavoured to collect our Squadrons as well as we could; but we were so much scattered that few could be got together, and with these few we retired slowly towards our own position, under a pretty severe fire, driving as many Prisoners before us as we could.

No Cavalry was opposed to that part of the Brigade with which I was; but I was told that the left suffered greatly when retiring from an attack of Lancers.

No Cavalry opposed to the right of the Brigade.

Our Infantry, which we had passed at the hedge, now proved of essential service to us. They had formed small bodies or squares following in the rear of the charge, and not only checked pursuit, but without their support and assistance I am satisfied we should not have got back so well as we did, and certainly we could not have secured one-half of the Prisoners taken in the charge. Many who had surrendered effected their escape, yet above 2,000 were secured and sent to the rear.

Support of the Infantry.

The French on this occasion behaved very ill, many of our soldiers falling from the fire of men who had surrendered, and whose lives had been spared only a few minutes before. I had a narrow escape myself. One of these men put his musket close to my head and fired, a sudden turn of the head saving my life, the ball taking off

Ill conduct of French soldiers.

the tip of my nose instead of passing through the head, as was kindly intended.

But to reply to your questions as well as, at this distance of time, I can.

The heads of the French Columns, which appeared to me to be nearly close together, had no appearance of having been *repulsed* or *seriously checked.* On the contrary, as I mentioned before, they had forced their way *through our line*—the heads of the Columns were on the *Brussels* side of the double hedge. There was no British Infantry in the immediate front that I saw, and the line that had been, I presume, behind the hedges (for I did not see it until the moment of charging) was wheeled by sections or divisions to the left, and was firing on the left flank of the left Column as it advanced.

In fact, the crest of the height had *been gained*, and the charge of Cavalry at the critical moment recovered it.

Had the charge been delayed two or three minutes, I feel satisfied it would probably have failed, and you, I daresay, are well aware there were no Infantry in reserve behind that part of the position, though there were on the Brussels road.

The pause after wheeling into line did not exceed a few seconds. The left of my Squadron (the centre one) being already in front of part of the Enemy's left Column, I brought it more so, and clear of our own Infantry, by inclining a little to the left. How the others got on I cannot say. I came in contact with the head of the Column on the Brussels side of the hedges as it was going about, after having given us a destructive fire at a distance of perhaps fifty yards. No preparation appeared to be made to receive Cavalry, nor do I think there could have been, as there was not above a hundred yards to go over *after we saw* each other.

The line was quickly lost where I was, the two Squadrons (I can only speak of the 1st and 2nd) endeavouring to keep collected to their own centres as much as possible, and getting round the Column as it

The heads of the Columns were on the Brussels side of the Wavre road.

Critical result of the Charge.

No preparation made by the French to receive Cavalry.

retired gradually, inclining and gaining ground to the front and left.

.   .   .   .

I can give no account of the 3rd Squadron. I rather think it charged the front near the Enemy's right, which must naturally have brought it and the Inniskilling Dragoons round the opposite flank to where I was.

The charge took place on the *crest*, not on the *slope* of the ridge, though it was followed up to the hollow ground between the two positions.

The Greys (2nd line) must have charged immediately after the 1st line, at least, they were up and mixed with the Royals long before we got half-way down the slope. No Cavalry checked the right flank of the Brigade. It retired from exhaustion, and from getting under the fire of fresh troops on the opposite ridge. It was not attacked in retiring, only fired upon. The left of the Brigade, I understood, was followed and suffered severely from a body of Lancers, but I did not see it.

Greys join front line.

Sir John Vandeleur's Brigade of Light Cavalry, which had been stationed more to the left of the Line, and under the ridge, moved to the right, advanced, and took up a position about one hundred and fifty or two hundred yards on the Brussels side of the double hedge. We retired behind them, re-formed in *two* Squadrons (Lieut.-Colonel Dorville and myself), and remained dismounted near a small wood in rear of the position until about three o'clock or half-past, when we were ordered to the right of the Brussels road, and placed in line on the crest of the position in rear of and rather to the left of the large Square of Foreign Infantry in which the Prince of Orange was wounded.

Retired behind Vandeleur's Brigade.

Brigade moved to the right of the Brussels road.

This was the most trying duty of the day. The Brigade, with the exception of two or three advances to check the Enemy's movements, and to encourage the Belgic* Square to keep together, being the greater part of

* *See* note, p. 68.

the next three hours *perfectly stationary*, and suffering severely from grape and musketry.

At the time I left the field, a little before seven (having received a second wound), the Regiment was reduced to one Squadron, and we had sent out a few skirmishers to meet those of the Enemy, more for the purpose of occupying the men than from any good they could do. At this time the Household Brigade was in line a little to our right, and about one hundred and fifty yards more retired from the front than we were.

Reduced to one Squadron at the end of the day.

Of the glorious Advance which took place almost immediately after I was obliged to leave the field, I, of course, know nothing.

A. K. CLARK KENNEDY,
Lieut.-Colonel, &c.

FROM THE SAME.

No. 37.

Leeds, July 14th, 1839.

. . . . .

Waterloo.
1st Charge.

I also met Lieut.-Colonel Phipps, then a Captain commanding a half of the right Squadron of the Royals. He assures me that the right Squadron (commanded by Lieut.-Colonel Dorville) passed through the 32nd Regiment. He had some conversation with an Officer of that Corps (Major Haynes), and was some time with them, his horse having been killed at the hedge where the other Captain (Windsor) and several men and horses fell.

The Greys should have been a supporting line.

If the Greys did not form a supporting line, which it now appears to be almost certain they did not, they ought to have done so. Colonel Phipps was close to the Marquis of Anglesey when he ordered the Brigade to wheel into line, and he heard him distinctly say, "The Royals and Inniskillings will charge, the Greys support."

Sir William Ponsonby was in front of the Inniskillings. I also saw Lieut.-Colonel Wyndham (then a Cornet) [in the Greys] in town. He tells me he does not think they ever formed a second line, but that they may have doubled a little behind the Inniskillings in the advance, on account of the nature of the ground. I confess that, until after reading your last notes, I never had a doubt on the subject.

. . . .

I did not see the Eagle and Colour (for there were two Colours, but only one with an Eagle) until we had been probably five or six minutes engaged. It must, I should think, have been originally about the centre of the Column, and got uncovered from the change of direction. When I first saw it, it was perhaps about forty yards to my left and a little in my front. The Officer who carried it and his companions were moving in the direction O, with their backs towards me, and endeavouring to force their way into the crowd. Capture of the Eagle of the 105th French Regiment.

Towards site indicated, p. 69.

I gave the order to my Squadron, " Right shoulders forward, attack the Colour," leading direct on the point myself. On reaching it, I ran my sword into the Officer's right side a little above the hip joint. He was a little to my left side, and he fell to that side with the Eagle across my horse's head. I tried to catch it with my left hand, but could only touch the fringe of the flag, and it is probable. it would have fallen to the ground, had it not been prevented by the neck of Corporal Styles' horse, who came up close on my *left* at the instant, and against which it fell. Corporal Styles was Standard Coverer; his post was immediately behind me, and his duty to follow wherever I led. When I first saw the Eagle I gave the order, " Right shoulders forward, attack the Colour," and on running the Officer through the body I called out twice together, " Secure the Colour, secure the Colour, it belongs to me." This order was addressed to some men close to me, of whom Corporal Styles was one. On taking up the Eagle, I endeavoured to break the Eagle from off the pole with the intention of putting it into the breast of my coat ; but I could not break it. Corporal Styles said, " Pray, sir, do not break it," on

ROYAL DRAGOONS.

which I replied, " Very well, carry it to the rear as fast as you can, it belongs to me."

What became of the other Colour without the Eagle I know not, but it is rather singular that I last autumn saw a dark blue silk flag with the words 105*me Régiment d'Infanterie de Ligne* in gold letters upon it in the hall at Abbotsford along with other military curiosities. How it got there I could not learn, the present Sir Walter Scott telling me he had no knowledge of how it got into his late father's possession, or where it came from. Could this have been the very flag that was along with the Eagle, or was it only a camp colour? The flag of the Eagle was red, white and blue; this all blue.

Saw a blue
silk flag at
Abbotsford
purporting to
have belonged
to the 105th
French Regi-
ment.

·   ·   ·   ·   ·   ·

The Brigade
took no stand-
ards into the
Field.

Please to recollect that *none of the Brigade took their Standards into the Field,* they were left at home by order.

·   ·   ·   ·   ·   ·

Yours, &c.,
A. K. CLARK KENNEDY,
Lieut.-Colonel 7th Dragoon Guards.

FROM THE SAME.

No. 38.

Leeds, July 27th, 1839.

·   ·   ·   ·   ·

Waterloo.
1st Charge.
French left
Column
previously
repulsed by
Kempt's
Infantry.

Until your last, I had no idea that the attack of the left French Column had been met and repulsed by part of Sir James Kempt's Brigade *before we* gained the crest of the ridge, or could see what was going on in front; and it is excusable, my mistaking in the momentary view I had of our Infantry crossing the hedges in apparently great confusion (in returning from their successful attack for the purpose of re-forming) for an involuntary movement before an advancing Enemy, the head of one of whose Columns had gained the height on my immediate left.

That at the time we wheeled into line our Infantry were in the act of crossing the hedges I am certain, but whether they formed in rear of them, or immediately advanced and re-formed in front, I cannot say, but there was apparently great confusion at the moment.

. . . .

The Brigade was most gallantly supported by the Infantry, both in advancing and in retiring, by numerous small squares or parties of from ten, to twenty, or thirty men each, who came down the slope of the hill after us. Several of those parties were Highlanders, but whether 42nd, 79th, or 92nd, I cannot say, perhaps some of them all and other Regiments, for as I mentioned in a former letter, troops of various descriptions got mingled together. One instance I can speak to, viz., a small party of the King's Dragoon Guards that had joined in the charge on the other side of the Brussels road, retired on the *proper left* of my Squadron, and regained the position along with it. Mistaking them for some of my own Regiment I called out to them, " Royals form on me." The reply was, " We are King's Dragoon Guards, not Royals," and they passed on. . . . . . .

The Brigade supported by the Infantry.

Some of the King's Dragoon Guards retiring by the left of the Royals.

Yours, &c.,

A. K. CLARK KENNEDY.

FROM THE SAME.

Leeds, October 28th, 1839.   No. 39.

. . . .

I was speaking a short time ago to Mr. Hope, the Adjutant of the Leeds Recruiting District, who was a Subaltern in the 92nd Regiment at Waterloo, who told me he never saw anything to equal the enthusiasm of both Corps when the Greys passed through the 92nd to charge —that they mutually cheered each other on—that the 92nd seemed half mad, and that it was with the greatest difficulty the Officers could preserve anything like order in the ranks.

Waterloo.

Enthusiasm of Greys and Highlanders.

With regard to the strength of the Brigade in the field on the 18th of June, I have never calculated it at more than 950, or at the utmost 1,000 swords. The

Strength of the Brigade at Waterloo.

numbers mentioned in the Duke's despatches, of course, include not only the Officers, but men, *General Officers'* Orderlies, hospital or Surgeons' Orderly, camp kettle men, Farriers, Trumpeters, &c., and they may be safely set down as 120 or 130 at least in the three Corps, but they were probably a good many more.

Yours, &c.,

A. K. CLARK KENNEDY.

THE 2ND OR ROYAL NORTH BRITISH DRAGOONS— SCOTS GREYS.

LIEUT.-COLONEL C. WYNDHAM.
LIEUTENANT SCOTS GREYS.
Ballincollig, 13th, [? April or May 1839.]

No. 40.

Waterloo.
1st Charge.

There is no doubt that before we wheeled into line we were in a hollow and had suffered from the Guns in question before we charged, and it was at this period (not in the charge, as your military correspondent tells you) that Sir T. Hankin fell off his horse. I saw him on this side of the hedge taken to the rear, and three or four others besides of the men.

I cannot have a doubt but what it was a Column on the other side the hedge in irregular order trying to arrive at the hedge to command us, after the Highlanders had fallen back a little; there must have been a strong body of French opposed to this Brigade, or why did they fall back?

First wound after crossing the hedge.

I can recollect the circumstance by having got my first wound a few yards on the other side of the hedge. We sabred a good many going down the hill; it is possible that I may not be correct with regard to the distance from one Column to the other of the French, but I know it

Second wound.

was not many minutes afterwards going into the second Square or Column I got shot through the foot and disabled.

Crawford tells me after this they [the Greys] went up the high ground and took the Guns, somewhere about 20, and sabred the gunners and drivers, but could not bring away the Guns. The Lancers of the French, in open column, came close by me, and were evidently going in pursuit of our wounded and dismounted men, but did not attack the small main body of our Regiment. If we had been supported here, many of our poor fellows would have been saved; these Lancers did much havoc, and at Brussels, some weeks afterwards, I found many of our men with 10 and 12 lance wounds in them, and one man, *Lock,* had 17 or 18 about his person, and lived afterwards to tell the story. The prisoners I have mentioned which were taken came from both Columns from the hedge onwards.

I will now try, if possible, to help you in respect to the *enigma,* for such it appears at present.

I cannot allow we supported the other two Regiments, but here I think the mistake lies, and there was plenty of work, whichever way it was, cut out for everybody. We came from the hollow you speak of, the fire from the Enemy's Guns becoming too warm. We moved up, and I think took ground to the left to get more under cover of the hill. This may account ·for our being in some degree detached from the other two Regiments. We afterwards wheeled into line and went, in not the most regular order, over and through the hedge in the best way we could, encountering at the same [time] the French fellows who had formed themselves at the hedge, and gave us their fire as we came up the hill. We had several killed and wounded at this moment from small shot, and our remark ever since that memorable day was the extraordinary manner in which the bullets struck our swords as we ascended. Colonel Hankin never crossed this ground, but was left in the hollow and taken to a farm house nearly in front of which we bivouacked.

In respect to the brushwood which you allude to, I am almost sure I saw it on our left. The circumstance,

SCOTS GREYS.

since you have mentioned it, brings to my recollection an unfortunate Officer, I think of the Highlanders, who was brought down the hill to this very ground, and was being carried in a blanket by five or six of his Regiment, when a shell came and fell near them and destroyed nearly the whole [party]. I had before imagined it had been a garden instead of brushwood, but no doubt you are right. Some gun horses I saw in a difficulty near this spot at the same moment.

Scene on the Road to Brussels.

I have often thought of the scene I witnessed in going to Brussels. What a droll model it would have made. The road was one varied scene from the time I left the village of Waterloo until I arrived at Brussels; men, women, and children were ridden over by the runaway Belgians, and a few of our own people—baggage waggons, Guns, &c., lying in the middle of the road.

I must say I was delighted with your Model in London, and I was always sorry my time was so short for viewing it; it requires some hours to look it well through, but I was amused with an old Sergeant of the 12th Lancers telling his story to some one of having gone down with his Regiment in the charge with the Greys. "And *we* took an Eagle?" There is an old saying to "lie like a trooper," but this is all fair game and helps to vary the "oft told tale."

Yours, &c.,

C. WYNDHAM.

FROM THE SAME.

No. 41.

Newbridge Barracks, March 14th [? 1839].

Waterloo.

Greys not engaged with Cavalry except the Lancers.

The Greys, and I believe the Brigade, were not engaged with the Cavalry beyond the Lancers cutting up our wounded stragglers, &c., and some who were rallying; but depend upon it there was no order of "parade," or any dressing of "lines." *Pêle-mêle* we went to work, and from the circumstance of our first, second, third, and fourth in command being *hors de combat*, rely upon it there was not the time for meditating who was to halt the Corps or Brigade. It was an affair of, you may almost say, a moment, but had its desired effect, though not according to Cocker or Hoyle.

SCOTS GREYS.
Four commanding Officers put *hors de combat.*

In the evening, as you know, we crossed the road to the right, and although very much exposed to fire, had to show front to the Enemy, and awe them by advancing and retiring; and although there was a large body of French Cavalry in front, still they did not, *fortunately* for us, attack.

Brevet-Major Cheney at night brought out of action four or five Officers, and under thirty men. It is a curious circumstance that we lost as many killed (nearly) as wounded, both in Officers and men. *The Lancers* did us as much mischief almost as the round shot and shell, as they got in our rear. We found men with ten and fifteen wounds, and one man had eighteen and alive at the time.

At the end of the day reduced to four or five Officers and under thirty men.

Yours, &c.,

C. WYNDHAM.

Extracts from accompanying Memorandum.

No particular Regiment supported. The charge was a charge of the Regiments in line.

No Regiment in support.

The 92nd Highlanders appeared to be giving way when the Greys came to the top of the hill where the hedge was situated.

The 92nd Highlanders passed through the intervals of the Greys, and several went down the hill from the hedge with the Regiment, and it was at this moment when the 92nd cheered the Greys, and cried, " Scotland for ever ! "

I cannot say, but presume the 42nd Highlanders were in the same Brigade with the 92nd and 79th Regiments.

In reply to a question whether any of the Greys passed through the 42nd.

.   .   .   .

In descending the hill, about three or four hundred yards from the hedge, the Greys came in contact with a 2nd French Column or Square, regularly formed, the fire

The Greys come upon a

from which they received [and which] did great execution.
The loss at this moment in men and horses was most
severe. This Column was nearly destroyed, and the remainder of it were taken prisoners.

.   .   .   .

The Eagle was taken from the leading French Column
by the Greys, and sent to Brussels.*

C. WYNDHAM,
Lieutenant-Colonel commanding 2nd Dragoons.

PAYMASTER W. CRAWFORD, SCOTS GREYS.
CORNET SCOTS GREYS.

No. 42.   *Ballincollig, June 12th, 1839.*

.   .   .   .   .

Waterloo.   I have no recollection of the Greys having been in
1st Charge.   support during any part of the charge made on the
Columns of French Infantry alluded to in your note. I
remember Lieutenant-Colonel Hankin's going to the rear
in consequence of his horse having fallen with him; but
this took place some time before we charged. In your plan
See plan, p. 38. which you have enclosed (and which I now return), in my
opinion the Greys are placed correctly. I perfectly
recollect the hollow from our having had two or three men
and horses severely wounded by cannon shot, and in
consequence of this, of our having been ordered to advance
a short distance so as to place us more under cover, where
we were for a short time, and then ordered to charge (the
French Columns which were causing our Infantry to retire),
upon which we advanced *direct*, and not as a supporting
body.

As we advanced we were met by a number of the
92nd joining   92nd Regiment, who turned and ran into the charge with
in charge.   us, and during which I don't remember seeing either
Royals or Inniskillings in our front.

* The Eagle of the 45th French Regiment was taken in the charge
by Sergeant Ewart of the Greys. Unfortunately, I cannot find the letter
giving the details. Early in the following year, Sergeant Ewart was
appointed to an Ensigncy in the 3rd Royal Veteran Battalion.—ED.

I do not recollect the patch of brushwood, nor do I remember the Guns which are said to have fired on us from the hedge; but a most destructive fire was kept up, and from which we suffered most severely, both in Officers and men, and also horses.

Yours, &c.,

W. CRAWFORD.

THE 6TH INNISKILLING DRAGOONS.

LIEUT.-GENERAL SIR JOSEPH STRATON, C.B., K.C.H.

KNOWN AT WATERLOO AS LIEUT.-COLONEL AND COLONEL J. MUTER, INNSKILLING DRAGOONS.

United Service Club, London, June 6th, 1839.   **No. 43.**

. . . .

Not wishing to trust to my own memory at this distance of time, and Colonel Madox being here, I sent for him. His recollections are that the 2nd Brigade Heavy Cavalry, composed of Royals, Greys, and Inniskillings, were in column, and wheeled into line; that Sir William Ponsonby, about mid-day (we were on the slope of a hill), rode to the crest (La Haye Sainte), called to me to come to him; that I returned to the Brigade, that Sir W. Ponsonby shortly afterwards touched or moved his hat; and that I advanced the Brigade in *line.* Sir W. P. did call me to the front, pointed to the French Columns, and told me when he saw the fit moment he would make the signal for advancing; and I confess to you that my impression was that Madox's recollections of advancing in *line* were substantially correct. He commanded the right Squadron.

I afterwards saw Lt.-Col. Linton, who says that we stood in column and wheeled into line; that shortly the French Artillery annoyed our left, and that the Greys were moved to a second line, and that in the charge on the Columns of French Infantry the Greys were in

Waterloo.
1st Charge.
See plan, p. 38.

Signal for the
advance.
See No. 32,
p. 63.

support. He recalled several incidents, such as Lt.-Col. Hankin of the Greys having fallen from his horse, the circumstance having been reported to me; my looking round, &c., a Trumpeter being killed, and I am almost inclined to think the Greys were formed in a second line for a time; but whether afterwards brought up into line with the other two Regiments, or whether the Greys continued in support, I can hardly take upon me to say. Certain it is that the Royals and Inniskillings were in line, and in the first, if there was a second.

With deference, I should say that the military maxim of a support was more applicable to partial Cavalry charges than to the operations of a general Action, and therefore I should not be much swayed by the maxim in deciding whether the Greys were in support or in the first line. I have since seen Col. Madox, but he, being on the right, can fix nothing as to the Greys, who were on the left. He recollects the Artillery bearing on us before we advanced. I was in front of the centre Squadron of the Inniskillings, and had the conducting of the movement in advance by signal from Sir Wm. Ponsonby, so that the Royals and Inniskillings advanced simultaneously there can be no doubt.

Conducted the advance.

As to passing through the Infantry—part wheeled back to make room for the Cavalry—part passed through the intervals of Squadrons, and some, I fancy, got through rather irregularly. I recollect most distinctly the attack on a Column of Infantry by the Inniskillings. One circumstance I cannot forget—an Infantry French soldier on his knees, deliberately taking aim at the Adjutant of the Inniskillings, who was close to me, in the *midst* of one of the French Columns, and sending his bullet through his head.

The Adjutant, M. M'Clusky killed.

A squadron takes the Prisoners to Brussels.

? As to the Inniskillings taking an Eagle.

A Squadron of the Inniskillings was sent to the rear (Brussels, I believe) with the Prisoners; but whether they took more prisoners than the other Regiments I cannot say. As to taking Eagles, much might be said. A Private (Penfold, I forget his Christian name), *now living* at Brighton, can give some strong proof on that head.

It may be proper to mention that Colonel Hamilton of the Greys stood above me, but somehow, neither Sir W. Ponsonby or myself adverted to it.

.   .   .   .

I have, &c.,

JOSEPH STRATON,

Lieutenant-General.

Sir William Ponsonby was killed after the charge through the Columns of French Infantry (I was close to him). Colonel Hamilton was seen in advance, and never afterwards heard of. I succeeded to the command of the Brigade, and continued in command of it till wounded, very near the termination of the Action; about four or so in the afternoon we had moved to the *right* of the road. About six I was wounded, and Sir Arthur Clifton had command of the Brigade, then Lieutenant-Colonel of the Royals.

Death of Ponsonby, and of Col. Hamilton of the Greys.

Col. Muter succeeds to the command of the Brigade until wounded, about six p.m.

Lt.-Col. Sir A. Clifton, of the Royals, succeeds in the command.

FROM THE SAME.

U. S. Club, London, June 17th, 1839.   **No. 44.**

Waterloo. 1st Charge.

I give you my own recollections, and those of Lieutenant-Colonels Madox and Linton, in reply to the Queries contained in your letter of the 10th.

The Inniskillings came in contact with the French Columns of Infantry almost immediately after clearing the hedge and (I should call it) *chemin creux*. We all agree in thinking that the French Columns had nearly gained the crest—perhaps twenty to thirty yards down the slope. We think there were three French Columns.

The French Column did *not* attempt to form square, nor was it, so far as we could judge, well prepared to repel an attack of Cavalry. Our impression is that, from the formation of the ground, the Cavalry was not aware what they were to attack, nor the Infantry aware of what was coming upon them. Sir William Ponsonby knew, and I knew, he having called me to the front; other individuals

The Cavalry came unexpectedly on the French Infantry.

may also have known, but not the mass. I have always considered it a splendid illustration of the maxim that the attacks of Cavalry against Columns of Infantry should be unforeseen and unexpected.*

I could give an example, in the Peninsular War, of a similar result from the formation of the ground, as also of opposite results where the Infantry saw, and prepared accordingly.

The French Infantry had no time to throw themselves into square.

Our recollections are that the French skirmishers must have rejoined their Columns before, or at the moment of our clearing the hedge. We do not recollect seeing them.

The right and centre Squadrons of the Inniskillings certainly came in contact with a French Column. The left Squadron may have had to bring up its left shoulders to come on the flank of the Column, but I rather think the French Column extended as far as our left.

Our left Squadron cut off (if I recollect) about 2,000 Prisoners.

I shall send your query to Lieutenant-Colonel Miller, and let you know.

I am inclined to think that the Artillery by which our left was annoyed must have been placed on the opposite heights. We do not recollect coming on any Guns accompanying the French Columns, nor do I think that the

The French Guns were on the opposite height, not with the attacking Columns.

French Artillery got to the hedge. If there were any, they must have made off.

We cannot say that the Inniskillings were checked by any body of Cavalry in line, but rather think that, flushed by extraordinary success, they went on with so

---

* The Cavalry, on reaching the crest, or a moment before that, saw, from being a little raised on horseback, the solid Columns, and increasing their speed, attacked with great impetuosity, cheering by the three countries, England, Scotland, and Ireland. The French Infantry made good use of their musquets and fire, but had no time to throw themselves into square; any attempt to do so would, I think, have been frustrated by the momentum which the Cavalry had [gained] by plunging over the hedges, and their increased ardour by this time acquired.

much impetuosity, and suffered severely, both in pursuit and return, from Pelotons, Clouds, or small bodies of French Lancers.

After charging through the Infantry, there was no line preserved—imperfect, at any rate.

.   .   .   .

I have, &c.,

JOSEPH STRATON.

LIEUT.-COLONEL F. S. MILLER.

MAJOR AND LIEUT.-COLONEL INNSKILLINGS.

TO SIR JOSEPH STRATON.

Radway, June 11th, 1839.

MY DEAR SIR JOSEPH,—

.   .   .   .

As I perceive the Royals and Greys have an Eagle on their Standards, &c., I think application should be made for the Inniskillings to be granted the same distinction, as I have always considered them as much entitled to it as either of the other Regiments.

.   .   .   .

When we took [up] our position on the 18th, the Royals were formed on the right, the Inniskillings on the left, the *Greys in reserve,* and so formed we charged. I commanded the *left* Squadron, Madox the right, and Browne the centre. My Squadron was composed of Holbeck's and Douglas' Troops. In charging the French Column I was bayoneted in two places slightly, and lost my horse. In returning to the rear I met Sergeant Small, who had lost his own horse, and was leading one which had belonged to a French Officer of Lancers, and on that I rode, with the Lancer's appointments, for the rest of the day. I then found out Rickatts, got some sticking-plaster put on my bayonet wounds, and rejoined the Brigade— then reduced to three Squadrons, some having been

No. 45.

Thinks the Inniskillings entitled to the distinction of an Eagle on their Standards, as well as the Royals and Greys.

Inniskillings.
Assist.-Surgeon W. H. Rickatts, Inniskillings.

sent to Brussels with prisoners — behind the little wood.

From thence, after some time, we were ordered to the right of the Genappe road, moved up to the front, and there I was again wounded, and left them under the command of Madox, you commanding the Brigade. As to time I cannot pretend to any accuracy whatever. I should *guess* we charged about twelve—Ponsonby was killed at that time—that we moved towards the right about four, and that I left the field about five. I was wounded shortly *before* you, and, I believe, also before Lord Anglesey—but of that I am not certain.

Wounded a third time.

.   .   .   .

As to Penfold taking an Eagle, I only know what I *heard* at the time, that he took an Eagle which was by some means dropped or lost, and brought off by a man of the Greys or Royals. But Penn says that Penfold *told* him that after we charged he saw an Eagle, which he rode up and seized hold of; that the person who held it would not give it up, and that he dragged him by it for a considerable distance; that the pole broke about the middle and Penfold carried it off; that immediately afterwards he saw Hassard engaged by himself, and went to his assistance, giving the Eagle to a young soldier of the Inniskillings, whose name Penn now forgets; and that a Corporal of the Royals persuaded that young soldier to let him have it, and he carried it off, and Penn says he *saw* an Eagle broken as described going to Brussels with the prisoners.

Story of Private Penfold taking an Eagle.

Penn appears to have been a private or non-commissioned officer of the Inniskillings.—Ed.

Lieut. A. Hassard, Inniskillings, wounded.

.   .   .   .

Believe, &c.,

F. S. MILLER.

FROM THE SAME TO THE SAME.

Radway, June 18th, 1839.   No. 46.

MY DEAR SIR JOSEPH,—

. . . .

You may remember that when we advanced, and the men *Waterloo.* began to fall from the fire of the Artillery, we dismounted *1st Charge.* and marched up the hill on foot, and on reaching the top *Moved up the* we mounted, and I then perceived the enemy's *close* *hill on foot.* *Columns advancing* near the hedge.

On seeing us they hesitated, and were inclined *to turn.* *See* No. 17, A person in plain clothes, standing near the hedge close to p. 36. the left of my Squadron, cried out, "Now's your time," The Duke of Richmond's so over the hedge I went, and waited a moment or two for *exclamation.* the men to collect, and then we were into the Column in a second. There it was I received my bayonet wounds, and lost my horse. From our scattered state in getting over the hedge, I do not conceive we should have made any impression on *our* opposing Column had they not been inclined to *retire,* and had they reached the hedge we could have done nothing with them.

So you will perceive it was at the top of the hill that my Squadron came in contact [with them]. They were in square when I first saw them. I saw no skirmishers. The Square fired at us very irregularly, after we got over the hedge. But they seemed altogether taken by surprise, and did not offer the resistance they ought to have done. And we did not *stand long* to be shot at.

. . . .

My Squadron certainly completely broke one Column, *His Squadron* and I always understood, took a number of prisoners, and *broke one* the Eagle which afterwards got into the possession of one *Column, took* of the other Regiments ; therefore it is, (I think it will be,) *a number of* very hard upon the Regiment if they are to remain the *an Eagle (?).* only one of the Brigade without the distinction.

As I was on the left of our front line I heard no word of command, and only did what I saw done on my right until I got in sight of the Enemy. So I was rather behind the rest of the line, when we advanced after mounting, and therefore *might* come more unexpectedly on the Enemy, and after the skirmishers had been called in.

.   .   .   .

Believe, &c.,
F. S. MILLER.

Penn is not now with me, but keeps a public-house of mine, and has put up the *Inniskilling Dragoon* for his sign, which was before the *Red Horse*.

I conceive there were *three* or more Columns or Squares charged by the Brigade, *one* by my Squadron, supported by the Greys.

DÖRNBERG'S CAVALRY BRIGADE.

The 3rd (Light) Cavalry Brigade was composed of the 1st and 2nd Light Dragoons of the King's German Legion, and of the 23rd Light Dragoons. It was commanded by Major-General William Dörnberg.

On the 17th, the 1st and 2nd Light Dragoons formed part of the right Column of Cavalry in the retreat, whilst the 23rd was with the centre Column, which passed by the road through the town of Genappe. After acting as a support to the 1st Life Guards during their charge at Genappe, it became the last Regiment in the rear guard, and continued so during the remainder of the retreat.

See General Plan, No. 1.

At Waterloo the Brigade was first posted in rear of Sir Colin Halkett's Infantry in the Allied right centre, and was engaged during the day in several successful combats with the French Cavalry attacking that part of the line.

At the time of the advance of the second Column of the Imperial Guard, a Squadron of the 23rd Light Dragoons, under Lieut. J. Banner (Captain P. Z. Cox having just been disabled) charged and overcame the Cuirassiers, which were annoying the British Batteries, pursuing them round the rear of the Column, until checked by the *See* General fire of French Infantry. The 2nd Light Dragoons Plan, No. 2. of the German Legion also greatly distinguished itself.

The letters are solely from the 23rd Light Dragoons.

No. 47 refers to the march on Quatre Bras, and to the retreat on 17th June, the remaining letters to Waterloo.

23RD LIGHT DRAGOONS.

BREVET-MAJOR J. BANNER, 93RD HIGHLANDERS.

LIEUTENANT 23RD LIGHT DRAGOONS.

Lakefield House, Hawkeshead, Lancashire,　　　No. 47.
April 15th, 1837.

Severe domestic affliction, which I have experienced since I had the pleasure of seeing you, must plead my excuse for not having sooner forwarded to you the enclosed Memorandum of my remembrances of the 16th and 17th of June, 1815.　.　　.　　.　　.　　.

I am sorry I cannot lay my hands upon some papers, containing a few particulars of the Campaign, and an old map of the Netherlands, wherein I had marked all the marches performed by the 23rd Dragoons in that country, with the cantonments which they occupied there, consequently I cannot positively name the places in the enclosed statement. But *Gonicke* or *some such name* was the village at which my Troop was stationed when ordered to march upon Quatre Bras ; it was about seven miles from Brussels.

I am, &c.,

JOHN BANNER.

MEMORANDUM.

16th June.

On the morning of the 16th of June, 1815, at two o'clock, the different detachments of the 23rd Light Dragoons, that were in cantonments about seven miles from Brussels, received orders to assemble at the Head Quarters of the Regiment with all possible haste, for the purpose of proceeding to Quatre Bras, where the British troops were directed to concentrate, intelligence having been received that the outposts of the Allied Army had been attacked, and were forced to fall back, and that Napoleon with the French Army was advancing upon that point.

The 23rd Light Dragoons being collected moved off from its headquarters shortly after daybreak, and on its march came up with several Dragoon Corps; the 13th Light Dragoons was the Regiment immediately in its front.

When we arrived within a few miles of Nivelles a brisk cannonading was plainly heard, which indicated that a general engagement was going on; the Cavalry had to proceed through bad roads, which retarded their progress exceedingly, but they trotted whenever the road admitted of their moving at that pace, and pressed forward with the greatest alacrity to participate in the glories of the Field of Action.

On reaching Nivelles it was in the greatest possible state of excitation and confusion, the inhabitants from distant parts of the neighbourhood having come there for security; every house was filled with ladies and well-dressed females, who crowded to the windows, waved their handkerchiefs, and cheered the troops as they passed along the streets, in the most enthusiastic manner; the spectacle was encouraging beyond description.

Never was a sight more touching than that on approaching nearer to the Field of Battle. The road sides close to Quatre Bras were covered with the slain, and a vast number of gallant fellows in their last moments of agony.

The British Cavalry having a long march from their cantonments did not reach Quatre Bras until near six o'clock in the afternoon of the 16th June, about the close of the Action. The 23rd Light Dragoons was one of the first Regiments that arrived ; it took up its position on the rising ground to the right of the Namur road at the entrance to the Field of Action from Nivelles. Almost immediately on the 23rd entering the field, a reconnoitring party, under the charge of an Officer, was despatched across a large plain of high standing corn close to the edge of an extensive wood to watch and ascertain the movements of the main body of the Enemy, which was lying behind it.

Cavalry reach Quatre Bras about six p.m.

See plan No. 2 of Quatre Bras.

From six o'clock (the hour about which the Cavalry joined or came up) the firing gradually diminished until nine o'clock, when it altogether ceased at Quatre Bras, but towards Ligny, where the Prussians were engaged, the cannonading continued until 10 o'clock. The 23rd Light Dragoons furnished a strong picquet that night, under the command of Lieut. Banner, which was posted on the sloping ground to the right of the Namur road, opposite to and not far distant from the wood near the entrance of the Field of Battle. Colonel the Earl of Portarlington was the Field Officer on duty, and Captain Dance was the Captain of the day. The night passed off quietly, nothing material taking place in the immediate vicinity of Quatre Bras until 10 o'clock, when a most tremendous cheering, which continued for several minutes, was heard towards the right of the French position, and which was supposed to be the Enemy's demonstration of joy for the fancied victory they had obtained in the hard fought Battle of Quatre Bras, but in the morning it was ascertained that the acclamations and shouts of joy were proclaiming the decisive advantage they had gained over the Prussians at Ligny, in forcing them to abandon their position.

At ten p.m. French Troops cheering for the Battle gained at Ligny.

The Enemy did not renew the attack at Quatre Bras

The Retreat on 17th June.

the next morning, nor was any attempt made to disturb the troops while they remained in that position. When the Duke of Wellington received on the morning of June 17th intelligence of Marshal Blucher's defeat, and that the Prussian Army was retiring, the British and Belgian troops were immediately put in motion and ordered to fall back upon Waterloo. The Infantry commenced moving from Quatre Bras early in the morning, and the Cavalry, ordered to protect the retreat, remained in that position until the rest of the Army had proceeded some distance to the rear. The Cavalry began its march about two o'clock in the afternoon, when the Enemy immediately afterwards emerged from the woods and pursued the Allied rear guard with the greatest enthusiasm. The rear guard had not marched half a mile from Quatre Bras when it was overtaken by a storm of thunder and rain, the latter falling in such abundance that it rendered the roads and ground over which the troops retreated scarcely passable.

The Infantry commence their retreat early.

The Cavalry about two p.m.

Defile of Genappe

There being only one street by which the Army could pass through Genappe, the progress of the troops was consequently retarded at that village, and during this stoppage some of the Cavalry Regiments moved a short distance to the right of the entrance to Genappe to be ready to form and meet any attack that the French advance guard, which was rapidly approaching, might make upon our Columns while they were delayed at this defile, but all our troops entered Genappe before the French came up.

The Artillery which accompanied the French advance guard to Genappe was immediately planted at the left side of the town on the bank of the river which passes through it, from which station the Enemy opened a heavy and incessant fire upon our Cavalry when ascending from Genappe, by which they were exceedingly galled and sustained some loss; our Artillery being all at the period considerably in front, we were without a cannon to return a shot. The Enemy's Cavalry, having entered Genappe,

began to press upon our rear guard, the last division of
which had scarcely quitted the town when the Earl of
Uxbridge came to the rear to reconnoitre, and placing
himself upon the elevated ground on the right of the road
leading from Genappe, perceiving the boldness of the
French, directed the 7th Hussars to charge in order to
check their advance; the 7th Hussars, being animated by
the *presence of their Colonel*, rushed on the Enemy with
the greatest spirit and intrepidity, and drove the French
advanced divisions back into the street of Genappe upon the
main body of their Cavalry which occupied the town, where
a most obstinate conflict commenced, each party fighting
with the utmost desperation. The French, being backed
by a long dense Column of Cavalry flanked by the houses
on each side of the street, were enabled to make a most
formidable resistance; notwithstanding this numerical
superiority, it was only when menaced by such a heavy
force pressing forward that the 7th Hussars were obliged
to retire, but although they fell back the fault did not lie
with them, nor was it in consequence of the lightness of
their horses, as has been insinuated. The conduct of this
Corps on this occasion was heroic in the extreme; their
spirit and ardour was universally admired and acknowledged by all who witnessed the gallant affair. The French
became exceedingly elated in thus having repulsed the
7th Hussars in this, the first attack made by the British
Cavalry.

Immediately on the 7th Hussars falling back the whole
French Column raised the war cry and rent the air with
shouts of *En avant! En avant!* and evinced the greatest
impatience to follow up this momentary advantage, and
attack us in return at this favourable moment when a
great many of our Columns in the rear were experiencing
considerable annoyance from the well-directed and effective
fire from the Enemy's Guns on the bank of the river. The
French Cavalry being thus emboldened, several divisions
pressed on rapidly with a view to fall upon our rear guard.
The 23rd Light Dragoons being then the Regiment next

7th Hussars
ordered to
charge the
advancing
French
Cavalry.

7th obliged to
retire.

Enthusiasm of
the French.

The 23rd Light Dragoons in the rear, nearest Regiment to the Enemy.

Open out to permit 1st Life Guards to pass.

to the Enemy, were halted and ready to receive them, but the Earl of Uxbridge, desirous to afford the 1st Regiment of Life Guards, which was immediately in front of the 23rd Dragoons, an opportunity of charging, directed that Corps to be brought back; the 23rd Dragoons opened out to permit them to pass.

During the interval of time which had elapsed between the attack made by the 7th Hussars and the Life Guards coming from the front and forming in the rear, the French had debouched from Genappe, and when their leading divisions had ascended a little more than half way up the hill, the Life Guards were ordered to charge, and this

Gallant charge of 1st Life Guards.

charge was perhaps one of the most effective ever made by any troops. Although the French sustained the attack with firmness, they were quite unable to stand their ground in such a situation, advancing up the hill against the flower of the British Cavalry.

The French were overthrown with great slaughter, and were literally rode down in such a manner that the road was covered with men and horses scattered and sprawling in all directions down to the main body of the Enemy's advance guard.

After the charge the 23rd again the rearmost Regiment, and for the rest of the Retreat.

The 23rd Dragoons supported the Life Guards on this occasion, and after this successful and most brilliant charge, the 23rd Dragoons became again the last Regiment in the rear guard, and continued so during the rest of the retreat, and while it was proceeding leisurely along the road near the summit of the hill, not far from a house that was on the left-hand side of the *pavé*, this part of the road being much exposed to the Enemy's fire, a Staff Officer who was passing called out to Colonel the Earl of Portarlington, who commanded the 23rd Dragoons, to trot and push forward, but his Lordship, with his usual *sang-froid*, gave the word of command in the most emphatic manner for his Regiment to walk, and replied that " the 23rd Dragoons should never trot before an enemy," the French advance guard being at the time only a very short distance off.

From this period until the 23rd Dragoons entered
on the position at Waterloo it was not much harassed;
the Enemy merely pressed on twice or three [times], and
made preparations to attack, but never carried their
intentions into effect. The last time when their advance
guard showed any serious disposition of doing so was in
the hollow before reaching La Haye Sainte, when the
23rd Dragoons formed in line on the ground on the left-
hand side of the road to *bid* them an *affectionate* good-
night, but they would not come on to receive the proffered
salutations. During this last ceremony the Guns from the
position at Waterloo, and those which accompanied the
French advance guard, were playing over the heads of the
Cavalry. Thus closed the proceedings of June 17th,
1815.

JOHN BANNER,
Major and Captain, 93rd Highlanders.

FROM THE SAME.

TO COL. D'AGUILAR, DEPUTY ADJ.-GEN., DUBLIN.

DEAR COLONEL D'AGUILAR,—

Rochdale, Sept. 3rd, 1835. No. 48.

.   .   .   .

The 23rd Dragoons, to which I had the honour of Waterloo.
belonging, were posted towards the right of the British
Line at the Battle of Waterloo, when Major Cutcliffe,
having left the field wounded, between four and five o'clock
in the afternoon of that day, the command of the
Regiment devolved upon Major Lautour, who received an
order between five and six o'clock to send part of it towards
the centre to the relief of a Brigade of Guns, which was
considerably annoyed by the repeated charges of the
French Cavalry, and in obedience with that order a
Squadron to which I belonged was despatched, under the
command of Capt. Cox, who was soon after obliged to
leave the field in consequence of having been previously

severely stunned in a charge by his horse falling on him.

The French Cavalry that made the last effort to silence the Guns above-mentioned were repulsed and driven back by this Squadron of the 23rd Dragoons to a Square of French Infantry, which was formed considerably to the front, and behind which the French Cavalry took refuge. *See* General Plan of Waterloo, No. 2. This Square opened a heavy fire on the 23rd Dragoons on their retiring, and in consequence of their experiencing a similar annoyance on approaching the British line, they were induced to move to its flanks, which movement brought the greater part of this Squadron of the 23rd Dragoons along the front of Sir Hussey Vivian's Brigade. After clearing the Brigade I re-formed the men belonging to the 23rd Dragoons, and proceeded in the direction of Sir Hussey's Brigade, which had just before advanced, and on my coming up with the 18th Hussars on the summit of the French position, I went to the Honble. Col. Murray, who commanded that Corps, and informed him of my having brought up a division of the 23rd Dragoons which had been separated from its Squadron in a previous charge, and requested to be allowed to advance with his Regiment, upon which he replied that he had no control over me. I therefore continued to march with the 18th Hussars until we halted to bivouac for the night, when Captain McNeill and Lieut. Dodwell, with a few men, reunited with my division. The other Officers of the Squadron were Cornet Blathwayte and, I believe, Cornet Hemmings. Cornet Blathwayte was with my division.

.　　.　　　.　　.

I am, &c.,
JOHN BANNER,
Captain 93rd Highlanders.

LIEUT.-COLONEL P. A. LAUTOUR, H. P. 23RD
LANCERS.

MAJOR 23RD LIGHT DRAGOONS.

Boulogne, February 28th, 1835. No. 49.

.   .   .   .

On the evening of the 17th of June the 23rd Light
Dragoons having formed part of the rear-guard, entered
into position and bivouacked in a barley field just in
rear of the Nassau Brigade of Infantry, the 1st and
2nd German Light Dragoons having joined us that
evening, which composed our Brigade under the command
of Major-General Baron Dörnberg. Major-General Sir
Colquhoun Grant's Brigade being to our right.

On the morning of the 18th the Brigade moved up Waterloo
in column of Squadrons to the ridge of the position
occupied by part of the Royal Horse Artillery, as a
support to the Guns, one of the German Light Dragoon
Regiments forming on our immediate left, and the other
a little to our left rear ; and in rear of our Brigade
was formed a Regiment of Belgian Heavy Cavalry,
where the Brigade remained dismounted until the French
Lancers and Cuirassiers advanced to attack our Guns
and the position we occupied, when the Brigade mounted, Repulse   an
and led by our gallant General Dörnberg (who was attack
French
severely wounded in that charge), repulsed the Enemy Cavalry on
our Guns.
with great loss, and when the 23rd Light Dragoons,
animated and borne away by this success, pursued its
advantage a little too far, crossed a very wide and deep
ravine into which several of the rear rank horses fell,
driving back the Cuirassiers and Lancers on their own
Guns, and throwing the French gunners into the greatest
confusion.

After re-forming the Regiment (Lieut.-Colonel Cutcliffe
having been severely wounded), I moved it up in advance
of its first position, and to the support of the 33rd
Regiment, commanded by Colonel William Elphinstone,

Led by Lord
Anglesey,
advanced and
drove back
the Enemy's
Cavalry.

which Regiment was formed in square prepared to receive
the French Cavalry. Immediately after that movement
the 23rd Light Dragoons (the Marquis of Anglesey at their
head) advanced again and drove back the Enemy's
Cavalry from their immediate front, and during which
advance I found it necessary to move the Regiment to
the right to give an opportunity to the Belgian Heavy
Regiment of Dragoons in our rear to deploy (which I
had reason to believe afterwards they did not do), and
to prevent our being outflanked, as the Enemy were
deploying at that moment a reserve to take us in flank,
which by this movement was frustrated.

The 23rd Light Dragoons in this charge forced the
Enemy's Cavalry to abandon the eminence they had
obtained a momentary possession of, and which they
appeared very jealous of maintaining. From that period
the Regiment remained on the eminence supporting the
Infantry until about five or six o'clock in the evening,

In the even-
ing the 23rd
is formed on
the left of
Somerset's
Brigade.

when, it being much weakened, I formed it on the left of the
Household Brigade, commanded by Lord Edward Somerset,
and where we remained until the evening [when the
Enemy] on our right, led on by the Imperial Guards,
advanced again to force the position occupied by the
British, and in which they were successfully repulsed ;
and it struck me, as well as I could judge from the
immense smoke and confusion at that moment, that a
part of the Imperial Guards were overthrown and driven
back by the 52nd Light Infantry.

Lord Angle-
sey obtains a
troop horse
from the
Regiment.

It was almost immediately after that attack that
the Marquis of Anglesey rode up to the Regiment,
and requested me to let him have a troop-horse, his
own being tired out or wounded, which request I immediately complied with by dismounting Sergeant-Major
Stride, giving his Lordship the Sergeant-Major's mare,
which his Lordship instantly mounted and galloped some

And is
wounded
immediately
afterwards.

yards to our front on, when he met with his wound.
Perceiving his Lordship to have fallen, and on galloping
up finding it proceeded from a severe and dangerous

racture, I ordered a small party to assist in removing his Lordship from the ground, and reported the circumstance to Major-General Lord Edward Somerset.

About, or just previous to this time, Major-Generals Vandeleur's and Sir Hussey Vivian's Brigades advanced, when the 23rd Light Dragoons forming a support to the former, advanced with it the remainder of the evening and bivouacked next to the 11th Light Dragoons on that night.

The 23rd form a support to Vandeleur's Brigade.

In this statement I have not troubled you with the details of the several affairs in which the 23rd Light Dragoons were specially engaged during this memorable day, but it is a duty which I owe to the Officers and men whom I had the honour on that occasion to command, to state that the charge which they made down into the ravine, to which I have alluded, and in several other charges which in the course of the day they made, especially in one in which they rode over a body of French Cuirassiers and Lancers, they displayed in a high degree the cool steadiness and determined bravery of British soldiers.

I cannot conclude without naming a circumstance relative to the Earl of Portarlington, at that period the Lieutenant-Colonel of the Regiment, which I feel it a justice due to his Lordship (as a more gallant Officer never existed) to state, and to account for his absence from the 23rd Light Dragoons during that day, that in consequence of his Lordship having been taken *dangerously* ill with spasms and a violent bowel attack during the night of the 17th (when the Regiment slept on mud from the torrents of rain that fell), which obliged him to be removed from the ground very early on the morning of the 18th, and when he was conveyed to Brussels in a dangerous state; but having during the day recovered a little, and hearing of the Action, he came up in the evening, and at the moment the 18th Hussars were charging, and advanced with them, and had his horse severely wounded under him in that charge, and which illness will account for his

Illness of its Colonel, the Earl of Portarlington.

He comes up in the evening, and charges with the 18th Hussars. His horse severely wounded under him.

Lordship not having been with the 23rd Light Dragoons during that day.

I have, &c.,

P. A. LAUTOUR,

Lieutenant-Colonel H. P. 23rd Lancers.

LIEUT.-COLONEL H. GROVE.

CAPTAIN AND BREVET-MAJOR 23RD LIGHT DRAGOONS.

No. 50.   *Tonbridge Wells, January 8th,* 1845.

Waterloo
Vivian's
advance.
Death of
Major
Howard, 10th
Hussars.

See No. 75,
p. 176.

I saw Vivian's Brigade trot gently up in a Column of Divisions in the most perfect order, with Vivian, Thornhill, Keane, and others at the head. Poor Howard was in the rear, and we nodded to each other as they passed, within a few minutes of which he was killed—and a very fine, handsome fellow he was; but he evidently looked as if his time was come.

Yours, &c.,

H. GROVE.

VANDELEUR'S CAVALRY BRIGADE.

The 4th (Light) Cavalry Brigade consisted of the 11th Light Dragoons, the 12th, or Prince of Wales', Light Dragoons, and the 16th Light Dragoons. It was commanded by Major-General Sir John Vandeleur, K.C.B., up to the period of Lord Uxbridge being wounded in the evening at Waterloo, when the latter was succeeded in the command of the Cavalry by Sir J. Vandeleur, and the command of the 4th Brigade devolved upon Lieutenant-Colonel J. W. Sleigh, of the 11th Light Dragoons.

On the 17th June, Vandeleur's Brigade (with

the exception of a detached Squadron of the 11th Light Dragoons) and Vivian's formed the left Column of Cavalry in the retreat. It was drawn up in rear of Vivian's Brigade, and, on the latter being pressed by the Enemy, it crossed the Genappe river at the bridge of Thuy, so as to leave the passage open for Vivian.

Nos. 52 and 55 formed part of a correspondence in which exception was taken by some Officers of the Brigade to the description given in the first edition of Captain Siborne's History (Vol. I. p. 261 and following), to the effect that Vivian expected that Vandeleur was to support him until pressed by the Enemy, and then let him retire through his (Vandeleur's) Brigade, the latter taking the rear guard in its turn.

The pursuit of the Enemy being checked at the river, the two Brigades retired without further molestation to the position at Waterloo.

On the 18th, Vandeleur's Brigade was posted *See* General Plan, No. 1. in the morning on the left of the position behind the Wavre road, and in rear of the farms of Pape-lotte and Ter la Haye.

At the time of the first attack on Picton's *See* Plan, p. 38. Division, and of the charge of Ponsonby's Brigade, Vandeleur's was moved to the right to support the latter, but was delayed by the nature of the ground it had to pass over in coming up. The 12th Light Dragoons, the leading Regiment, charged down into the valley, and broke the only French Column remaining intact after Ponsonby's charge. It then took in flank the French Lancers who were pursuing the remains of the Heavy Brigade.

The 16th, led by Vandeleur, also charged the Lancers, but more in their front, the two Regiments driving them back to the foot of the valley. The 12th sustained heavy losses, and the Commanding Officers of both Regiments were very severely wounded. The 11th had been kept in reserve on the brow of the hill.

Later in the day, on the advance of the Prussians being ascertained, the Light Cavalry was moved from the left to the other side of the main *See* General road. Vandeleur's Brigade was drawn up in rear Plan, No. 2. of the Infantry Brigade of General Chassé's Dutch-Belgian Division, and by its attitude prevented the latter from quitting the field at the time of the final attack of the Imperial Guard.

See General In the General Advance the Brigade moved Plan, No. 3. forward to the left of Hougoumont, and encountered further on a large Column of Infantry forming square to receive them, which they charged and broke. The 11th Light Dragoons captured the last Battery which kept up its fire in the French left wing. The 12th came upon the Regiment of Grenadiers à Cheval, which was in perfect order, not having been engaged all day, but were too weak, after their previous losses, to make an impression on it.

Nos. 52, 55, 56, and 60 refer to the retreat on the 17th, No. 55 and all the remaining letters to Waterloo.

GENERAL SIR JOHN VANDELEUR, G.C.B.

MAJOR-GENERAL AND K.C.B., COMMANDING 4TH CAVALRY BRIGADE.

MEMORANDUM.   *No date [? October,* 1836].   No. 51.

On the morning of June 18th, Vandeleur's Brigade, Waterloo.
consisting of the 11th, 12th, and 16th Light Dragoons, Position of
was formed on the extreme left of the Infantry (Picton's at the com-
Division), being separated from the Infantry by a ravine, the Battle.
and having the village or hamlet of La Haye Sainte *See* General
[La Haye] two hundred or three hundred yards in its Plan, No. 1.
front, occupied by Germans. Vivian's Brigade was
formed on the left of Vandeleur's Brigade. Observing
that the Enemy's shot reached us, Vandeleur's and (I
believe) Vivian's Brigades were ordered to retire behind
the brow of the hill and dismount.

About the time of commencing the Action, an order
arrived from Lord Anglesey to Generals Vandeleur and
Vivian to engage the Enemy whenever they could do so
with advantage without waiting for orders, and subsequently an order came from the Duke or Lord Anglesey
to close to the Infantry, which had left a vacancy by
closing to its right.

These two orders were the only orders received previous
to the first charge made by Vandeleur's Brigade.

This Brigade, upon receiving the order to close to the The Brigade
Infantry, passed the ravine in column with a small front. moves to the
It was then seen that Sir William Ponsonby's Brigade, Ponsonby's
after their most gallant charge, had been repulsed, and seen retiring.
was retiring precipitately and in disorder upon the left of 1st Charge.
Picton's Division, of which it masked the fire. Vandeleur's
Brigade was brought forward as quickly as was consistent
with order. The 11th Light Dragoons were ordered to The Brigade
be the reserve and remain on the hill, the 12th and 16th brought
being in line, the 12th on the left. forward.

Sir William Ponsonby's Brigade, followed closely by the
Enemy's Lancers in column, were so near to the left of
Picton's Division, and to the right of Vandeleur's Brigade,

that it was impossible to form a line perpendicular to the Enemy's flank in order to charge him in flank perpendicularly without exposing the left of the Brigade to a flank attack by a part of the Enemy's Column. The two Regiments were therefore ordered, " Squadrons Right half wheel, charge."

And drives back the French Lancers.

The Enemy was driven back, and the two Regiments were ordered, previous to the charge, not to pass the hollow ground in front. Sir Hussey Vivian's Brigade followed Vandeleur's over the ravine, but could not arrive in time to cover the retreat of Sir William Ponsonby's Brigade. It formed on the left of the ground from which Vandeleur's had charged. The pass across the ravine was narrow and required some time to pass, which was the reason that Sir J. Vandeleur left the 11th in reserve.

The Brigade ordered to the rear of the Infantry behind Hougoumont.

It supports Vivian's Brigade when charging the retiring Enemy.

It relieves Vivian's Brigade, and charged and broke the last French Infantry which preserved order.

After this the Infantry left a considerable space of ground vacant on the left by closing to the right, and forming four deep, squares, &c., and Vandeleur's Brigade was ordered to the rear of the Infantry on the great road behind Hougoumont, where it remained till the Enemy made his last great effort, and was repulsed. It then supported Vivian's Brigade, which made several charges on the left of the retiring Enemy. Vandeleur's Brigade then relieved Vivian's Brigade, pursued, charged, and broke the last Infantry which preserved its order near La Belle Alliance. It was then quite dark and the troops remained on the ground.

After this it was so dark that a collision with the 1st German Hussars nearly took place.

It was so dark at the end of the last charge that the 1st German Hussars, coming up in rear of Vandeleur's Brigade, were mistaken for the Enemy till reconnoitred, which prevented any collision.

FROM THE SAME.

No. 52.

The Retreat on the 17th.

Dublin, Nov. 1st, 1845.

I had the pleasure to receive your letter of the 23rd ult., and am perfectly satisfied with your proposal contained therein, viz., that the last declared opinion of the

late Lord Vivian was that Sir J. Vandeleur had received no instructions to support his, Sir Hussey Vivian's, Brigade on the 17th of May [June], and with the alterations you propose to insert, and which Colonel Childers approves of, namely, adding the following sentence :—
" Vivian not being aware that Vandeleur had previously received orders to retire and leave the road clear for the retreat of the Cavalry in his front."

I remain, &c.,

J. VANDELEUR.

THE 11TH LIGHT DRAGOONS.

LIEUT.-GEN. J. W. SLEIGH, C.B.
LIEUT.-COLONEL COMMANDING 11TH LIGHT DRAGOONS.

Shirley House, near Southampton, Nov. 11th, 1841.　No. 53.

In acknowledging the receipt of your letter of the 5th inst., received this morning, I shall be happy in replying to your queries, so far as my recollection will allow; the first as regards Sir John Vandeleur's Brigade covering the retreat of General Ponsonby's after his attack on D'Erlon's Columns. The Brigade was formed that day, the 16th Dragoons on the right, 11th in the centre, the 12th on the left. When Sir John Vandeleur ordered it to advance I was directed to remain on the brow of the position as a support, the 12th being the left Regiment of the whole line advanced by itself under Sir Frederick Ponsonby; the 16th with Sir John Vandeleur at their head proceeded rather to the right, but in going down closed on the 12th, and I am pretty sure some of the 16th charged with the 12th.

The 16th, however, broke off to the right, leaving a considerable distance between the Corps, through which interval and the 11th Dragoons the chief part of the Greys retired, excepting one Squadron under Colonel Cheney, which fell back in very perfect order to the right of the 16th Dragoons.

With reference to the Belgian Cavalry, who joined in covering the retreat, there were some in the rear of our

Marginal notes:
Waterloo. 1st Charge. When the Brigade advanced to cover the retreat of Ponsonby's Brigade, the 11th were left in support on the brow of the hill.

The Belgian Cavalry.

Brigade to the left, a few of them went down following the 12th Dragoons; but I cannot say I observed them to take any part in the attack, nor would the ground admit of their doing so on the left, as the 12th advanced close to the hedge from which they suffered the severe loss the Regiment sustained.

In the evening the Brigade was supporting and encouraging Belgian Squares in rear of the Guards.

With regard to the second query, the Brigade moved towards the close of the day to the right upon the crest of the position, giving cover [? support] to some Belgian Brigades who were in rear of (I think the Guards), and which timely support restored order to these troops, who were from the press made at that period upon this part of the position in some confusion and unsteady.

The Duke came up and said, " Tell them the French are retiring."

The Duke came up and said, " Tell them the French are retiring," and I imagine from this [? time] gave the order for the General Advance. This is (as near as the distant period will allow of my stating) my observation on this part of the day.

. . . .

In the General Advance Vandeleur's Brigade was on the right.

Took the last French Battery and received the last fire.

Vandeleur's Brigade in the Advance was the right of the whole, Sir Hussey Vivian's being on our left. We took the last Battery, and received their last fire, which was given when the Brigade, then under my command, was so close that I saw the Artillerymen fire their Guns; fortunately the ground was undulating, and we only lost by the fire Lieutenant Phillips [? Phelips] of the 11th Dragoons, and Hay of the 16th Dragoons. It was after this, when continuing our advance, that the 1st Hussars came up in the rear of the Brigade, and from its being nearly dark were all but in collision with the 11th and 16th, which Regiments, knowing there was a Brigade of French Cavalry on our right, went Threes about, and were in the act of charging, when they recognised the 1st Hussars by knowing their cheer; it was very dark, and the men knew of the French Brigade being behind them.

The 11th and 16th all but in collision with the 1st German Hussars.

. . . .

I am, &c.,

J. W. SLEIGH.

FROM THE SAME.

Shirley House, November 20th, 1841. No. 54.

. . . .

The statement given you by an officer of the 12th, I Waterloo.
have no doubt is correct, as I afterwards ascertained we
were close on Buonaparte when he was getting away.

The Brigade of French Cavalry is the same as you Colonel Sir
mention. It was poor Colonel Harvey who rode up and told Felton
me where they were, but they never came down, and I Light
imagine must have gone to the rear on the road to Dragoons,
Charleroi, or the Regiment mentioned by the 12th officer Qrtr.-Master
may have formed one of this Brigade.

> I am, &c.,
>
> J. W. SLEIGH.

Colonel Sir Felton Harvey, 14th Light Dragoons, Dep.-Assist. Qrtr.-Master General.

COLONEL M. CHILDERS.

CAPTAIN AND BREVET-MAJOR 11TH LIGHT DRAGOONS.

FORWARDING AN EXTRACT FROM A LETTER BY LIEUT.-GEN. SLEIGH.

Floors Castle, Kelso, September 23th, 1845. No. 55.

I have the honour to acknowledge the receipt of your The Retreat
letter (with its enclosures) of the 25th inst. I do not on 17th.
know Major-General James Hay's address, but I wrote to
Lieutenant-General Sleigh. An extract from his letter I
herewith send you :—

"Your letter of the 4th reached me this morning
(September 10); in reply I will state, as well as my recollection permits, the circumstances attending the paragraph
in Captain Siborne's History.

"Previous to the two Brigades retiring, the 4th was Previous to
formed in rear of the 6th some short distance. We re- retiring,
ceived instructions to send an Officer to ascertain where we Brigade was
could cross the Genappe River, and to commence our retreat in rear of
as soon as this had been found. Before the Officers re- Vivian's.
turned who had been sent from the two Brigades and

11th Light Dragoons.

Moved off to the bridge over the river, but took up no new position till the Brigade had crossed.

Dyneley's Guns (I think), that tremendous rain commenced. We moved off, and gradually proceeded to the Bridge, Vivian's Brigade and the Guns following. We took up no new or commanding position until the Brigade had crossed. The 11th Dragoons was the leading Regiment when they broke into column to pass, and I fully remember Sir J.

Ordered to leave room for the Guns and rear Brigade to pass.

Vandeleur desiring me to form as soon as I could find an open space, leaving the road clear for the Guns and rear Brigade. This was done, and the 4th Brigade remained till Lord Vivian's and the Guns had passed; and this is shown, I believe (if I recollect right), in Siborne's statement, as it will be found we were the last Brigade that got

Vandeleur's the last Brigade that arrived at the Waterloo position.

to the final position; then, if Sir J. Vandeleur had received instructions to allow the rear Brigade to pass and relieve them, he did so the moment he could, and at the most material point."

This is the extract from Lieutenant-General Sleigh's letter, and only shows how hopeless it is to expect (after such a lapse of time) an account from those who were actors in what then took place, in which all should agree. For my own part I do not recollect even the Bridge to which the Lieutenant-General alludes.

·   ·   ·   ·   ·   ·

Waterloo.

Colonel Tomlinson is kind enough to say, respecting Sleigh and myself (he, S., was then Lieutenant-Colonel commanding the 11th Dragoons), that we assisted in restoring order in a Belgian Square of Infantry which had commenced crumbling to pieces. I perfectly recollect the circumstance, for Colonel Sleigh was hit by a spent ball in the stomach at the moment, and I thought was killed. You may either mention it or not as you may think fit. It is not for me to publish or make mention of these matters.

I have, &c.,

M. Childers.

P.S.—I do not recollect any particular Regiment of French Cavalry more steady than the others, nor do I remember the Grenadiers à Cheval.

LIEUT.-COLONEL J. A. SCHREIBER.

CAPTAIN 11TH LIGHT DRAGOONS.

Melton, near Woodbridge,
Oct. 21st, 1839.

No. 56

. . . .

On the evening of the 16th June I was ordered on Picket to Quatre Bras in command of a Squadron of the 11th Dragoons, and remained there till about one o'clock p.m. on the 17th, when I received an order to retire, forming the rear-guard. This I did at a foot's pace without the least molestation from the Enemy's Cavalry. On arriving within about two miles (as near as I can recollect) of the town of Genappe, I was directed to leave the high road to make room for the 7th Hussars, I think by Lord Anglesey himself. On proceeding a short distance I discovered the 7th Hussars formed in close column of Divisions on the *Chaussée.* Having passed them I resumed my position on the high road, and retired quietly *through* the town of Genappe. At about a quarter of a mile on the Brussels side of it the 7th Hussars passed us at speed, right and left of the road in all directions, having been evidently much harassed.

[margin: Sent on picket evening of 16th at Quatre Bras.]
[margin: Retreat on 17th June.]
[margin: 17th retires through Genappe.]

I immediately halted and fronted, and when they were clear, charged and drove the French Cavalry back into the town of Genappe. We were then obliged to retire, which was perfected in good order, and I rejoined my Regiment the same evening about nine o'clock.

*[margin: The account of this charge is contradicted by Lord Anglesey. ED *See* No. 4, p. 6.]*

. . . .

I have, &c.,

J. A. SCHREIBER.

THE 12TH, OR PRINCE OF WALES', LIGHT DRAGOONS.

MAJOR-GENERAL THE HON. SIR FREDERICK C. PONSONBY, K.C.B., G.C.M.G., K.C.H.

LIEUT.-COLONEL AND COLONEL COMMANDING 12TH LIGHT DRAGOONS.

No. 57.   *Curzon Street, July 29th*, 1836.

Waterloo.

See General Plan, No. 1.

The statement which you have sent me respecting the charges made by Sir William Ponsonby's and a part of Sir J. Vandeleur's Brigades at the Battle of Waterloo appear to me to be very correct. I will, however, give you my own impression of these charges.

General Vandeleur's Brigade was bivouacked on a cross road in rear of General Picton's Division on the night of the 17th. On the morning of the 18th it was directed to move about nine o'clock to the extreme left of the position about three-quarters of a mile from the left of our Infantry (General Pack's Brigade, I believe). Here it remained, in company with General Vivian's Brigade and a Battalion of Nassau Infantry till the Battle commenced, when it was ordered to close in and form near our Infantry. During this short movement the heavy rattling of musketry showed that a serious attack was in progress, and when my Regiment, the 12th, was formed on its new ground, I had a view of the plain between the two Armies, and of the whole of the French position.

Position of Vandeleur's Brigade.

Brigade moved to the right towards Picton's Division.

1st Charge.

Danger in which were Ponsonby's Dragoons near the crest of French position.

12th and part of 16th charge the French Infantry.

Lieut. W. Osten, 16th Light Dragoons.

I saw considerable bodies of French Infantry and Cavalry in some confusion in the plain, and a good many scattered Dragoons in red nearly on the crest of the French position. I felt that these were in the utmost peril unless some support was immediately afforded, and the 12th, accompanied by some of the 16th Dragoons, charged and penetrated a mass of unsteady Infantry on the plain below. I say some of the 16th, for I saw Baron Austen and Sergeant-Major Blood of that Regiment in the *mêlée* which took place. The confusion was very great in the *mêlée*, as a body of French Lancers and Chasseurs had entered into the conflict.

French Lancers and Chasseurs enter into the conflict.

I endeavoured to draw off my Regiment, but being wounded and completely disabled, I soon fell to the ground upon the crest of the French position, and in the near vicinity of some Guns which probably had been abandoned during the charge of General Ponsonby's Brigade, as several men, I think of the Royals, were found in the same spot where I was picked up in the following morning.

Wounded and disabled on the crest of French position.

The French soon resumed the ground they had lost. I believe the ground on which I fell was the extreme right of the French position, and it was occupied the remainder of the day by French Light Infantry. Some Squadrons of Prussian Cavalry passed over it late in the day.

Fell about the extreme right of French position.

I cannot take upon myself to say who gave the order for the charge. There can be no question that it was well timed, and it must have been, if not by the order, at all events with the sanction of Sir J. Vandeleur. What part of the 16th charged I cannot say, but some certainly did. If I may venture an opinion it would be that the 12th and a Squadron of the 16th charged, and that the remainder of the Brigade acted as a support to the charge.

My personal adventures have nothing to do with the narrative, except as establishing the fact that some of the Royals, some of the 12th, and some of the 16th were cut down close to some Guns on the French position.

The time of my charge was immediately after the charge of General Ponsonby, which I suppose took place between 11 and 12, and the French troops in the plain must have been a part of those returning from the unsuccessful attack on General Picton's position.

The time of the charge of the 12th immediately after that of General Ponsonby.

I have said that a good many men fell on the crest of the French position. I know we ought not to have been there, and that we fell into the same error which we went down to correct, but I believe that this is an error almost inevitable after a successful charge, and it must always depend upon the steadiness of a good support to prevent serious consequences. In a great battle the support is at

12TH LIGHT DRAGOONS.

hand, and I am therefore firmly of opinion that although we sustained a greater loss than we should have done if our Squadrons had remained compact, the Enemy suffered a greater loss, was thrown into more confusion, and required more time to re-establish order, than if greater regularity had been preserved.

You are at perfect liberty to make what use you please of this letter. The opinions may be erroneous, but I pledge my honour that the facts are correct.

I have, &c.,

F. PONSONBY,

M.-General.

MAJOR A. BARTON, 12TH ROYAL LANCERS.
CAPTAIN 12TH LIGHT DRAGOONS.

No. 58.

Waterloo.

Birmingham, November 3rd, 1834.

Major Barton, 12th Royal Lancers, presents his compliments to Mr. Siborne, and agreeable to his request, returns his plan of the Field of Waterloo, on which he has, to the best of his recollection, marked the two principal positions of the Regiment on the 18th of June. He has also enclosed a few recollections of that eventful day.

To the rear of Papelotte.

See General Plan, No. 1. Vandeleur's Brigade.

This was the first position taken up on the morning of the 18th of June. The Regiment was formed in close column of three Squadrons, left in front, in a field of peas or vetches in the left rear of the British line of Infantry, having in its immediate front the troops of Nassau.

1st Charge.

The left of our line being attacked by a strong Column of Infantry, commanded by General Durutte, the Regiment was ordered to advance by its Lieut.-Colonel the Hon. Fredk. Ponsonby, who, I believe, had orders to act discretionally. We advanced unperceived by the Enemy, and on passing the hedge-row, occupied by the Highlanders, immediately made a flank attack on the French Column. This attack was successful, and threw

12th attack the French Infantry.

the Enemy into disorder, who retreated in the greatest confusion followed by the Regiment till we were stopped by their standing Columns of reserve on the opposite side of a ravine.

Stopped by French Columns of reserve on opposite side of the valley.

During the whole of this time an indiscriminate fire was kept up by the French Artillery on the Regiment as well as on their own retreating Battalions. We were in considerable confusion, being mixed up with the Enemy's broken Infantry, suffering at the same time from a heavy cannonade, and before we could regain the position for formation, we were charged by the 3rd and 4th French Lancers, who advanced from behind their own Columns of reserve. From this charge and the heavy fire to which we had been before exposed we suffered great loss, having nearly one hundred killed and wounded; amongst the latter was our gallant Lieut.-Colonel, who at the time was reported "killed."

12th attacked by the French Lancers, this and the heavy fire causing great loss.

This was our position at about 7 p.m. We were at this time formed into two Squadrons, owing to the great loss the Regiment had sustained in its attack on Durutte's Column. We were standing in a field of trampled corn, in the right rear of the rising ground held by the Guards, to which point Sir John Vandeleur's Brigade had been moved from the left of the line, as nearly as I can recollect, about five o'clock.

The site indicated is exactly in rear of the House of Hougoumont, and close behind the Nivelles road, after the Brigade had been moved towards the right of the position.

On the Brigade taking up its position, the Regiment stood on the left, and in its immediate rear was a deep quarry or sandpit. I can call this circumstance more particularly to my recollection from Lieutenant-Colonel Stawell (then Captain) remarking the awkward position in which the Regiment stood in the event of a retrograde movement becoming necessary, and suggested we should take up a more advanced alignment, which was accordingly done; this consequently placed us some distance in front of the Brigade. We had elevated ground in our front, from which the shot directed on the Guards ricocheted, passed over our heads, and took effect on the other Regiments of our Brigade; we were at this time so close to the Enemy that some of our men were wounded by grape.

The Brigade advanced over the scene of the struggle between the French and British Guards.

On the failure of the Enemy's last attack the Brigade advanced, passing over the ground on which the struggle had taken place between the French and English Guards. The scene here was terrific from the great number of killed and wounded. Bodies were lying so close to each other that our horses could scarcely advance without trampling on them, and a great many were wounded in the fetlocks from the bayonets and other weapons that were scattered about on the field.

It is impossible for me at this moment to state positively on which side of Hougoumont the Regiment passed during its advance, indeed, I do not think any individual of the Regiment could at this day, or even the day after the Battle, decide the fact; such a scene of devastation and rout had never before been witnessed by any of us, but I am disposed to think, from our inclining towards our left

Advanced by the left of Hougoumont. *See* **General Plan.**

during the Advance, that we must have left Hougoumont to our right. The Enemy was in full retreat, and our Brigade followed them, skirting the wood at the Observatory *close to our right.*

The only attempt to make anything like a stand against us or interrupt our pursuit, was made by a *weak* Regiment of Infantry which halted and fired a few shots at us, after which some of the men threw themselves down on their faces in the standing corn, and others effected their escape into the wood on our right. At this time we saw to our left front, at no great distance, a strong Regiment of

Meeting the Grenadiers à Cheval who retire in perfect order.

Cavalry, which we soon ascertained to be the Grenadiers à Cheval of the Imperial Guard; they were formed in a dense close column, and appeared to take but little notice of our advance, when opposite their flank they fired a few pistol or carbine shots.

We were some distance in front of our Brigade, and being too weak to make an impression [on them], they literally walked from the field in a most majestic manner.

I had subsequently an opportunity of learning from a

French Officer that this Regiment, as well as the Red Lancers of the Guard, was not in action during the day. I can only account for their steadiness in such a perilous situation, by ascribing it to a wish to cover their Infantry and Cavalry that were retreating in such great disorder, and by their perceiving that we had outmarched our Guns.

The Brigade continued its pursuit of the Enemy still further, and when we were ordered to retire a short distance for the purpose of taking up our bivouac, rather an extraordinary circumstance occurred. While retiring we met the 1st Hussars, King's German Legion, advancing. We mutually mistook each other for the Enemy, and were on the point of attacking when the error (by which an Officer of our Brigade was slightly wounded) was discovered.

Averted collision between the Brigade and the 1st Hussars, K.G.L.

THE 16TH LIGHT DRAGOONS.

MAJOR W. TOMKINSON.
CAPTAIN 16TH LIGHT DRAGOONS.

Willington, Nathwich, April 2nd, 1835. No. 59.

.   .   .   .

The Brigade went out at the left of the position, supported the charge, and covered the retreat of the Heavy Brigade, viz., Royals, Greys, and Inniskillings. The appearance of the Enemy at this time in our front, being about one o'clock, was having their Light Troops in advance of the hills they occupied in our front, with parties of Cavalry and Infantry in different places without forming any line.

Waterloo. 1st Charge.

The arms of the French Infantry charged by the Heavy Brigade lay in two lines, nearly as regularly as if laid on parade. They had advanced diagonally to our position, their right (I think) considerably advanced. I did not ascertain this on the 18th, but find the following in my Journal :—

Arms of French Infantry, charged by Ponsonby's Brigade, lying in two regular lines on the ground.

" On going over the ground the following morning I

saw where two lines of Infantry had laid down their arms, whose position was accurately marked from the regularity the muskets were placed in."

Brigade remained on the left until arrival of, and attack by, the Prussians.

The Brigade remained on the left until half-past five or thereabouts, and having seen the advance and commencement of the Prussians' attack, moved in rear of our Line, crossed the Brussels and Genappe road (our Line being at this time greatly reduced, and having large intervals), forming with our left on the road the instant we passed it.

Formed in rear of some Belgian Infantry, and prevented their going to the rear.

There was a Regiment of Belgian Infantry a little in advance of the left of the Brigade in square, which during the last attack on our Line, which was immediately in our front, commenced firing their muskets in the air, meaning to move off in the confusion. Colonel Childers of the 11th and myself went and urged them to be steady, the Duke riding up and doing the same.

. . . .

Joined in the pursuit of the French.

In pursuit when the Line advanced, we moved in line to the crest of the position, when we broke into a Column of half-Squadrons to pass the Infantry. When on the crest of the position the whole French Army was in full retreat, their Infantry in confusion running at the bottom of the hill.

Yours, &c.,

W. TOMKINSON.

FROM THE SAME.

No. 60.

Willington Hall, Chester, February 10th, 1845.

I beg to forward you a reply from my Journal relative

Retreat on 17th.

to the retreat on the 17th, which, I believe, is a correct representation of what occurred.

I have no doubt Sir Hussey Vivian expected us to cover him, and so we were ordered to do; but the events I mention changed that purpose, and rendered it impossible.

. . . .

I remain, &c.,

W. TOMKINSON.

June 17th, 1815.

The Duke rode up at daylight to Quatre Bras, and we soon heard that, in consequence of the attack made on the Prussians last night, they had retired on Wavre, and that we were also to retire to a position in our rear to cover Brussels. The Infantry withdrew quietly, leaving the Cavalry to cover their retreat. We remained on the ground [on which] we had passed the night until one o'clock, when, in consequence of the Enemy showing some Cavalry, we turned out, forming in three lines to the left and rear of Quatre Bras.

Retreat. begun.

The two Brigades of Hussars were in the first line, General Vandeleur's Brigade in the second line, and the Heavy Cavalry in support some distance to the rear.

Two Brigades of Hussars in first line or rear line, Vandeleur's in second. Heavy Cavalry in support.

The intention of Lord Uxbridge was to keep the Hussars [? in hand] to take advantage of any favourable chance, and on the Enemy advancing in such force as to oblige us to retire, they were to pass through the second line (our Brigade), and it to cover the retreat.

Lord Uxbridge intended the Hussars to pass through the second line when pressed.

I saw the French Cavalry when turning out of their bivouac, and I thought, from their numbers, we must either bring all our force to oppose them and keep our ground, or that, if a retreat were determined on, the sooner we marched the more prudent.

They came out Column after Column, and in greater force than I ever recollect seeing together at one point. They advanced in very large bodies, and Lord Uxbridge soon saw that, so far from having any chance of charging, he had nothing left but to get his troops away with the least possible delay. We, the second line, were ordered away immediately, and retired, leaving Genappe on our left (in retiring). The first line got away without much loss, retiring with the Heavy Brigade Cavalry on Genappe, but had not time allowed it to retire through the second line as at first intended.

The great numbers of the French Cavalry.

There was not time for the Hussars to pass through our Brigade, the Enemy was so close upon them, and had

No time for Hussars to pass through second line.

we not got off with the least possible delay, the Hussars and our Brigade would have been in one confused heap. We had learnt the necessity of making way for those in front when we and they were retiring.

The Infantry being all clear, and the Enemy showing so large a force of Cavalry, we ought not to have waited so long. Retreat being our object, the more easily it was effected the more prudent it would have been.

MAJOR J. LUARD.

LIEUTENANT AND ADJUTANT 16TH LIGHT DRAGOONS.

TO COLONEL JAMES HAY, 2ND DRAGOON GUARDS.

No. 61.

Waterloo.

No date.

Extract of a letter from Major Luard (late of the 16th Light Dragoons) to Colonel James Hay, Commanding 2nd Dragoon Guards (late of 16th Light Dragoons).

.   .   .   .

On the morning of the 18th, I don't think we mounted our horses much before 9 a.m. You may recollect my coming to you for orders; you were in a small house. Lieut. Richardson was in the same room with you, and *was very sick.* When the Regiment was formed we moved and were placed under the brow of a hill nearly on the left of the British Line. The Hussar Brigade was on our left, a little to the front. We then dismounted, and while in this situation, at about eleven o'clock, the cannonade became spirited, and the Battle appeared (from what we could hear, for under the hill we could see nothing) to be becoming general. A group of Officers were talking together with their horses in hand, when a shell dropped in the middle of them and killed Captain Swetenham's horse.

The fire of all arms was now increasing and drawing near, and shot and shell passed thickly over us. We were ordered to mount. The 12th Light Dragoons were detached from our Brigade to the left, while we moved more to the right, to support a charge made by Sir William Ponsonby's

1st Position of Brigade on left of the line. *See* General Plan, No. 1.

Moved to the right to

Brigade. On our moving over the hill, the Greys made a most gallant and desperate charge, overthrowing everything opposed to them, and pursuing their success to the height of the French position. Upon returning to reform, of course broken and divided, they were pursued by the Enemy's Lancers, which the 16th charged in front and drove them back upon their own Infantry, while the 12th Light Dragoons charged in flank. At this moment Colonel Hay, who commanded the 16th Light Dragoons, fell desperately and dangerously wounded, and Lieutenants Osten and Crichton were also wounded. The Regiment was on the point of making another charge, when orders were received to move more to the right. We moved some distance, passing the remains of Sir William Ponsonby's and Lord Edward Somerset's Brigades, and formed under the brow of a hill in *échelon* of Regiments, left forward. The Hussar Brigade was formed on our left. A Corps of Foreign Infantry (I believe Dutch) formed in our front, partly covered, like ourselves, by the hill; in front of them, on the top of the hill, was formed our line of Infantry.

The fire now became tremendous, particularly of musketry. I had at this moment my horse shot in the head by a musket-ball, and Lieutenant Phillips [? Phelips] of the 11th, while condoling with me on seeing me mounted on a troop horse, had his head shot off by a cannon-shot. The fire became every moment hotter, and from the rapid way in which it approached us, appeared as if the Enemy was carrying the hill by which we were partially covered, and I confess I thought at that moment the day was going hard with us, that the Infantry were beaten, and that we (the Cavalry), by desperate charges, were to recover what they had lost.

The Foreign troops in our front appeared to think so also, but certainly had not resolved to recover the day, for they began to give way rapidly. We closed our squadron intervals, and would not let them pass through, and by the persuasion of Sir John Vandeleur, other Officers, and

support Ponsonby's Brigade.

1st Charge.

16th charge the French Lancers.

Colonel Hay dangerously wounded.

Brigade moved to the right.

Posted in rear of Dutch-Belgians.

Period of the attack of the 2nd column of the Imperial Guard.

The Dutch-Belgians prevented from giving way.

myself, they again formed to the front. The fire now
rapidly slackened, the Duke of Wellington appeared in our
front in great spirits, and we moved to the front at a
smart trot, in a Column—open Squadrons left in front.

Brigade
moved to the
front.

We passed the scene of carnage where our Line had been
formed, moved down the hill with great rapidity, passed
our own Infantry as well as broken Columns of the French,
and pursued Cavalry of all arms mixed, the ground
strewed with cuirasses thrown away to lighten the
Cuirassiers in their flight. About a mile and a half from
our position, a road runs through the valley, on the opposite
side of which a Column of French Infantry formed square
to oppose us. We instantly wheeled into line, received

Charges and
disperses a
square of
French
Infantry.

10th and 18th
charging on
the left at the
same moment.

their fire, and charged, taking or destroying the whole. In
this charge Captain Buchanan and Lieutenant Hay were
killed, and Captain Weyland wounded. The 10th and
18th Hussars charged a Column of the Enemy at the same
moment to our left.

Averted col-
lision with
1st German
Hussars.

We now saw houses on our left on fire. We continued
to pursue the Enemy until we came upon some huts, which
had been the Enemy's bivouac the preceding night. The
day now closed, and as we were returning nearly in the
dark, the 1st German Hussars, taking us for the Enemy,
were preparing to charge us, when other Officers and myself
rode forward and prevented them, by stating what we were.

Having taken some waggons laden with provisions and
brandy, I, as Adjutant, collected a number of canteens of
each Troop, and filled them, to be divided equally amongst
all the men. We then bivouacked near a wood, but
exactly where that wood is I don't know.

Commenced
the march on
Paris at 10
next morning.

We moved at ten o'clock the next day, and continued
marching until we reached Paris.

.   .   .   .

GRANT'S CAVALRY BRIGADE.

The 5th (Light) Cavalry Brigade consisted of the 7th Hussars, the 15th, or King's, Hussars, and the 2nd Hussars of the King's German Legion, but as the latter Regiment was still on the frontier, it was replaced by the 13th Light Dragoons taken from the 7th Brigade (in which remained only the 3rd Hussars, King's German Legion). It was commanded by Major-General Sir Colquhoun Grant, K.C.B.

In the retreat on the 17th the Brigade, with the exception of the 7th Hussars, formed part of the right Cavalry Column. The 7th furnished at first the rear guard to the centre Column, which held the Enemy in check until the other troops of the Column had passed the bridge and town of Genappe, when it also retired through the same.

On the Enemy's advanced guard of Lancers appearing at the other entrance of the town, the 7th charged it, and an obstinate conflict ensued, with great loss on both sides.

At length the 7th were withdrawn, and the Enemy's Column, the rear of which was already beginning to retire from the town, was driven through it by a charge of the 1st Life Guards. A brilliant charge was made in the evening by a Troop of the 7th Hussars, as the two Armies were taking up their respective positions at Waterloo.

On the morning of the 18th, Grant's Brigade was posted to the right of all the other Cavalry, and in front of the Nivelles Road, near the junction of the latter with the Wavre Road. One and a half Squadrons of the 15th Hussars were detached to the right of the position with Vedettes thrown out.

See General Plan, No. 1.

Between three and four p.m., the 13th Light Dragoons and 15th Hussars were ordered to the right to attack a body of Lancers, who were menacing that quarter, and in the meantime the 7th Hussars (with other Regiments) charged and repelled the French Cavalry attacking the Infantry Squares in front. Grant, observing that these attacks were being repeated in great strength, and that the movements of the Lancers were a diversion to draw him away from them, returned to his original ground, leaving a Squadron of the 15th in observation as before.

The Brigade was then employed in charging and repelling the French troops attacking the Allied Line, and, with alternate success, according as the French were driven back, or, bringing up strong supports, forced it to retire.

In the General Advance the Brigade attacked bodies of Cavalry and Infantry, and contributed to the rout of the French.

Nos. 65 and 67 refer to the retreat on the 17th, all the remaining letters to Waterloo.

LIEUT.-COLONEL J. THACKWELL, FOR LIEUT.-GENERAL SIR COLQUHOUN GRANT, K.C.B., G.C.H.

Major-General Sir C. Grant, K.C.B., Commanding 5th Cavalry Brigade.

No. 62.

Waterloo.

Gloucester, July 9th, 1835.

Having been requested by Lieut.-General Sir Colquhoun Grant (owing to his inability in consequence of a severe family affliction) to reply to your printed letter of 28th October, 1834, soliciting information with respect to the proceedings of the 5th Brigade of Cavalry in the

Battle of Waterloo, I beg leave to state, in connection
with a former communication relative to the movements *See* No. 68,
of the 15th Hussars that, with reference to the query, p. 141.
"What was the formation of the 5th Cavalry Brigade,
&c. &c. ? "

The Brigade about this time was formed in line of Position of the
Squadrons at or about AA, *a*1, *a*2, in the Plan, according Brigade at
7 p.m.
to report and the best of my belief and recollection ; but
there might have been a Square of our Infantry between
the 15th and 13th, and their position might have been
50 or 80 yards more to the left. I must, however, here
remark that the relative situation of the three Regiments
was not the same throughout the day, the 13th being for a
great part of the conflict on the left of the 15th. The
Squadrons at this time did not probably amount to 30
files each. I should also perhaps explain here that the
13th Light Dragoons had joined the Brigade that morning
in consequence of the 2nd Hussars of the Legion not
having returned from the frontier, that the 15th Hussars
had a squadron in a ravine at *a*1, and a picket at *a*2, from
the beginning to the end of the Battle, which detachments
suffered some loss by cannon fire and skirmishing ; and
that the 7th Hussars were very weak, having suffered most
severely on [the] debouch of the French Cavalry from
Genappe the preceding afternoon.

With regard to the second query, " What was the
formation of that part of the Enemy's Forces immediately
in front of the Brigade ? " The Enemy's troops, Cavalry Formation of
and Infantry, were in column, the former at perhaps half French troops
in front of it.
or quarter distance. It is a difficult matter at this distant
period to trace the Enemy's formation more particularly,
but a large force of his Cavalry was in this part of the
field.

In reference to the general proceedings of the Brigade
I beg to state that it was under the crest of the position,
in rear of the angle at Hougoumont, until about three p.m., About 3 p.m.
when the 15th Hussars and 13th Light Dragoons were 13th and 15th
moved to
moved to the Ravine D between the Nivelles road and the right of

attack Lancers on French extreme left.

Braine-la-Leud, for the purpose of attacking 10 squadrons of Lancers in two lines, forming the left of the French Army at E. Whilst dispositions were making for the attack the Lancers began cheering, and on looking towards the position we had quitted, the cause of cheering

Attack by French Cavalry upon our Infantry and Guns in the left rear of Hougoumont.

was discovered to be an impetuous attack by the French Cavalry upon our Infantry and Guns, the limbers of which were going rapidly towards the Nivelles road. The French Cavalry passing between the Squares of the Infantry were charged and driven back by the Cavalry of the 3rd Brigade [Dörnberg's] and the 3rd Hussars of the Legion.

Grant returns to repel the same.

This attack was several times repeated, and Sir Colquhoun Grant, judging that the attack of the Lancers was only a secondary object, most judiciously took upon himself the responsibility of taking the two

Charge of the 13th and 15th.

Regiments back to the ground they had left, the 13th leading, which Regiment formed line to the front, and at or about the spot marked B, charged a body of Cuirassiers, who were driven back for more than 300 yards to the low ground beyond C; the 15th also formed to the front, to the left of the 13th, and charged a mass of Cuirassiers, which were likewise driven back for a like distance upon heavy masses of Cavalry, who beginning offensive operations in front and on the flank,

The two Regiments retire before superior numbers, but the Enemy's advances checked.

compelled the 13th first and afterwards the 15th to retreat to their own line, where the steadiness of the two Regiments had the effect of checking any further serious attack upon this point for some time; but the skirmishers of the 15th were employed against the Cuirassiers and other Cavalry in front, who were kept at some distance.

More to the left, however, the Enemy's Cavalry made some demonstrations in advance and attacks. Between six and seven o'clock a Column of nearly 1,000 Infantry had advanced to within 150 yards, or less, of the first line, to near the spot F on the plan, supported by a large body of Cuirassiers and other Cavalry about C. This Square was charged by the two squadrons of the 15th Hussars and its further advance was checked. Shortly after some Light Cavalry and Lancers, who incommoded the front of the adjoining Squares of Infantry, were charged and driven back by the same Corps. The 7th Hussars and the 13th Light Dragoons were also most actively engaged, and on the General Advance the Regiments of the Brigade made several attacks on Cavalry as well as Infantry, in one of which Colonel Kerrison of the first named Regiment had a horse killed under him, and Major Griffiths, of the 15th Hussars, was killed in charging the latter; and these attacks contributed greatly to the loss and confusion of the Enemy. Sir Colquhoun Grant had five horses killed and wounded under him. He was in Hussar uniform, and rode, at about seven o'clock, a very fine, large, chestnut horse, which was wounded.

Between 6 and 7 p.m. a French Square charged by two Squadrons of the 15th.

7th and 13th also actively engaged.

In the General Advance the Brigade made several attacks on Cavalry and Infantry.

Maj. Griffiths, of the 15th, killed.

Sir C. Grant had five horses killed and wounded under him.

The prompt, judicious, and fortunate movement of the Brigade, from the designed attack of the Lancers to that of the Cuirassiers before-mentioned, restored confidence to this part of the Line, which seemed to be in some danger, and may justly be considered an event of the utmost importance.

I should imagine it was previous to the return of the Brigade that the Cavalry attack witnessed by Major Mercer occurred. However, I saw no Cavalry in the ravine leading to Braine-la-Leud from the time we quitted the angle of the position to that of our return, except the 13th and 15th passing along it, although there might be Cavalry at the spot stated by Major Mercer. It might have taken place afterwards, for I know, by report at the time, that a body of Cuirassiers passed between the Squares of Infantry to our left, and being unable or unwilling to return, retreated down the Nivelles road, and passed the small post of the 15th Hussars; but those who escaped were said to be not more than about thirty, some having been knocked down by the fire of the 51st, the direction of which prevented their being charged by the above detachment. But a difficulty occurs here, as at this

See No. 89, p. 216.

See No. 133, p. 316.

A body of Cuirassiers passed between the Infantry Squares and down the Nivelles road. Not more than thirty escaped.

time a considerable part of Lord Hill's Corps had joined the first line, and probably Major Mercer with it. I think I heard this body was charged, but never knew when, or by what Corps. It is certain that no attack by Cavalry had been made on the position near Hougoumont until after the two Regiments had quitted that part of the field to move against the Lancers, and it is therefore probable some mistake may have occurred as to time, and that the circumstances mentioned may have originated in the same affair.

I trust I need not apologise for this long statement, confiding in the hope that you have received Sir Colquhoun Grant's note intimating that he had desired me to transmit it after having perused and confirmed all the events of moment therein mentioned.

.   .   .   .

I have, &c.,

JOS. THACKWELL,

Late Lieut.-Col. 15th or King's Hussars.

THE 7TH HUSSARS.

LIEUT.-COLONEL T. W. ROBBINS, HALF-PAY,
CAPTAIN 7TH HUSSARS.

No. 63.   *Castle Malwood, Stony Cross, Hants.   March 31st, 1835.*

.   .   .   .

Waterloo.

On the first advance of the French Cavalry on our position (on the left of Hougoumont), I conclude between six and seven o'clock, I was wounded and fell. When I was able to rise my own Regiment was gone, the Enemy we had been opposed to were gone, and some close Columns of Infantry, I think one of them was a Battalion of Guards, had changed their ground also. Being then obliged to leave the field, of that part of the Battle to which you particularly allude I am unable to give any account.

On the night of the 17th the 7th Hussars bivouacked

Wounded between 6 and 7 o'clock.

on the left of the high road leading to Genappe, above La Haye Sainte, which I have marked No. 1. Early on the following morning the Regiment was moved across both the high roads to No. 2, where it remained dismounted until the commencement of the Action. On our way we passed many Regiments of all arms moving to their places in position. I think I am correct in marking this spot, as I recollect on our left was a mound or hillock, which I conceive to be the spot I have marked X. A little in our rear was a hedge, and a rather hollow roadway.

No. 1 is 200 yards to the left of the Genappe road, and 200 yards in rear of the Wavre Road.

No. 2 is about 370 yards in front of Merbe Braine.

X is the rise of ground shown by contour 125.

Soon after the commencement of the Action we moved to No. 3, remaining there some time; but being much annoyed by shot and shells, and still seeing no Enemy, yet losing many men and horses, we were again moved to No. 4, formed in line under cover of a bank, from which some Guns of the Horse Artillery had just been obliged to withdraw, the Enemy's Guns from Mon Plaisir having exactly got their range and doing great execution.

No. 3 is just across the Nivelles road and in a line with the outer boundary hedge of Hougoumont.

No. 4 is behind the Wavre Road, not far from its junction with the Nivelles road.

At the alarm that the French Cavalry was advancing up the hill on the left of Hougoumont, the 7th were mounted, and rapidly moved from their left; then wheeling into line they almost immediately charged the leading Regiment of the Enemy at No. 5 (Lancers). They came on in three distinct lines. In this charge I fell, and from that time am unable to state anything that occurred. During the short time we were in motion my attention was too much occupied with my own men to have been able to pay much to what was going on around us. Yet I distinctly saw the three lines of the Enemy's Cavalry advancing rather *en échelon*, as steadily as if on a field day, at the time we were brought up to oppose them, passing some of our Guns and some Squares of Infantry whose fire they must have sustained. Some other Regiments of Cavalry came up at the moment, and, I conclude, charged with us. But from [the] place I occupied, commanding the centre Squadron of the 7th, I am unable to say more.

No. 5 about 200 yards left of No. 4.

Charged the French Lancers.

French Cavalry advanced steadily in three lines.

.   .   .   .

As long as I remained in the field I can with confidence

say we never scarcely saw an enemy, up to the time I have mentioned already. I shall ever regret having been so unfortunate as to have missed seeing the end of that glorious day.

.   .   .   .

Allow me, &c.,

THO. ROBBINS,

Lieut.-Col. H.-Pay, late Capt. 7th Hussars.

LIEUT.-COLONEL S. O'GRADY,

LIEUTENANT 7TH HUSSARS.

No 64

Cahir Guillamore, March 18th, 1835.

.   .   .   .   .   .

Waterloo.

I believe, however, that the time you fix is that when the *last attempt* to force the British position was made by (I think) Ney, on the Brussels road. If so, the 7th were ordered from the right to assist in repelling that attack, and consequently were on the right centre at that time, but from the great confusion that prevailed consequent upon the flight of some Belgian Dragoons, who ran through our ranks, I find it very difficult, and indeed, except by guess, impossible to fix upon the precise spot we occupied.

The 7th were posted on the ground above Hougoumont, and, with the 13th and 15th, drove back the French Cavalry, who attacked the British and Brunswick Squares.

The 7th, who were in advance of the left centre on the night of the 17th, were moved very early on the 18th to the ground above Hougoumont, and occupied various positions there during the day, and assisted by the 15th Hussars and the 13th Light Dragoons, drove back the French Cavalry, who attacked the Squares of British and Brunswickers immmediately above Hougoumont, and rather late in the day. If your query has reference to that charge I think I could place the 7th accurately for you.

The French Cavalry were in the first instance Cuirassiers, and in squadron, but they soon became mixed with Cavalry of all arms, and acted in masses of more or less size. After clearing the front of our position we were ordered to our left to assist in repelling the *last attempt* of the Enemy to which I before alluded. After that we moved to about midway to our former position, from which we moved at the General Advance, and sweeping the ground to Hougoumont, entered the Enemy's Line on his left, and charged down his Lines until we met Sir Hussey Vivian at the head of his Brigade.

In the general advance the 7th charged down the Enemy's Lines from his left until they met Vivian's Brigade.

The 7th having in these various encounters lost a great many men, and being reduced to a Squadron, and having separated from the 15th Hussars and the 13th Light Dragoons, joined Sir Hussey and continued to act with him until the next morning.

.   .   .   .

You will perceive that as we occupied the ground above Hougoumont no Infantry penetrated to us, though we were perpetually menaced, and often attacked by the Enemy's Cavalry, who advanced in column and formed squadrons of attack.

.   .   .   .

I have, &c.,
STANDISH O'GRADY.

FROM THE SAME.

Hampton Court, April 10th, 1837.

No. 65.

.   .   .   .

On the occasion of our last advance at Waterloo I believe we commenced it from the right centre of our Line, and consequently we left the house, &c., of Hougoumont on our right. None of our Cavalry were during the day on the ground beyond (or at the Nivelles side of) Hougoumont. The road to Nivelles was stopped by felled trees, and the 51st Regiment protected it.

Waterloo.

None of the Cavalry were, during the day, on the ground on the Nivelles side of Hougoumont.

As respects the retreat of the Army on the 17th from Quatre Bras, I am aware that much misconception existed in the minds of many at the time, and of many more since, as to the conduct of the 7th Hussars who covered the retreat on the main road to Brussels through Genappe, and

Retreat from Quatre Bras.

Commanded a
Troop sup-
porting the
skirmishers.

on this subject I ought to be qualified to speak, as I had
the command of the Troop on the high road, supporting
the skirmishers, and consequently was an anxious and
interested observer of all that took place. My first impressions I see no reason to alter, and I believe no
Regiment could have done more or done better than the
7th did upon that day. Facts are, however, what I
apprehend you want, and I will give them as shortly
as I can.

Early in the morning of the 17th the Army was drawn
up to show a front, and soon afterwards the Infantry
began to move to the rear. When they moved off,
leaving the Cavalry, Sir C. Grant called the Field Officers
together, and spoke to them for some time. When Major
Hodge (who was in command of the right Squadron, to
which I belonged) returned, he called me aside, and told
me that the Prussians had been beaten and obliged to fall
back, and that we must make a similar movement to
prevent the two Armies from being disunited; that our
Brigade was to retire by Regiments from the left, and that

The 7th was
to have the
post of honour
in the Retreat.

the 7th had the post of honour, the main road to cover and
protect; that Sir William Dörnberg was to take charge of
the skirmishers of the Brigade, and that our Squadron was
to skirmish. There was at this time no appearance on the
part of the Enemy of an advance, and we were to hold our
ground until driven from it.

We did so and (though I cannot pretend to accuracy in
point of time) I think it was twelve before their advance put

Right Troop
of Major
Hodge's
Squadron
thrown out to
skirmish.

Supported by
the left Troop
under Lieut.
O'Grady.

us in motion. We threw out the right Troop to skirmish, and
Major Hodge went with them. I held the high road with
the left Troop, and had from time to time to send them
assistance, and frequently to advance to enable them to
hold their ground, as their movements were difficult
through ploughed fields so soft that the horses were sunk
up to their knees always, and sometimes to their girths.

Whilst I was so employed Sir William Dörnberg joined
me. Thus we continued to dispute every inch of the
ground until we came within a short distance of the town

of Genappe. Here Sir William Dörnberg told me that he must leave me; that it was of the utmost importance to face the Enemy boldly at this spot, as the bridge in the town of Genappe was so narrow we must pass it in file; that I should endeavour if possible to obtain time for the skirmishers to come in, but that I was not to compromise my Troop too much. Sir William had been riding with me some hours, and when he bid me farewell he shook my hand, and I saw plainly he never expected to see me again.

I then called in the skirmishers and advanced at a trot up the road. The troops opposed to me went about, and as I followed them they did not stop as soon as I did. I continued advancing and retiring alternately, until I saw all my right Troop safe on the road in my rear, and then I began to retire at a walk, occasionally halting and fronting until I turned the corner of the town of Genappe. I then filed the men from the left and passed through the town at a gallop, no enemy in sight. When I arrived at the opposite entrance of the town I found the 7th drawn up on the road in a column of divisions, and having re-formed our Squadron we took our place between those already formed and the town.

Here I met Sir William Dörnberg, who appeared surprised to see me, and asked me how we had effected our retreat, and if we had saved any of the skirmishers, and when I told him we had not lost a man or a horse, he exclaimed, "Then Buonaparte is not with them; if he were, not a man of you could have escaped."

Here we remained drawn up about twenty minutes before any of the Enemy appeared, and then only a few stragglers, some of whom rode into us and were found to be quite drunk. As well as I can guess, the Cavalry Column by which we were pursued, and which moved slowly, but shouting loudly along the high road, were about fourteen Squadrons. Occasionally I was able to count them, but not accurately. They might have been eighteen. And this Column now showed its head within the town. This head consisted of a Troop of Lancers, all very young men, mounted on very small horses, and commanded by a fine-looking and a very brave man.   For about fifteen minutes they remained in the jaws of the town, their flanks being protected by the houses ; and the street not being straight, and those in the rear not knowing that the front were halted, they soon became so jammed that they could not go about.

In this state of affairs Lord Anglesey gave us orders to charge them, which we immediately did.   Of course, our charge could make no impression, but we continued cutting at them, and we did not give ground, nor did they

move.   Their Commanding Officer was cut down, and so was ours (Major Hodge), and this state of things lasted some minutes, when they brought down some Light

At length
French Light
Artillery
strikes the
rear of the
charging
Squadron of
the 7th, and it
was retired
by Lord
Anglesey.

Artillery, which struck the rear of the right (the charging) Squadron and knocked over some men and horses, impeding the road in our rear.   We then received orders to go about from Lord Anglesey, who was up with us, but not on the road during all this time.   The Lancers then advanced upon us, and in the *mêlée* which ensued they lost quite as many as we did, and when at last we were able to disengage ourselves they did not attempt to pursue us.

The 7th re-
tired through
a Regiment of
Light
Cavalry.
Lieutenant
O'Grady takes
back his
Squadron to
recover the
wounded.

We retired through a Regiment of Light Cavalry, and the first pass we found off the road we took, and formed in the field by the road side.   I then got the remnant of the right Squadron and moved them down towards the town of Genappe to look after any of our wounded, whom it might be in our power to save.   When I saw the ground upon which we had charged it was strewed with men and horses, but I saw very few fighting men of the Enemy. In the meantime the Light Brigade having been removed from the road where they were when we passed through

them, the Life Guards came down the road and charged into the town.

I could not, of course, see what they did, but I believe they fell upon the rear of a retiring Column, impeded by the narrowness of the bridge, and did their duty manfully.

The Enemy did not again attempt to molest us, and we reached our position without further interruption, except some picket affairs in taking up our respective Lines, in one of which Captain Heyliger of the 7th made a very brilliant charge with his Troop, and when the Duke of Wellington sent to stop him he also desired to know his name.

Charge by Captain Heyliger with his Troop near the position of Waterloo.

I thought at the time, and I still think, that when we charged the Enemy at Genappe their entire Column was in the town, and that being the case it is clear that as soon as they found the head of their Column engaged, they commenced clearing their rear out of the town.

If this be the case it is obvious that the success or failure of the 7th in their charge was simply a matter of time. A little delay and they would not have had to charge, but to pursue. This as well as I recollect was Sir Wm. Dörnberg's opinion at the time when he objected to charging before their flanks were open to us. I feel, however, that I have no right to pursue this, and satisfy myself that I have given you, as well as I can now recollect them, all the facts as they came before me. A few minutes before we charged, one of the heaviest showers of rain I can remember fell, which, as it wet everybody and everything, rendered fire-arms useless, and though the French fired a few pistol shots, I don't think they did any damage; our engagement was therefore one of sabre and lance.

See No. 4, p. 6.

I have only to add that we lost our Commanding Officer, Major Hodge killed, and Captain Elphinstone, who commanded the right Troop, wounded and taken. Our Adjutant was killed also, but not in the charge, but as we never could find either Major Hodge or Adjutant Mayer, I only say they were killed because I hope it.* In answer to a flag of truce that evening they said they had taken a Major, a Captain, an Adjutant, and an A.D.C., which latter was Captain Krockenberg, A.D.C. to Sir Wm. Dörnberg.

Officers of the 7th killed and wounded in the charge at Genappe.

---

* That is, in fighting.—ED.

You will perceive that the right Squadron under Major Hodge was the only one of the Regiment engaged, and that it was Captain Elphinstone's Troop, which had been engaged skirmishing throughout the day, that charged afterwards at Genappe.

.   .   .   .   .   .

Believe, &c.,
STANDISH O'GRADY.

.   .   .   .   .   .

THE 13TH LIGHT DRAGOONS.

MAJOR D. DOHERTY, 27TH REGIMENT.
LIEUTENANT 13TH LIGHT DRAGOONS.

No. 66.

Waterloo.

Dublin, 19, Stephen's Green North, Nov. 14th, 1834.

*Operations of the 13th Light Dragoons on the 18th of June, 1815, at the Battle of Waterloo.

On the morning of the 18th June, 1815, the 13th Light Dragoons being in Brigade with the 7th and 15th Hussars, and under the command of Sir Colquhoun Grant, moved up to their post in the position, being thus situated on the immediate left of the Nivelles road, and in support of the Château de Hougoumont.

In the morning the 13th were ordered to the extreme right of the position.

Soon afterwards back to their original ground.

Previous to the attack on Hougoumont the 13th Dragoons were ordered to cross the Nivelles road, and take post on a rising ground on the extreme right of the position, to which post also the 51st Regiment were ordered. The 13th Dragoons were soon afterwards ordered back to their original post, when the Action commenced.

From this time until I suppose about one or two o'clock they remained under a heavy fire of Artillery, when the 13th were again ordered across the road, and remained in the hollow for about an hour. They were then for the first time called upon to act, and re-crossing the road moved up to the crest of the position, and formed in line, opposed to a line of French Heavy Dragoons, which were immediately charged and routed. On returning after the charge the Regiment re-formed in rear of the Columns of Infantry, and again moved half way up towards the top of the position, when a large Column of French Cavalry appeared in front of our left Squadron, which they immediately charged in the most gallant manner, commanded by Captain Gregory, and checked their advance, and [they] were subsequently obliged to retire, I suppose from seeing the force of Cavalry ready at hand to support the left Squadron.

Charged and routed a body of French Heavy Dragoons.

The left Squadron charged French Cavalry again.

French Cavalry obliged to retire.

On arriving at the crest of the position the 13th were again opposed to the Enemy's Cavalry, and forced them back, and afterwards retired under the brow of the position, where they remained for a short time.

13th again opposed to Enemy's Cavalry

The 13th again moved and retook a Brigade of Guns that had been momentarily taken by the Enemy, and after driving back the Enemy's Cavalry the Regiment again retired to their former position.

The 13th retake a Battery which was momentarily in possession of the French.

It was at this period that Lieutenant-Colonel Dalrymple of the 15th Hussars lost his leg, and the same cannon shot that struck him also passed through the body of Sir C. Grant's horse. The Officers of the 13th and 15th were almost all assembled together and talking to Sir C. Grant, when the ball bounded from the top of the hill and came into the midst of them.

Lieut.-Col. Dalrymple, 15th Hussars, wounded.

Not long after this the 13th were again called upon, and on advancing in line up the position, Lord Anglesey and Lord Hill were observed by the Regiment, the latter with his hat off, cheering them forward, and on reaching the crest of the position, the centre Squadron of the 13th, commanded by the late Major Doherty, found itself opposed to a strong Column or Square of Infantry.

Captain J. Doherty, 13th Light Dragoons.

The cheering cry of their old General, Lord Hill, "At them, my old friends, the 13th," was quite sufficient, and instantly the centre Squadron dashed into them, and completely upset them, dispersed them, and with the assistance of the rest of the Regiment nearly annihilated them.

13th opposed to a Column of Infantry.

Broke and dispersed it.

13TH LIGHT DRAGOONS.

Obliged to
retire before
superior force
of French
Cavalry.

This slaughter continued until a Regiment of Polish
Lancers on our left, and a Regiment of Cuirassiers in
our front came to their assistance, which obliged the 13th
to retire, and which they only did at the last moment, and
then retreated in rear of two Squares of Infantry, one of
which was composed of the German Legion, and as Sir C.
Grant's horse was wounded, *he* was obliged to enter the
Square for safety.

French Cav-
alry suffering
from fire of
our Infantry;
charged and
pursued by
the 13th.

The Cuirassiers and Lancers suffered severely from the
fire of the Infantry, and as soon as the 13th Dragoons were
again reformed, and finding the Enemy's Cavalry so much
broken from the fire of the Infantry, they again advanced
and pursued and cut down the Enemy's Cavalry as far as
they could prudently follow, when they again retired under
cover of the position.

Lt. Doherty
severely
wounded at
the time of
the Crisis.

The 13th remained there until the Crisis, when they
again moved up the position, and on nearly arriving at the
top, a large Column of the Enemy's Infantry was observed
to the left of their Line, and immediately 1 was struck
by a grape shot in the stomach, and instantly afterwards
by a musket ball through my head, which so completely
took away my senses that I have no recollection of what
occurred subsequently, but I have always heard that on the
Regiment arriving at the top of the position, the Enemy
gave way, and the rout became general.

G. DOHERTY,

Major 27th Regt., late of the 13th Lt. Dragoons.

Severe losses
of the 13th.

N.B.—The 13th Dragoons went into action on the
morning of the 18th June, 1815, with three complete
Squadrons, and I have been informed that at the close of it
they could only muster one weak one.

LIEUT.-COLONEL A. T. MACLEAN, HALF-PAY.

LIEUTENANT 13TH LIGHT DRAGOONS.

United Service Club, Nov. 4th, 1844. No. 67.

As it is more than probable that your work on the Waterloo Campaign may have a second edition, I take leave to bring to your notice that the 3rd German Hussars were not in action on the 18th* (as stated in page 91), and did not join the British Cavalry till the 20th, near Binche. The 13th, in absence of that Corps, was attached to Grant's Brigade (the 7th and 15th Hussars), and did duty with it on the 17th, and throughout the Action on the 18th, a Troop of it covering the retreat of the Brigade, and having orders to move parallel with the 7th on the left of Genappe on the former day, on which occasion it was so hard pressed by the Enemy that the 2nd half-Squadron, under Major Macalister, was ordered to its support, and engaged with the Enemy till skirmishing ceased. *Retreat on 17th June. A Troop of 13th covers the retreat of the Brigade.*

Lieutenant Drought mounted picket at Hougoumont that night, but was withdrawn early next morning, when [it was] occupied by the Guards, and the right Troop of the Regiment was posted in the circular road leading to the Château, where it made several charges in column of Divisions, capturing some prisoners and horses, and continued until the Brigade was ordered off to the extreme right; when Major Moray, 13th—not 17th—Dragoons (A.D.C. to General Grant), directed the Troop to join the Brigade (and was hard hit in giving the order). Lieut.-Col. Boyse commanded, not Doherty, † who was left sick in the rear at Castros [?] on the 15th, till his horse was shot, falling on him, and so disabling him that he was compelled to give the command to Brevet-Major B. Lawrence, who had three horses shot under him, and held it during the *13th furnished a picket at Hougoumont night of the 17th. Morning of the 18th the right Troop was posted near Hougoumont, where it made several charges, capturing some prisoners and horses. Major Moray wounded. † Lieut.-Col. and Col. P. Doherty, 13th Light Dragoons. Lieut.-Col. Boyse disabled.]*

* This is an error, as there is a letter from an Officer of the 3rd Hussars giving an account of the operations of the Regiment at Waterloo, where it arrived the same morning from Brussels.—ED.

13TH LIGHT DRAGOONS.

Major Lawrence commanded the Regiment for remainder of the day.

remainder of the Action.   General Grant had four horses shot under him.

Your account of the charge made when the Brigade resumed its ground left in front is most correct.   The 13th only had time to wheel into line, and though the charge was successful, we were flanked on the left by Infantry, which occasioned our retiring *hurriedly.*   The second advance was made in line by the Brigade, and in this instance we suffered most by the concealed skirmishers in the wheat we passed over to get at a body of Cavalry gradually retiring on our approach.   The Brigade took ground to its right, and here each Corps in succession had opportunities of charging with advantage bodies of Cavalry, invariably Heavy.

Brigade well up with Vivian's at close of the day.

Towards the close of the day we were well up with Vivian's Brigade till halted for the night, when we were unable to obtain water.

Having been with the Regiment in these momentous days, and being the Officer ordered in search of the 3rd Hussars on the 20th, I have a perfect recollection of *when* I found old Baron Arentsschild and his Corps, and the kind reception they gave me.

.   .   .   .

Yours, &c.,

A. T. MACLEAN,
Lieut.-Col. H.P., 13th Dragoons.

.   .   .   .

I was the Officer who commanded the rear guard on the 17th, and held the approach to Hougoumont on the 18th. I am not aware that you make any mention of the 7th

Combat of 7th Hussars at Genappe.

Hussars and their fight on the 17th in Genappe, when they so gallantly checked the Enemy's advance by repeated charges when it was impossible for them to penetrate the dense Column that pressed them through the narrow long street of that village, flanked by a nasty marshy ravine hardly practicable from the torrents of rain that fell at the time.

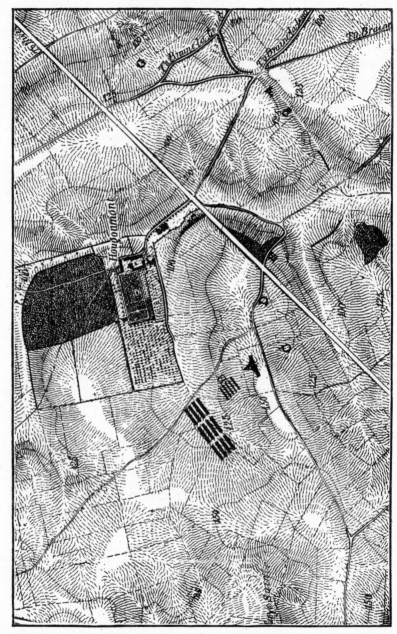

PLAN SHOWING POSITIONS AND MOVEMENTS OF 15TH HUSSARS.

I witnessed the charge made by the Life Guards when the 7th made way for them, thus allowing the French Cavalry to clear the village and form up in its front, when they were more easily vanquished than when checked by the 7th.

Charge of 1st Life Guards.

.   .   .   .

It occurs to me this instant that in the second advance made by the Brigade, when it suffered so severely, *one* Troop of the 13th lost all its officers—Captain Gubbins, Lieutenants Geale and Pym.   I mention this as I observe you specify Officers' names of other Corps, and when they fell.

The former killed, the two latter wounded.

THE 15TH OR KING'S HUSSARS.

LIEUT.-COLONEL J. THACKWELL.
CAPTAIN 15TH HUSSARS.

Gloucester, December 20th, 1834.   No. 68.

.   .   .   .

Before I reply to your queries I had better here state that the Squadrons of the Regiment were not more than from fifty-two to fifty-five files, including Officers (each), and that one Squadron and a Division of another were detached from the Regiment on the morning of the 18th of June, and did not rejoin, except for a short time, during the day.   This detached body was posted in observation in front of the valley leading to Braine-la-Leud, and as its operations were confined to skirmishing, its loss was trifling.

Waterloo.

A Squadron and a Division detached to the right in the morning. Remained in observation all day.

1st, With respect to the query, "What was the particular formation, &c. &c.?"

Answer.—I beg to trace the formation of the 15th Hussars at A in the plan; on its flanks were British Infantry in Square, but I am not certain of what Regiments, as part of Lord Hill's Corps from the second line were then in the first line; and I am not sure whether the site of the traced position is not a little too much in

Formation at 7 p.m.

advance. The 13th Light Dragoons were either to the right or right rear of the 15th, but as the troops were at the time closely concentrated in this part of the position, it was a difficult matter to distinguish particular Corps.

2nd, "What was the formation of that part of the Enemy's forces, &c. &c. ?"

Formation of the Enemy in front of the 15th.

Answer.—At B I beg to trace, according to the best of my recollection, a body of about 1,000 Infantry in Square, supported by a large body of Cuirassiers and other Cavalry. This Square was charged by the three Troops of the 15th Hussars, as it was halted and in fine order, a little before or about the time of the advance of the Imperial Guard;

Severely wounded about the time of the advance of the Imperial Guard.

but as I was then severely wounded, I did not observe in what manner these troops were supported on their flanks, or how their retreat was conducted, but very large masses of Cavalry were in their rear.

.   .   .   .

Positions of the 15th earlier in the day.

In the early part of the day the position of the main body of the 15th Hussars was, in the plan, at C, that of the right Squadron at C 2, and that of a Picket at C 3; but after the Battle had begun until about half-past 2 p.m. it was at D; and for nearly an hour afterwards it was at E, whence it moved with the 13th Light Dragoons to about F, for the purpose of attacking 10 Squadrons of Lancers posted in line in rear of a deep ravine at G. It then joined the right Squadron of the Regiment, but owing to the impetuous attack of the French Cavalry on the right centre of the British position, the intended attack of the Lancers was given up, and the Regiment, leaving the right Squadron where it was originally posted, retraced its steps to the

Charging the Cuirassiers and other Cavalry.

vicinity of the position A, and was immediately engaged in the attack, by charge and skirmishing, of Cuirassiers and other Cavalry, and this lasted until the Enemy's Cavalry found it could make no lasting impression on this part of the position.

The Enemy's Cavalry and Infantry moved in column in advance and retreat, the former being at about quarter distance, and I understood when the British Line advanced the three left Troops of the 15th charged a body of Infantry as well as some Lancers.

The position of the Regiment being in rear of Hougoumont, the masses of Infantry which would have closed on its post were intercepted by the troops defending that place, and none of the Enemy's Infantry, to the best of my recollection, passed its enclosures, and the first I saw of that force in the immediate front of the 15th Hussars was the Column charged by my Squadron; but I witnessed the advance of many heavy masses of Infantry which attacked Hougoumont, although soon after the firing began the distant movements of the Enemy's Column were from this part of the position but indistinctly seen, owing to the smoke which hung lazily on a surface saturated with rain.

The left of the Enemy's Infantry [? Cavalry] extended to the Nivelles road nearly in line with the letter G in the plan, from whence a heavy fire of Artillery was kept up for the chief part of the engagement upon the angle of the British position.

The extreme left of the French line extended nearly in line with G on Plan.

.   .   .   .

I have, &c.,

JOSEPH THACKWELL,
Late Lieutenant-Colonel commanding
15th or King's Hussars.

LIEUT.-COLONEL H. LANE.

LIEUTENANT 15TH HUSSARS.

Thorpe Arch, near Wetherby, March 24th, 1835.   No. 69.

.   .   .   .

Two Squadrons of the Regiment were placed upon the position near our own Squares of Foot Guards, and one Squadron was detached to the right in rear of Hougoumont, having a Subaltern's picket placed on the high road leading to Nivelles at the point which I have marked.

Waterloo.

Position of 15th.

On the Nivelles road in due front of E in foregoing Plan.

I cannot answer the two leading questions you propose as to the appearance of the Enemy at seven o'clock. Large masses of troops in column advanced very near our lines,

15TH HUSSARS.

till shaken by the severe fire they sustained from our Artillery they wavered, and upon our whole Line advancing to meet them, fled in utter confusion.

. . . .

Saw the first shot fired about 11 o'clock.

I saw the first shot fired from our lines about eleven o'clock; it struck the Column of the Enemy advancing upon Hougoumont, and caused some confusion and delay.

See p. 124.
A little to the left front of C 2 in foregoing Plan.

The 15th Hussars was moved soon after to the ground on the right of the position, where I have marked a Squadron as placed, and where the Enemy showed a strong body of Lancers, which we were preparing to attack. The Enemy made this diversion for the purpose of drawing off our force from the right centre of the position, which, in fact, was successful, for we were no sooner off that ground than the first attack made by the Cuirassiers took place upon the spot we had quitted. We at once returned to our former position,. leaving one Squadron to keep the French Lancers in check.

Returning to the position, charged the French Cavalry with success.

We were no sooner on our ground than we advanced in line, and charged the Grenadiers à Cheval, who fled from us. Our next attack (in line without reserve) was [on] a square of French Infantry, and our horses were within a few feet

Also a Square of Infantry, but failed.

of the Square. We did not succeed in breaking it, and, of course, suffered most severely. In short, during the day we were constantly on the move, attacking and retreating to our lines, so that, at the close of the Battle, the two Squadrons were dreadfully cut up.

See No. 133, p. 316.

When the Cuirassiers made their first attack, they passed through the Squares considerably in rear of our lines, and in retiring a body of them followed the high road to Nivelles. They came unexpectedly to the *abatis* marked on your map, and a Regiment of Infantry hidden there gave them their fire, which destroyed them all.

I am, &c.,

HENRY LANE.

VIVIAN'S CAVALRY BRIGADE.

The 6th (Light) Cavalry Brigade was composed of the 10th or Prince of Wales's Hussars, the 18th Hussars, and the 1st Hussars of the King's German Legion. It was under the command of Major-General Sir Hussey Vivian, K.C.B.

In the retreat on June 17th, the Brigade formed the rear portion of the left Cavalry Column. It had some skirmishing with the French Cavalry previous to crossing the Genappe, or Dyle, River at the bridge of Thuy, where the advance of the latter was checked, and the Brigade then marched to the position at Waterloo without further molestation.

On the 18th it was posted on the extreme left of the Line, where it remained until the advance of the Prussians rendered its presence there no longer necessary. *See* General Plan, No. 1.

The Brigade was then moved to the immediate right of the Brussels-Genappe road, and was drawn up in support of some German Infantry which was being greatly harassed. Here it was exposed for some time to a tremendous fire of artillery and musketry.

On the repulse of the Imperial Guard, the Brigade moved round by the right of Maitland's Guards, and advanced towards the French position. On arriving about half-way, the Regiments were ordered by Vivian to form line on their leading half-Squadrons, the 10th in front, the 18th and 1st Hussars in support. Owing to the fast pace of the leading half-Squadrons, they advanced rather in *échelon* than in line. The 10th was inclined to the *See* General Plan, No. 3.

See General
Plan, No. 3.

right, and its three Squadrons successively encountered bodies of the French Cavalry, overthrew
and dispersed them.

The 18th were then directed towards the left
against some of the Cavalry of the Imperial Guard
drawn up in front of La Belle Alliance. Some
French Horse Artillery attempted to gallop away
across the front of the Regiment, but were overtaken, the gunners and drivers cut down, and the
Guns secured. The 18th then charged the Cavalry
and completely dispersed them, and also drove
some more Artillerymen from their Guns, the whole
flying in disorder.

Meanwhile, the 10th on the right had gone on
in pursuit of the Enemy's Cavalry, excepting about
a weak Squadron collected by Major Howard.
Vivian, calculating upon the support of some
Infantry which was approaching, ordered this
Squadron to attack a French Square of Infantry.
This was carried out with great gallantry, but also
with great loss, amongst the killed being Major
Howard, as our Infantry had gone in pursuit of a
separate Column. The Hussars, however, kept
pressing the Square, and forced it back for some
distance, until it finally broke up, and its ranks
joined the other fugitives.

The remaining portion of the 10th, after returning from the pursuit of the French Cavalry,
came upon about half a Battalion of the Imperial
Guard which had been rallied, and was supported
by Cavalry. The 10th charged both bodies, which
turned and fled.

The 10th and 18th having become greatly

mixed up with the flying Enemy, were at length, and with difficulty, rallied and re-formed behind the 1st Hussars, which were brought up into front line, and ultimately the Brigade bivouacked for the night near the hamlet of Hilaincourt.

Nos. 70 and 71 refer to the receipt of intelligence of the advance of the French Army into Belgium.

Nos. 70 and 75 refer to the march on Quatre Bras.

Nos. 70, 71, and 75 to the retreat on June 17th.

Nos. 71, 74, 75, and 76 to the arrival of the Prussians at Waterloo, and all the letters to the Battle of Waterloo.

MAJOR-GENERAL SIR HUSSEY VIVIAN, K.C.B.

EXTRACTS FROM A LETTER TO LADY VIVIAN.

June 23rd, 1815. *First day's halt.*   No. 70.

On June 13th I went to Tournay to inspect the 1st Hussars. I there heard that the whole French Army had concentrated at Maubeuge, and the persuasion in France was that Buonaparte would arrive from Paris and advance on the 15th. We treated this with contempt, supposing that he would hardly dare such a thing, &c. On the 14th I returned to my quarters at Neder Boulire [?], and on the 15th I went to Brussels to attend a ball to be given by the Duchess of Richmond, and I should here notice that so little did the Duke of Wellington expect an advance of the Enemy, that he was to have given a ball on June 21st, the anniversary of the Battle of Vittoria.

At dinner on the 15th, however, he heard that the Enemy had advanced and driven the Prussians, who were at Binche, out of that place. At the ball reports came

13th June.

At Tournay heard that the French army had concentrated at Maubeuge.

15th June.

Duchess of Richmond's ball.

Duke of Wellington was to have given a ball on the 21st.

At dinner the Duke heard

SIR H. VIVIAN.
of the French
advance.
More reports
at the ball.

which proved the Enemy were advancing in very great force. Things became serious, and most of the Officers, about twelve or one o'clock, left Brussels to join their respective Corps.

We received orders to march at daybreak upon Enghien—twelve miles from Grammont. From Enghien we moved by Braine-le-Comte, twelve miles more, to Nivelles, twelve more; the roads dreadful.

.   .   .   .

We threw out our pickets and skirmished on the Field of Battle.

The next morning, the 17th, the French and we stood looking at each other, neither party appearing disposed to move, Lord Wellington waiting for the junction of his whole army, Lord Hill's Corps not having arrived, when he would have attacked the French.

.   .   .   .   .   .

Retreat on
17th.
The Cavalry
to cover the
retreat;
Vivian's
Brigade on
the left.

Orders were given accordingly, and the Cavalry left to cover the retreat, the Hussars in front, Grant's Brigade on the right, mine on the left. We remained quietly on the ground until about two o'clock, when immediately on my left I observed a great dust, and by looking a little nearer I discovered an enormous Column of Cuirassiers, Lancers, Hussars, &c., moving over a hill into the high road which

Enemy's
Cavalry drive
in pickets.
Artillery fire
begins.
Enemy moved
to attack the
centre Column
also.

was on my flank. My pickets were soon engaged and driven in. A Brigade of the Enemy trotted up the road and formed opposite to me, a little ravine separating us. I opened upon them with my Horse Artillery. They very soon returned the compliment with theirs. A large body also moved up the road to attack our centre, where General Dörnberg was posted with the 7th Hussars and 23rd.

The line of Heavy Cavalry and Light Dragoons in our rear had by this time received orders to fall back, and we in advance were to do the same. This I did very *contre gré*, for at this moment a Brigade of Lancers and Chasseurs à Cheval were about to attempt crossing the ravine in my front, and my fingers were itching to have a lick at them. However we retired quietly enough. They cannonaded my rear, and pressed my rear Squadron until we crossed a little river, the Dyle, which runs by Genappe, and then I formed the 10th to support my rear guard, and they molested me no more. Not so the poor 7th, &c. &c.

18th. . . . .

I arrived in the rear of the Infantry just at the time that several small Squares of Foreign troops were giving way. In fact my wheeling into line in their rear and cheering them actually halted two of them, and gave them confidence. Lord Edward Somerset with the wretched remains of the two Heavy Brigades, not 200 men and horses, retired through me, and I then remained for about half an hour exposed to the most dreadful fire of shot, shell, and musketry that it is possible to imagine. No words can give any idea of it (how a man escaped is to me a miracle), we every instant expecting through the smoke to see the Enemy appearing under our noses, for the smoke was literally so thick that we could not see ten yards off. But we at last began to find that the shots did not come so thick, and I discovered that the Enemy were, instead of advancing to gain our position, retrograding on theirs. The moment to attack was arrived, and I received orders to advance.

. . . .

Having cleared the smoke I observed the French retiring up the hill and along the high road covered by their Guns—two large bodies of Cavalry, and two Squares of Infantry, whilst our Infantry were gallantly moving on also after them.

I led the head of my Brigade diagonally across the ground for the left body of Cavalry. The Enemy, seeing this, opened a fire upon me from the Square, and with grape from their Guns, and I suffered some loss. But every man was at his post. We gave them a cheer in reply, and I instantly ordered the Regiments to form line on their front half-Squadrons. They did it to admiration. I led the 10th against a body of Cuirassiers and Lancers, much superior to them in force, on the French left, and having seen them fairly in, the Enemy flying and falling under

---

Sir H. Vivian
His rear Squadron pressed.

18th June.
Waterloo.
Brigade moved to the right and placed in rear of Foreign troops encourages them. *See* General Plan, No. 2.
Remains of Heavy Brigades pass through Vivian's Brigade.

General Advance.

Brigade charges French Cavalry.

See General Plan, No. 3.

their swords, I rushed to the 18th, and with them attacked
the Cuirassiers and Chasseurs who formed the French right
in support of the Square and Guns. They were routed by
the intrepidity and gallantry of this Regiment, and the
artillerymen cut down at their Guns. From this moment
not another cannon shot was fired. By this time the
remains of the 10th had again formed The 1st Hussars,
still in reserve, determined that the glory of ending the
day should end [? rest] with the Regiment of my Royal

The 10th
charge
Infantry.

Master, I ordered the 10th to charge the Square of Infantry
still steady and close to us. This they did most gallantly,
and as gallantly was the attack received.   .   .

The 10th cut down the French in their ranks, some few
then escaped under cover of a hedge, but from this time
every man was in retreat, and eventually every man was
taken during a pursuit which lasted as long as we could
see, so long, indeed, until from actually having cut down

Gave pursuit
up to
Prussians.

some Prussians, we were obliged to desist and give them
the pursuit.   .   .   .   .   .   .

We marched in pursuit on the 19th to Nivelles, 20th
to Binche, 21st to Bavay, 22nd Le Cateau. From daybreak until sunset have we been marching. Now the
Infantry are so fatigued that it has been found absolutely
necessary to rest.

FROM THE SAME.

(Lieut.-General, G.C.B., G.C.H.)

No. 71.

O.O. [Ordnance Office], June 3rd, 1839.

In the U.S. Journal for this month is a paper headed
" Popular Errors Respecting the Battle of Waterloo," which
is not in itself perhaps exactly correct. As you are about
to write a History perhaps the following remarks may be of
some use to you.

As regards the
Duke being
taken by
surprise.

1st. In respect to the Duke being taken by surprise.
That he must have been aware the Enemy was concentrating there can be no doubt. I myself on the 12th

13th June.

and 13th visited Tournay and Mons. I found in front of

Tournay, where there had been a picket of French Cavalry, they were replaced by Douaniers. I spoke to them, and they did not hesitate to say that their Army was concentrating, and that if they did not attack us they expected we should attack them, and this, on my return to my quarters, I communicated both to Lord Anglesey and Lord Hill.

On the 15th I went to Brussels and dined with Lord Anglesey. After dinner Sir Pultney Malcomb came to us from the Duke, where he had dined, and said that the French had advanced, and I think he said had taken Charleroi. At night we all went to the Duchess of Richmond's ball. It was only during the ball that the Duke called several of those who commanded Divisions or Brigades together, and told us to be prepared to move in the morning, and it was during the night only that orders were issued for the actual march of the British troops from the right towards Nivelles, and it was on the march that we received orders to continue our march on Quatre Bras. That the Duke must have been aware, therefore, that the French were concentrating there can be no doubt. That the uncertainty of the front on which they would make their attack prevented his concentrating his force sooner I think is equally clear, and that he did not expect the attack quite so soon I am very much disposed to believe. And he was probably led to this from the fact of information having only about the 14th, I think, reached him of the Imperial Guard having left Paris, and from his not calculating that they could have so soon arrived with the Army, and been in a state of readiness to advance.

2nd. That the Prussians were seen advancing to our support long before their arrival on the field there can be no doubt. (The French at first took them for Grouchy's Corps.) That its being an understood thing between the Duke and Blucher that they were to support us, and that such understanding was a necessary part of our remaining in our position and risking a battle is equally certain. Any attempt therefore to throw doubt on the combination

15th June.

News that the French had advanced and taken Charleroi.

Duchess of Richmond's ball.

Orders to march on Quatre Bras.

The Duke did not expect the attack so soon.

Waterloo.

The Prussians were seen advancing long before their arrival at Waterloo.

by which their assistance was afforded to us is quite absurd, and the writer who attempts to correct the error is perfectly right in what he says on this part of the subject. That the *tardy* arrival of the Prussians rendered the victory more complete is, I feel confident, quite correct. Had the French been engaged earlier in the day with them, the last body that attacked us would not have been so committed. So far the delay of the arrival was most fortunate. Still, however, had they arrived earlier we might have beaten the Enemy sooner, and had more daylight to take advantage of our victory.

Their *tardy* arrival rendered the victory more complete.

3rd. That the position of Waterloo is by no means a strong one cannot for a moment be disputed. How far the statement that the Duke had the year before selected it is correct I will not pretend to say, but I will mention an anecdote told me by poor Sir Fredk. Ponsonby after the Battle, and what I heard him often repeat. He said " he knew it to be a fact that the Duke had himself halted some Regiments in position on the Brussels side of Genappe, meaning to have halted his Army there, having that town and the small river that runs through it in his front, but that Delancey, his Quartermaster-General, who had been sent to the rear, came to him and described to him the position of Waterloo, and that the Duke determined to retire from that on which he was then halted to take up that on which the Battle was fought."

The position of Waterloo is not a strong one.

Report that the Duke intended fighting on the Brussels side of Genappe.

Col. Sir Wm. Delancey, K.C.B., Dep. Quart.-Master General, killed at Waterloo.

Colonel Delancey's report of the position of Waterloo determined his adopting it.

The French made a great mistake in attacking the position of Waterloo. They should have masked Hougoumont and penetrated with all their force between us and the Prussians by attacking our left, or else they should have attacked Hougoumont in a different manner than that in which they did attack it, not advancing against the garden and wood, but occupying in force the height above it and driving our troops out with their Artillery, and then turning our right altogether, advancing, getting possession of the road to Brussels at the point of junction with that from Nivelles and that from Genappe. They might thus have bothered us terribly.

Mistakes of the French in their attacks at Waterloo.

Sir H. Vivian.

4th. With respect to the meeting of Wellington and Blucher I see a note refers to what I said in the Gawler controversy. I cannot turn to that correspondence, but I have no doubt in my own mind that when I saw the Duke he had met Blucher. I think his words were, on my telling him (after congratulating him on his victory) that my Brigade was in perfect order, reformed after their attack, and ready to pursue : " Our troops have had a hard day's work ; the Prussians will pursue the Enemy ; do you bivouac your Brigade." I am not quite certain, but I believe he said he had settled it with Blucher the Prussians were to pursue. Certain I am that what he said conveyed that conviction to my mind that he had seen Blucher.

Meeting of Wellington and Blucher.

Arrangement that the Prussians were to pursue the French.

The morning after the Battle, at or soon after daybreak, I proceeded from the hamlet of Hilaincourt over the Field of Battle to Waterloo to see Lord Anglesey. I called on the Duke, it must have been about or soon after four o'clock ; he had just got his breakfast. He asked me many questions about the field, which I had just passed [over], and was very much surprised, indeed, when I assured him of the very large number of the Enemy's Guns that I had seen on the ground. He told me no Returns he had received had at all amounted to what I had described, and I am quite certain he was not at that time aware of the full extent of his Victory. He told me, I recollect full well, that as far as he had then heard, the Prisoners sent to the rear were about 1,200.

19th June.

Called on the Duke, who was surprised at the extent of his victory.

I believe you have my Journal of the proceedings of my Brigade, but I am not certain if I have gone into all the detail, or mentioned some interesting anecdotes of what occurred in front of Quatre Bras before our retreat.

On the morning of the 17th at daybreak, or soon after, the Duke came to Quatre Bras. I believe he had slept at Genappe. I was on horseback near the house at Quatre Bras, looking about. Some few of the Enemy's vedettes only were to be seen, and my Brigade being on the left, I had two strong pickets out,

17th June.

Vivian's Brigade on the left

one of the 18th on the Namur road and one of the 10th Hussars in front. The 1st Hussars had only joined me from Tournay in the night after an immense march.

The Duke asked me what account I could give of the Enemy. I told him all I knew, which was not in fact much, for they had been very quiet. He then desired that I should send half a Squadron with an A.D.C. of his (Col. Gordon) on the Namur road. I did so and in about an hour, or rather more, they returned, reporting that the Enemy was to be seen on the right of the road about two miles distant, where they had been engaged with the Prussians the preceding day, but that they could not learn that they had crossed the road. This patrol, how-ever, seeing the Enemy on the right, had not ventured to push on very far, from a fear of being cut off. Soon after the patrol was sent off the Duke received some despatches from England, and shortly after that I think he gave orders for the retreat, having satisfied himself that although the Enemy were not in motion, still they were preparing to move. He then lay himself down on the ground, covered his head with one of the newspapers he had been reading, and appeared to fall asleep, and in this way he remained some time; when he again rose and mounted his horse and rode down the field in front of Quatre Bras a little distance, and looked about through his glass, and I perfectly well remember his expressing his astonishment at the perfect quiet of the Enemy and his saying it was "not at all impossible that they also might be retreating."

He remained for some time longer anxiously looking out, when on a sudden on the road to Namur at a con-siderable distance, I should say about three miles, we saw something glittering in the sun, which was rising bril-liantly. The Duke at first said they were the French bayonets, but on looking through my glass I saw they were Cuirassiers, moving on the road and forming in the field by the side of it. Very shortly after the picket of the 18th Hussars began skirmishing as did that of the 10th

Lieut.-Col. Sir A.Gordon sent with a patrol along the Namur road.

Owing to the extreme quiet of the Enemy in front, the Duke thinks their retreat-ing possible.

Cuirassiers seen advanc-ing on the Namur road.

in our front, and also that of the 7th Hussars (I believe) on our right. My Brigade with their Guns formed on the left of the house of Quatre Bras, Vandeleur's in their rear and on their right somewhat. Presently the 18th picket came galloping in, followed by two or three Squadrons of French Cavalry, on which my Guns opened a fire, and if I am not mistaken, some Guns of another Brigade on the right did the same. This checked the advance of the French, but we presently saw them very active in bringing up Guns, and soon a fire was opened on us.

Vivian's Brigade formed on left of Quatre Bras, Vandeleur's in their rear.

Pickets driven in.

French advance checked by Artillery fire, which the Enemy replied to.

The Duke had by this time left us to go more to the right. Lord Anglesey, who remained, told me we were to retire, and that Vandeleur's Brigade would support mine, and he then left me. I saw the Enemy pressing on in vast numbers, not only on my front, but left flank. I therefore ordered off the Guns at once. Fortunately, I had early in the morning sent an Officer of the Artillery, Lieut. Swabey, to reconnoitre the passages of the little river Dyle, and he had discovered a bridge to which a road parallel to the high road led from the rear of Quatre Bras, and which was a little higher up [lower down] the river than Genappe. To this bridge, then, he at once moved ·at a trot with his Guns, and passed without interruption from the Enemy. I put my Brigade about and retreated in line, covered by skirmishers. Across a small dip in the ground, and standing rather on a commanding position, Vandeleur's Brigade was drawn up distant from me about six hundred or seven hundred yards. I fully calculated on his allowing me to pass through and his taking the rear. The Enemy had brought some Guns to bear on us, and I recollect a soldier of the 18th being killed by a shot immediately before me in the ranks of that Regiment as we were retiring.

Retreat on 17th.

Lieutenant W. Swabey, R.H.A.

The guns sent across the Genappe River.

Brigade retreats in line.

On my arriving within about fifty or sixty yards of Sir J. Vandeleur, he put his Brigade about and retired, upon which I moved to the ground he had occupied, and directed the 1st Hussars to cover the left flank and left front. In this manner we stood some time skirmishing

Vandeleur's Brigade retires on the approach of Vivian's.

with the Enemy, and during which Lieut.-Colonel Thornhill, A.D.C., came from Lord Uxbridge to me to see what we were about. I told him I had enough upon my hands, but that I hoped to get my people all well off, and I sent an A.D.C. to Sir J. Vandeleur to desire he would as fast as possible get his Brigade over the bridge, in order that I might have no interruption in my retreat in case I was hard pressed.

The thunderstorm came on, rendering the ground very difficult for movement.

About this time the most tremendous storm I almost ever witnessed came on, in a very short time rendering the ground so deep that the horses had some difficulty in moving quick through it. To this I am persuaded I am in a very great degree indebted for the little loss I experienced in the retreat to the bridge. The Enemy began to relax in their preparations for enveloping me, which considerable bodies assembling on my left appeared preparing to do; those in my front were contented with simply skirmishing.

10th and 18th pass over the bridge.

Some 10th men dismounted to defend it with rifle fire.

1st Hussars left as rear Guard.

I sent off the 18th Hussars and 10th, ordering both Regiments to form on the other side of the bridge, and the 10th to dismount some of their men who were armed with rifles to defend it, and prevent the French from pursuing our rear guard over it should they press us hard, and I remained with the 1st Hussars (K.G.L.). This Regiment had now taken the whole of the rear guard of our left, and skirmished with the Enemy, but no charge took place.

The greater number of the Enemy pass by the high road.

On the high road to our right skirmishing was also going on, and I observed the greater portion of the Enemy's Cavalry were directed to that road. After some time I sent off a Squadron of the 1st Hussars towards the bridge, and when we began to do this the French again pressed on so much as to interpose between the left Squadron and the body of the Regiment, and oblige that Squadron to pass the little river (Dyle) higher up [lower down] than the bridge over which we passed.

1st Hussars cross the river.

When I found all was ready, I galloped off down the road to the bridge with the remaining Troops of the

Hussars. The French followed us cheering, and took a Sergeant whose horse was wounded. On our passing the bridge and the Enemy's arriving at it, some of the dis-mounted men fired, and from that moment no attempt was made to molest us. I halted my Brigade some little time on the ground beyond the bridge, and then moved quietly on the narrow lane which runs parallel to the high road by an old Abbey, I think called the Abbey of [? Ayanors], to the hamlet of Verd Cocou, where I bivouacked, the officers occupying three small houses.

Enemy checked by fire of dis-mounted men.

. . . .

I don't know if I sent you a long series of extracts I made from different French writers speaking of the Battle [Waterloo], in which they all attribute the com-plete disorder (the *sauve-qui-peut* state) into which the French were thrown at the end of the day to the attack of these six Regiments of fresh Cavalry (Vandeleur's and Vivian's Brigades). Now, without meaning to take from the merits of my friend Vandeleur, I must claim for my people their due. I assert positively that, when I advanced I left Vandeleur's Brigade standing on the position, and they cheered me as I passed. The 10th charged, the 18th charged; the Squadron or more of the 10th under Howard formed and charged again, and I had myself ordered the 10th and 18th to be re-formed and to follow me. Having placed myself at the head of two Squadrons of the 1st Hussars, two other Squadrons being in support, and was advancing in pursuit of the broken Enemy, when I found on my right and front the 11th Regiment, part of Vandeleur's Brigade.

Waterloo.

Opinions of French writers,

Who attribute their complete rout to Vivian's and Vandeleur's Brigades.

Vivian's ad-vanced first, and had the principal share in it.

Charges of the 10th and 18th.

So completely had I found myself alone with my Brigade prior to this, that I had actually some time before sent my A.D.C., Captain Keane, to Sir J. Vandeleur to request he would come on and support me, and the gallant old Soldier, for he is as brave an old fellow as ever lived, was very angry with me for so doing, saying "that I had no business to send orders (which I did not) to my senior Officer." . . . . . .

Vivian sent an A.D.C. to ask Vandeleur to support him. Reply of the latter.

SIR H. VIVIAN.

I wish I could tell you anything of Napoleon during the day, but I neither saw or heard anything of him, excepting before the attack began, when, with a large suite of Officers, he rode amongst the Columns forming in the front of the British left, and was hailed with shouts of *Vive l'Empereur.* I fancied looking through my glass I could distinguish the little Hero, and, indeed, have little doubt of it, but he very soon returned towards the centre of his position, and certainly after that never again, I should say, came to that part of the French line.

With his glass saw Napoleon before the Battle began.

Ever, &c.,

HUSSEY VIVIAN.

FROM THE SAME.

No. 72.   *Memorandum.*   *Jan.* 18*th,* 1830.

.   .   .   .

Waterloo.
Criticisms of the *Quarterly Review* on the conduct of the Cavalry.

In one of the Numbers of the *Quarterly Review* the conduct of the British Light Cavalry in the Battle of Waterloo is noticed in the most slighting terms. Everything is attributed to the Heavy Cavalry, which arm alone is stated to have had power enough to meet the French Cuirassiers. Now, I have no wish to take from the great merits of the Heavy Cavalry on the occasion. The Life Guards and Blues, with the 1st Dragoon Guards, gallantly met and repulsed the charges of the Cuirassiers in the very heat of the Action, and the losses of these Regiments afford evident proofs how severely they must have been engaged. Whilst about the same time the desperate attack of the Brigade of Heavy Cavalry under the command of Major-General Sir William Ponsonby on the Columns of French Infantry advancing against our position on the left of the road, and its complete success, had an influence on the Battle infinitely greater than has ever been admitted; indeed, having myself witnessed from my position on the left the complete success of the charge, and the consequences to the French Infantry, I cannot but consider *it as one of the most important features of the Battle.*

The important results of the charge of Ponsonby's Brigade.

SIR H. VIVIAN.

But after these attacks of the Brigade of Life Guards and Sir William Ponsonby's, they became non-effective, and the other Cavalry of the right having suffered most severely, there remained only the Cavalry of the left, Sir J. Vandeleur's and Sir H. Vivian's Brigades, effective.

Owing to the losses of the other Cavalry, Vandeleur's and Vivian's Brigades only were effective in the evening.

These Brigades, then, were moved to the right, and arrived at a most opportune moment. The effect of their formation immediately in the rear of the line of Infantry on the position, was to give confidence to the troops almost worn out with the protracted and murderous combat, and to the effect of the [? their] charge the following quotations from French authors (for they at least have done them justice, and those who feel the blow may be supposed to know, under such circumstances, from whence it came) will bear testimony.

French authors ascribe the total rout of their Army to these two Brigades.

The detail of the proceedings of Sir H. Vivian's Brigade will show that the Cavalry referred to is this Brigade, and this only. *Sir J. Vandeleur's did not charge until some time after on the remains of a broken Square of Infantry that had collected,* and most of whom were made prisoners by it. That Sir J. Vandeleur's Brigade did not attack any of the French Cavalry, nor indeed until they had been all driven from the field, is proved by their having taken no horses, whilst a very large number, nearly two hundred, were captured by Sir H. Vivian's Brigade. The principal loss sustained by Sir J. Vandeleur's Brigade occurred whilst formed on the left of the road, and in support of Sir William Ponsonby's Brigade. There, indeed, its loss had been great, and especially in the 12th Light Dragoons. The attack that was made at night on the body of French Infantry that had collected, was made by the 11th and part of the 16th Light Dragoons.

In reality it was mainly owing to Vivian's.

The time between the attack of the first, 6th, Brigade and the advance of Sir J. Vandeleur's must have been at least twenty minutes, if not thirty. It may be judged of from the following facts: the 10th had charged and rallied; the 18th had charged after the order to halt was given to the 10th; the order to halt had been given to the 18th; the rallied body of the 10th had charged, and it was after this that Captain Keane was sent by Sir H. Vivian to Sir J. Vandeleur to beg him to move on in his support; and Sir H. Vivian was in the act of moving on with two Squadrons of the 1st Hussars when Sir J. Vandeleur, with his Brigade, passed by his right flank, and a conversation took place between them.

I have been thus particular in stating these facts, because it will be seen by some of the following extracts that the confusion occasioned by the attack of the Cavalry from the left is attributed to an attack of both these Brigades, whereas in fact it was one only that made the most important impression.

Vandeleur's Brigade had suffered severely earlier in the day.

In saying this it is not my object to take from the merit of the conduct of Sir J. Vandeleur's Brigade. That Brigade had been much exposed and had suffered severely and behaved gallantly early in the day, whilst mine was comparatively in security.

It was therefore right that the brunt of the last attack should fall upon Vivian's.

It was fair and right, therefore, that the brunt of the Battle should at last fall upon me [? us], and having so fallen it is equally fair and right we should have credit for it.

Truth is history, and history without truth does not deserve the name; and I am anxious for the sake of the gallant men I commanded, that one day at least the truth may be known.

. . . .

HUSSEY VIVIAN

FROM THE SAME.

No. 73.

No date.

Waterloo.
First Prussians that came into action.

The first Prussians that came into action I should say were the advanced guard of a Corps not exceeding two Regiments, and supported by another; they passed the hedge of Papelotte, drew up across the valley in line almost at right angles with us. They were directly under where I stood, and I saw the operation as plainly as if at a field day.

The French at once advanced against them (their left flank rather), and drove them back. They then occupied the village of Smohain or Papelotte, I forget exactly the name. This must have been somewhere between five and six o'clock. I should say nearer five. It was a considerable time after this that the Prussians appeared in force. They [we] remained long enough for me to see the French reserve and right form line *en potence* in order to meet the attack on Planchenoit, and I was surprised to see the tremendous fire the French were able to direct against the Prussians. It was just as this took place that I moved to the right.

.   .   .   .

If anyone can tell you exactly about the time we advanced it will give you the time of the Prussians being generally engaged, but I should certainly say that they were before Planchenoit very soon after half-past seven, if not as early. This I saw then, when with the 18th Hussars I got into the high road beyond La Belle Alliance. Some Prussians also had reached it, and I have no doubt some were cut down by the 18th for French, for I myself saw two or three who were wounded with the sabre on the road the next morning.

The Prussians were generally engaged at the time of the British Advance.

Met Prussians on the high road beyond La Belle Alliance.

Some mistaken by the 18th for French and cut down.

I have no doubt Gawler is quite correct as to when he saw the Prussian Artillery—that is some few Guns; but I do not think any large force of Prussians reached the high road short of Belle Alliance. I am certain some came along the French original position, from the direction of the fire. The fact was that after the attack of the Prussians, theirs might almost be called the general Action —fighting had in a great degree ceased along our Line, excepting on one front—*i.e.*, the attack of the Imperial Guard, so that the Prussian Army must of course cut a conspicuous figure at the moment chosen for representation on the Model.

In truth, I care not what others may say, we were

LORD VIVIAN.

The Prussians coming on the right and rear of Napoleon gave us the Victory of Waterloo.

The attacks of the 10th and 18th threw into confusion the French troops covering the retreat of their left.

Whilst Adam's Brigade had before routed the Reserve covering the attack of the Imperial Guard.

Not the slightest ground for jealousy of the Prussians.

greatly indebted to the Prussians, and it was their coming on the right and rear of Napoleon that gave us the Victory of Waterloo. We might have held our ground, but we never could have advanced but for the Prussian movement.

The advance of my Brigade and the attacks of the 10th and 18th no doubt threw into confusion all those French troops formed to cover the retreat on their left of the road around La Belle Alliance, whilst Adam's Brigade had before routed the body of reserve covering the attack. I can very easily believe that the movement of the 52nd, &c., did not occupy more time than Gawler mentions.

You are quite right in saying there is not the slightest ground for jealousy, and I must say those are most unjust to the Prussians who refuse them their full share of credit for their most effective aid at the end of the day. I must conclude. Ever, &c.,

H. VIVIAN.

FROM THE SAME (LORD VIVIAN).

Bodmin, November 27th, 1841.

No. 74.

In the details of what took place under such circumstances as the advance of my Brigade at the end of the day of Waterloo, it would be a miracle if all parties in the same

See No. 75, p. 173.

Regiment [? Brigade] ever agreed. It is very possible that both Colonel Taylor and I may be right, and yet not exactly agree. Indeed it is extraordinary that we all (I mean all the Officers of my Brigade) agree so generally.

That I ordered the advance at a trot, and that the leading Squadron moved off at a trot, and went down the hill into the flat at a trot, *I cannot have the slightest doubt.* That Taylor, who commanded the centre Squadron of the 10th, might have galloped in order to preserve his distance, perhaps from not having moved off the position at the same moment is very possible. There is one circumstance to which I have I think to you before adverted, that proves the advance was at a trot and not a hurried one. The leading half-Squadron as we were moving off the position, on approaching some of our Guns wheeled to the right instead of to the left, and was consequently moving to the rear. I was on the flank of the Squadron. I immediately (I recollect perfectly well), with a *considerable degree of emphasis, &c., and a good hearty damn,* galloped to the flank of the second half-Squadron, and said that it was *towards the Enemy* and *not from the Enemy* they were to wheel. I then took the flank Officer's place and I led the Column down the hill in the direction I wished it to move until the leading half-Squadron was brought back into its place, when I went to the flank of that half-Squadron, and in this way conducted the Column some little distance. Now had our advance been at any very rapid pace the half-Squadron which had wheeled from us and been left behind, somewhat perhaps confused and entangled with the Guns, would never have returned to its place in so short a time.

Then as to what happened when we arrived in the plain at the bottom of the hill. That there was a pause, and I may say a halt in the front I can positively affirm; the very circumstance of Sir Colin Campbell coming to me from the Duke and desiring me to halt, and the conversation which took place (the affair of a minute, or perhaps moment only, I admit), proves it. When I moved on again, and ordered the formation on the leading half-Squadron, and the advance and attack, the order was to form line on the front half-Squadron; but that the formation was rather *en échelon* of Squadrons than in line I think is much more than probable, and if any halt occurred in the next Squadron it was [illegible] at once, for I well recollect the instant it was in line giving the order to charge, and the others no doubt took it up in succession. I sent orders to the 18th to remain steady in support. I charged with the 10th, and as

10TH HUSSARS.

soon as we were well into the Enemy and mixed up, the French making off, I gave the word "halt," and galloped off to the 18th.

Attacked by a Cuirassier.

En route I was attacked by one of the Cuirassiers whom we had passed. I was fortunate enough to give him a thrust in the neck with my left hand (for my right was in a sling, and I was just capable of holding the reins with it only*), and at that moment I was joined by my little German orderly, who cut the fellow off his horse. I then went to the 18th, and what happened afterwards I have before described to you.

.   .   .   .

The circumstance of the Squadron of the 2nd Light Dragoons, K.G.L., having been attacked by some Lancers when passing across our front you will recollect I have before described to you. I believe I also mentioned a circumstance that occurred at that time, which made a great impression on me, which was that a man of that Squadron having had his horse wounded, and struggling to get from under him, and a French Lancer immediately before me blowing his brains out.   .   .   .   .

Ever, &c.,

VIVIAN.

10TH OR PRINCE OF WALES' HUSSARS.

LIEUT.-COLONEL T. W. TAYLOR, 10TH HUSSARS.
CAPTAIN 10TH HUSSARS AND BREV.-MAJOR.

TO SIR HUSSEY VIVIAN.

November, 1829.

No. 75.   MY DEAR SIR,

I am afraid that I cannot pretend to exactness as to the proceedings of the Hussar Brigade under your command on the 16th, 17th, and 18th June, 1815, but at your

* In consequence of a wound received at Croix d'Orade, near Toulouse.—ED.

request will do my best to relate what I remember of the
proceedings of the 10th Hussars, which may be useful in
recalling to your mind the general movements of the
Brigade.   Many of my opinions may be erroneous; I
have never seen the ground since we galloped over it, but I
fancy that if I was there I could point out the exact course
we took, in spite of Belgic Lions and Tombs, &c., with
which they say the ground is now encumbered.   If I use
the vowel of which Lord Erskine was accused of being
so fond, it is only because I relate what I saw or thought,
and it must be excused.

On the 15th June I rode home from Brussels to 15th June.
Vivorde by myself in the evening, and found that there
were orders for a field day next morning.   On the 16th, 16th June.
at about half-past four a.m., my servant called me and said
the Regiment was ordered to turn out in full marching
order to change quarters.   The Brigade assembled on the
road from Vivorde to Grammont.   We waited some time March on
Quatre Bras.
for the 18th Hussars.   When assembled we commenced
our march (I think) about seven.   We proceeded through The Brigade
marched
about 7 a.m.
Grammont and Enghien, falling in with other Corps of
Cavalry on the march.   At Enghien Lieut. Parsons of my
Troop joined, having come across from Brussels, where I
had left him the day before; he informed me of the
advance of the French, that the troops had turned out
from Brussels, and that there would probably be an action
in the course of the day.

After some hours' march, we turned off the road to
the right, dismounted and fed, and the men and Officers
dined on what they had in the haversacks or could procure—
continued the march to Braine-le-Comte.   In passing
through a deep wood beyond that town, we began to hear
firing; on our issuing from the wood it became quite
distinct, and soon we were enabled to see the line of smoke
of the Action at Quatre Bras from the high banks of
the road.   An order arrived from Lord Uxbridge to throw Ordered to
trot at nine
miles an hour
towards
Nivelles.
away our hay and to trot at nine miles per hour, towards
Nivelles, which we did accordingly.   We passed through

10TH HUSSARS.
After passing Nivelles proceeded along the Namur road.

Nivelles, in which we saw several waggons with wounded. We had then an order to proceed two miles on the Namur road, and the Brigade, with its Horse Artillery trotting up the *chaussée* made no small clatter.

We met several wounded coming out of action; when we got near the left of the wood at Quatre Bras the firing was still going on and some cannon shot passed us; a horse of the 18th I heard was killed. We formed half-Squadrons and were then ordered to canter, and in this way advanced to the Field and halted. Our horses, in spite of the long march—between 30 and 40 miles I should think for some of the Corps—were very fresh; one horse of ours broke his neck by falling into [a] hollow road we passed, in consequence of his pulling and throwing up his head.

Arrival at the Field of Quatre Bras.

The Action now over.

The Action was now over, only a Gun firing now and then and a few occasional shots of tirailleurs. We heard of the Duke of Brunswick's death, and of the Battle of Ligny, and that the Prussians had retired. We retired and dismounted and bivouacked in a wheat-field behind the left of the wood in which the Guards had been engaged.

17th June. A patrol of the 10th ordered out with the Duke's A.D.C. Sir A. Gordon.

* Not 5. (signed) H.V.

17th. About two a.m., a Troop was ordered to mount to patrol with Sir A. Gordon, the Duke of Wellington's A.D.C. Captain Grey's Troop went, they had 12* miles out and as many back, most of it at a smart trot as I heard, but were I believe unsuccessful in communicating with the Prussians. Firing commenced at daybreak between the pickets of Infantry and lasted with little intermission to near 12. Major Howard's Squadron had been on picket during the night at a farm in front and to the left of Quatre Bras, whither we all went in the morning by squadrons to water, and then returned to the brow of the hill and dismounted, and breakfasted, having a good view of the Infantry skirmishing.

Retreat on 17th.

The Infantry, Guns, and baggage commenced retiring, the pickets were withdrawn, and the firing ceased. At about 12 o'clock the French Infantry began to cook, as we saw by their fires. Our Regiment mounted and was moved down to the low ground, where it stood in *échelon* of squadrons, a picket of the 18th where the road came through the enclosures in advance of us. About this time we saw the French Cavalry filing over the rising ground in front beyond the pickets, and forming their columns of assembly.

The Duke of Wellington and Staff with Lord Uxbridge came down to look at them, and stood near the front of my (the centre) Squadron. I heard the Duke say, " Well I suppose we shall fight them here," and I understood Lord Uxbridge to answer that he did not think it a favourable situation, as there were defiles in our rear, &c. The Duke then said, stretching himself and yawning, " Then I suppose we must retreat." Just after the Cavalry forming two lines along the brow of the rising ground to the left of the road (to Namur I believe) the Heavy Cavalry in second line, we were ordered to retire and form in our place in Brigade.

The French Cavalry then commenced its advance, the 18th picket falling back, not by the road, but in line across the fields under us, a Squadron of Lancers advancing upon them, both having skirmishers out. When the Enemy's Cavalry were pretty thick in the opening between the fences our Brigade of Horse Artillery Guns gave them a few rounds, apparently with effect, knocking men and horses off the road.

Both lines of Cavalry were then ordered Threes about, and retired in line over the cornfields. On our getting rather into a hollow the Enemy's Guns opened upon us, throwing shells which fell over us. I saw one burst near the 18th. Just then commenced a thunderstorm worthy of the tropics for the loudness of the thunder and violence of the rain. This with the sort of ballet of war of the retiring and advancing Cavalry, and the French Guns firing, altogether made a picturesque and grand scene.

Our Brigade then filed off into narrow roads and through a village, the 18th leading (I think), the 10th in

10TH HUSSARS.

The rear of the Brigade pressed by the Enemy.

the centre and the 1st G. Hussars following. I heard that their rear was attacked by the Enemy just as we entered the narrow roads, but the French soon left us for the main road. On issuing from the village there was a hollow way with an ascent commanded by high banks. Here Sir H. Vivian formed a division of the 10th on the bank, in rank entire with carbines advanced and ready to fire into the hollow way and check pursuit, had the Enemy come on, but as they did not, the division resumed its place, and the

After passing the hollow way (? bridge over the Genappe), the Brigade retires unmolested.

Brigade marched quite unmolested through narrow roads, hearing occasional cannonade on the main road, and the shouts of the attacks that took place. Lieutenant Smith of the 10th was sent across to the main road, and was present at the affair between the 7th Hussars and the French Lancers; during which, at considerable risk to himself, he

Lieut. Smith saves Lieut. Gordon of the 7th on the main road.

saved Lieutenant Gordon of the 7th, who was wounded, from capture or death, by dismounting and lending him his horse to carry him to the rear till he could meet his own led horses. Lieutenant Smith escaped being taken by leaping over the ditch off the *chaussée,* till the Lancers being driven back he got his horse again.

Towards evening we reached a coppice near some cottages to the *left* of Waterloo with reference to the

Bivouacked in rear of the position of Waterloo.

position. Here we halted and bivouacked in the coppice, it still raining hard. Some of the Officers made a fire and lay down round it, some got into cottages. I was warned by the Adjutant for picket with my Squadron. After some time I found Lord Robert Manners and some of the Officers in a cottage drying their clothes and picking and broiling fowls. Finding shelter I lay down and got a good sleep, after which went to see when my picket was to turn out. Towards morning I received the order, and at daylight marched with my Squadron to the brow of the

* Papelotte.
—H. V.

His Squadron sent on picket.

hill over a village (Ohain* I believe, from inquiries I made of an inhabitant), where I relieved a Squadron of the 18th commanded by Captain Grant; they had an advanced post the other side of the village, and their chain of vedettes on the rising ground beyond it. I went round with Captain Grant and saw the post and vedettes relieved. We were to communicate with the 1st Hussars picket round to the left, and (I think) Infantry on the right. In going round my vedettes I saw two Corps of French Cavalry in close column dismounted within carbine shot of them, and looking from the ridge of the hill into a hollow beyond, I saw a strong patrol of French Heavy Cavalry winding up a road that led away to our left, probably going to feel for the Prussians.

Having seen the chain secure I moved the Squadron into a road of the village in the bottom, when a Prussian Officer with a patrol arrived at my post and desired me to inform the Duke of Wellington that General Bulow with his *Corps d'Armée* was advancing to join us, and that he was *trois quarts de lieue* distant. Having communicated with our Army the Officer was to return directly. I sent Lieutenant Lindsay to Headquarters with this intelligence.

We then established ourselves in a house in the village, which was deserted, and getting some fowls killed, put them to boil in a pot with some bacon we found. I mention this, as a ridiculous thing occurred which relates to this. One of my men came in from the advanced post, saying "there were three great Squadrons right in upon us." I mounted immediately and galloped to the front, where I saw the vedettes withdrawing steadily and falling back to the advance party. Serjeant Guedule [?], who was one of the captors of Lefebre and Benevente, was conducting them. I saw two or three Squadrons of Cavalry advancing towards the village and a general movement along the opposite slope, troops and Guns taking up their positions.

I called in my men and mounted the rest, and knowing that the village was well garnished with Infantry, retired through it, and formed on the plain space above, one Troop in advance ready to charge any Cavalry that might attempt to push through or round the village, placing more vedettes to command the hollow way and the valley.

Battle on the
left flank
begun by
tirailleurs
skirmishing.

Artillery fire
commenced
about 11 a.m.

* Nassau.
—H. V.

Just then the Action commenced on that flank by
tirailleurs skirmishing in the valley and about a farm-
house. Some French Guns opened on the village, and the
troops on the hill to our right (Belgic* I believe), whose
Guns returned the fire. I think this was about 11 o'clock.
Just then we heard a tremendous fire distant on the right,
which I suppose was the first grand attack. I had notice
sent me that we were not to fire on troops coming up
from the left, in consequence I suppose of the intelligence
brought by the Prussian Officer.

The Squadron
rejoins the
Brigade which
was formed on
the crest of
the hill.

See General
Plan, No. 1.

The remainder of the Regiment and Brigade came up
from the rear, and my Squadron was ordered to join the
Brigade, which then took ground to the right and formed
on the crest of the hill, the 10th with their right to a
hedge which ran at right angles to the position and a road
rather sunk in the slope of the hill. The Horse Artillery
were advanced to the brow of the hill, but did not fire,
though some Belgic Guns there (or Hanoverian) did.
Some French Guns were either attracted by their fire or our
position, as for several rounds they constantly struck the
ground in front of mine and Major Howard's Squadrons,
or fired just over our heads. A cannon shot had struck
one Squadron and caused some casualties; here Lieut.
Hardman, the Adjutant, who had gone forward to look,
received a severe contusion from a musket shot.

The Brigade
moved to the
right to
support
Vandeleur.

While in this position we saw movements of Cavalry at
a distance to our right and a good deal to the rear, as if
some of ours which had attacked were retiring and rallying.
We next moved through the hedge into the low ground
behind the ridge, and advanced in line to the top of the
hill to support an attack of the Light Brigade, General
Vandeleur's. While on the ridge of the hill there were a
good many shells sent over us or pitched near us; the
latter did no harm, as they buried in the mud and burst
upwards. We had been all this time looking out for the
Prussians; we had seen the French throw out vedettes at
[an] angle with the right of their position, and looking
towards where the Prussians were expected by us. They

The French
preparing for
the approach
of the
Prussians.

had Guns and troops in reserve as if waiting for them.
Some Staff Officers came occasionally to the left, to see if
there was any appearance of them. I remember seeing
Captain [Lieut.-Colonel] Percy, the Duke's A. D. C.

At last we remarked the French vedettes in some com-
motion, and some Prussian tirailleurs began skirmishing
with their right to the village in the bottom, and after a
considerable time the Prussians began to come up and
form with their right to the village, Corps after Corps,
extending to the left in a line at right angles with the
French Line. They established Batteries which opened,
and the French reserves formed to oppose them opening
their Guns also. The Prussians kept their right stationary,
but pushed on their left getting round the Enemy, so that
before we moved to the right, their right formed an acute
angle [? with our Line]. I do not think the Prussians
commenced seriously till about four o'clock, or later.

The Prussians begin to come up and form at right angles with the French Line.

Their Artillery and that of the French become engaged.

The Prussians keep pushing forward their left.

After having supported the Light Dragoons, we took
(I think) ground to the left again, resumed our first position,* then moved to the right again, and for some time
were formed on the face of the hill, just above the hollow
road in which our Horse Artillery were. We dismounted
for some time; there was a heavy cannonade at this time.
I heard that a shell fell through the limber box of one [of]
our Guns without exploding it, which was fortunate, if true,
for the Guns were just under us. While in this position I
remember a very sharp attack on the Infantry to our right
near the trees, which was, I believe, the position of Sir T.
Picton's Division. The Enemy, however, were driven back.

* No; we never passed back through the lane.
—H.V.

Soon after we were mounted, and advanced along the
crest of the hill in open column of half-Squadrons, there
was a good deal of fire, and I remember seeing Captain
Grey's mare in the right Squadron hit in the head; she
was killed after by another shot. We took ground
towards the rear of the position by Threes right, so as to
get under the shelter of the hill, and passed through a
coppice of low brushwood behind the hill, and after halted
in close columns just behind, and with our left to the end

Brigade moved to the right.

Affords support to the Infantry.

of a ridge.   Here we saw the Infantry warmly engaged, and took open column after a little time, and, bringing up left shoulders, moved along the rear of the Infantry, and the Infantry being rather pushed by the Enemy, who kept up a heavy fire, we wheeled into line and supported, about fifty yards in rear of them ; they rather fell back upon us, and one Battalion of Brunswick Oels in close column, retiring, being [in] want of ammunition, I˙believe, but in good order, was near passing through us between my Squadron and Major Howard's.   Just then two or three Battalions to the left of it advanced at double quick, their drums rolling, and drove back the Enemy.   The Brunswick Oels faced about and advanced at the charge also, Sir H. Vivian and Captain Shakespeare,* &c., cheering them on.

* Capt. Shakespeare I had ordered out of the ranks to attend me as an extra A.D.C. on the occasion.
—H. V.

A cloud of tirailleurs being close up to our Infantry, behind which we were, and keeping up a heavy fire, we had many casualties here, particularly numbers of horses hit, some in two or three places.   Captain Gurwood, of my right half-Squadron, was struck in the knee, the shot wounding his horse, which was killed as he was going to the rear.   Captain Wood was shot through the thigh, and I think Captain Grey was wounded here.   The men behaved with great steadiness in a position rather trying for Cavalry.

Capts. Gurwood, Wood, and Grey wounded.

Great steadiness of the men under a heavy fire.

Brigade moved still further to the right.

The attack being repulsed, we wheeled by half-Squadrons to the right and moved on, then took ground to the rear by Threes, passed by a farm-house, I believe Mont-St.-Jean, took ground to the left (of the position) a short way, fronted, and after advanced in column again right in front, crossed a *chaussée* in front of the farm-house,† and moved on towards the right of our position bringing up the left shoulders rather.   About this time I saw the Marquis of Anglesey and his Staff, and some miserable remnants of the Cavalry of the right.

† This was before the Nassau troops attempted to pass us, and not after, and it was before the casualties mentioned in the last page.
—H.V.

Brigade halted in rear of some Guns.

We halted in open column in rear of some Guns. Troops in front warmly engaged, a heavy fire.   As I was sitting close to Lieut. Hodgson, who had taken my right half-Squadron after Captain Gurwood, his horse was shot in the body, staggered forward, and fell. We either went Threes left from column or wheeled into line, and when we had come close up to the rear of a Battery, were ordered to pass through it by Threes, and when through to wheel up. This brought my right half-Squadron with its right flank to the muzzle of a Gun ; either the Officer of Artillery had not ordered them to cease firing, or it was not attended to, for I saw the man with the portfire apparently about to fire, and roared out to him not to blow my half-Squadron away ; he answered, " Out of the way, then, and let me have my shot." I gave the word to rein back, and as soon as my horse's nose was clear of the line of fire he fired, the shock shaking all the horses, and the shot must have all but grazed some of the horses' noses ; luckily it was round shot. Lieut. Arnold had been in the same predicament with his half-Squadron, I heard, and when the Gun fired the flannel of the cartridge struck on the neck of his horse. After we advanced, an Officer has told me since, he saw one of our men knocked forwards off his horse by a cannon shot, probably from our zealous friends, who had so good a sight of the French retiring that they did not like to cease firing.

Ordered to advance through Napier's Battery

Zeal of Napier's gunners.

Just then, the last attack of the French being repulsed, we were ordered to advance in column right in front and to gallop. A Staff Officer met us (Colonel Harvey, I think) and said " Come along," when I told him in passing that our right Squadron was behind and begged him to rectify it. This I believe he did, or probably told Sir H. Vivian, for the right Squadron came up at a great pace and took its situation at the head of the Column. Before we passed the Guns I remembered [saying] to Lord R. Manners that there was no Squadron Officer to the right Squadron. Sir G. Quentin having been wounded, Lord R. Manners took the command of the Regiment, which vacated the Squadron. I think he ordered Lieut. Arnold to command it. I do not remember Major Howard changing from the left.

Brigade ordered to advance at a gallop.
See No. 74, p. 163.

Colonel Sir G. Quentin being wounded, Lieut. Lord R. Manners takes command of the 10th.

As we advanced at a gallop we saw the French Army

10TH HUSSARS.
Picturesque view of the French retreating.

Lord Uxbridge wounded.

10th attack French Cavalry.

See General Plan, No. 3.

* Light Germans from the right; these and a Squadron of Belgians were the only Cavalry I saw in advance.
—H. V.

The French Cavalry broken and flies.

retiring in confusion up the hill, presenting a most picturesque sight of a mixture of all arms and uniforms. Some Guns in their rear were firing, and there was also some musketry. At this time I conceive Lord Uxbridge was wounded near the left of our Regiment. One of our Officers told me he saw him fall. The Guards and other Infantry were advancing in close columns on our left and cheered. I believe the Duke of Wellington was near them, observing our advance. There were some Corps of French Cavalry—one very conspicuous with red [uniforms] or red facings and red crests, also Dragoons in green and French Lancers *white,* formed to the right to protect the retreat.

Sir H. Vivian led us towards these, bringing up the left shoulders rather and gave the order—Front form line. Each Squadron formed, but the head was going so fast that we scarce got into line, rather *en échelon* of Squadrons.

As we neared the Enemy, a Squadron or half-Squadron of a Light Dragoon Regiment with red facings, either the 23rd* or some Germans, pushed rather in advance of our right rather obliquely. The Lancers couched their lances, made a gallant charge down the hill and turned them. Our right Squadron came upon the Lancers and sent them about; the Dragoons in green charged to support the Lancers, and the centre Squadron came upon them, and the whole broke and fled, our men cutting in among them.

Bringing up the right shoulders rather and passing over a hill we were halted and rallying. A Square of French Infantry was formed rather in a hollow under the road. Sir H. Vivian appeared to be preparing to attack them with the 18th. I do not know the result, as Lord R. Manners led us on in pursuit up the hill across the road, where we passed Infantry, who surrendered, and abandoned Guns. Coming to the brow of the hill we found three or four Companies about, rallied and formed with Cavalry close behind them. They commenced a fire on us. Lord R. Manners halted a minute to form and charged. They turned and fled, and our men pursued to the brow of a hill with a steep dip beyond it on the opposite side. On a knoll another Square of Infantry was formed. Our men being much scattered I began to collect them and retired to join the rest of the Regiment, which I found halted and forming, telling off, &c., and commenced collecting and telling off my Squadron.

Before I left the last hill my horse was so knocked up he could hardly go, and I was going to change him for a French one. But Sir H. Vivian coming up and expressing himself satisfied with the Regiment, and that we should have no more to do that night, I desisted from changing my saddle.

Just as I was coming back I saw about thirty of the 18th pass dash down into the hollow and gallantly, though uselessly charge the Square on the hill, by which they were repulsed. It was now dusk and I remember several shells pitching at no great distance, whether thrown by friend or foe was difficult to say. In a little time we advanced and met many prisoners* under the escort of Light Dragoons. We halted on rising ground. There was now fine moonlight. The course of the fugitives could be discerned by the occasional fire of the Prussians pursuing, and shouts and clamour, which gradually died away. A Regiment of Prussian Uhlans advancing in pursuit here passed us. After a little time we were ordered to bivouac, which we did in a wheatfield near the Observatory * as they called it. The Officers sat down under a hedge, and we got some beer from a farm-house not far off, and got what we could to eat. My batman coming up with the led horses agreeably surprised me by producing two boiled fowls and some bacon, which, on my inquiring, he told me he had secured by going into the village where my picket had been on the left, as soon as the French ceased to cannonade it. There he found all quiet, and our pot boiling away and the fowls

10th attack French Infantry with the same result.

* These were men taken by Sir J. Vandeleur's Brigade, which had advanced after mine had attacked and were reforming.—H. V.

* The Brigade bivouacked at Hilaincourt. —H. V.

and bacon done, which he brought away, and very welcome they were.

We lay down under the hedge, and I believe all slept soundly till daylight.

Next morning, the 19th, we fed in a clover field near a farm-house, which was full of Officers writing to England. I wrote to my friends. Lieutenant Smith of the Regiment went with a burying party to the field, and then it was, I believe, Major Howard's body was recognised and buried by Serjeant Plowman, by whom it was afterwards taken up and removed to England.

Attack on a Square of Infantry by Major Howard's Squadron.

With regard to the attack on a Square of Infantry by Major Howard's Squadron, in which he was killed, having received three wounds—Lieutenant Arnold was shot through the body, and Lieutenant Bacon through the thigh—I do not describe that, not having seen it, but I understood that the charge had been successful, and that the Square was broken, and Sir H. Vivian gave the Regiment credit for it in Orders. The account I have had of it

* I was by the side of Major Howard, and myself advanced with the Squadron; the communication with the Infantry was after the attack to desire them to cease firing. It was a Regiment of Hanoverians. —H. V.

from an officer was this : that Sir H. Vivian had directed Major Howard to co-operate with some Infantry that were coming along the road in attacking this Square ; that he, Major Howard, sent to the Officer of Infantry to say so, who for some reason declined ; that Major Howard asked this Officer of the Regiment what he thought of it, who said that without co-operation of the Infantry it was better not as the Square was well formed, but other troops coming up and surrounding them, they must surrender.* Major Howard said that having been ordered to attack he thought it a ticklish thing not to do it, and gave the order

Major Howard killed and afterwards struck by a French soldier with the butt end of his musket.

Lieut. Gunning killed.

accordingly and did it with effect, though the Enemy stood well, the Officers being wounded close to the bayonets, and Major Howard falling so that a man in the ranks struck him with the butt end of his musket.

Lieut. Gunning, of my left half-Squadron, I always understood to be killed in the charge by a musket shot, but my batman says he saw him fall in an attack on a Square from which they were repulsed.

The Duke of Wellington in his despatch, I think, says the Earl of Uxbridge was wounded by the last shot that was fired. After which we had Major Howard and Lieut. Gunning killed, and Lieuts. Arnold and Bacon severely wounded, and Major Harris.

Major Harris, Lieuts. Arnold and Bacon severely wounded.

It is curious to remember that little notice was ever taken of the charge of this Hussar Brigade in English accounts, whereas there is scarcely a French account in which the Corps of Cavalry that came from the left and completed the rout, [and] which Buonaparte saw cutting into the thick of his troops, is not mentioned as the final blow that decided him to be off.

The charge of this Brigade so little noticed in English accounts, whereas French writers say it was owing to it that Napoleon left the field.

I was generally so much occupied with my own Squadron (because I think that if every Officer keeps his immediate charge in order all will go well), that I cannot speak as to the proceedings of the 18th and 1st Hussars. The latter were, I believe, sometimes supporting in second line, but what I have written may, in spite, I dare say, of some erroneous notions, assist you in recalling the general movements of the Brigade.

About twelve o'clock on the 19th, we marched to Hautain-le-Mont, next day to Merbes-Ste-Marie, next day across the Sambre, so on to Paris.

19th June. Brigade begins the march on Paris.

The day Paris surrendered I was going on Squadron picket from Bourget to Grandrancy [?] to relieve Kranckenberg of the 1st Hussars, when you sent for me and told me my vedettes were not to fire.

I cannot read this over, not wishing to delay it longer.

In some places I mention you by name, which you must excuse in a letter addressed to yourself.

Believe, &c.,

T. W. TAYLOR.

18TH HUSSARS.

MAJOR-GENERAL THE HON. H. MURRAY, C.B.

LIEUT.-COLONEL 18TH HUSSARS.

No. 76.   MEMORANDUM.   *Jan.*, 1835.

.   .   .   .

Waterloo.
See General
Plan, No. 1.

The 10th and 18th were on the left at the commencement of the Battle.

The 18th had bivouacked at Verd-Cocou the night of the 17th, throwing out a picket to Ohain.

Coming down upon luxuriant crops, the Brigade took up its position, the 10th being on the right of the 18th in line.

Beginning of
the Battle.

The Action soon commenced, and General Vivian rode forward to observe its progress.

The Brigade stood under cannonade frequently, but not attended with serious casualty.

To us on our regimental posts the prevailing fire seemed towards the centre of the Armies, and to our right, very heavy and continued.

It is impossible at this distance of time that I can trace step by step the progress of the Brigade from the left to the right, but I will mention as consecutively as I can the chain of events which constitute my recollection of it.

Intelligence of
the advance of
the Prussians.

A Prussian Officer came with the intelligence of the advance of that army.

After some time, Major [Lieut.-Col.] the Honourable Henry Percy, one of the Duke of Wellington's Aides-de-Camp, came to ascertain how soon the Prussians might be expected.

Major Percy told us of the fall of Sir William Ponsonby, and the severe wound (or supposed death) of Colonel Frederick Ponsonby.

After a time we joined General Vandeleur's Brigade again to our right.

I may here mention that when we were thus moving to our right the day had improved, and whilst ourselves were less exposed to fire, we had a better view of the Action.

When with General Vandeleur's Brigade, we heard of the wound (then supposed mortal) of Colonel Hay of the 16th Light Dragoons.

Afterwards the 6th Brigade quitted General Vandeleur's and proceeded right in front, and passing a little to the rear, went on again more towards the right.

Brigade moved to the right.

About this time I believe Colonel Quentin, of the 10th, was wounded.

About the time we crossed the Genappe road there was a wonderful Column of French pouring down from their position.

But that Column could not have been engaged with the right of the British forces so soon as the period when we first replaced the Household Brigade in our position.

I mention this because I have been told that it was seven o'clock when we passed Lord Edward Somerset's Brigade, but I have no idea that it could be seven till some time afterwards.

The Brigade now began to tread the ground of devastation ; the pavement of the Genappe road was torn up and scattered.

Lord Edward Somerset's Brigade, strengthened by the addition of what had been Ponsonby's, was dwindled to two various Squadrons.

Reduced state of Somerset's and Ponsonby's Brigades.

General Vivian asked, " Lord Edward, where is your Brigade? " " Here," said Lord Edward. The ground was strewed with wounded, over whom it was hardly possible sometimes to avoid moving.

Wounded or mutilated horses wandered or turned in circles. The noise was deafening, and the air of ruin and desolation that prevailed wherever the eye could reach gave no inspiration of victory.

Lord Uxbridge, in Hussar uniform, mounted on a common troop-horse (his own being exhausted), rode with General Vivian a short time in our front.

Colonel Sir Felton Harvey came to exchange his

wounded horse, and in the act of mounting a troop horse of the 18th exclaimed, "Lord Wellington has won the Battle, if we could but get the d—d —— to advance." Then galloped to the front.

Advance of the Brigade at the Crisis.

We moved in column of half-Squadrons to the right, parallel to the position. Then wheeled the head of the Column to the left, so as to proceed perpendicularly to the front.

In the first part of this movement wounded British Infantry were lying on the ground, when we changed into the new direction; General Vandeleur's Brigade (I believe) on our right cheered.

We were cannonaded upon our right flank, and some casualty I think took place amongst the 10th, who were leading. I have an uncertain recollection, but believe it must have been somewhere about this time I saw Sir Colin Campbell.

See No. 74, p. 163.

As the fire, by which we were inconvenienced when about to form to our front, proceeded partly from our own Artillery's mistaking us when thus advanced, it was understood General Vivian had sent to remedy this mistake.

This was when the Brigade, after having moved from the left of the British position, was drawn up in support of the Infantry on the right of the Brussels-Genappe Road. —ED.

I cannot determine the time, nor exactly what we were doing, when some Nassau troops with white caps fell back upon us, and were forced forward, in which I remember my Adjutant instrumental; nor can I state when it was that I either heard myself, or was told at the moment, the Infantry was advancing. Perhaps it is not irrelevant to mention that when we were proceeding in column of half-Squadrons to the front, the earth thrown up by a cannon-shot falling under my horse struck me hard in the face and breast.

See No. 48, p. 98.

In forming line to our front some of the 23rd Light Dragoons and Germans came rapidly across, and the right Squadron of the 10th was attacked by Cuirassiers. Some casualty from fire happened too amongst the 18th.

General Vivian (who I think had then changed from his own horse to a grey troop-mare of the 10th) had just been giving directions with regard to our formation.

Ordering the 18th to remain where we were, the General went on with the 10th to direct their charge.

The charge of the 10th I believe was in a direction diverging to the right, and bringing their left shoulders forward. The 18th remained under fire, until Sir Hussey Vivian's return to them.

18th remain halted under fire during the charge of the 10th.

I remember Sergeant-Major Jeffs and others making use of the expression which General Vivian mentions* before we moved off to charge; the General being a great favourite with the 18th.

Where we stood in line there were (as I have reason to think) in our front French Artillery, Cavalry, and Infantry near us. General Vivian himself accompanied me to give me the original direction, and in that direction when put into it the Regiment proceeded onwards.

That direction diverged to the left (as the 10th charge had to the right), bringing our right shoulders forward.

See General Plan, No. 3.

It may be mentioned that I led from the centre Squadron in front of Captain Luard (who very ably commanded it), and whose coverer was Sergeant Colgan.

Charge of the 18th.

However slow the description of a charge of Cavalry, the grass has no time to grow under their horses' feet.

I understood that Major Harris was wounded in our charge, but when, I am not aware. His animation I well remember when things looked worst.

On proceeding onwards in the direction that had been given us for our charge, we soon crossed a *chaussée* or road (the horses clattering as they went over at a gallop). When coming from our left and slanting towards our right some French Artillery made a push to cross us at a gallop. But it would not do, we were on them (I ordered

They cross the *chaussée*.

---

* To the 18th I said: "Eighteenth, my lads, you will, I know, follow me"—on which the Sergeant-Major, Jeffs (afterwards Adjutant of the 7th), who was near me answered: "Yes, General, to h—ll if you will lead us."—*Extract from a letter by Sir H. Vivian.*

Intercepting
and taking
French Guns.

Closed with
the French
Cavalry.

The Enemy
routed.

the Guns to be secured, the drivers not hurt); when again
we were in with some Cavalry (on our right formed up,
Cuirassiers and other Cavalry, and, as I think, some Guns),
an Officer in front of them rode forward and fired at
me, but the 18th were among them with their swords.
The Enemy gave way and were forced over the
field.

The charge then ceased to be compact, for the assailants and those who were in retreat were intermingled
pell-mell, and that as hard as they could ride.

Diverging
nature of the
charge.

The Cavalry, in trying to escape, rather bore to their
right hand, than went quite straight to the rear. So that
the original direction of the 18th having been to the left,
and that direction (leaning down to intercept the French
Artillery coming from the left) having been still further
increased, was altered by a sudden swerve to the right
hand to attack the Cavalry formed to our right, and that
alteration more or less increased in pursuit. As this was
a chase, compactness was out of the question.

The 18th come
upon French
Infantry
retreating.

Coolness of
men of the
Old Guard.

But soon we came into ground entirely covered with
French Infantry retreating, not in a body, but individually,
yet with none of that hurry and confusion that might be
imagined when thus suddenly ridden in upon, and especially some of the Ancienne Garde might be remarked
for their coolness and bold countenance (one nearly
bayonetted me as I passed). Numbers of these were cut
down, and my Orderly (a man named Dwyer) cut down
five or six in rapid succession, the pursuit of the Cavalry
continuing.

Squares of
French
Infantry to
the right of
the line of the
charge.

The 18th first
pulled up.

On our right were some Squares of French Infantry,
but out of the stream of attack of the 18th as they
pressed on the heels of the Cavalry.

The first pull upon their horses was where a party of
the 18th, with Lieut. Woodberry I know (perhaps with
Lieut. Waldie), were well formed up. Though few, ready
and anxious to act.

The field they had passed was cleared, and a considerable distance had been traversed as hard as the horses

could go, and now they stood with some Squares of French on the opposite bank halted.

There was a dip or hollow in the ground between the party of the 18th and the Squares, perhaps a fence, but quite close.

The Squares so posted were inaccessible with any prospect of making impression upon them by even a much larger force of Cavalry than the party I have mentioned, especially with troop horses after so hard a gallop.

I moved them a little to the left, where the ground favoured them more, and others joined us.

However, as I was told that the signal had been given for us some time before to retire—as this was too close to the Enemy for forming up the Regiment after a charge, and nothing was immediately in our power to do—which was evident to all—I put them about in order to fall back upon our reserve.

The charge, as also the previous movements, had been attended with casualty, but retiring with a view to formation proved infinitely more destructive. For as the light was uncertain, they crossed upon some fire, whether the Enemy's or Prussians' (perhaps the latter), which mowed them down many at a time more than once.

In returning there was a party of men with me at first; so many fell I do not think another man remained. This happened near a barn or farm building on our right as we came back. I then joined others of the 18th, and the first person of the Brigade I met and spoke to was Sir Robert Gardiner [Capt. and Lieut.-Col. R.H.A.].

Lord Robert Manners was forming the 10th when the 18th came to form up with them; Major Grant, I remember, assisting me in doing so.

The attention having been directed to the Artillery on our left, it was more as the Cavalry formed on the right drew out in their escape that their description was observable to those who had charged them.

It must also be observed that there is not leisure

nor opportunity for remarking what is even at an inconsiderable distance whilst engaged in charge or pursuit.

Did not observe any British Infantry in the pursuit, being too far advanced.

I am not aware of having seen any British Infantry whilst we were employed in the pursuit. Where our pursuit ended I do not imagine that any of our Infantry could be in our front, that front being occupied by French Squares.

But not having been subsequently over the ground on which the Battle was fought, I cannot give any guess at the place where the charge which I was concerned in terminated, but that it was far from the place whence we had started for the charge there can be no doubt.

The various little occurrences I can call to mind would occupy some minutes, and the rate of going, taking divergence and check into calculation, must have been at the rate of ten miles an hour at the least, probably more.

The 10th and 18th formed up together, and after a time were moved still further to the right, and, the action having concluded, bivouacked.

The 1st Hussars were in reserve during the attack.

Sir H. Vivian addressed the Brigade in commendation of its conduct.

In the attack the 1st Hussars had been in reserve.

In the course of the day the Brigade had moved from left to the right.

Sir Hussey Vivian severally addressed the Regiments that night in commendation of their conduct.

.   .   .   .

HENRY MURRAY.

ROYAL ARTILLERY.

The whole of the British and German Artillery was under the command of Brevet-Colonel Sir George A. Wood, Kt., and the Horse Artillery was commanded by Lieut.-Colonel Sir Augustus Fraser, K.C.B.

The six Troops of Horse Artillery were at Waterloo detached from their respective Brigades of Cavalry, with one exception, that of Sir Robert Gardiner's, and, with the two reserve Troops, were generally employed as Batteries of position, so to speak. One of the five Field Batteries (Rogers's) was also moved away from its Division to other positions.

To avoid confusion, therefore, the letters from the Troops and Batteries of Artillery have all been placed together in one series, instead of being included with those of the Brigades or Divisions to which they belonged.

At Quatre Bras only two British Batteries were engaged, Lloyd's and Rogers's, the latter with Picton's Division near the left of the position, while the former at a critical period succeeded, with great loss, in silencing two French Batteries in the Bois de Bossu, and in forcing back into it a strong Column of French Infantry.

In the retreat on the 17th the Troops of Horse Artillery accompanied their Cavalry Brigades, frequently coming into action, and checking the advance of the French Cavalry. On the arrival of the rear of the Army at Waterloo, Lloyd's Battery (and Cleeve's of the King's German Legion) were employed in driving back some Columns of French Infantry which were approaching too close to the position.

At Waterloo Gardiner's Troop remained all day with Vivian's Cavalry Brigade, accompanying it in the General Advance at the end of the day.

Rogers's Battery, after being engaged in resisting D'Erlon's first attack on Picton's Division, was moved to the right of the main road, and finally assisted in the repulse of the French Imperial Guard.

The Rocket Sections of Whinyates' Troop supported the charge of Ponsonby's Cavalry against D'Erlon's Columns, and subsequently his Guns remained in position in front of Kempt's Infantry Brigade, and were more or less in action for the remainder of the day.

Ross's Troop was at first posted on the crest of the Position in rear of La Haye Sainte with two Guns on the Main Road, but on the loss of that farmhouse and its surroundings, it was obliged to move more to the right.

In the adjoining plan I have endeavoured to indicate the positions of the remaining Troops and Batteries on the right of the Main Road, as far as can be gathered from the replies to the Circular Letter, and the situations indicated by the writers on the plan that accompanied it, and which positions varied but little during the course of the day.

As a rule, they were stationed along the crest of the position in front of the Infantry, and their fire was directed upon the assaulting Columns of French Cavalry and Infantry from the period of their formation until their near approach compelled the Artillerymen to abandon their Guns for the moment, and to take refuge in or behind the Infantry Squares.

One remarkable exception to the latter proceeding was that of Mercer's Troop, which two or three times, by its own unaided fire, repelled the charges of French Cavalry upon it.

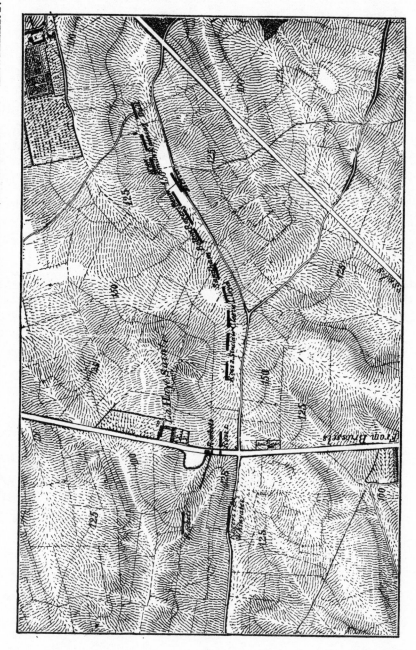

During the intervals between these attacks the fire of the Guns was mainly directed against the French Batteries.

In the General Advance, most of such Troops and Batteries, or portions of them, as were in a condition to be moved, joined in it, and took advantage of favourable opportunities for opening their fire upon the retreating French.

Numbers 80, 81, and 98 refer to the march on Quatre Bras.

Numbers 98, 100, and 101 to Quatre Bras.

Numbers 80, 81, 85, and 98 to the Retreat on the 17th; and all the Letters, except No. 101, to Waterloo.

COLONEL SIR JOHN MAY, K.C.B.

Lieut.-Colonel, Assist. Adjutant-General Royal Artillery.

MEMORANDUM.   *Woolwich, Dec. 24th,* 1834.   No. 77.

.   .   .   .

At the middle and end of the day, the British Horse Artillery was much with the Cavalry, to which it was attached. The Reserve Horse Artillery on the ridge of the hill, and the Troops and Brigades* attached to Infantry Divisions were with the same under the Generals commanding.

Towards, however, the latter end of the day even the Artillery in the second line were ordered to the front, and the whole so disposed of on the ridge as to play upon the immense close Column of Foot Guards advancing, and constituting the last effort of the French.

As the Artillery were shifted according to circumstances,

Waterloo.

Positions of the Artillery.

Towards the end of the day the Artillery in 2nd line ordered to the front.

And to play upon the Imperial Guard.

---

* At the period of Waterloo Horse Artillery Batteries were called Troops, Field Batteries either Brigades or Batteries of Foot Artillery.
—Ed.

BULL'S TROOP.

it would (if it were even possible) create much confusion in detailing their situations on the ground.

. . . .

No one person can speak correctly about the movements of the Artillery throughout the day. The Officers, or Captains commanding Troops and Brigades (who survive), if referred to, will be the best able to point out their several positions at different periods of the day, and the Field Officers commanding the same may throw much light on the subject.

ROYAL HORSE ARTILLERY.

MAJOR BULL'S TROOP.—HEAVY 5½-INCH HOWITZERS.

CAPTAIN AND BREVET-MAJOR R. BULL, R.H.A.

TO LIEUT.-COLONEL SIR AUGUSTUS FRASER, K.C.B., COMMANDING
ROYAL HORSE ARTILLERY.

No. 78.
June 24th, 1815.

Waterloo.

SIR,—Having received your directions through Lieut.-Colonel Macdonald to render a report of the manner in which the Troop of Horse Artillery under my command was employed during the Battle of the 18th inst., I beg to

At first formed on the right flank of Ponsonby's Cavalry Brigade.

inform you we were ordered from our bivouac at half-past eight o'clock a.m., and formed on the right flank of the Heavy Brigade of Cavalry, commanded by the late Major-General Sir William Ponsonby, K.C.B., to the left of the road leading from Waterloo to Genappe, where we remained

Ordered to the right by Lord Uxbridge.

Came into action on the height in rear of Hougoumont.

Dislodged the Enemy from the wood of Hougoumont.

about an hour, when we moved by order of Lieut.-General the Earl of Uxbridge to the heights on the right of our first line, and immediately came into action with spherical case shot with the intention of dislodging the Enemy's Infantry from the left of the small wood and the garden and the farm called Hougoumont adjoining, and at about 1,000 yards' distance from our front, in which I have reason to believe we succeeded, for our Infantry were enabled to enter the wood.

We then ceased firing for a few minutes by order of the Commander of the Forces on account of our troops occupying the wood, but on the Enemy reinforcing it, and again obliging them to retire, we recommenced our fire, and in a short time our Infantry again entered it, reinforced by another Regiment, when we directed our Guns on some strong Columns of Infantry in rear and support of the wood with common and spherical shells, which immediately caused them to retrograde.

Fired on strong Columns in rear of the wood.

The Guns opposed to us at this time were about sixteen in number, twelve in our front and four on our right flank beyond and above the before-mentioned farm on the road to Lillois, and when we obliged their Columns of Infantry to move, they brought up six more Guns in our front, all of which were well served, and annoyed us considerably. It was from one of the flanking Guns that Major Cairnes was unfortunately killed, a few minutes after we got into our position.

French Guns opposed to the Troop.

Major Cairnes killed.

We continued in this situation firing on their Guns and Columns until near two o'clock, when we ceased firing and received an order to retire the Troop, and form on the right of Major Ramsay's in the second line to enable us to repair our casualties and complete our ammunition. Whilst thus employed Lieutenant Smith, two men, and two horses were wounded. As soon as everything was completed we moved forward with Major Ramsay's Troop to resume our former position in the front line, but at that instant the first charge of the Enemy's Cavalry took place against our first line, and we formed and got into action between the Squares of Infantry of the second line.

Ceased firing at 2 p.m., and moved to the rear to complete ammunition.

Lieut. Smith wounded.

Moved forward again.

First charge of French Cavalry on British right.

As soon as their attack was repulsed we again attempted to regain our former position, but the second charge of the Enemy's Cavalry took place at the instant of our getting up, and we had only to prepare to defend ourselves with our swords from another situation on the side of the hill; but as the Enemy's Cavalry were again driven back we followed them, and once more got into action on our original ground in front of the wood, but about

Second charge of French Cavalry.

Got into action 200 yards in front of original position.

two hundred yards further advanced, Major Ramsay's Troop firing on our left, from which position we maintained a most severe cannonade as well as receiving the fire of the Infantry from the Column protecting the retreat of their Cavalry, which latter, however, lasted but a short time. The Guns on our right galling us extremely, I directed Lieutenant Louis to turn his two Guns towards them, and we shortly succeeded in silencing them, which, as they enfiladed our position from the right, was of considerable advantage to us during the remainder of the day.

Lieut. Louis's two Guns silenced the French flanking Guns beyond and to the right of Hougoumont.

About this time I myself was wounded, and from feeling much pain and losing a good deal of blood I went to the rear to have my arm tied up. During my absence (about half an hour), Lieutenant Louis maintained the same ground, and shortly after my return the advance and attack of our Army took place, and we advanced in support of them, as far as the eligibility of the ground would admit.

Major Bull wounded.

Returns to the Troop.

It was shortly after my return to the Troop that some of my Guns being short of ammunition, several of my men volunteered to assist Major Ramsay's Guns on our left. The early part of the morning our Guns being directed against the wood, the natural effect could not be so well distinguished, but on inspecting the ground afterwards it fully justified the opinion we had formed of it in the morning.

The effect of our Guns upon the Enemy's Column was plain and decisive; and Major Ramsay on our left, who could see it more accurately than ourselves, sent me word some of the shells opened a perfect lane through them; one in particular strewed the ground on the opposite side of the Column. I have also reason to think our fire on their Artillery had its effect, particularly on the two enfilading Guns on our right. Our fire on their Cavalry appeared to add considerably to their confusion whilst retiring.

The effects of the Troop's Guns.

I believe I have now stated, as nearly as possible,

the manner in which the Troop under my command were
employed during the whole period of the Battle. We
remained on the field until ordered to march at 3 p.m., on
the 19th.

Of the conduct of the Officers and men I think it Conduct of Officers and men.
unnecessary to add more to the statement already given
in; nothing could surpass their coolness and steadiness
throughout the day, or their cheerfulness whenever called
upon for particular exertion. I beg to add that the
effect of the spherical shells generally appeared very Effects of spherical shell.
great, and I observed but two shells out of the number
fired that did not burst well.

ROBERT BULL,
Commanding 1st Troop.

LIEUT.-COL. WEBBER-SMITH'S TROOP.—LIGHT 6-POUNDERS.

MAJOR-GENERAL J. WEBBER-SMITH, C.B., R.A.
CAPTAIN AND BREVET-LIEUT.-COLONEL R.H.A.

Dublin, August 29th [? 1835].   No. 79.
Waterloo.

I first came into action in the field near Hougoumont
with my right close to the road and a little in front of the
sunken road. Bull was then very much to my left, being
on the ridge above the orchard. When I had got my
harness, &c., &c., in order in the hollow way I got into
position a little to the left of Bull.

I think Ramsay was between us, and no charge or
attack of Cavalry had taken place before I was in action
there.

Believe, &c.,
J. WEBBER-SMITH.

LIEUT.-COLONEL E. Y. WALCOTT, R.H.A.

CAPTAIN R.H.A.

No. 80.   *Winckton, Ringwood, January 18th, 1835.*

. . . .

16th June.
Marched on
Quatre Bras.

Marched on the morning of the 16th June, 1815, with Lieut.-Colonel Webber-Smith's Troop of Royal Horse Artillery, of which I was Second Captain, from Haltert, a small village near Alost, to join the advanced posts of the Army.   Troop reached Quatre Bras about ten o'clock

17th June.
Arrived at
10 a.m., and
joined Grant's
Cavalry
Brigade.
Retreat on
17th.

a.m., Saturday the 17th.   Troop joined the Brigade of Cavalry it was attached to under the command of M.-General Sir Colquhoun Grant, consisting of the 7th Hussars, 15th Hussars, and 2nd German Light Dragoons.

Detached with
two Guns
during the
retreat.

The remainder of this day I was detached with *two* Guns of the Troop, and retired into the position on which the Battle of Waterloo was fought, with the right of the Cavalry.

Waterloo.

Sunday, June 18th, 1815.

At 11 a.m. I rejoined my Troop, then under arms, close to the road leading from Nivelles to Brussels and a little to the rear and left of Hougoumont.   At half-past eleven o'clock the Enemy showed himself in considerable force,

Troop ordered
into action in
support of
Hougoumont.

and threatened the Château of Hougoumont.   Lieut.-Colonel Webber-Smith's Troop was ordered into position to protect the château and the Enemy came on in force. We (the Troop) continued hotly engaged and suffered severely from a Battery in support of the attack, until the French troops arrived in close action with the troops in the grounds of the château, the buildings of which and the trees surrounding it prevented our longer annoying

Retired in rear
of right of
first line.

the Enemy, in consequence of which the Troop was withdrawn, and remained a short time in rear of the right of the first line.

I cannot recollect hours, but the Troop had been but a very short time so posted when it was ordered to join the position of the Troops of Horse Artillery immediately in front. From this spot I for the first time saw the whole position of the French and their attacking Columns coming on. No sooner had the Troop got into action, having on its right Lieut.-Colonel Bull's and Major Ramsay's Troops, and on its left Captain Mercer's, than a Column of the Enemy's Cavalry came directly towards us. From the nature of the ground, and to protect the British Infantry from the fire of the Enemy's Artillery, they were formed in squares behind us on the slope of the undulating hill, the crest of which we occupied. These Squares consisted of the Guards, and I believe German Legion.

Ordered to join other Troops, R.H.A., in front line.

Attacked by French Cavalry.

That magnificent order which directed the Artillery-men, when from the closeness of the Enemy they could no longer fire canister, to leave their Guns in position and fall back in a line with the Squares did not reach my ears, and I continued directing a Gun of the Troop, till looking up when it was ready, I found the skirmishers of the attack-ing Column, French Imperial Guard—for they had not the cuirass, and wore black fur caps—close upon me. Two of them contrived to upset me, and when up again seeing [? saw] all my men in a line with the Squares, and the Squares ready to advance, our absence from the Guns en-abling them to do so freely, as well as to fire and resist Cavalry without killing us. I cannot recollect whether on this occasion the Column topped the hill or not, but no sooner was the demonstration over than we rejoined the Guns, which were again in full play.

Ordered to leave Guns in position, and the gunners retire to the protection of the Infantry.

Capt. Walcott upset by the Grenadiers à Cheval.

Soon after this attack a second, much more serious, was made by Cavalry supported by Infantry. On this occasion the same fine manoeuvre was resorted to. The French Cavalry came right through the line of Guns, and so far to the rear as to kill and wound men and horses of the Troops of Artillery with the *limbers* and *ammunition* carriages of those Guns in action on the crest of the hill. The French Infantry followed quick the attack of the Cavalry. The Artillerymen fell back. The Squares of Infantry advanced, and gloriously driving back the

Second attack of French Cavalry sup-ported by Infantry.

GARDINER'S TROOP.

attacking Columns, gave us the opportunity of playing over the heads of our own, and *into* the retiring and beaten mass of the Enemy.

Another similar attack.

Another similar attack being made, the day continued more or less wildly, and much more severe towards our left until the last attack of the French. The last shots made by Webber-Smith's Troop, and the expenditure of all our ammunition then immediately with us, were directed into the head of this last attacking Column of the Enemy towards our left.

And the final attack of the Imperial Guard.

Lieut.-Colonel Webber-Smith's Troop was not ordered in pursuit. At half past nine p.m. I received orders to collect a list of killed, wounded, and casualties of the several Troops of Horse Artillery stationed in the different parts of the field, and a most interesting sight it was, and at half-past two a.m., on a tired trooper (my charger being taken prisoner) and a *lost shoe,* after plenty of brandy from both *Prussians* and British, I made my report to Colonel Sir Augustus Fraser, my commanding officer.

Capt. Walcott sent to collect a list of the casualties in the Horse Artillery.

Ever, &c.,

E. Y. WALCOTT.

LIEUT.-COLONEL SIR ROBERT GARDINER'S (K.C.B.) TROOP. LIGHT 6-POUNDERS.

CAPT. W. B. INGILBY, R.H.A.

LIEUTENANT R.H.A.

No. 81.

Woolwich, April 25th, 1838.

16th June.

Temath, June 16th. Marched before daylight, orders having been given in the night to place ourselves on the great road between Ninove and Alost. A fresh order while on the march directed us to proceed to Enghien. At Enghien we were joined by, or met with, the main body of the Cavalry, and were finally ordered to be attached to Sir H. Vivian's Brigade of Hussars. We bivouacked

Troop marches on Quatre Bras.

Attached to Vivian's Cavalry Brigade.

late in the evening at Braine-le-Comte; there was a heavy cannonade in front.

Some of the Cavalry Regiments pushed on for the purpose of getting into the field. We must have marched this day between fifty and sixty miles by a most irregular and circuitous route, which must show how uncertain the Duke must have been of the movements of the Enemy. At night a drizzling rain came on.

17th. We marched before daylight, passed through Nivelles, meeting many wounded on the road, and arrived at Quatre Bras, where the affair of yesterday had been. The whole Army was gradually and successively arriving, and the French appeared in considerable force in our front. About noon Lord Arthur Hill, Aide-de-Camp to the Duke, mentioned that the Prussians had been defeated, and that their Army was in retreat. In the afternoon there appeared a considerable bustle among the Enemy's troops in our front, as if preparing for a move. The whole of our Infantry at this time were moving off to a position we understood to be a few miles to our rear.

17th June.
Arrival at Quatre Bras.

The Cavalry formed in three lines : the Hussars in the first line, the Light Cavalry in the second, and in the third line the Heavy Cavalry. It suddenly became insufferably hot and close, and the sun became absolutely darkened by a very black cloud, while at the same time a heavy cloud of dust rising, showed the advance of a very large body of Cavalry coming to reinforce the Enemy ; they came from a direction on the right of the Enemy.

Retreat on 17th.

I had heard the same Aide-de-Camp say that Lord Uxbridge had positive orders not to have an affair of Cavalry.

The French Cavalry I have before adverted to now advanced boldly in great force, and for some time partially under cover of a wood, until their vedettes fired on our front line. We commenced a cannonade, which was promptly returned, and as the Enemy continued to advance and, I think, had commenced a deployment, an affair seemed inevitable.

Troop's Guns open on the French Cavalry.

The interest and even silence, until the Guns and skirmishers opened, up to this moment was intense, for it was not generally known that the Cavalry General was to avoid an affair.

The retreat of the British Cavalry begins.

At the last moment the order was given, and the whole commenced a rapid retreat in three Columns and by different roads. At this instant the heavy black cloud broke with a tremendous clap of thunder and torrent of rain. We formed the left Column in retreat. The road and ground became so quickly deluged with the heavy rain that was falling, that it became impracticable for the French Cavalry to press our Column in any force. In fact, out of the road in the track of our own Cavalry, the ground was poached into a complete puddle. Seeing this, and having lost the shoe from off a Gun horse, I halted and had it put on in spite of some skirmishers who began to press on us, but were kept at bay by our own skirmishers forming as if to charge them. This will show how impracticable it was for them to press us on this cross road. But at this moment I could see the centre Column on the main road on my right, and they apparently charging, accompanied with much cheering. (This was the affair of the 7th Hussars, who were not successful, but the matter was retrieved by the Life Guards.) In our Column not a man was lost. The retreat for the Guns the whole way, with the exception of the Gun mentioned, was at a hard gallop for six or seven miles until we came upon the Infantry, in and getting into position. The rain continued very heavy throughout the night.

The thunderstorm, after which the ground became so saturated that the French Cavalry could not press on in force.

At this moment saw the engagement on the main road between the 7th Hussars and the French.

The Guns retreated at a gallop to the position at Waterloo.

Lieut. Ingilby ordered to search for a line of retreat for Vivian's Brigade, in case of necessity, through the wood of Soignies, and parallel to the Brussels road.

The same night I received instructions to set out by times in the morning to find a practicable road which should lead parallel to the main road, and through the wood of Soignies and by the left of Brussels, so that in case of further retreat Sir Hussey's Brigade might retire covering the left flank of the Army.

18th. I left the bivouac just at dawn, and succeeded in making myself acquainted with a road practicable for our light Guns (six-pounders) and Cavalry. At a village

I fell in with a body of four or five hundred Prussians, At a village evidently of different Corps, and seemingly fugitives; how- falls in with ever, they appeared as if collecting to march in the sians (?). direction of the cannonade, which was commencing to be rather heavy. Numberless of the peasants had taken and were taking refuge in the wood of Soignies, with their women and children, cattle, pigs, sheep, and whatever valuables they could carry off. I went into Brussels; the streets were wholly deserted, except by the wounded that Deserted state were straggling in from the Cavalry affair of yesterday of Brussels. and at Quatre Bras the day before; many were lying and seated about the steps of the houses as if unable to proceed further in search of a hospital. I managed to get a hasty breakfast in the Hotel d'Angleterre with a gentleman anxious for news, and who proved to be Admiral Malcolm. I carried off a cold fowl for the Troop, who I knew had nothing, and which I reached about half- Returned to past ten o'clock, and immediately proceeded to make my 10.30 a.m., report to Sir Hussey Vivian. I found Sir William and made his Delancy with him, and it was at this time I became Vivian. acquainted with the instructions he was receiving from the Duke of Wellington, through Sir William Delancy, for the operations of his Brigade during the day.

.   .   .   .

Believe, &c.,

W. B. INGILBY.

FROM THE SAME.

Island Bridge, November 20th, 1834.   No. 82.

.   .   .   .

Sir William Delancy was with Sir H. Vivian, and I   Waterloo. learned the ultimate position of the Brigade was to be on the extreme left of the Line, and that Sir H. Vivian would be in communication with the Prussians, for whom a look-out was to be kept, and who would arrive on our left.

At about eleven o'clock Sir H. Vivian moved his

This must refer to the advanced pickets in and about Smohain. *See* No. 75, p. 170. —ED.

Brigade forward in observation, and shortly after, about noon, the French Columns, which in the meanwhile had crowned the opposite heights, were in motion, and making a simultaneous push forward, neared our whole Line, and immediately the Battle commenced by a heavy cannonade from both sides. The right Column of the French was almost abreast with Sir H. Vivian before he retrograded and took his position in the general Line, on the extreme left of the whole Allied Army.

We could at this time distinguish a stationary picket or a patrol of Prussians, with our glasses, at a considerable distance, on an eminence to our left.

Some Nassau troops were a little in advance, occupying the hedge rows in our front, and near the village of Papelotte, supported by the fire of three or four Guns. To the right we could see a considerable way along the front of our Army. Immediately to our right was a round height (Mount St. Jean), on the slope of which, and adjoining Sir H. Vivian, was the German Legion and their Artillery.

Vincke's and Best's Hanoverians.

D'Erlon's first attack on Picton.

The cannon of both Armies after commencing maintained a continued roar, and the French having a very long line of Guns at their right centre, near the main road, soon after, supported by the fire from this Battery, advanced a Column of Infantry, shouting " *Vive l'Empereur,*" and attacked the line along the whole face of Mount St. Jean.

Charge of Ponsonby's Brigade.

Our troops recoiled, and some Highlanders were in confusion; but the thick rolling fire of the musketry, adding to the smoke from the Artillery, I could not perceive the further result until after a time, when a Brigade of our Cavalry appeared charging and to carry all before them, and the Infantry, apparently then relieved of the pressure of the attack, again advanced and resumed its first ground. A body of French Cavalry, having a second (which appeared clothed in red) in support, proceeded diagonally from the right of the French Army to aid their repulsed and seeming routed Infantry.

Our Cavalry (Sir William Ponsonby's Brigade) also advanced diagonally to their left, and then charging the French in line and in the greatest order, completely overthrew them and appeared to annihilate the French Cavalry. An inconsiderable party of Sir William Ponsonby's Brigade after this success, or in continuation of the charge, wheeled to their right and rode amongst the Guns of the right flank of the great French Battery, and kept undisturbed possession of them for a quarter of an hour or twenty minutes, and as they abandoned them again, apparently only at their leisure (for the red Column of French Dragoons fairly trotted to their rear, and left their front line to its fate), we remarked had those brave men been furnished with spikes and acquainted with their use, several of the Guns of the great Battery could have been rendered useless the rest of the day.

This must refer to the advance of Vandeleur's Brigade. *See* No. 57, p. 113. —ED.

Although as I had learned when in Sir William Delancy's presence that Sir H. Vivian's Brigade was not to engage, and be kept entire, until the arrival of the Prussians, the desire to assist Sir William Ponsonby seemed irresistible, therefore Sir R. Gardiner advanced with two Guns, and being myself included with them, the slope of the ground also favouring, I had a clear and very near view of the charge. The ground, however, was so saturated with the rain, and so little capable of bearing the horses without sinking up to their girths nearly, that we had some trouble in bringing the Guns into action at all; but scarcely had we opened a fire, when a shell from the great French Battery (which from its elevated position and large calibre of the Guns directed an accurate fire) blew up, by passing through the ammunition boxes of one of the two Guns. The French set up a general Hurrah and *Vive l'Empereur* at this explosion. The charge being over, the Guns rejoined the Troop, and the limber was replaced complete from a waggon.

Two Guns of the Troop advanced.

On coming into action the ammunition boxes of one of the Guns blown up by the French Artillery fire.

The weather was still dull and wet. The cannonade mixed with musketry never intermitting, it was only occasionally when the wind freshening and partially cleared away the smoke, that other charges of the Cavalry and movements in both Armies, and the Infantry in columns or squares, and then again in line firing volleys or in a continuous roll, could be distinguished, amidst which the Hurrahs and shouts of *Vive l'Empereur* were frequently revived.

The position of Sir H. Vivian, and consequently of Sir R. Gardiner's Troop of Horse Artillery, continued stationary on the left, during which several announcements were made by Prussian Officers, sent on for the purpose, of the arrival of their Army ; and on the other hand two or three times Officers from the Duke's Staff came to ascertain if their troops had actually made their appearance. Nothing more was yet visible of them but their fixed picket in the distance. At length, however, about 5 o'clock, the advance of a Prussian Corps did make its appearance, hurrying up in a direction to pass the village of Papelotte.

Announcements of arrivals of the Prussians.

At 5 o'clock a Prussian Corps appeared.

The French up to this time, upon the whole, had succeeded so far, that it was on a plain or flat in advance of the ground on which they had commenced the Battle their line now fired from—but their numbers were evidently greatly diminished, as well as our Line, for by closing in as the ranks became thinned, a large space was left between the right of Sir H. Vivian's and the left of the German Legion.

Up to this time the French had a certain amount of success.

The Prussian Corps, when their front had halted, in contact with the French skirmishers, arriving in successive straggling and broken parties, gradually formed, and at about six o'clock (not being then in any great strength or sufficiently collected) made a brisk advance perpendicular to the French Army to attack its right. The French had perceived the arrival of the Prussians, and we saw them prepare for this attack by wheeling some troops to the right from their Reserves, and taking Guns from the right of their great Battery. They then advanced against the Prussians and very quickly repulsed them. This took place exactly in our front, but without the effectual range of our 6-pounders, and as the slope of the ground des-

About 6 o'clock the Prussian Corps attacked the French right.

But were quickly repulsed.

cended [? ascended] towards us, we had a flank bird's-eye
view of both the Prussians and French in their movements,
and that Corps of Prussians made no further progress,
or any effort that I saw, during the remainder of the
Battle.

The weather now took up, and it became a very
fine afternoon. Matters did not appear advanced either
way.

About half-past seven o'clock Sir H. Vivian made a
circuit to his right and placed his Brigade in line, about 20
paces in rear of the Infantry in front of Mt.-St.-Jean,
and thus formed in two lines, the whole steadily advanced
to attack. This movement of Sir H. Vivian's Brigade
gave rise for a moment to misgiving as to the result of
the Battle, that it was to cover the retreat of the Army.
From the details, casually heard in the presence of Sir
William Delancy, I expressed a different expectation,
which was soon proved. For some while we could see
nothing whatever from behind the Infantry (which advanced slowly, step by step) on account of the dense smoke
from their musketry.

This account, including that of the final advance, differs from all the others from Vivian's Brigade.—ED.

The advance of this Infantry was admirable. By-and-
bye they ceased to fire, broke from line into open column,
and Sir H. Vivian's Brigade quickly passed through
the intervals. We had now the French in full view
before us, completely routed and flying, in the greatest
confusion.

Sir Robert Gardiner brought his Guns to fire upon the
fugitive crowd instantly, and from that period acted independently from the Brigade of Cavalry, alternately
advancing rapidly and halting to fire, whenever we found
we had a clear front from our Cavalry (which charged in
separate bodies or divisions, and frequently became mixed
with the French) and the beginning (more than dusk) of the
evening permitted.

The Troop fires on the French fugitives,

As we commenced our pursuit, at about half-past eight
o'clock, a Prussian Corps arriving near the spot Sir H.
Vivian had occupied during the day, their Horse Artillery

And by mistake is fired on by a Prussian Battery.

opened a fire, and by mistake directed two or three shots upon us at a moment the Troop was limbering up to move forward. However, as the Prussians had never probably seen British troops before, it was not extraordinary that they should take us to be the Enemy in the *pêle-mêle* sort of confusion that was presented to their view at first coming up. Previous to this and as we first emerged from behind the Infantry, we could perceive another fire of

The Prussians at Planchenoit.

Artillery in the direction of Planchenoit, which had opened upon the right rear of the French. These were Prussians also, so that there appeared three Corps or bodies of Prussians on the Field at this time. The first had been easily kept in check, and the two last appeared too late to be actually aiding in the Battle, but as their approach when perceived (requiring to be provided against) at a critical juncture added to the difficulties of the French, it probably deprived them of every hope of withstanding the attack we had already commenced.

State of the field after the Battle.

In traversing the field, following the flight of the French, it was hardly possible to clear with the Guns the bodies of both Armies which strewed the ground, and afterwards late at night (the Troop had halted in bivouac near the wooden observatory at about half-past ten o'clock) when despatched to bring up some ammunition waggons, it was with difficulty we could avoid crushing many of the wounded on the road near La Haye Sainte, that had crawled there in hopes of more ready assistance. There were some in whom life was not yet extinct that we supposed the French Artillery had crushed by passing over in their retreat.

I may add a remark in confirmation of the necessity for the allowance offered in your Circular, that on the foregoing occasion, when I rejoined the Troop and stated how numerous I found the dead and wounded throughout every

At first it was not realised by the Troop that a great Victory had been gained.

part of the field I had passed over, and that I had seen full 50 Guns abandoned by the French, and then hazarded an opinion that we must have won a great Battle, there was thought to be some exaggeration, so little confident did we feel as subordinate actors on the spot, in our capability at once and immediately to estimate to its full extent the magnitude of the event we had a part in achieving.   .   .

And have, &c.,

W. B. INGILBY,

Captain R.H.A.

MAJOR E. C. WHINYATES' TROOP.—LIGHT 6-POUNDERS AND ROCKETS.

COLONEL E. C. WHINYATES, C.B., K.H., R.A.

BREVET-MAJOR R.H.A.

TO COLONEL SIR HEW ROSS, K.C.B., DEPT. ADJUTANT-GENERAL R.A.

Carlisle, March 10th, 1841.   No. 83.

MY DEAR SIR HEW,—

.   .   .   .

When the bugles of the Army sounded the turn-out my Troop, with others of the Horse Artillery, assembled on the low ground behind the position on the left of the road leading to La Belle Alliance, and there awaited orders. The men were dismounted, and stood near their horses.

Waterloo

I was in front of my Troop when I observed a stir amongst the Cavalry. I was personally advanced before the line of Cavalry, but not in its front, and watched with interest the General of Cavalry making the preparation. My Troop was further back than the Dragoons, but I should certainly say not in their rear.

Position of the Troop in the morning.

I suddenly received a communication that the Cavalry was going to advance, and that I was to move forward. Whether at this moment my men were on or off their horses I do not recollect, but as they were alert, active, and knew their business well, that would make very little difference. I moved forward.

Ordered to move forward with Ponsonby's Cavalry Brigade. 1st Charge.

The Cavalry in all probability had the start, having been prepared before I received my order, and they certainly were across the *chemin creux* before us, as a hollow road with two banks and two hedges would require a little examination and consideration where and how to pass it with Guns, and the greatest care to avoid accidents. At this

On arriving at the Wavre Road, ordered to leave the Guns and move forward with the Rocket Sections.

moment, however, Colonel Macdonald of the Horse Artillery came up, and ordered me to leave my Guns and advance with the Rocket Sections, which I did, down the slope in front of the position until the ground on the

Advanced to a favourable position.

French side gave a more favourable chance of effectual rocket practice.

In passing over this ground there were no English or French Dragoons, at least I saw none; there were a few French Infantry* soldiers laying about and asking quarter.

Fired some ground rockets.

On dismounting to fire the ground rockets some very high grain crops interposed and screened the Enemy's line, and after firing some discharges of rockets I received an order to rejoin the position. The Troop accordingly moved back,

Rejoined the Guns.

steadily and in perfect order and unpursued, and rejoined their Guns.

I remember in going down the slope I saw a Guidon, or Flag or Colour near a Frenchman, and though most anxious to get possession of it, I proceeded rapidly on to come into action. I mention this to show that when the mind is intent, and engrossed by such paramount duties, it is not likely that the observation can wander to that which is only of subsequent interest. The Guidon was close to my horse's feet.

Troop had advanced clear of the Cavalry,

According to my recollection of circumstances (passed so long ago) the Troop, from the moment of getting into motion, moved straight forward clear of the Cavalry, who were to my left (for I should not have advanced in rear of Cavalry when an open space was on their flank, for if they wanted my support they would have masked my Guns, or, if checked, the Dragoons would have been amongst and crippled us); it may, however, have inclined to the left or right, actuated by circumstances of ground, or the

And other troops.

position of troops in its way, or in nearing the hedge to

---

* I thought they were Infantry.

convenient openings in it. Or it may not have been parallel originally to the position. I do not at all know where the Dutch Battery had been placed, or the relative position of other Batteries; events passed rapidly, and we did and occupied what seemed most advantageous and eligible.

The high growing corn through which we fired the rockets gave no indication, that I am aware of, of Cavalry having passed through it, and I never heard that the rockets went amongst the English Dragoons, which I think I should have done had the case been so.

The above relation will perhaps answer in some way the points inquired about, and remarks on them; but to speak more specifically to Mr. Siborne's inquiries (which are about six), I should say, in regard to his first paragraph and question, "Whether some little interval of time did not elapse between the charge of Cavalry and discharge of rockets?" that time did elapse and must have been occupied in forming the Sections and moving down the slopes, and that the Cavalry must have been well engaged before any rockets were fired, but I cannot say that the Dragoons were then retiring as Mr. Siborne suggests; indeed from the quickness with which everything was performed I am led to think they were not, though they might have been. Colonel Macdonald might have seen them retiring, I did not.

The Troop did not advance at the same moment as the Cavalry.

The next reference is Captain F. Warde's letter. My opinion was that the foregoing transactions were from one to two hours earlier in the day, and with respect to the French Brigade of Cavalry (whether they were Lancers or Cuirassiers I do not know) stated to have been put into disorder, the only observation I can make is that they did not follow us, and that about five or six years ago I was told that a Major of English Dragoons was left wounded near the French line, and that he had said he heard the rockets passing and the French swearing (in their way) at them, and the English for wishing to burn them alive, and that they did not like them at all.

See No. 86, p. 210.

Effect of the Rockets on the French.

Troop
directed its
Guns on some
French
Artillery with
effect.

Some French Guns were annoying, causing us casualties, which obliged the Troop to direct their attention to them, when they became much less troublesome. I had not an opportunity of seeing that Battery at the close of the day. I regret I cannot give any remarks that can be satisfactory to Mr. Siborne as he requests me to do, for I did not see the French Artillery gallop into action, but it seems probable that the checking of the Brigade of Enemy's Cavalry must have been about the period the rockets were discharged, but I will not assume or presume that it was checked by rockets. Captain F. Warde says "soon after coming into position." I should have written this, "*on* coming to the position," &c.

Two Guns of
the Troop sent
to the *abatis*
on the main
road.

The two Guns of the Troop were not sent to the *abatis* until after the charge of the Cavalry (Ponsonby's Brigade) and the return of the Rocket Troop to their Guns after firing.

The last paragraph of Mr. Siborne's letter is replied to in the commencement of mine. If on nearing the position Major Rogers's Battery, or any other description of troops had been, or were directly in my front, I should have been obliged to find open space for my Guns, and not have proceeded to ground already occupied. My object, of course, was to get forward and be useful. In the first page of Mr. Siborne's letter, he supposes the case that the Rocket Sections "advanced down the slope simultaneously with the Cavalry." They did not so advance. They did not after coming to the position move simultaneously with the Cavalry at all.

In advancing,
no Guns or
other troops
in his front.

Did not
advance
simultane-
ously with the
Cavalry.

．　　．　　．　　．　　．　　．　　．

I am, &c.,

E. C. WHINYATES.

FROM THE SAME.

Carlisle, 20th November, 1842. No. 84.

. . . .

In answer to the question, " Had you a certain number *Personnel* of the Rocket Troop. of men employed *exclusively* in managing the rockets, in addition to the ordinary numbers attached to other Troops? and if so what was the probable amount of that additional strength?" I have to state that the mounted Rocket Sections were also Gun Detachments and were *not* exclusively employed in managing rockets.

When Colonel Macdonald ordered the advance with rockets all the Gun Detachments (except the two dismounted men at each Gun, who are called limber gunners, and which two are carried on the limbers and have no horses) left their Guns behind them and moved quickly, Method of coming into action. being on horseback, down the slope in front of their Guns. When halted and brought into action, they dismounted from their horses to fire *ground* rockets, that is rockets not laid at angles of elevation, but rockets that ricochéd along the ground. There were crops of high standing grain in front of the Rocket Sections when the men dismounted, which screened all objects in front, and the rockets were fired through them in the direction of the Enemy's troops in position.

. . . .

With respect to the costume and equipment of the Costume and equipment. Rocket Troop at the Battle of Waterloo, the men were dressed like the Horse Artillery, viz.: with a laced jacket (having three rows of buttons in front) and helmet. Their appointments (both of horse and man), however, differed from those of the Horse Artillery. They had a pouch belt, which the Horse Artillery had not. Each mounted man carried a fasces of three or four rocket sticks in a bucket in a manner similar to the mode lances and Dragoon carbines are carried. These sticks were carried on the right side of the horse. Besides these the centre of Threes carried a small trough on his saddle bag, in which the rocket was laid when fired, and every man in the Rocket Sections carried rockets in his holsters. Should you entertain any intention of representing the costume of the troops the small flag attached to the rocket stick should not be introduced. It was added by the Captain as an ornament, and was discontinued, and not part of the real equipment. The Horse appointments were those of the Light Cavalry, and the N.C. Officers and gunners had blue shabraques laced with yellow.

.   .   .   .

I am, &c.,

E. C. WHINYATES.

FROM THE SAME.

No. 85.

Waterloo.

Detached Rocket party under a non-commissioned officer.

Carlisle, 19th December, 1842.

I beg to acknowledge your letter of the 12th inst., and in respect to your reference whether the party alluded to by the Staff Officer* was the one detached under Capt. Dansey, as I know nothing of the circumstance personally will state that the Troop *when united* did not fire any ground rockets, except at the time of their first advance at the commencement of the Action, when they went down the slope in front of the position, and at which time they had no support, and there were none of our troops [illegible] the fire. I conclude therefore that the party seen by the Staff Officer was composed of some of Captain Dansey's men after that Officer was wounded, and that the uncertainty of the N.C. Officer as to his orders arose from

---

* *Extract from a letter from Sir Horace Seymour of 4th Dec.*, 1842 :—
"About the middle of the Action I was returning . . . from the Enemy's position some small distance to the left of our centre, and had arrived at the foot of the rising ground, when I met a non-commissioned officer of the Artillery in charge of a party of about eight or ten men armed with rockets ; he was passing to the right of our line. Whether he spoke to me first, or I to him, I do not recollect ; but I remember perfectly he in the coolest manner dismounting his men, and firing a succession of rockets into a Column of Infantry on the crest of the French position, each of which seemed to take effect."

his knowing that his men were also Gun Detachments, and
that the Guns would be useless without them, and if he
detached himself.

I am sorry I cannot give you certain information on
these points, for I was with the Troop in the same position
from the beginning of the Action until the total rout of
the Enemy, and having seen the day won, went to Mont-
St.-Jean to have my wound examined, and having the **Major**
next morning been sent to Brussels for cure, lost hearing **Whinyates wounded.**
many of the particulars of the Action, not having joined
again until Paris was occupied by the Allies.

With respect to the proceedings of the Troop on the 17th, **Retreat on the 17th.**
when the rear was falling back from Quatre Bras to occupy
the position of Waterloo, a very few rockets were fired, **A few single rockets were fired.**
and those singly on the *chaussée*. I did not consider the
rockets bad, for I think they cleared the *chaussée*, but
single rockets never have the imposing appearance of
ground rockets fired together, when the general effect and
mass only is observed, whereas rockets when fired singly
have their deviations exposed and visible.

I am, &c.,

E. C. WHINYATES.

CAPTAIN F. WARDE, R.A.
LIEUTENANT R.H.A.

Lauriston, May 27th [? 1840]. *Dover.* **No. 86.**

. . . .

I was not on duty with the Rocket Troop at Waterloo, **Waterloo.**
but with the adjoining Troop of Horse Artillery, com- **Not with the Rocket Troop**
manded by Sir Hew Ross in the line of position resting **at Waterloo.**
upon the right of the Genappe road. The Rocket Troop **(But I think he joined it**
upon our left, the road separating us, with a Brigade of **shortly after-**
Guns—Foot Artillery—I had an opportunity of observing **wards.—ED.)**
the Rocket Troop, and gladly afford you a correct recol- **Belonged to Sir Hew**
lection of such. But although Colonel Whinyates, Major **Ross' Troop.**
Dansey and Capt. Strangways were severally wounded, I **Major Whin-yates, Capt.**

Dansey, and Lieutenant Strangways wounded.

Troop took up ground vacated by a Dutch Battery.

Composition of Troop.

Rocket Sections advanced to check Enemy's Cavalry, which was dispersed.

French Horse Artillery came into action against the Troop, which retired to reply with its Guns, and disabled the former.

From 250 to 300 rockets fired.

should recommend your applying to them for a detailed report. I can only offer you my observation.

About twelve o'clock the Rocket Troop, commanded by Major Whinyates, took possession of the ground vacated by a Dutch Brigade of Artillery on the left of the Genappe road. The Rocket Troop was composed of five light six-pounders, and the Troop told off into thirteen Sections, each Section carrying eight six-pound rockets. Soon after coming into position, Major Whinyates received orders to advance with the thirteen Sections, with the view of checking the advance of a Brigade of the Enemy's Cavalry. Major Whinyates moved at a trot within a range of three hundred yards, and fired volleys of rockets, and in ten minutes the French Brigade were in total disorder and dispersed, when a Brigade of French Horse Artillery, consisting of eight pieces of eight-pounders, galloped into action from the rear of the broken Brigade of Cavalry. Major Whinyates then retired upon his Guns in the original position, which the Troop maintained with most exemplary spirits (though with severe loss) during the whole of the Action. The Brigade of French Horse Artillery in front of the Rocket Troop were, by the Guns of the Rocket Troop, totally disabled before five o'clock, and left a wreck upon the ground at eight.

There were about two hundred and fifty or three hundred rockets used during the commencement of the Action.

I beg, &c.,

F. WARDE,
Captain of Artillery.

LIEUT.-COLONEL C. C. DANSEY, R.A.

LIEUTENANT R.H.A.

No. 87.

February 2nd, 1843.

. . . .

Waterloo.

I think the advance of the Rocket Troop to the double hedge did not take place until the results of the charge of

Cavalry were pretty nearly consummated, and that when the Rocket Troop came up very few of the Cavalry remained out in front upon the Enemy's ground. My general idea of that crisis of the Action is that a grand attack of the Enemy upon that part of our position on our left of the high road was steadily met by a Brigade of Infantry (I think Scotch) who were in line somewhat in rear of the double hedge, and that the defeat of that attack (which had been so far successful that some of the Enemy were at one time actually on the very ground that the Guns of the Rocket Troop were on afterwards, namely, the double hedge) was completed by the opportune charge of the Cavalry. Rogers' Artillery formed part of the defence against which that attack was made, and it removed to another part of the position, I think on the right of the high road; but at what period relatively to the above-named attack of the French I cannot say. I only know that Rogers' Artillery was early in action there, for before the Rocket Troop came up I had been up to the ground and spoken with the Officers, the Guns being then in action, and I know that when the Rocket Troop came up, Rogers' Artillery was no longer there, and the Rocket Troop came into action on, or very near to, the ground where Rogers' Guns had been.

The advance with the rockets, when the Guns were left unlimbered on the position, was directly to the front, and I am not aware that it was connected with any other movement. When I was detached from the Troop, I had two Guns as well as rockets, and I went to the front along the high road to look for a place, or rather to form an opinion as to where it would be best to come to action, and I went near to the *abatis*, and the fire of musketry was very hot, and I resolved not to attempt to bring the Guns up. I went back and ordered the men to get their rockets and follow me on foot with them. Lieut. Wright took a rocket under his arm, and we all went to the front to the *abatis* and stuck the rockets among the bushes of it. The moment we began firing I was wounded by a musket ball,

Thinks the Rocket Troop did not advance until the Cavalry (first) charge was nearly concluded.

His general idea of D'Erlon's attack and its repulse.

Rogers' Artillery joined in the repulse, and then went to the right of the main road.

He was subsequently detached from the Troop with two Guns as well as rockets.

Left the Guns behind and advanced with the rockets to the *abatis*.

Directly they began firing

them he and
Lieut. Wright
were wounded

and Lieut. Wright had some of the buttons knocked off his jacket; we were the only persons of the party mounted, and were both hit; this makes me think the more that the Guns could not have been brought up.

Thinks this
was after the
French had
taken La
Haye Sainte.

I think it was after the French had gained possession of La Haye Sainte that the rockets went up to the *abatis*, because, to the best of my recollection, I saw Sir A. Barnard and Sir Hew Ross and Colonel Parker on the ground above the high road (which is cut through there, you know) on my right, and there was no one *on* the road, and some one asked me with earnestness where I was going, and I think they were these, having fallen back, as you mention, upon the main position. The *abatis* was some distance in front of where these Officers were, perhaps forty or fifty yards, and if the situation of the *abatis* with regard to what you allude to as the main position, to which you say the 95th were forced to fall back, corresponds with my impression of its situation with regard to the position where I saw those Officers, then it may be inferred that it was upon the main position that they were, and that they had fallen back to it (for I am sure that the rockets went to the front of any troops of ours), and that it was after they had so fallen back, and consequently after the gaining possession of La Haye Sainte by the French, that the rockets went to the *abatis*.

See note to
No. 85, p. 208.

I believe that after I went to the rear, Lieut. Wright rejoined the Troop; possibly some of the party may have got separated from him, and, if so, may have been those seen by the A.D.C. of Lord Anglesey, but I had never before heard of the circumstance until Colonel Whinyates mentioned it to me as having heard it from you; indeed, it is the only way I can at all account for it, for there could not have been any party away from the Troop before my being detached without either of us knowing it, whereas it might have been so afterwards from our both being wounded.

I have a slight recollection of some Guns (not English) being at perhaps about a hundred or two hundred yards on

our left when we were at the double hedge, but I cannot
speak as to their being deserted.

. . . .

I am, &c.,

C. C. DANSEY.

FROM THE SAME.

Woolwich, February 23rd, 1843.   No. 88.

We had with the Troop a great awkward lumbering   Waterloo.
carriage, with an apparatus called a Bombarding Frame for   Rocket Troop
heavy rockets; my impression is that at the time of our   Equipment.
advance with the Guns, this carriage did not go to the   The Bombarding Frame.
front with us, but I recollect our seeing it, with its great
long frame cocked up in the air, at an angle of about
45 degs., firing away.   It was on our left, but whether so
far from us as to create the impression of its being a
separate party from us, I cannot say; perhaps it might.
But I am sure that the non-commissioned officer in charge   Brought into
of it did bring the carriage into action quite of his own   action by the
accord, without any orders from Major Whinyates what-   non.-com.
ever.   As to what he might have been firing at, 'tis hard   officer without
orders.
to say; to be sure, rockets in those days were not what
rockets are now, but I should think that if those rockets
that were fired from the frame went as they would now,
they must have gone about a mile and half, and Major
Whinyates ordered him to cease firing, as there were some
Foreign Cavalry of our side between him and the Enemy.

. . . .

I am, &c.,

C. C. DANSEY.

LIEUT.-COLONEL SIR ALEXANDER DICKSON'S (K.C.B.)
TROOP.—9-POUNDERS. COMMANDED BY CAPTAIN A. C.
MERCER, R.H.A.*

BREVET-MAJOR A. C. MERCER, R.A.
CAPTAIN R.H.A.

No. 89.   *Devonport, November 26th, 1834.*

· · · · · · ·

Night of 17th June bivouacked at the Farm of Mont-St.-Jean   The night of the 17th, together with two other Troops of Horse Artillery, we bivouacked in the orchard adjoining the farm of Mont-St.-Jean. The whole of the adjacent ground forming the reverse of the position (that is, the northern slope from the crest of the ridge occupied during the Battle by the first line of our Army) was covered with Corps of all arms in Bivouac. Most of these Corps were **Waterloo.** still on the same ground some hours after daylight on the 18th, but having gone into the Farm for a short time (perhaps about 10 a.m.), I was surprised on returning to find my own Troop alone in the Orchard, and the whole neighbourhood a complete solitude; scarcely a man appearing in any direction. At the same time, a heavy fire of Cannon and Musketry was going on upon the ridge.

Drawing the Troop out of the Orchard, we remained, according to Orders just then received, for some time in the Position A, but how long, I cannot say. During this **The Duke of Richmond arrived from Brussels.** anxious period the only individuals we saw were the Duke of Richmond and his sons, who, arriving from Brussels, crossed our front, and galloped away towards the Right.

I think it must have been past noon when the Adjutant of the Horse Artillery came to conduct us to the Position B, **Troop moved to the right.** on the extreme right of the 2nd Line, or what I then considered as such. Here we formed up facing towards **Formed up in front of Merbe Braine, and facing the Cavalry on the extreme French left.** Nivelles, *en potence* as it were to the 1st Line, having a Ravine (if I may so call it) in our front, running from

* Sir A. Dickson was detached from the Troop, and in command of the Battering Train.—ED.

Plan Showing
Positions and Movements
of Mercer's Troop, R.H.A.

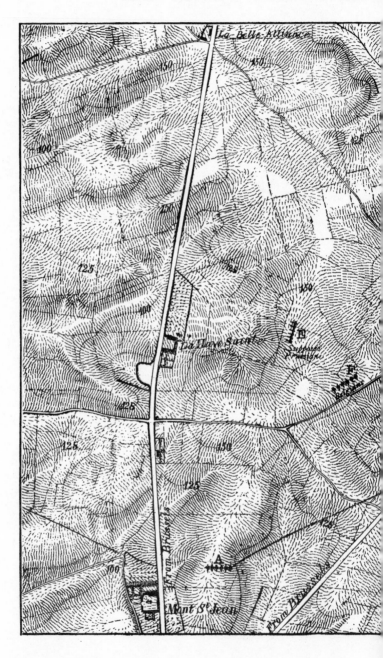

Hougoumont in the direction of Merbe Braine, in which, as well as I can remember, were Riflemen or Light Infantry and some Cavalry of the German Legion.

On our left, extending towards the Nivelles road, and somewhat in advance, was a Battery of Foot Artillery, commanded by Captain Bolton, who was killed shortly after our arrival; what other troops there might have been beyond, I do not remember. There were none of any description on our right. In rear of us was the 14th Regiment of Infantry lying down in square.

Beyond the Ravine the ground ascended at first rather abruptly, and then continued in a gentle slope for a considerable distance. Up this ran the great road to Nivelles, having extensive corn-fields on either side of it, interspersed (if I recollect right) with a few clumps of wood; and, on what appeared from our position, the summit of the slope, was drawn up a large body of Cavalry, consisting principally, if not entirely of Lancers, as marked in the Plan. On their right were several Batteries of both heavy and light Guns, the latter of which kept up a constant fire on us; but the former seemed held in reserve, since they only opened once, and then but for a short time, ceasing immediately with the cause that had drawn forth their fire. Our orders were to observe this line of Lancers, and not to fire unless they attempted to cross the ravine, but as they never did this we had ample leisure to remark all that was passing around us, which I much regret not having noted down at the time instead of trusting to a treacherous memory.

A continued skirmish was kept up amongst the corn near the Nivelles road by the riflemen, &c., whilst the Cavalry in the bottom sent from time to time small detachments up the opposite bank, which, after advancing a short distance towards the line of Lancers, retreated again, and rejoined their main body.

Of what was transacting in the front of the Battle we could see nothing, because the ridge on which our first line was posted was much higher than the ground we occupied.

Bolton's Battery on the left front of the Troop.

The Cavalry and Guns on the French left.

Of that line itself we could only see the few Squares of Infantry immediately next us, with the intervening Batteries.

French Cavalry charges on the Squares in front line between which the former penetrated.

From time to time bodies of Cavalry swept over the summit between the Squares, and, dispersing on the reverse of the position, vanished again, I know not how.

One of those bodies, however, came over in more compact order, and was holding its course directly towards us,

One body of them came towards the Troop and 14th Regt.

when a Regiment of Cavalry (I think of the German Legion), debouching from the ravine at D, formed up to attack them. The French Corps, immediately aware of

It charges a Regt. of Allied Cavalry.

this danger, wheeled to the left into line, and, both advancing to the charge, literally came in collision at full gallop. The shock appeared tremendous, yet there was no check, each party passing through the other, and closing their files immediately on being clear.

The charge was not renewed, and the two Corps disappeared like the rest, I forget how.

Several avalanches of this sort had already occurred,

About 2 p.m. another general charge of French Cavalry on the front line of Squares.

when (perhaps about 2 p.m.) such a burst took place that the whole right of the first line appeared to have been overwhelmed by it. I can compare it to nothing better than a heavy surf breaking on a coast beset with isolated rocks, against which the mountainous wave dashes with furious uproar, breaks, divides, and runs, hissing and boiling, far beyond up the adjacent beach. In a moment such shoals of Lancers and others came sweeping down the slope

The interval between the first and second lines covered with French Cavalry.

that the whole interval between the lines was covered with them, a mixed and various multitude, all scattered and riding in different directions.

The 14th Regiment immediately stood to their arms and closed their Square, whilst we made a disposition to support them with the left division of our Battery.

Nothing to be seen of the first line but the deserted Guns.

Of the first line we could see only the deserted Guns still in position on the ridge, but of the Infantry Squares nothing ! Every living soul seemed to have been swept away by this terrible burst, and so dismal was the appearance of things that an Officer of rank who happened to be

standing with me at the time expressed his serious apprehension that all was over.

Whilst anxiously watching the movements of the confused *mêlée* that thronged the plain, our attention was
suddenly called to the direction of Merbe Braine by loud
and reiterated shouts, that we found proceeding from
several Columns of Infantry, which, debouching from that
place, were rapidly crossing the fields towards us. Still,
however, the line of Lancers remained immovable, which
seemed inexplicable. The advancing Columns had all the
appearance of being French, and we prepared to give the
best reception in our power to the double attack which we
expected, when to our no small joy a mounted Officer of the
14th, who had on the first alarm gone down the hill to
reconnoitre, returned with the intelligence that they were
Belgians who had been ordered up into line. The Belgians
advancing
from Merbe
Braine.

In the meantime the scattered bands of horsemen had,
like all those that preceded them, begun to evaporate, and
things were reassuming the same appearance as before their
irruption, when Lieut.-Colonel Sir Augustus Fraser, who
commanded the Horse Artillery, came in great haste to
conduct us to a position in the first line; accordingly,
limbering up to the left, we moved off at a gallop in
column of sub-divisions, taking the route indicated in your
plan.

On the way Sir Augustus informed me that a serious
attack was meditated against that part of the line to which
he was leading us ; that in all probability we should be
immediately engaged with the Enemy's Cavalry, in which
case should they charge home, it was the Duke's positive
order that the men should be withdrawn from their Guns
into the nearest Infantry Squares. Then, having indicated
our position between two Squares of the Brunswick Infantry, he left us. The ground we were to occupy was
two or three feet lower than that immediately in our front,
so that the bank where this difference occurred *abruptly*,
and along which ran a narrow open road, formed a sort of
genouillère to our Battery. Beyond this road extended a Troop moved
up into front
Line between
two Bruns-
wick Squares.

tolerably level surface for about 40 or 50 yards; and thence the ground descended rapidly towards the plain that divided the two Armies.

Our leading sub-division had scarcely arrived on the position, ere it became evident that the Duke's order could not be complied with, for a heavy Column of Cavalry composed of Grenadiers à Cheval and Cuirassiers, had just ascended the Plateau and was advancing upon us at a rapid pace, so that there scarcely appeared time even to get into action, and, if caught in column, of course we were lost.

Hardly time to get into action before the French Cavalry was close upon it.

However, the order was given to deploy, and each Gun as it came up immediately opened its fire; the two Infantry Squares at the same time commencing a feeble and desultory fire; for they were in such a state that I momentarily expected to see them disband.

Disordered state of the Brunswick troops, who were mere boys.

Their ranks, loose and disjointed, presented gaps of several file in breadth, which the Officers and Sergeants were busily employed filling up by pushing and even thumping their men together; whilst these, standing like so many logs, with their arms at the recover, were apparently completely stupefied and bewildered. I should add that they were all perfect children. None of the privates, perhaps, were above 18 years of age. In spite of our fire the Column of Cavalry continued advancing at a *trot* until separated from us by scarcely more than the breadth of the little road, but at the very moment when we expected to be overwhelmed, those of the leading Squadrons suddenly turning, and endeavouring to make way to the rear, confusion took place, and the whole broke into a disorderly crowd. The scene that ensued is scarcely to be described. Several minutes elapsed ere they succeeded in quitting the Plateau, during which our fire was incessant, and the consequent carnage frightful, for each Gun (9 Prs.) was loaded with a round and case shot; all of which, from the shortness of the distance, size of the object, and elevation of the ground on which they stood, *must* have taken effect.

French Cavalry advances in spite of the close fire of the Troop.

But suddenly turns and retires in confusion.

Many, instead of seeking safety in retreat, wisely

dashed through the intervals between our Guns, and made
their way as we had seen others do ; but the greater part,
rendered desperate at finding themselves held, as it were, in
front of the Battery, actually fought their way through
their own ranks, and in the struggle we saw *blows* ex-
changed on all sides.   At last the wreck of this formidable
Column gained protection under the slope of the hill,
leaving the Plateau encumbered with their killed and
wounded, and we then ceased firing, that our men, who
were much fatigued with their exertions, might rest themselves and be fresh against the next attack, which we saw
preparing ; for they had not retired so far down the hill
but that the tall caps of the Grenadiers of the leading
Squadrons were visible above the brow.

Leaving the ground encumbered with their killed and wounded.

The second attempt was preluded by a cloud of skirmishers, who, advancing to within a very short distance
of our front, did us considerable mischief with their
carbines and pistols, but their intention being evidently to
draw out our fire, no notice was taken of them.

A second attack preceded by skirmishers.

At length the Column being re-formed, again ascended
the Plateau, and advanced to attack us, but this time their
pace scarcely exceeded a walk, or at most a gentle trot, too
many obstacles lying in their way to admit of more rapid
movement without confusion.   This was in our favour.
Experience having shown us the unerring and destructive
effects of a close fire, we allowed the leading Squadrons to
attain about half the distance between the brow of the
slope and the road in our front before we commenced.   It
is scarcely necessary to say that the result was precisely
similar to what has been already detailed.   Again they fell
into confusion, and again for several minutes were exposed
to a deliberate fire of case shot within 20 yards, so that the
heap of killed and wounded left on the ground, before
great, was now enormous.

Exposed to the fire of case shot at 20 yards, they leave an enormous heap of killed and wounded.

I think three times (of this I am uncertain) these
attacks were renewed, always with less prospect of success
because our position became more and more inaccessible
after every attack.   Be that as it may, the last had just

been defeated and we were still busy at the work of destruction, when the Duke arriving from the rear rode along our front and obliged us to cease firing, although the remains of the Cavalry had not yet quitted the Plateau.

? Advance of Adam's Brigade.

His Grace was soon followed by a line of Infantry, who ascending the slope with *ported* arms, ankle deep in a tenacious clay and struggling with the numerous obstacles encumbering the ground, presented but a loose and broken front, whilst the feeble hurrahs they sent forth showed how much they were out of breath with their exertions. Arrived on the summit, these disorders were rectified, although the fire that now opened upon us from the Enemy's Batteries caused considerable loss, and the whole (our neighbours of Brunswick included) descended the hill towards the plain.

General Advance of the Line.

I suppose this movement must have been general; for, at the moment it took place the cannonade slackened all along the line, and the smoke clearing away in a great measure, enabled me for the first time to get an extended view over the field.

The summit and declivity of the opposite position were covered with dark masses of troops, and others were in movement on the plain, but my recollection is too confused to admit of attempting to particularise.

The Line having descended sufficiently to permit of it, we had just commenced firing over them at the masses in the plain, when under cover of the smoke a Battery came (we could not conjecture whence) and established itself a little in advance of our left flank, from which it could not have been distant more than four hundred yards (marked E in the Plan), and thus almost enfilading our line, besides being on higher ground; the fire it poured in upon us was the most destructive we had yet experienced, and could not have failed to annihilate us, had we not been saved by a Battery of Belgic Horse Artillery which came up soon after on our left (F), and thus taking them almost in flank, soon drove them from their position.

The Troop enfiladed by a Battery on its left front, and a most destructive fire.

The Troop supported by a Belgian Battery, which drove the former from its position.

Before the arrival of these Belgians, however, we had

turned two Guns against our adversaries in the hope, if not
of silencing them, at least of rendering their fire less
deadly. Hardly had this been done, when an Officer in a
black Hussar uniform came to inform us that we were The hostile
killing our friends the Prussians. It was useless repeating Battery as-
serted to be
to this man that in such a *mêlée* we could only know the Prussian.
tree by its fruit, and that our friends the Prussians had
already treated us very scurvily, of which abundant testimonials lay around. We even ceased firing altogether to
convince him, but to no effect, although during the interval
he witnessed the continued and dreadful fire kept up by his
countrymen. At last we persuaded him to ride round and
endeavour to stop the fire of the other Battery, but we
heard no more of him, and, as I said before, were only
saved from annihilation by the Belgians, who, by the bye,
were all drunk, and would have fired upon us, too, had we
not taken some pains to put them straight.

My recollections of this period of the Battle are rather
confused, but I think that soon after, our Infantry appearing in the plain, all firing from the Batteries ceased, and
about the same time we saw the Enemy's masses dissolving
and streaming from the field in confused multitudes.

Just then an Aide-de-Camp galloped up, shouting to us
with all his might, " Forward, Sir! Forward! It is of the Troop
utmost importance that this movement should be supported ordered to
support the
by Artillery!" We could only point to the miserable General
Advance. Im-
remains of our Battery, a glance at which was sufficient, possibility of
and he rode on. moving.

When all was quiet, I found that, except ourselves and
Major Bull's Troop of Horse Artillery, no other Corps
remained on the Position; but soon after several Batteries
of Prussian Artillery marched up and established their
Bivouacs near us.

With respect to the appearance of the Field after the
Action, not much can be said, for night closed in upon us
very shortly, and we were too glad to lie down to think
of looking about. That the ground was everywhere thickly
strewed with the dead and dying (Men and Horses), wrecks

of Gun and Ammunition Carriages, Arms, Caps, &c., will occur as a matter of course. I should, however, add that

Heap of slaughter in front of the Troop greater than in any other part of the Field.

the heap of slaughter was far greater in front of our Battery than on any other part of the Field, so much so that Colonel Sir Augustus Fraser told me two days afterwards at Nivelles that in riding over the French Position he could distinctly see where G (our Letter) Troop had stood from the dark pile of bodies in front of it, which was such as even to form a remarkable feature in the Field.

Exhausted state of the Troop.

The depth of the ground and the exhausted state of the few men remaining at the Guns had latterly prevented the possibility of running them up after each round, so that when the Action ceased, their recoil had brought them together in a confused heap—as well as I can remember, something like this

the two Guns employed against the Battery on our left having recoiled upon the others.

In filling up the Plan, from not exactly understanding your method of marking the feature of the ground, I may have committed mistakes, which your more recent acquaintance with the localities will readily enable you to correct. I cannot presume to do more than guess, and where to place the (*soi-disant*) Prussian Battery has particularly puzzled me. It was about *four hundred yards obliquely to our left*, and, as well as I can remember, on more elevated ground.

I have thus endeavoured to give you as exact a detail as possible of every circumstance connected with the Troop I had the honour of commanding on that memorable occasion, which I trust may be sufficiently explicit for your purpose. . . . . . .

I have, &c.,

A. C. MERCER,
Captain Royal Artillery, Major.

MAJOR W. N. RAMSAY'S TROOP.—9-POUNDERS.

CAPTAIN P. SANDILANDS, R.H.A.
LIEUTENANT R.H.A.

Woolwich, December 15th, 1834. No. 90.

I beg to return you the Plan of Waterloo. I commanded Major Ramsay's Troop of Horse Artillery at seven o'clock, the period of the Battle which you have selected for representation, and I think I may say that its position and formation at that hour (viz., oblique *échelon* to the left) is accurately marked on the Plan.

The fire of Major Ramsay's Troop I caused to be directed against the Enemy's attacking Columns from the moment of their formation near La Belle Alliance until their arrival on the crest of our position near La Haye Sainte; it then ceased, as the Duke of Wellington, who had brought up three Infantry Regiments from the right, deployed them on the flank of the French Columns, and shut them out from our view.

Marginal notes: Waterloo. Major Ramsay was killed earlier in the day.—ED. *See* Plan, p. 186. Fire of the Troop directed against the Columns of the Imperial Guard from the moment of their formation to the attack of Adam's Brigade.

. . . .

I have, &c.,
PHILIP SANDILANDS,
Captain Royal Horse Artillery.

LIEUT.-COLONEL SIR HEW ROSS' (K.C.B.) TROOP.— 9-POUNDERS.

COLONEL SIR HEW D. ROSS, K.C.B., R.A.
CAPTAIN AND BREVET LIEUT.-COLONEL R.H.A.'

Carlisle, January 27th, 1835. No. 91.

. . . .

With respect to my own Troop, it was posted at the commencement of the day—

Two Guns on the road at the Quarry, and four on the heights to its right, where it was exposed to a destructive

Marginal notes: Waterloo. Position of Troop.

Ross' Troop.

Three Guns disabled.

fire, by which three Guns were disabled, and when the Enemy's Cavalry forced that part of the position, several men were cut down before they could take shelter behind the Infantry. After the Enemy got possession of La Haye Sainte, it was no longer possible to remain in our

Troop moved to the right, after the French took La Haye Sainte.

See Plan, p.186

first position, and the Troop was ordered to take ground to its right. At the moment the French Imperial Guards reached the crest of the position in their last attack, it occupied, as near as I can now judge, the situation I have marked upon the Plan, though I cannot speak positively as to the precise spot; and on the repulse of the

The 3 serviceable Guns join in the General Advance.

Enemy, the three Guns then movable joined in the pursuit to the heights beyond La Belle Alliance.

I have, &c.,

H. D. Ross,

Colonel Commanding R.A., N.W. District.

FROM THE SAME.

Extracts from a Memorandum by Sir Hew Ross.

No. 92.

Waterloo.

Woolwich, March 22nd, 1841.

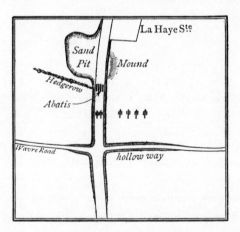

During 1st charge of Cuirassiers,

When the first charge was made by the Cuirassiers, the men serving the 4 Guns in front of the Hollow-way retired into it or endeavoured to shelter themselves under the Guns. Sir Hew Ross believes both the Guns on the high road were disabled at this time.

The earthen mound referred to afforded some shelter, but he does not recollect that many availed themselves of it.

The four Guns were in action soon after Somerset's Heavy Cavalry charged down the slope in pursuit of the French Cavalry. . . . . .

The Hollow-way was partly blocked up by the wounded horses and limbers of his Troop.

H. D. Ross.

Major G. Bean's Troop.—Light 6-Pounders.

CAPT. J. E. MAUNSELL, HALF-PAY, R.A.
Lieutenant R.H.A.

Cheltenham, November 30th, 1834. No. 93.

. . . . . .

Major Bean's Troop, under my command, was formed on the ridge a good deal to the right of the Brussels road, immediately in front of the Imperial Guards, and continued firing on the advancing Columns until our Infantry advanced to the charge, when a Battalion of the Rifle Corps passed through the intervals of our Guns; after this the Troop advanced to where the Duke of Wellington and his Staff took post, but did not fire. The Troop then took ground to the left and got upon the road, advanced, and took up a position on the right of the road, a good deal in advance, in front of which the road was cut through a hill. The Troop was prevented firing on the retiring mass as they passed through the gap by a Battalion of, I believe, the Guards forming line in front of the Guns, and before they could be got from our immediate front in the hurry of the pursuit, the Enemy had got behind the rising ground, when the pursuit ceased for the night.

. . . .

Col. Adye.

Major Bean and Lieut. Cromie killed, Capt. Webber wounded.

Sir James Bruce, Bart., of Down Hill, Londonderry, who was the only officer with me, will be able, perhaps, to give you further information, Major Bean having been killed, Captain Webber wounded, and Lieut. Cromie having had both his legs taken off.

I am, &c.,

JOHN E. MAUNSELL.

ROYAL ARTILLERY.

COLONEL S. E. ADYE, R.A.

LIEUT.-COLONEL R.A.

No. 94.

Woolwich Common, December 6th, 1834.

. . . .

Waterloo.

Commanded Artillery of 1st Division, including Sandham's Battery.

See Plan, p. 186.

Fire directed on French Troops behind Hougoumont.

Just previous to the General Advance furiously charged by the Cuirassiers.

I have to inform you that I commanded the Artillery attached to the 1st Division of the 1st Corps, and that it consisted of two Batteries of six Guns each : Captain Sandham's British Foot Artillery, and Major Kuhlman's Horse Artillery, King's German Legion.

The Batteries were formed, as nearly as I can guess, where I have placed them in pencil on the Plan, on a byeroad running from the Nivelles road along the position, and their fire was chiefly directed on the masses of the Enemy's troops, formed on the rising ground to the right and behind Château Goumont.

The Guns continued in nearly the same position the whole day. A short time previous to the advance, they were suddenly and furiously charged by a body of Cuirassiers, and some of the Guns in the confusion fell back on the road in their rear, leading from Brussels to Nivelles. They afterwards resumed their original position nearly.

. . . .

I am, &c.,

STEPH. E. ADYE.

CAPTAIN SANDHAM'S BATTERY.—9-POUNDERS.

BREVET-MAJOR C. F. SANDHAM, HALF-PAY, R.A.

CAPTAIN R.A.

Kurdell, Shoreham, May 19th, 1835.　No. 95.

．　　．　　．　　．　　．　　．　　．

I have endeavoured to mark, as nearly as I could, the *Waterloo.* position of my Battery, and believe I have nothing more *See* Plan, to add than about the time alluded to in your circular p. 186. letter, that it was charged by a Column of Cuirassiers. Battery charged by

Colonel Adye, who commanded the Artillery of the Cuirassiers. 1st Division, was with the Battery the whole of the day, and from whom it received its orders, has probably been able to afford you fuller information.

I have, &c.,

CHAS. F. SANDHAM,

Brevt.-Major, H.P.

CAPTAIN BOLTON'S BATTERY.—FOUR 9-POUNDERS AND TWO HOWITZERS.

CAPTAIN G. PRINGLE, R.A.

LIEUTENANT R.A.

74, George Street, Edinburgh, November 25th, 1834.　No. 96.

．　　．　　．　　．　　．　　．

Captain Bolton's Battery was contiguous to the Foot *Waterloo.* Guards, with the right of whose line it formed an angle of The Battery about 140°. was posted close to and

The Enemy advanced in heavy close column, with the on the right intention of penetrating the position at the right of the of the Guards. Foot Guards. They were within the angle formed by the Battery and the Foot Guards before they went about, so that at last the right Gun could not conveniently be brought to bear upon the *head* of the column. The Battery Repulse of the fired case shot from the moment they appeared on the first attacking Column of the crest of the hill (about two hundred yards), and during the Imperial advance along the plateau, from which they suffered Guard.

severely, the Column waving, at each successive discharge,
like standing corn blown by the wind.   .   .   .

I have, &c.,

G. PRINGLE,

Captain Royal Artillery.

LIEUTENANT WM. SHARPIN, HALF-PAY, R.A.

LIEUTENANT R.A.

No. 97.   *Beccles, December 6th,* 1834.

.   .   .   .

Waterloo.

First positions of Battery.

See Plan of Capt. Mercer's, p.214, for 1st position of Capt. Bolton's Battery.

Captain Bolton's Battery was attached to Lord Hill's
Corps d'Armée, and formed part of Sir Henry Clinton's
Division.

At the commencement of the Action we were stationed
about six or seven hundred yards behind Hougoumont,
where we remained till between two and three o'clock in
the afternoon. Whilst we were in this position marked on
the map A, three of the Guns under Captain Napier were

Three Guns detached to silence a French Battery firing on Hougoumont.

Effected this in about an hour.

detached to the point B for the purpose of destroying a
French Battery of six Guns that was committing great
devastation amongst our troops in and near Hougoumont.
This they effected in about an hour, and then rejoined us.
About three o'clock we moved to position C, the centre
of the front line of the Army.   .   .   .   .

See Plan, p. 186.

Battery moved to position in front line on the right of the Guards.

You may perhaps more precisely ascertain our position
at the period chosen for your Model by my stating that on
our left was a Brigade of Guards lying down under a low
bank.

A few minutes before the French Imperial Guards
made their appearance the Duke of Wellington rode up

The Duke's instructions to the Battery just before the last attack of the Imperial Guard.

to our Battery and hastily asked me who commanded it; I
replied that Bolton did, but that he was just killed, and
that it was then under Napier. His Grace then said,
"Tell him to keep a look to his left, for the French will
soon be with him," and then he rode off.

I had scarcely communicated the Duke's message, when

we saw the French bonnets just above the high corn, and within forty or fifty yards of our Guns. I believe they were in close Columns of Grand Divisions, and upon reaching the crest of our position they attempted to deploy into line, but the destructive fire of our Guns loaded with canister shot, and the well-directed volleys from the Infantry, prevented their regular formation.

Destructive effect of the Battery's fire.

They remained under this fire about ten minutes, advancing a little, but finding it impossible to force our position they gave way, and went to the right about, upon which the Duke ordered a general charge to be made, and in a moment our Infantry and the French were so mixed together that an end was put to our firing for the day.

The French give way.

Captain Bolton at the time he was killed was on horseback. I was standing on his left side with my hand on his stirrup talking with him. The shot from a French Battery at that time flew very thick amongst us, and one passed between me and Bolton, upon which he coolly remarked that he thought we had passed the greatest danger for that day ; but scarcely were the words uttered before another ball, which I saw strike the ground a little in front of us, hit him in his left breast. The shot having first severely wounded the horse in the left shoulder caused the animal to stagger backwards, thereby preventing my catching poor Bolton as he fell from his horse.

Capt. Bolton's death.

You will perceive that in position C I have only marked five Guns instead of six, the usual number. The deficiency arose from the Howitzer of the left division of the Battery, having been loaded by mistake with canister shot whilst in the first position ; and no opportunity offering when there to discharge it, I ordered the non-commissioned officer as we were moving into our last position to take it aside and get the shot out, and join us immediately, but from some cause or other he did not find us again till after the Battle. Four nine-pounders, therefore, and a Howitzer on the right of them composed the Battery in position C.

In last position only five Guns,

A Howitzer being temporarily disabled by a mistake in loading.

Captain Napier, Lieutenant (now Captain) Pringle and

myself were spared till nearly the close of the Action, but
at the time the French gave way, or rather just after our
troops were mixed with them, a Gun was fired from our
Battery, loaded with shrapnel shell, which, bursting in the
Gun, wounded poor Napier very severely in several places.

Capt. Napier
wounded by a
shell bursting
in one of his
Guns.

We remained in position C all the night, and in the
morning the Field of Battle presented a frightful spectacle
of killed and wounded, both of men and animals of each
party.

Appearance
of the Field
next morning.

.   .   .   .

I beg, &c.,

WM. SHARPIN.

MAJOR LLOYD'S BATTERY.—9-POUNDERS.

MAJOR S. RUDYARD [? H.P.R.A.].
CAPTAIN R.A.

No. 98.   *United Service Club, London, May 6th,* 1838.

.   .   .   .

16th June.

At daybreak on the morning of the 16th the 3rd
Division, under Generals Baron Alten and Halkett,
belonging to the 1st Corps, commanded by the Prince of
Orange, moved on from the neighbourhood of Braine-la-
Leud, Braine-le-Comte, or thereabouts, on towards
Quatre Bras. Majors William Lloyd and Cleeves were
the two commanding Batteries. We were halted for some
hours after arriving on the Nivelles road until the French
had been well driven back over the said road, otherwise
we should have come up in their rear. It might have
been about noon or an hour later, when Colonel Harvey,
A.D.C. to the Duke of Wellington, ordered the Division
to move on the scene of action without delay.

The Battery
marched with
the 3rd
Division on
Quatre Bras.

Ordered to
the scene of
action.

See Plan of
Quatre Bras.

G indicates
where the
Bois de Bossu
skirts the
Nivelles road.

On that part of the Nivelles road I have marked G,
we were halted and directed to form line, the Enemy
being descried in the wood on our right, and close to us.
I was with two Guns attached to the 69th, Lieutenant-

Detached with
two Guns.

Colonel Morice, and placed myself on their right, when I was directed to follow the four other Guns of Major Lloyd's Battery ordered into action in front of the farm of Quatre Bras, on the Charleroi road, to the support of the Duke of Brunswick. I had hardly quitted the 69th when the Cuirassiers charged from the wood, and before the 69th could get into square they were rode over, broken, and sad havoc made among them, their only Colour taken, the other being "in the Hospital of Invalides at Paris, taken at Bergen-op-Zoom," and but for a Battalion of British Guards coming up to ·their support, and, throwing in one of their destructive fires, compelling the Cuirassiers to return to the wood, not a man save the Colonel and Adjutant would have escaped but for this timely aid, as Colonel Morice stated to me before he fell at Waterloo, having there received four musket ball wounds.

Rejoined the Battery on the Charleroi road.

See No. 136, p. 322.

On my reaching the farm at Quatre Bras, two of Major Cleeves' Guns enfiladed the Charleroi road, and had literally macadamised it with the carcases of the Cuirassiers and their horses, who had made a most desperate charge in great force, but never returned to it.

Battery ordered to the right front of Quatre Bras.

At this moment Major Lloyd's six Guns were ordered to the point marked D to support the Duke of Brunswick's troops who were getting severely handled by the Enemy, particularly from two Batteries in the wood marked E. Colonel Kelly, Q.M.G.D., ordered us to take up the position we did under this heavy fire, and before we unlimbered some three or four horses of each Gun and waggon were killed, some wheels disabled, and literally some of our gunners were cut in two, for we were not more than from four to five hundred yards from the Enemy's Batteries.

D is facing wood, half way between it and road, and about same distance on Quatre Bras side of rivulet.

E E French Batteries in skirts of wood, one on either side of angle formed by boundary.

We succeeded in silencing them, and also in obliging a solid mass of French Infantry, marked F, to retrograde and return to the wood. Finding ourselves now alone without any support, except a few Lancers of the Brunswickers, and the duty executed that we were ordered upon, we limbered up and walked off towards the Quatre

Silenced the Batteries, and drove back into wood a body of French Infantry—F —on right of

Bras farm and joined our Division. Major Rogers'
Battery of British had been up some time earlier in the day
than we were, and had been engaged with the Enemy.
These were the only *two* British Batteries at the Battle of
Quatre Bras. Major Cleeves' and other Batteries of the
German Legion were up.

Battery, be-
tween wood
and road.

Lloyd's and
Rogers' the
only two
British Bat-
teries at
Quatre Bras.

Having sustained much damage from the Enemy's fire,
we were occupied the whole night in repairing broken
axle-trees, wheels, &c., and had just finished in time to
move off the field, in view of the whole line of French
Cavalry, when a cannonade between our Horse Artillery
and theirs commenced, and continued at intervals the
whole retirement we made towards our position at
Waterloo. By General Picton's orders, our six Guns were
united to those of Major Cleeves and took up a position
on the height, close to the Brussels road, right leading
from the wood, and we opened our fire upon the French
Infantry who had followed us up rather too close, and
[were] disposed to continue. The range we had was
La Belle Alliance, or just where the road widens into a
quarry or open space (at that time). There we dealt out
our round shot liberally and caused much destruction, as
the head of the Enemy's Columns were unable to retrograde
from the pressure in their rear, and did not extricate themselves for some time, and were about half an hour under
fire, and must have suffered much. Two Batteries of
French Horse Artillery played upon us at the time, but
not with much effect. The shot holes in La Belle Alliance
(which you have seen, perhaps) were perforated at this
period. By order of the Duke, we ceased firing and remained on our ground until morning, when we took up our
position for battle on the 18th in front of Hougoumont.

Occupied the
whole night
in repairing
damages.

Retreat on
17th June.

Retired to the
position of
Waterloo.

Lloyd's and
Cleeves' Bat-
teries ordered
to fire on
French
Infantry,

Which must
have suffered
much.

Two French
Horse Artil-
lery Batteries
replied with-
out much
effect.

．　　．　　．　　．　　．　　．

I remain, &c.,

S. RUDYARD.

FROM THE SAME.

Whitby, January 6th, 1835.   No. 99.

. . . .

Early on the morning of the 18th our position was
taken up on the very crest of the slope in front of our
Division; the Regiments were 69th and 33rd in our rear;
the grain, I can't say whether wheat or barley, it was above
our heads, but soon trodden down. From this position we
never moved one instant until the Battle closed; the
Batteries contiguous to ours were Major Sandham's Royal
Artillery on the right, Major Cleeves' King's German Legion
[on] our left. Major [? Sinclair's] Royal Artillery and a
Dutch Battery were in reserve, and came into action late in
the day. At seven o'clock, when the Imperial Guards
advanced, our Guns were still in line. The French advanced
in masses of Infantry, upon which we directed our fire.
Never during the Action did we return the heavy fire kept
up upon us by their Artillery. Our fire was ever oblique
towards the ground in front and right of Hougoumont.

When at the close the British Infantry advanced in
line to the charge, it very much resembled the curvature of
the surf upon the shore. You ask me for any local
remarks as may assist in the accuracy of the Model. My
horses, ammunition waggons, were in rear of our Guns
under cover of a little hollow between us and our Squares of
Infantry. The forge cart, artificers' stores, and such like
were in the rear of all out of fire. When ammunition was
to be replenished, a Subaltern conducted such waggons as
could be spared. They were supplied from the depôt in
the wood, and returned without delay. The ground we
occupied was much furrowed up by the recoil of our Guns
and the grazing of the shot, and many holes from the
bursting of shells buried in the ground. As horses were
killed or rendered unserviceable, the harness was removed
and placed on the waggons, or elsewhere. Our men's
knapsacks were neatly packed on the front and rear of our

Side notes: Waterloo. Battery posted on the crest in front of the 69th and 33rd. Never moved from this position all day. Between Sandham's and Cleeves' Batteries. Fired upon the French Imperial Guards. Details of the service of the Battery.

LLOYD'S BATTERY.

limbers and waggons, that they might do their work more

Every Gun and carriage struck.

easily. Every *Gun*, every carriage, spokes carried from wheels, all were struck in many places.

The French Cavalry charged the Battery six or seven times.

The Cuirassiers and Cavalry might have charged through the Battery as often as six or seven times, driving us into the Squares, under our Guns, waggons, some defending themselves. In general, a Squadron or two came up

Effects of the Battery's fire on them.

the slope on our immediate front, and on their moving off at the appearance of our Cavalry charging, we took advantage to send destruction after them, and when advancing on our fire I have seen four or five men and horses piled upon each other like cards, the men not having even been displaced from the saddle, the effect of canister.

The Duke and his Staff frequently in rear of the Battery under a heavy fire, also the Prince of Orange.

The Duke and all his Staff were frequently in our rear under the heaviest fire, also the Prince of Orange. I saw the fore-legs taken from the horse of one of his Highness's A.D.C.'s at the shoulders, and [he] continued rearing for some time with his very fat rider, dressed in green. My own horse was shot through by a 9-pounder shot behind the saddle flap, and did not fall for some time. Some of the Cuirassiers were left, every charge among our Guns, killed.　.　　.　　.　　.　　.　　.

Believe me, &c.,

S. RUDYARD.

CAPTAIN F. WELLS, R.A.

LIEUTENANT R.A.

No. 100.

Kingsbridge, Devon, March 13th, 1837.

.　　　.　　　.　　　.　　　.　　　.

16th June.
Marched to Quatre Bras,
And immediately brought into action.
See No. 98, p. 231.

I have, therefore, to inform you that Major Lloyd's Brigade of Artillery marched to Quatre Bras on June 16th with the third Division of the Army, to which it was attached, and was immediately brought into action in a field in front of the houses on the high road at Quatre Bras, adjoining the Bois de Bossu, and was attacked by two Brigades of French Artillery, who were in the wood, and was about to be charged by their Infantry, who were coming out of the wood, but were driven back by its fire. It suffered very severely, many of its men and horses were killed and wounded; two of its Guns could not be taken off the field till the Action was over, so many horses being killed. Suffered so severely from the two French Batteries that two of its Guns became immovable from the horses being killed.

With respect to the memorable June 18th—the Brigade was in the same position at seven o'clock p.m. as it took up at the commencement of the Battle, viz., on the left of two other Brigades of Artillery—Major Sandham's, of the British Artillery, and Major Cleeves', of the German Legion, in front of the Squares of Infantry and a little to the left of Hougoumont. It was opposed the whole day to the French Artillery, drawn up as well as ourselves in the front of each Army, and was frequently charged by the Polish Lancers and Cuirassiers. Waterloo. Position of the Battery. Frequently charged by the French Cavalry.

Our loss on the 18th was also very considerable. Major Lloyd received a mortal wound from an Officer of the Imperial Guard, and Lieutenant Harvey lost his arm. Major Lloyd killed, Lieut. Harvey lost an arm.

.   .   .   .

I remain, &c.,

FORTESCUE WELLS,

Capt. R. Artillery.

MAJOR ROGERS' BATTERY.—9-POUNDERS.

COLONEL T. ROGERS, C.B., R.A.

CAPTAIN AND BREV.-MAJOR R.A.

Woolwich, February 25th, 1837.   No. 101.

.   .   .   .

About the time the Division took up its position at Quatre Bras, or very soon after, we were engaged with some French Artillery, which opened a heavy fire upon us, in addition to that of the musketry, killing and wounding several of our men and horses; the Artillery being as we supposed at about the distance of 500 or 600 yards in Quatre Bras. Loss of men and horses.

See Plan of Quatre Bras, No. 1.

the direction of the wood, and to *their* left of the piece of water described in your Plan. The number of Guns, we could not judge of with any degree of precision, as they were partly concealed by the wood ; and we* think they were stationary during the Action, as we did not observe them advancing or retiring. We were at one time menaced by a body of Heavy Cavalry, but not charged by them.

* He and Capt. Maule.

Position of the Battery.

Our original position was on the left of the 5th Division, not in front of it. In regard to the movement of the latter by Sir Thomas Picton in squares, as referred to by you, our recollection does not furnish us with sufficient distinctness to enable us to give any detail of particulars. Our attention was much engaged in firing spherical case shot at a Column which, passing near the piece of water I have mentioned, attempted to turn our left flank. We saw no Allied Battery in the vicinity of our post, but believe that a Hanoverian Battery of the King's German Legion was in the field. . . .

Engaged in firing spherical case at French Infantry.

> I have, &c.,
>
> T. ROGERS,
> Colonel Royal Artillery.

FROM THE SAME.

No. 102.

Woolwich, February 9th, 1837.

. . . .

Waterloo.
See next letter.

Having read the account referred to by you as given to you by Captain Maule of my Battery at Waterloo, I have little to add, and the following is principally drawn from his notes, assisted by our mutual recollections.

D'Erlon's attack on Picton.

During the attack on our left, by the Count D'Erlon's Columns, the position of the 5th Division under Sir Thomas Picton, to which my Battery was attached, must be too well known to you to need repetition. During the formation of those Columns, and of numerous Batteries of Artillery, the latter occasionally opened their fire upon the Artillery of the Division, by which we lost some horses, but were restrained by Sir Thomas Picton from returning it.

In reply to your inquiry as to the manner in which that attack was met and repulsed, I have to state, by the fire of the Artillery of the Division, as long as it was possible to continue it; and on the Enemy coming into close contact with us, by the Infantry of the Division passing between the Guns, and receiving them at the points of their bayonets. These were almost immediately supported by a body of our Heavy Cavalry, advancing in column, as it appeared to us, parallel to and along the road from the right, but the smoke became so dense and the *mêlée* so complete, that it is impossible, at this distant period of time, to describe with sufficient accuracy the movements of any particular body of the parties engaged.

Manner in which it was repulsed.

Probably the 2nd Life Guards.

About this moment, Sir Thomas Picton was killed, close to one of the Guns of my Battery.

Picton killed close to the Battery.

A sand, or gravel pit, was a little to the right in front of the position of my Battery, and if by the " mound," you mean the little rising ground directly above the edge of the pit, neither Captain Maule nor myself recollect to have seen any Guns posted on that spot.

We were, shortly after, ordered to the right of the road, on the high ground a little to the right of and in rear of La Haye Sainte, where, and afterwards more to the right, the Battery continued in action until the General Advance, opposing by its fire the advance of the Enemy, and finally of the French Imperial Guards, in their last attempt to force the position.

Afterwards the Battery was ordered to the right of the main road, and later to the right of the Guards, continuing in action, and opposing the last attack of the Imperial Guard.

At the time referred to in your printed Circular, as that chosen for your Model, the formation of my Battery was *five* Guns, in line, and in action, as nearly as Captain Maule's and my own recollection enable us to fix the spot, where I have marked it in your Plan, the 52nd Regiment being near our right, and our fire taking the advancing French Columns diagonally on their left front.

At 7 o'clock only five Guns were in action. The Battery was on the left of the 52nd Regiment, and its

In the final advance of the English force, and retreat

ROGERS' BATTERY.

fire took the
French
Column
diagonally.

The Battery
joined in the
final advance.

of the French, the Battery limbered up, and joined in the
pursuit. Owing to the depth to which the wheels sank in
the heavy field we traversed, and some horses being more
exhausted than others, the rear Guns could not keep up
with those leading the Column. I therefore directed my
Second Captain to bring up the rear of the Battery, with
the ammunition carriages; and advanced with Captain
Maule and the leading Guns, diagonally across the field,
partly upon the small cross road, until we came to the
Genappe road, which we ascended until a little way beyond
the house of La Belle Alliance, where we fell in with the
Prussian troops, close to the left of the main road, and
the pursuit being continued by the Prussians, bivouacked
there for the night.

A remark in your letter as to " the position of the
three remaining Guns about half-past seven p.m.," leads
me to consider some misconception possible, of the information you received from Captain Maule, which it may
be as well to provide against.

One Gun had
been spiked
by its non-
com. officer
when Picton
was killed.

One Gun was spiked by its non-commissioned officer, at
the time Sir Thomas Picton was killed, and was afterwards sent to the rear to have the spike drilled out, but
though, from casualties amongst the horses, and the heaviness of the ground, one or two Guns may have been
momentarily prevented from getting into a new position so
soon as the rest, the other *five* Guns of the battery were
never separated, except as I have described, *in'the pursuit,*
in which Captain Maule fully concurs.

．　　　．　　　．　　　．　　　．　　　．　　　．

I have, &c.,

T. ROGERS,
Colonel Royal Artillery.

CAPTAIN G. S. MAULE, R.A.

LIEUTENANT R.A.

Woolwich, December 30th, 1834. No. 103.

.   .   .   .

You may remember I read to you an extract from my Journal written the day after the Action of 18th June, when the three days' work were, as you may suppose, pretty fresh in my memory.

On reference to it and what I bear in mind to this day, I have no hesitation in affirming that the three principal positions, or rather stations, my Battery took up on the 18th were—1st. Close in front of the 5th Division, that is, behind the hedge along the lane *to the left* of the Brussels and Genappe road, where Sir Thomas Picton was killed and we had a Gun spiked.

Three principal positions of the Battery.

1st, in front of Picton's Division, and to the left of the main road.

2nd. We then moved to reinforce the Artillery to our right on the other side of the said road, and were engaged some time.

2nd, to the right of the main road.

3rd. We were ordered to, and took ground considerably more to the right, coming to action with three Guns (two more being disabled by the loss of horses) at the angle formed by the Guards in line on the left, and General Adam's Brigade, 52nd, 95th, 71st, whose right flank had been thrown forward on our right. When there I perfectly remember the French Guard coming up in front, and *nearly to* our Guards, and their being taken in flank by Adam's Brigade and my Guns.

3rd, to the left of Adam's Infantry Brigade.

Battery assisted in repelling the French Imperial Guard.

Before, or rather on their arrival with our Guards, they were repulsed, and our Cavalry at this moment as well as the whole Line advanced, and I accompanied with two Guns the Cavalry along a country road diagonally in front of the original, or grand position, coming to action several times on the retreating French until we gained some houses on the main (Brussels and Genappe) road, where a French park of Artillery had been.

Two Guns joined in the General Advance, and kept up with the Cavalry.

Captain Bloomfield, R.A., on the Staff of Sir George

Wood, perfectly remembers my advancing along this road, and my keeping up with the Cavalry, having during the day taken the precaution of re-horsing my Guns from other carriages as they became disabled.

· · · · · · ·

Faithfully yours,
GEORGE S. MAULE.

CAPTAIN SINCLAIR'S BATTERY—FIVE 9-POUNDERS, AND ONE 5½-INCH HOWITZER.

CAPTAIN J. A. WILSON, R.A.
LIEUTENANT R.A.

No. 104.   43, *York Place, Edinburgh, November 27th*, 1834.

· · · · · · · ·

Waterloo.

Positions of the Battery.

Came into action in the right rear of La Haye Sainte.

At the commencement of the Action Captain Sinclair's Brigade was posted near a windmill in a field on the left of the Brussels road, and in rear of the village of Mont-St.-Jean. When we were ordered into action we proceeded along the Nivelles road, took ground to the left, and formed on the right rear of La Haye Sainte between two and three hundred yards in front of the footpath laid down in your Plan.

The smoke was so dense that I could not see distinctly the position of the French, being at that time ordered to direct my fire over the dead bodies of some horses in front.

About 3 o'clock the Battery was charged by Cuirassiers, who were driven back by the 1st Royals.

About three o'clock, our ammunition being nearly exhausted, we were charged by the French Cuirassiers, who in their turn were driven back by the 1st Dragoons (Royals). We retired behind the Squares formed in our rear. I heard the word given to them in German. The Gun on the left without the limber having been surrounded by the Enemy's Cavalry, remained in their possession. Having received a supply of ammunition, we returned to our former position and recovered the Gun.

We were almost immediately ordered to the right, near Hougoumont. Whilst moving along the ground I could see the French advancing, apparently against the right, in heavy masses of close columns. We remained in our last position until twelve next day. The ground on which we were posted was covered with the killed and wounded of the Imperial Guard. A wounded Officer, who lay near me, told me he belonged to that body.

In our first position we passed through deep mud, our wheels being up to the naves; in our second the crops were grain.

The Battery, which consisted of one 5½-inch howitzer and five 9-pounders, was formed in line in both positions.

.   .   .   .

I have, &c.,

J. A. WILSON,
Captain R.A.

Marginal notes: Battery ordered to the right near Hougoumont, And to the ground on which the Imperial Guard had attacked.

MAITLAND'S INFANTRY BRIGADE.

The 1st Infantry Brigade was composed of the 2nd and 3rd Battalions of the 1st Foot Guards and was commanded by Major-General P. Maitland.

The Brigade arrived at Quatre Bras about half past six o'clock on the evening of the 16th June, and was at once employed in driving the French out of the Bois de Bossu. Arriving at the southern extremity of the wood, and pursuing the Enemy beyond it, it was forced back by the French Artillery as far as the rivulet which crosses a portion of it.

It then formed line to its left as far as the Charleroi road, and, after engaging the Infantry in its front, its left flank was assailed by the French Cavalry, whereupon it quickly retreated to the ditch which bounded the wood, and from thence poured in a most destructive fire on the Cavalry which, together with a flanking fire from a Square of Brunswickers, drove them from that part of the field. It and the 2nd Brigade remained at night in possession of the Bois de Bossu.

See Plan of Quatre Bras, No. 2.

At Waterloo the Brigade was posted on or behind the ridge of the position between Halkett's and Byng's Brigades, and its Light Companies in the wood and orchard of Hougoumont.

See General Plan of Waterloo, No. 1.

Here the latter sustained such a severe and continued contest with the French troops, that about two o'clock there were hardly any of them remaining.

During the day the Brigade was exposed to an incessant cannonade, and to the attacks of the French Cavalry. Towards evening the advanced Square of the 3rd Battalion was at one time much galled by the fire of a mass of Tirailleurs, when it quickly formed line, charged, and drove them off, rapidly re-forming square in readiness to receive the approaching French Cavalry.

The head of the 1st attacking Column of the Imperial Guard was directed against this Brigade. The Guards awaited its approach, lying down in four deep order under shelter of a bank, and, on its arriving within a distance of fifty paces, stood up, and poured such a destructive fire into it, that in one minute's time 300 of the French lay dead and dying. The Column then began to waver, when it was at once charged by the Guards and driven down the hill in complete disorder.

The Brigade having advanced so far as to have its flank menaced by the 2nd French attacking

Column, the order was given to face about and retire, but owing to the noise it was misunderstood, and a false alarm of Cavalry being raised, the Brigade was thrown into confusion and hastily retired to the original position, where order was speedily re-established.

The head of the 2nd Column of the Imperial Guard was directed against the extreme right of Maitland's Brigade, which brought forward its left shoulder, and poured a galling fire into the Column until it was dissolved and driven away by the flank attack of Adam's Brigade.

Maitland's Brigade subsequently joined in the General Advance of the Army.

No. 108 refers to the march on Quatre Bras.

Nos. 106 and 108 to Quatre Bras.

No. 108 to the retreat on the 17th June, and

All the letters to Waterloo.

LIEUT.-GENERAL SIR P. MAITLAND, K.C.B.

Major-General P. Maitland, Commanding 1st Infantry Brigade.

Brighton, November 24th, 1834.　　**No. 105.**

In compliance with your request I transmit to you, for　Waterloo. your own eye only, a concise Memorandum hastily drawn up, of events that occurred in the course of the last attack made by the French on our position at Waterloo.

.　　.　　.　　.　　.　　.

The position of the Duke of Wellington must have been near to the 1st Brigade, as he was present with us while the Grenadiers of the French Guard were advancing up the slope.

I have, &c.,

P. MAITLAND,

Lieutenant-General.

Memorandum of some events that occurred in the course of the last attack made by the French on our position at Waterloo.

Brigade
formed to
meet the first
attacking
Column of the
Imperial
Guard.

About seven o'clock p.m., the Duke of Wellington, aware of the Enemy's preparations for a new attack, desired me to form the 1st Brigade of Guards in line four files deep, His Grace expecting that the French Cavalry would take part in the affair.

The formation of the Brigade was scarcely completed before the advance of the Enemy became apparent. The force employed by the Enemy in this service consisted of two strong Columns of Infantry; a third Corps, consisting of both Cavalry and Infantry, being in reserve.

The attacking Columns were alike composed of the Infantry of the Imperial Guard, the Grenadiers forming one Column, the Chasseurs of that Corps the other.

As the attacking force moved forward it separated, the Chasseurs inclined to their left. The Grenadiers ascended the acclivity towards our position in a more direct course, leaving La Haye Sainte on their right, and moving towards that part of the eminence occupied by the 1st Brigade of Guards. Numerous pieces of ordnance were distributed on the flanks of this Column.

The Brigade suffered by the Enemy's Artillery, but it withheld its fire for the nearer approach of the Column.

The Column
halted at
twenty paces
from the
Guards.

The latter, after advancing steadily up the slope, halted about twenty paces from the front rank of the Brigade.

The diminished range of the Enemy's Artillery was now felt most severely in our ranks; the men fell in great numbers before the discharges of grape shot, and the fire of the musketry distributed among the Guns.

The smoke of the Artillery happily did not envelop the hostile Column, or serve to conceal it from our aim.

With what view the Enemy halted in a situation so perilous, and in a position so comparatively helpless, he was not given time to evince.

The fire of the Brigade opened with terrible effect.

The Enemy's Column, crippled and broken, retreated with the utmost rapidity, leaving only a heap of dead and dying men to mark the ground which it had occupied.

The Column, broken by the fire of the Guards, retreated,

The Brigade pressed on the retreating Column, and was in some measure separated from the general line of our position.

and was followed by the Brigade.

The Enemy's second attacking Column advanced towards that part of our position which had been vacated by the second Brigade of Guards, when it moved to Hougoumont.

The advance of the 2nd attacking Column.

Supposing the prolongation of the front of the 1st Brigade of Guards, the Enemy's Column had already advanced across the line of extension on the right of the Brigade.

The Brigade began to change front towards its right.

The Light Brigade under Sir F. Adam occupied the ground vacated by the 2nd Brigade of Guards, and opened its fire on the Enemy's Column. The latter retreated with the utmost haste pursued by Sir F. Adam's Brigade.

Which is repulsed by Adam's Brigade.

So ended the last offensive effort of the Enemy.

The Allied Army advanced.

The General Advance.

The 1st Brigade, after passing several pieces of ordnance abandoned by the Enemy, received orders to halt.

The Prussian Cavalry advanced along the Brussels road, saluted as they passed, their bands playing, " God save the King," and took up the pursuit.

1st Foot Guards—2nd and 3rd Battalions.

•

MAJOR-GENERAL LORD SALTOUN, K.C.B., G.C.H.

Captain and Lieut.-Colonel 1st Foot Guards.

The Hill, Brampton, Cumberland, January 29th, 1838.   No. 106.

•   •   •   •

I can give you little or no information regarding Quatre Bras. On that day I commanded the Light Companies of the 1st Brigade of Guards, and the post we occupied was in and about the wood on the right of the Field of

Quatre Bras.

1st Foot Guards.
This Plan was a tracing from an imperfect foreign map, the only one available at the time.—Ed.
See Plan of Quatre Bras.

Battle; but from the circumstance of your Plan of the ground not being shaded, I am unable at this distance of time to trace our operations upon it.

When we debouched from the wood, which we had cleared of the Light French troops, we had on our right a deep ravine, or perhaps I should rather call it a hollow, and about 150 yards to our left, and about half that distance to the rear was a low scrubby hedge, behind which the 33rd Regiment was posted. This point I cannot make out in your sketch of the ground, but as far as information goes it is not of much importance. That was the extreme point we advanced to, as did also the Brigade, and although we were driven back from it we recovered it again and held it till the firing ceased at dark.

I perceive you have a small brook or marshy bottom running through the wood, but as far as my recollection serves me, we met with an obstruction of that description much nearer the Nivelles road, from which we commenced our advance, than it appears to be in your Plan. But I most likely am wrong in this, for hurried into action as we were, into a large and in some parts thick wood, without any instructions and nothing to guide me in my advance but the fire of the Enemy, it is not likely at this distance of time that I should retain a very clear recollection of distances.

Waterloo.
Hougoumont.

Next with respect to Hougoumont. From the first attack to the period mentioned in your letter (till about two o'clock), during the whole of which time I was at that post, the whole was a succession of attacks against the front of that post attended with more or less partial success for the moment, but in the end always repulsed; and it was in one of these attacks when I had been driven from the front hedge of the orchard to the hollow way in the rear of it, that they [the Enemy] occupying the outward side of the front hedge with Infantry, brought a Gun along the line marked by you *a b,* to a point I have marked D on that line. This Gun I endeavoured to take, but failed. I, however, regained the front hedge of the orchard, and from which I never was again driven.

See Plan of Hougoumont, p. 263.
Unfortunately I cannot find the Plan here referred to.—Ed.

Whether the Enemy had Artillery at the point C, I am unable to state. We suffered very little from Artillery on the post, but it is quite clear that the house and farmyard of Hougoumont was set on fire by that arm.

Your next point is "the attack (as you call it) of the 1st Brigade of Guards against a body of Infantry previous to the attack of the Imperial Guards, &c." You seem to have mistaken the advance, not of that Brigade, but of one Battalion of them—viz., the 3rd Battalion Grenadier Guards, and have concluded that this was an attack against a regular body of Infantry. But that was not the case. The circumstances were as follows :

During the Cavalry attacks on the centre a great number of the Enemy's sharpshooters had crept up the slope of the hill, and galled the 3rd Battalion, who were in square, very severely. At that time the 2nd Battalion of Grenadier Guards (the other Battalion of the Brigade) was likewise formed in square about 100 yards in rear of the 3rd Battalion. The 3rd Battalion, who suffered severely from this fire, wheeled up into line and drove them down the hill and advanced to a point I have marked E, and there re-formed square. A small body of Rifles were at a point I have marked with an x, and the 52nd in line at F G G.   .   .   .

The 3rd Battalion forms line from square, and drives away the French sharp-shooters.

Re-formed square, and

In this position we received the last attack of Cavalry I saw that day, who, refusing us, passed between us and the *inward rear angle* of the orchard, receiving our fire ; did not charge between us and the 52nd, where the Rifles were, but rode along the front of the 52nd with a view of turning their right flank, and were completely destroyed by the fire of that Regiment.

After this we, the 3rd Battalion, retired to our original position in square, as I conclude the 52nd did also, as the next I saw of them was their attack with the rest of General Adam's Brigade on the 2nd Column of the Imperial Guards. As to any attack made at that time by the outward angle of the orchard of Hougoumont I could not from my position see or know anything about it.

Retired to its original position.

The momentary confusion of the Guards after driving back and following the 1st attacking Column of the Imperial Guard.

Your next point is with respect to what took place towards the close of the Action, and during the momentary confusion that took place in the 1st Brigade from the cry of " Form square."

It will not do in an account such as yours to put down any order that was not given, however scientific it might be, still less to make me give an order to retire when that was the last thought that came into my head at that moment.

The word of command passed was " Halt, front, form up," and it was the only thing that could be done. Any other formation was impossible, and as soon as this order was understood by the men it was obeyed and everything was right again.

. . . .

The left shoulders were then brought forward, and we advanced against the second Column of the Imperial Guards, but which body was defeated by General Adam's Brigade before we reached it, although we got near enough to fire if we had been ordered so to do; and as far as I can recollect at this distance of time we did fire into that Column.

The 2nd Column defeated by Adam's Brigade.

Did not hear the Duke say, " Up, Guards, and at them!" or ever heard of anybody that did.

Your last point is whether the Duke made use of the words " Up, Guards, and at them." I did not hear him, nor do I know any person, or ever heard of any person that did. It is a matter of no sort of importance, has become current with the world as the cheering speech of a great man to his troops, and is certainly not worth a controversy about. If you have got it I should let it stand. . . . .

I remain, &c.,

SALTOUN.

LIEUT.-COLONEL AND COLONEL R. ELLISON, GRENADIER GUARDS.

LIEUTENANT AND CAPTAIN 1ST FOOT GUARDS.

Royal Barracks, March 1st, 1835.　　No. 107.

On the evening of 17th of June about six o'clock, four Light Companies of the Guards, one of which I commanded, were suddenly ordered from our bivouac to take possession of the farmhouse, garden, orchard, and wood of Hougoumont.

Evening of the 17th four Light Companies of the Guards sent to occupy Hougoumont.

The two Light Companies of the 1st Brigade occupied the orchard, the two Light Companies of the 2nd Brigade the farmhouse and garden. During the whole of the night we were occupied in making the position as strong as our means would allow. I was on picket that night. The French brought up their advanced posts close to ours, but gave us no molestation.

Those of the 1st Brigade occupied the orchard, those of the 2nd the garden and house.

In looking on the Plan, I cannot help thinking that the wood at Hougoumont is represented as much thicker and closer than it actually was. It had no underwood, and was easily traversed in all parts by Light Infantry, and the communication of files kept up with the greatest facility.

See Plan of Hougoumont, p. 263.

I can speak to this point, as I was sent at one time of the day (I believe about two o'clock) from the orchard with some Light Troops to drive the French Tirailleurs back, who had become very annoying to the farm, and were gradually gaining ground, particularly on the right flank of our position.

Sent to drive French Tirailleurs out of the wood.

We drove them quite out of the wood upon three French Columns, which were posted at the bottom of the hill outside the wood, ready to move up and renew their attack upon the farmhouse, two of these Columns just beginning to move, the third unpiling arms and falling in to the support. We, of course, were driven back immediately.

Which done, came upon three French Columns— driven back again.

Believe, &c.,

ROBERT ELLISON,

Lieut.-Colonel and Colonel Grenadier Guards.

CAPTAIN H. W. POWELL.

Lieutenant and Captain 1st Foot Guards.

No. 108.   *Foxlease, Lyndhurst. No date.*

Extracts from Journal.

March on Quatre Bras.

June 15th, 1815. Two o'clock p.m. Dragoon brought word that the French were crossing the frontier, and to hold the Brigade in readiness to move. Eight o'clock—A second dragoon arrived with intelligence that the Prussians had been forced across the Sambre. Orders were issued for the right wing of the 3rd Battalion to remain at Hove with the left wing, having been moved to that village on the first order. I find I have forgotten to state that the 2nd Battalion were quartered in the town of Enghien, and that the right wing of the 3rd Battalion was at the village of Mark, and the left wing at the village of Hove.

June 16th, half-past one, a.m. Drums beat to arms, the Battalion and baggage ready to move at two. At three the order came for the Brigade to assemble at Hove. Heavy stores and hospital ordered to Brussels. At four, the order was given to move to our left, over the position of Steenkirke, in the direction of Braine-le-Comte, where it arrived about nine o'clock, having been joined by the second Brigade (2nd Battalion Coldstreams and 2nd Battalion 3rd Regiment) on the march. We halted on the eastern side, having had great difficulty in getting through the town in consequence of the numberless waggons and baggage confusedly huddled together in the street.

About twelve, General Cooke returned from a reconnaissance to the southward, and (as said at the time) on his own judgment ordered the Division to move to the left towards Nivelles. The heat was excessive, and the men suffered much from the weight of their packs. At about three p.m. the Division arrived within half a mile of Nivelles, and took up a position looking over the town, supposing our day's work was done. We were, however, scarcely halted, and the men disencumbered of their loads, when an Aide-de-camp brought the order to advance immediately.

The Division were under arms in a minute, and started double quick down the hill into Nivelles, supposing that the Enemy were entering it at the other side, for the firing had by this time become very heavy, and apparently very close. We continued our march through the town to Hautain-le-Val, where we halted to collect the stragglers and to let the Artillery pass to the head of the Column. We then continued along the *chaussée* from Nivelles to Namur. On the march the order was given to untie ten rounds ammunition and to see the flints in order, then for the Officers to join their Companies and fix the bayonets. On the road we met many wounded, and Major Jessop, of the 44th (Q.M.G. Department) shot through the foot; who urged us to get on as the Action was going on badly.

As we advanced the wounded became more and more [numerous] along the sides of the road. At nearly five p.m. we arrived at the head of a wood that abutted on the *chaussée* to the right, when the Light Infantry of the Brigade, under Lord Saltoun, were ordered into it, and as the head of the 2nd Battalion 1st Regiment came up, they were also ordered in, two Companies at a time, to support and assist the Light Infantry till the whole Battalion were in the wood.

This wood was called the Bois de Bossu, and might on an average be about three-fourths of a mile long and three hundred yards broad. A small stream ran across it. On the left side and close to the edge was a hollow way running along the eastern side. The men gave a cheer, and rushing in drove everything before them to the end of the wood, but the thickness of the underwood soon upset all order, and the French Artillery made the place so hot that it was thought advisable to draw back to the stream, which was rather more out of range. A great many men were killed and wounded by the heads of the trees falling on them as cut off by cannon shot.

Ordered to form outside and to the left of the wood,

And advanced to a certain point.

A Battalion of Brunswickers following.

The French Cavalry charges the line of Guards, and drives them into the wood.
They throw in such a destructive fire as nearly to annihilate the Cavalry.
The Brunswickers form square beautifully, and contribute to the destruction of the Cavalry.

Buried in the Bois de Bossu, Capts. Grose, Brown, and

The order was then given to form line outside the wood to our left. By this time our 3rd Battalion had come down the wood, and together we formed with our right on the wood and our left towards the *chaussée* from Brussels to Charleroi.

As all order had been lost in passing through the wood, the men formed up as they came out and extended the line into the standing corn. A great many men of other Regiments who had been engaged before we arrived, very gallantly left the wood and fell in with our men. The line again advanced, but never could get beyond a certain point. Here we stood firing at the Enemy in front, who deployed most steadily under our fire, whilst the French Cavalry kept moving about for an opportunity of charging us.

During our advance a Battalion of Black Brunswickers (so called from their black uniform, being [in] mourning, as we heard, for their Duke killed at Jena, and from their Teutonic custom of blacking their faces) had followed in the open field along the outside of the wood, and were manœuvring to form on our left when the French Cavalry charged our left and drove us all into the wood on the right. The hollow way now covered us from the Cavalry, and from it the men threw in so destructive a fire as to nearly annihilate them, whilst the Brunswickers (whose front became uncovered by our retreat into the wood) formed square beautifully, and did their part most effectively in their destruction. Many men and horses were taken who fled for shelter into the wood, which supplied our mounted (or rather dismounted) Officers with fresh horses. In this charge Lord Hay was supposed to be killed.

The *tiraillerie* continued during the daylight, and General Maitland took the 3rd Battalion to the end of the wood which the Enemy now no longer disputed, and having thrown out pickets for the night, directed the 2nd Battalion to retire to the *chaussée* at the end of the wood.

17th June. The early part of this day was employed in bringing the wounded out of the wood, and in burying the four Officers we had lost—Capt. Grose, Capt. Brown,

Lord Hay and Barrington—which was done under the large tree on the right of the wood nearest towards Nivelles.

There was now much moving of troops from one point to another, but as it was ultimately determined to retire, the Divisions moved off along the *chaussée* towards Brussels. The 1st Division left their ground a little past eleven.

Nothing particular occurred to us on the march to the position of Mont-St.-Jean. The day was excessively hot and the road very much crowded, but yet there was but little confusion and the stoppages but short. The only material one was from the narrowness of the bridge over the Dyle at Genappe.

After a march of perhaps eight miles we were ordered to take along a cart track to the left, which soon brought us behind a country château and farm with a garden and orchard, but separated from us by a deep hollow way (the continuation of the cart road). Here we halted supposing we were fixed for the night. However, orders came shortly afterwards to order us to move to our right over the standing corn up the rise, and on to the next rise till we got to the *chaussée* from Nivelles to Mont-St.-Jean. Here we had hardly been five minutes when there came on a storm of rain that deluged us, and continued through the greater part of the night.

We afterwards found that we had halted under the Château of Hougoumont.

We remained on the Nivelle *chaussée* till a quarter before eleven (by my watch), when the first cannon shot was fired, and the different Divisions immediately moved to their different stations in the Line.

I have, &c.,
H. WEYLAND POWELL.

FROM THE SAME.

No. 109.   *Foxlease, Lyndhurst, April 21st,* 1835.

.   .   .   .

Waterloo.

I shall now quote my Journal in answer to your first question, because having been written when the thing was strong in my recollection, [it] will probably have more weight with you.

Owing to the advance of the Prussians,

"Between five and six the Emperor was so much pressed by the Prussian advance on his right that he determined to make a last grand effort, and as he had tried every other Corps without effect, there only remained to him the 'Garde Imperiale.' With these he resolved to

Napoleon resolves to play his last stake.

play his last stake and to ensure success. His Artillery were ordered to concentrate their whole fire on the intended point of attack. That point was the rise of the [our] position about half-way between Hougoumont and La Haye Sainte.

"The Duke of Wellington had but a short time *previous* rode down to see what was doing at Hougoumont, and in

The Duke orders the Brigade to move to the left, and form line four deep.

returning had ordered the 1st Brigade of Guards to *take ground to its left and form line four deep*, which poor Frank D'Oyley did by wheeling up the sides of the Square, putting the Grenadiers and my Company (1st Battalion Company) in the centre of our line. What would Dundas have said!!!

The Brigade sheltered behind a bank from the cannonade which preceded the attack of the Imperial Guard.

"This brought the Brigade precisely on the spot the Emperor had chosen for his attack. There ran along this part of the position a cart road, on one side of which was a ditch and bank, in and under which the Brigade sheltered themselves during the cannonade, which might have lasted three-quarters of an hour. Without the protection of this bank every creature must have perished.

The approach of the 1st attacking Column.

"The Emperor probably calculated on this effect, for suddenly the firing ceased, and as the smoke cleared away a most superb sight opened on us. A close Column of Grenadiers (about seventies in front) of la Moyenne Garde, about 6,000 strong, led, as we have since heard, by Marshal

Ney, were seen ascending the rise *au pas de charge* shouting '*Vive l'Empereur.*' They continued to advance till within fifty or sixty paces of our front, when the Brigade were ordered to stand up. Whether it was from the sudden and unexpected appearance of a Corps so near them, which must have seemed as starting out of the ground, or the tremendously heavy fire we threw into them, *La Garde*, who had never before failed in an attack *suddenly* stopped. Those who from a distance and more on the flank could see the affair, tell us that the effect of our fire seemed to force the head of the Column bodily back.

Unexpected appearance of the British Guards in its front.

The Column stops.

"In less than a minute above 300 were down. They now wavered, and several of the rear divisions began to draw out as if to deploy, whilst some of the men in their rear beginning to fire over the heads of those in front was so evident a proof of their confusion, that Lord Saltoun (who had joined the Brigade, having had the whole of his Light Infantry Battalion dispersed at Hougoumont) holloaed out, '*Now's the time, my boys.*' Immediately the Brigade sprang forward. La Garde turned and gave us little opportunity of trying the steel. We charged down the hill till we had passed the end of the orchard of Hougoumont, when our right flank became exposed to another heavy Column (as we afterwards understood of the Chasseurs of the Garde) who were advancing in support of the former Column. This circumstance, besides that our charge was isolated, obliged the Brigade to retire towards their original position.

Deadly fire of the Guards.

The Brigade charges and drives the Column down the hill.

The Brigade's right flank menaced by the 2nd attacking Column,

And retires to its original position.

"Opportunely, Sir F. Adam's Light Brigade had in the meantime come round the knoll between the position and Hougoumont, when we had been ordered to take ground to our left, and were advancing under the hedge and blind line along the northern side of the orchard at Hougoumont. As soon therefore as we had uncovered their front we halted and fronted.

Advance of Adam's Brigade,

"The two Brigades now returned to the charge which the Chasseurs did not wait for, and we continued our forward movement till we got to the bottom of the

And of the Guards.

valley between the positions. Here our Brigade halted to restore its order by calling out the covering Sergeants and forming Companies. As soon as the Column was

Proceeded towards the Charleroi road, where they found nearly sixty Guns abandoned.

formed we proceeded towards the *chaussée* (to Namur) [to Charleroi], where we found nearly sixty pieces of Artillery jammed together and deserted. Whilst we were halted in the valley the Light Troops and Cavalry had passed us and gone in pursuit."

.   .   .   .

I have, &c.,

H. WEYLAND POWELL.

LIEUT.-COLONEL H. DAVIS,

LIEUTENANT AND CAPTAIN 1st FOOT GUARDS.

No. 110.   *Elmley Park, March 19th, 1835.*

.   .   .   .   .   .

*Waterloo.
Position of Brigade.*

The Brigade of Guards to which I belonged, consisting of the 2nd and 3rd Battalions of the 1st Regiment, were posted above and to the left of Hougoumont, a little behind the crest of the position, so that they were nearly out of sight of the Enemy until close

*The Infantry formed in squares by order of the Duke.
After the attacks of French Cavalry had been repelled, an attack of French Infantry also.*

to them. The Infantry in that part of the line were formed in hollow squares by the express order of the Duke of Wellington at the commencement of the Action.

About the middle of the day, after the attacks of the Enemy's Cavalry had been repelled, a strong force of French Infantry was pushed forward, who kept up a galling fire on the part of the line where the Battalion to which I belonged was posted. In order to drive them back the Battalion, not waiting to deploy into line (which in consequence of large masses of the Enemy's Cavalry still hovering about would have been unsafe), opened from the centre of the rear face of the Square, that face and the two flank faces bringing their right and left shoulders forward until in line with the front face, thus forming an irregular line of four deep. They then advanced, drove back the French Infantry, and in the midst of a murderous fire of the Enemy's Artillery, re-forming square with as much coolness as on parade, returned to their former position.

When the French Imperial Guards advanced to the attack, the same manœuvre was repeated by the British Guards, and the French Guards, whose attack was made in column, were broken and driven back with great slaughter, the field being literally covered with their dead.

Repulse of the 1st attack of the Imperial Guard.

I remain, &c.,
H. DAVIS.

CAPTAIN AND LIEUT.-COLONEL J. P. DIROM, GRENADIER GUARDS.

ENSIGN* 1st FOOT GUARDS.

21, *Usher's Island, February 27th,* 1835.   No. 111.

With regard to our formation, that of the Imperial Guard, and what took place, I feel as certain as if it had only occurred yesterday.

Waterloo.

The Brigade had been formed in line four deep, and ordered to lie down. When the Imperial Guard came in sight, the men were desired to stand up and cautioned at the same time not to fire without orders. The Imperial Guard advanced in close Column with ported arms, the Officers of the leading Divisions in front waving their swords. The French Columns showed no appearance of having suffered on their advance, but seemed as regularly formed as if at a field day.

Manner in which the 1st attack of the Imperial Guard was carried out.

When they got within a short distance we were ordered to make ready, present, and fire. The effect of our volley was evidently most deadly. The French Columns appeared staggered, and, if I may use the expression, convulsed. Part seemed inclined to advance,

When within a short distance it received a deadly fire from the Guards.

* Appears to have held also the rank of Lieutenant.

part halted and fired, and others, more particularly towards the centre and rear of the Columns, seemed to be turning round.

At this moment our line was ordered to charge, as I always supposed, by the Duke of Wellington himself, who was then immediately in our rear. On our advance the whole of the French Columns turned round and made off.

On being charged by the Guards the Column made off.

We were shortly after ordered to take up the usual pace and form column of Companies without halting; as soon as we had done so several Regiments of Light Cavalry passed us at full speed in pursuit of the Enemy.

I have, &c.,

J. P. DIROM,

Capt. and Lieut.-Col. Grenadier Guards.

BYNG'S INFANTRY BRIGADE.

The 2nd Infantry Brigade was composed of the 2nd Battalion of the Coldstream Guards and the 2nd Battalion of the 3rd Foot Guards, and was under the command of Major-General Sir John Byng, K.C.B.

The Brigade reached Quatre Bras on the 16th June, about half-past six p.m. It was moved round the Bois de Bossu whilst Maitland's Brigade was clearing the French out of the wood, and remained upon the Charleroi road until the close of the Action, when it was moved up to the front of the wood, and threw out pickets for the night.

See Plan of Quatre Bras, No. 2.

See Plan of Hougoumont, p. 263.

At Waterloo the Light Companies of the two Battalions were posted in the Château, Farm-buildings, and Gardens of Hougoumont, and in the wood in front of it. About twelve o'clock they were reinforced by four more Companies of the Coldstreams.

After a prolonged combat in the wood, in which the Guards were supported by the fire of the British Artillery when practicable, they were at length driven by overpowering numbers inside the range of buildings, but continued to hold them and the gardens for the remainder of the day.

The French Artillery having set fire to the greater part of the buildings, this added immensely to the difficulties of the defence, and caused an agonising death to many of the wounded, the flames and smoke having made it impossible to rescue them.

During the repeated struggles for the possession of the orchard between the Enemy and the Light Infantry of Maitland's Brigade, the fire of the Coldstreams from the garden wall invariably turned the scale against the French, and deprived them of any temporary footing they had gained.

Several Companies of the 3rd Regiment had been moved down to reinforce the Post, and about two o'clock the remainder of the Battalion was sent as a further reinforcement, and to replace Maitland's Light Infantry, of whom few or none remained.

The Battalion advanced twice to the front hedge of the orchard, on the second occasion being reinforced by some German Troops of Du Plat's Brigade, but was each time outflanked and driven back to the hollow way in rear of it, and each time the French were again dislodged by the fire of the Coldstreams.

On the third advance of the Battalion and the Germans, they not only remained in permanent possession of the front hedge, but two Companies and the Germans also forced a passage into the wood, and firmly established themselves in it.

The two remaining Companies of the Coldstreams had been left as a protection to the Colours, at first on the main ridge of the position and, after the advance of the French Cavalry, in the hollow ground behind it.

GENERAL SIR J. BYNG, G.C.B., G.C.H.
MAJOR-GENERAL AND K.C.B.

No. 112.

London, November 2nd, 1834.

Waterloo.
At 7 p.m. in command of the Division, Sir G. Cooke being wounded.

Was with the 1st Brigade during the attack of the Imperial Guards.

The 2nd Brigade was at Hougoumont with a reserve on the hill in rear.

．　　．　　．　　．　　．　　．　　．

I can hardly give you the precise formation of my Brigade at seven p.m., as I was at that time in command of the Division (Sir George Cooke being wounded), and was with the first Brigade, then attacked by the Imperial Guards. As far as my recollection serves, the 2nd Brigade were in Hougoumont and in the wood or orchard to its left, with a reserve on the hill in rear of that position.

At that time I think the third attack of the Enemy had been repelled, and they (the French) were in columns at a distance, with skirmishers in front, keeping up an irregular fire ; but I do not feel positive.

．　　．　　．　　．

Yours, &c.,

J. BYNG.

FROM THE SAME.

London, April 4th, 1835.　　**No. 113.**

I had only reached the position of the first Brigade of Guards but a few minutes before the attack commenced. I will not, therefore, take upon myself to trace out on your inclosure the precise line of their position.

We were at first, as you state, in rear of the road, and partly under cover, from which I moved them forward two or three hundred yards. You are correct also in your remark that the general attack was not commenced until after a short delay, say, ten or twelve minutes.

I think the inference you have drawn from information received is generally correct. . . but I fear giving too decided an opinion, as I was at the moment suffering much from the contusion I received.

Yours, &c.,

J. BYNG.

Waterloo.
The attack of Imperial Guards on the 1st Brigade.

The General Advance did not commence until ten or twelve minutes after the repulsion of the Imperial Guard.

THE COLDSTREAM GUARDS—2ND BATTALION.

LIEUT.-GENERAL SIR ALEXANDER WOODFORD, K.C.B., K.C.H.

MAJOR AND COLONEL A. WOODFORD, COLDSTREAM GUARDS.

Gibraltar, January 14th, 1838.　　**No. 114.**

At the time I was sent down to Hougoumont (about twelve o'clock or a little after), the Enemy had nearly got into the farmyard. We found them very near the wall, and charged them, upon which they went off, and I took the opportunity of entering the farm by a side door in the lane.

From that time there was much *tiraillerie,* some

Hougoumont.
At 12 o'clock the French had nearly got into the farmyard, but were driven off.

French Artillery set

fire to the barns.

cannon and howitzer shots, which last I always considered set fire to the barns.

Much annoyed by French tirailleurs, on the east side of the enclosures.

The tirailleurs on the rising ground along the eastern hedge never distinctly showed themselves, though they annoyed us very much by firing at the door which communicated between the courtyard and garden, and of which they could see the top.

Several cannon shots enter the building where the wounded Officers lay.

Several cannon shots went into the centre building, where some wounded Officers were lying.

Opinion of Jerome's Chief of the Staff on the French attacks.

In Corfu I had much conversation with General Guilleminot, who was Chef de l'Etat Major to Jerome Napoleon. He told me that all Prince Jerome's Corps was in, and at the end of the wood. The first attack he advised; the others, he said, he did not agree in. It always struck me that the subsequent attacks were feeble.

Several wounded men burnt in the conflagration.

The heat and smoke of the conflagration were very difficult to bear. Several men were burnt, as neither Colonel Macdonell nor myself could penetrate to the stables where the wounded had been carried.

A wounded French Officer grateful for not being fired at.

Baron de Cubières, Governor of Ancona, also talked to me much about Waterloo. He commanded a Regiment, and was wounded and unhorsed just under the wall. He says we forbore to fire upon him, and he owes us much for many good years since. I have some recollection of the circumstance, of which he always makes a great deal.

· · · · · · · ·

I beg, &c.,

A. WOODFORD.

FROM THE SAME.

Gibraltar, December 9th, 1838.

No. 115.

The Farm and Garden of Hougoumont were occupied by the Light Infantry of the 2nd Brigade of Guards on the night of the 17th, and loopholes were made, and platforms constructed with whatever material the premises afforded.

Hougoumon' Farm buildings and garden occupied by the Light Infantry of

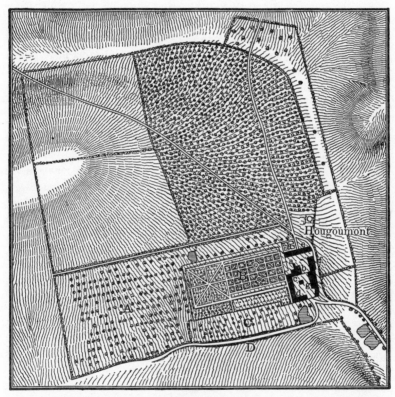

THE PLAN FACES TO THE SOUTH.

A, Great Orchard; *B*, Garden; *C*, Small Orchard; *D*, Hollow Way; *a*, Chapel; *b*, House; *c*, Farmer's House; *d*, Cowhouse and Stabling; *e*, Gardener's House, Stables, &c. ; *f*, Barn ; *g*, Great Barn ; *h*, Small Garden ; *j*, Haystack.

the 2nd Brigade on the night of the 17th.

The farm is well calculated for defence. The dwelling-house in the Centre was a strong square building, with

Description of the Post.

small doors and windows. The barns and granaries formed nearly a square, with one door of communication with the small yard to the South; and from that yard was a door into the garden, a double gate into the wood, under or near the small house, which I conclude you call the Gardener's house; and another door opening into the lane on the West.

There was also another carriage gate at the North-West angle of the great yard, leading into the barn, which conducted to the road to Braine-la-Leud.

The little garden to the South, fronting the wood, was occupied by the Guards; there were platforms in it, and I do not recollect that the Enemy ever got into it.

A few of the French penetrated into the yard, and were driven out.

Some few of the Enemy penetrated into the yard from the lane on the West, but were speedily driven out, or despatched.

The Enemy were, of course, in possession of the wood all night.

I have heard from a French General Officer, that on the 18th nearly the whole of Prince Jerome's Corps were directed against the wood. They came on in force several times, but did not attempt a general escalade; there was constant firing from the wood upon the garden, and from the men on the platforms and banks, and I think in some cases from the upper windows.

The French did not attempt a general escalade.

The French tirailleurs kept up an annoying fire from the rising ground to the south-west.

A rising ground commanded the south-west angle of the farm. The corn was high and concealed the tirailleurs, who kept a regular fire upon the doors of communication I have mentioned, and killed several men and wounded some Officers. There was but little cannonade directed against Hougoumont; in the afternoon, however, a shell or carcass was thrown into the great barn, and the smoke and flames burst out in a most terrific manner, and communicated with rapidity and fury to the other outbuildings. Some Officers attempting to penetrate into the stables to rescue some wounded men, were obliged to desist, from the suffocation of the smoke, and several men perished. The flames, as is well known, stopped at the little Chapel.

The great barn set on fire by a shell. The conflagration extended to the other buildings.

Many wounded perished in the flames, which stopped at the Chapel.

The French never, as far as I recollect, got into the garden. They were in the orchard, but did not scale the garden walls. The platforms did not extend all the way, as in some cases the bank was high enough to enable the men to fire over the walls. The platforms were, of course, rudely constructed, Colonel Macdonell having to work all night to collect materials and loophole the walls.

The French only penetrated into the orchard, not into the garden.

General Guilleminot was the Chef de l'Etat Major of the Corps, and was present at the several advances through the wood.

General Cubières, then commanding a Regiment, was wounded and thrown from his horse near the gardener's house, when the men nearest to him ceased firing at him, and.he has lived to acknowledge this; he has mentioned it to me several times.

The wood always appeared full of troops. From all I have heard from French Officers since, they considered Hougoumont as very formidable.

The French Officers considered Hougoumont as very formidable.

. . . .

Believe me, &c.,
ALEX. WOODFORD.

CAPTAIN AND LIEUT.-COLONEL C. W. SHORT, COLDSTREAM GUARDS.

ENSIGN, COLDSTREAM GUARDS.

London, March 5th, 1835.

No. 116.

Waterloo.

I cannot speak as to the position of any of the Companies of the 2nd Battalion otherwise than the 7th and 8th, to whom was confided the protection of the Colours. These two Companies remained in the original position to the immediate left of the three trees on the crest of the rise behind Hougoumont until the French Cavalry came on.

7th and 8th Companies detached with the Colours.

At first posted on the ridge to the left of the "three trees" in rear of Hougoumont.

We then retired by order of Sir J. Byng across the Nivelles road, and after two or three halts finally took our station in some hollow ground, which, as far as I recollect,

On the approach t

3RD FOOT GUARDS.

the French
Cavalry, re-
tired by Sir J.
Byng to the
hollow ground
in rear.

Remained
there till the
General
Advance.

commenced a little distance on our left and ran deeper in the direction of Braine-la-Leud.

.　　.　　.　　.　　.　　.　　.

On our right was posted a Regiment with green facing, the 51st or 55th, I think. Here we remained with the Colours until the General Advance took place, and we moved straight forward, and at the close found ourselves pretty nearly on the same ground as we stood on early in the day; rather perhaps in the advance, however, on the slope towards Hougoumont.

The Companies detached in and about Hougoumont joined us, and I went on picket in the wood.　.　.

Believe me, &c.,

C. W. SHORT.

THE 3RD FOOT GUARDS—2ND BATTALION.

MAJOR-GENERAL F. HEPBURN, C.B.

MAJOR AND COLONEL 3RD FOOT GUARDS.

No. 117.　　　　*The Hooke, near Lewes, November 22nd, 1834.*

.　　.　　.　　.　　.　　.　　.

Hougoumont.
I add a short narrative of the proceedings of the Battalion under my command on the 18th of June.

Several Companies of the 3rd Regiment Guards had been sent down to reinforce the Light Infantry of the 1st Brigade of Guards, who under Lord Saltoun were

About
1 o'clock
ordered
with the
remainder
of the Bat-
talion to
reinforce the
troops in the
orchard.

making a gallant defence in the orchard before mentioned. As near as I can judge, about one o'clock, Sir John Byng gave me orders to go down with the rest of the Battalion. The command was given up to me by Lord Saltoun, on my reaching the near hedge of the orchard, where there was a hollow way, which served us as a rallying point more than once during the day.

See Plan of
Hougoumont,
p. 263.

The hollow
way served as
a rallying
point.

After some time we advanced, crossed the orchard, and occupied the front hedge, which I considered my post, driving the Enemy through a gate at the corner of the garden wall into the wood. Soon after this the Enemy's

Cavalry passed close to our left, and ascended the position, at the same time we were warmly attacked, our left turned, and we were driven back to the hollow way, where we rallied; but when the attacking troops attempted to pass the orchard they received so destructive a fire from the Coldstream Guards, posted inside the garden wall, that they were completely staggered, and we meanwhile advanced and regained our post.

Advanced and occupied the front hedge of the orchard.

Outflanked and driven back to the hollow way.

Destructive fire from the Coldstreams in the garden on the attacking troops.

After some considerable time had elapsed, during which I presume the Enemy's Cavalry had been driven back, Columns of Infantry passed over the same ground on our left. We were again outflanked and driven back to our friendly hollow way, and again the fire of the Coldstreams did us good service, in fact, it was this fire that constituted the strength of the post.

We once more advanced, and resumed our station along the front hedge, from whence there was no further effort to dislodge us. But soon after Sir Henry Clinton having sent down some Landwehr (with offers of further reinforcements, if necessary), I sent them with two of my own Companies into the wood, where they kept up a heavy fire. I may remark here that the attacks made upon us were in general upon our flanks, and not in our front.

Advanced to front hedge again.

Same operations repeated.

Reinforcements received and sent together with two Companies of the Guards into the wood.

During this time I knew nothing of what was passing elsewhere. In about an hour or more after the last resumption of our post, a Staff Officer came from the left at full gallop, with orders for an immediate advance, stating that the whole Army were moving on to the charge. We passed the hedge and moved upon the troops in the cornfield, who retired in no order, and almost without firing.

Ordered to join in the General Advance.

The 3rd Guards joined in the general pursuit, till perceiving that the men were exhausted after their hard day's work, I halted, and took them back to a field in the rear of the house of Hougoumont, where we bivouacked for the night.   .   .   .   .

I have, &c.,

FRAN^s. HEPBURN,

Major-General.

CAPTAIN AND LIEUT.-COLONEL G. D. STANDEN, SCOTS FUSILIER GUARDS.

ENSIGN 3RD FOOT GUARDS.

No. 118.

33, *Old Bond Street.*

Hougoumont.

The Light Companies of the Coldstreams and 3rd Guards had the defence of the wood and Château.

An error as to D'Erlon. *See* next letter.

This point × is where the east edge of the wood is crossed by the diagonal path leading to the main road.

See haystack on Plan, p. 263. It served as a rallying point.

Between 1 and 2 the remainder of the Guards driven into the farm buildings.

A few French came in also, but were driven out again.

Barns, &c., on fire. Officers'

. . . .

" What was the particular formation, &c. ? "

I belonged to the Light Company of the 3rd Guards, which with the Light Company of the Coldstream, had the defence of the wood and Château of Hougoumont, after being driven into the house they remained there till the close of the Action.

" What was the formation of that part of the Enemy's forces, &c. ? "

Jerome Buonaparte attacked the wood and house with his Corps, consisting of D'Erlon's divisions, &c. See his speech in the Chambre des Pairs on the 21st or 22nd June. " At one o'clock we were in possession of the wood."

A tirailleur came within ten yards of × previous to the Action, and the corn concealed him till within that distance, by which path the Duke and his Staff left the wood half-an-hour before the commencement.

. . . .

I have marked . . . . where a haystack was set fire to in one of the attacks in which our Companies were repulsed, behind which we repeatedly formed and charged ; I cannot speak as to time, but Jerome put the earliest moment, but think between one and two the French drove the remaining few into the house. After a severe struggle the French forced the rear gate open and came in with us. We flew to the parlour, opened the windows and drove them out, leaving an Officer and some men dead within the wall.

During this time the whole of the barn and cart house were in flames. During the confusion three or four Officers' horses rushed out into the yard from the barn, and in a minute or two rushed back into the flames and were burnt. I mention this as I had always heard horses would never leave fire; perhaps some beam or large piece of wood fell and astonished them.

horses consumed in the flames.

The ditch at the corner of the wood leading into the orchard . . . was full of dead bodies (we had blocked up the gate), as the French strove repeatedly and gallantly to get through in defiance of the fire from the loopholes so close to them. The anecdote of the fire burning only to the foot of the Cross is perfectly true, which in so superstitious a country made a great sensation.

Ditch at left hand corner of the wood filled with dead bodies, the French striving to force an entrance at that point into the orchard.

I never saw such a "bullfincher" as the hedge in front of the orchard. I cannot tell how the barn was first fired, but there was an opening sufficient for a man to get through in the wall, by which the French might with the burning hay have fired it.

Story of fire stopping at Cross in Chapel true.

Barn might have been set on fire through an opening in wall.

.   .   .   .

Yours, &c.,

G. D. STANDEN.

FROM THE SAME.

Guards Club. No date. No. 119.

.   .   .   .

I thought Jerome did attack us first, from reading his speech in the *Moniteur* giving a description of the disastrous day, and that Reille, D'Erlon, &c., were under his immediate orders.   .   .   .   .   .

Hougoumont. D'Erlon commanded the 1st corps, Reille the 2nd, and Jerome a Division under the latter. —ED.

I heard voices, and the drummers beating the *pas de charge*, apparently belonging to Jerome's left Column. I was then in a small field like a crescent on the right flank of the house, adjoining the lane going to the Charleroi road from the house, but I am inclined to think they belonged to the right or centre Column.

The French advance against Hougoumont.

.   .   .   .

When we in turn retreated, our attacks became each time more feeble. Although we drove them out, our advances became shorter. They fed an immense force of skirmishers; we had no support.

The alternate attacks became more feeble on both sides owing to losses of men.

LOSS of men, the remainder not having been so keen as they were, therefore after the first or second charge it is impossible to say which Column of Jerome's they belonged to (*sic*). It was some time after the Action had commenced that a body of troops rushed into the wood from the field by the path leading to the Charleroi road. These came from Foy. They made a desperate attack and attempt to get into the orchard. Most were killed or wounded by the men inside the garden wall.

Gallant attempt of the French to get into the orchard.

. . . .

Quatre Bras. *See* Plans.

The Division of Guards marched right in front from the place we halted at, about five miles from Quatre Bras. We had proceeded some way by the edge of the wood, when we were halted by the Prince of Orange, who wheeled the first Brigade into the wood. They began firing directly. The French were by this time getting very close to the edge. They never were through or near enough to prevent the Prince of Orange from coming up the road. The first Regiment lost most of their men by shooting each other. Maitland has been much blamed for not clearing the wood with his two Light Companies, which he might have done. The consequence was, instead of halting and forming in a deep sort of ravine, they rushed out of the wood, got into temporary confusion, and were obliged to get back again.

The 1st Brigade become engaged in the Bois de Bossu.

Lose many of their men by shooting each other.

Rushing out of the wood get into confusion, and obliged to return to it.

They say the Duke sent to stop them, but the A.D.C. never arrived. I did not see any Belgians · or Dutch amongst the killed and wounded in the wood; we met some Cavalry (Belge) with lots of Good Samaritan Infantry taking care of them, perhaps sixty at the outside.

. . . .

Meanwhile the two Light Companies are sent on to Quatre Bras, then to the right towards 1st Brigade.

When the first Regiment were clearing the wood, our two Light Companies were moved to Quatre Bras, and then brought round to the right, in front of the left centre, with the First Regiment then debouching from the wood on our right. On our left, a little in advance, some Black Brunswickers received a charge of Cavalry with *great* steadiness. Our battalions remained till night on the *Chaussée.* Just before dark our Companies were put on the

Brunswickers repulse the French Cavalry with

3RD FOOT GUARDS.
great steadiness.
The French outposts fire during the night.

advance pickets owing to some mistake. The French having lit their fires and posted their sentries in the open field, began firing, which continued on their side frequently during the night whenever we stirred. Rather a curious thing that the sub-division to which I belonged was on the advance picket, the 16th and 17th both.

. . . . . .

Yours, &c.,
G. D. STANDEN.

ADAM'S INFANTRY BRIGADE.

The 3rd (Light) Infantry Brigade consisted of the 52nd Light Infantry, the 71st Light Infantry (Glasgow Highlanders), the 2nd Battalion, and two Companies of the 3rd Battalion of the 95th Rifles. It was commanded by Major-General F. Adam.

Previous to the commencement of the Battle of Waterloo it was posted between the village of Merbe Braine and the Nivelles road, but on the French moving to attack Hougoumont it was formed behind the Nivelles road in reserve to the Troops in the front line.

See General Plan, No. 1.

Towards the afternoon it was moved close up to the Nivelles road, and about four o'clock ordered by the Duke of Wellington to form a four-deep line, and attack the crowds of French skirmishers who had driven in the Artillerymen from the Batteries on the crest of the position.

The skirmishers were repulsed and the Brigade advanced and took up a diagonal position in the hollow to the left rear of Hougoumont. Here it was formed in Squares which successfully resisted several attacks of the French Cavalry, but during

See Plan, p. 288.

the intervals between these attacks, the Squares suffered greatly from the fire of the French Artillery, especially the two flank Battalions, the 2nd Battalion 95th Rifles, and the 71st. The portion of the 3rd Battalion 95th Rifles, attached to the 71st Regiment, most materially contributed, by its effective independent fire, in repulsing a Cavalry attack on the Square of the latter Regiment.

About six o'clock, the right of the Brigade being considered exposed to a flank attack from the enclosures of Hougoumont, the whole were withdrawn behind the crest of the main position, so as to be under cover from the Enemy's Artillery.

On the approach of the 2nd attacking Column of the Imperial Guard, which threw out a cloud of skirmishers in its front, the 52nd and 2nd Battalion 95th sent out a Company each to check them, but these were driven in by a body of Cuirassiers moved forward to attack the Batteries which fired on the Column. The Brigade, meanwhile, had been formed in line four deep, and brought up to the road running along the ridge of the position, and its appearance induced the Cuirassiers to retire, pursued by a Squadron of the 23rd Light Dragoons.

The French Column having diverged from its original direction somewhat to the right, so as to rather lend its left flank to Adam's Brigade, Colonel Sir John Colborne, commanding the 52nd, the centre Regiment, wheeled his left Company to the left, and formed the other Companies on it, so as to bring his front nearly parallel with the left

See General Plan, No. 2.

flank of the Column. The Imperial Guard halted, wheeled up its left sections into an opposing line to the 52nd, and opened a most destructive fire on that Regiment.

The Duke, seeing Colborne's movement, at once ordered the 2nd Battalion 95th, on the left, to conform to it. Colborne, after pouring a deadly fire into the French Column, which was quickly succeeded by that of the 95th, ordered his Regiment to charge the Column, and the 95th hastened to join in the charge. Meanwhile, Adam had galloped to the right to order the 71st Regiment and 3rd Battalion 95th to also conform to Colborne's movement, but they had so much ground to get over that they were not in time to fire into the Column before the charge commenced.

The French Column (excepting the two rear Battalions, which retired in a considerable degree of order) broke into the wildest confusion, and as the Brigade pursued them, its line became at first nearly perpendicular to the French position, a Hanoverian Battalion under Lieutenant-Colonel Halkett was advanced to give support to its exposed right flank. The French fugitives, meantime, bearing more towards La Belle Alliance, were being followed by the Brigade, when its front was crossed by the returning party of the 23rd Light Dragoons, at which, by mistake, some shots were fired, and immediately afterwards three French Guns on the prolongation of the right of the line of the 52nd began to enfilade it with grape, but were driven away by the right Section, which was wheeled up by Lieutenant Gawler for that purpose.

See General
Plan, No. 3.

The Brigade next came upon three Squares of the Imperial Guard, which were posted on a height with their right resting on the Genappe road, and the Duke ordered the Brigade to attack them. On the Brigade advancing, the Squares, after firing into it, were faced to the rear and retreated by word of command.

The Brigade, in its pursuit of the Squares, crossed the main road, and was threatened by a body of Cuirassiers, but Adam moved on in four deep formation, and the Cuirassiers declined the contest. On ascending the high ground in rear of La Belle Alliance, it was by mistake fired on by a Prussian Battery. Soon after this it dispersed some Infantry, and captured some Artillery, who were unaware of its approach, and the last (as supposed) French Gun fired that day was turned round by men of the 71st Regiment and fired by Captain Campbell (Adam's Aide-de-Camp) into the retiring Columns of the Imperial Guard.

The Brigade bivouacked for the night at or near the Farm of Rossomme.

Among the letters of this Brigade I have included that of General William Halkett, who led the Hanoverian Battalion which so effectively co-operated with it during the final Advance, and who captured General Cambronne, the Commander of the two rear Battalions of the Imperial Guard above referred to.

All the letters treat of Waterloo, and No. 123 relates also to the entry into Paris.

Sir F. Adam.

LIEUT.-GENERAL THE RIGHT HON. SIR FREDERICK ADAM, G.C.B., G.C.M.G.

MAJOR-GENERAL F. ADAM, COMMANDING 3RD INFANTRY BRIGADE.

Memorandum for Capt. Siborne.   *No date* [? 1838].

No. 120.

Waterloo.

I must premise by stating that having kept no notes at the time (in consequence of being wounded, and subsequently employed by orders of the Duke of Wellington while at Brussels), and never from that time to this having put anything on paper relating to the Battle, I have only my memory to trust to, and at this distance of time it is possibly not very accurate.

I may add that from the circumstance of my service since 1815, I have been little in the way of hearing the details of the Action discussed, and probably have not ten times during the three-and-twenty years which have elapsed, endeavoured to refresh my impressions for the purpose of stating in conversation the transactions which I witnessed on the 18th June, 1815. I wish these observations to be kept more especially in view as regards the hours of the day at which particular events took place. The relation of these events to others or their sequence, I can probably pretty accurately record, but the exact *time* of their occurrence must be fixed by the coinciding or preponderating testimony as to the hours of occurrence which may best [be] trusted to fix the precise period of the day.

The 3rd Brigade was bivouacked on the night of the 17th *en potence* to the main line of the troops. Merbe Braine was a little in front of its left.

The first position taken up by the 3rd Brigade was nearly that marked on the Plan, formed by Battalions in columns of Companies at quarter distance. In this position the Brigade remained in reserve with piled arms until the Enemy's Cavalry gained the crest of the position running from the [rear of] Hougoumont towards La Haye Sainte. When this was perceived the men stood to their arms, as we expected the Cavalry of the Enemy would break the

The Plan referred to is lost, and the "marks" are not designated in the letter. —ED.

See General Plan, No. 1.

small Brunswick Battalions which were down the slope. The contrary occurred, and the Brunswickers stood firm, and the Enemy's Cavalry retired.

Brigade advances to the Nivelles road.

Shortly after this the 3rd Brigade was ordered to advance, which it did in the order in which it was formed, to the Nivelles road, on the edge of which it remained for some time exposed to a fire of Artillery, by which a considerable number of men were disabled. After crossing the Nivelles road the Duke of Wellington personally directed that the Brigade should form line *four* deep " and drive those fellows away," meaning some French Infantry. There was not space to form the 52nd in line with the 71st and 95th, and the 52nd consequently was a sort of reserve to the Brigade.

Brigade ordered by the Duke to form line four deep, and drive away some French Infantry.

The Enemy's Infantry were very soon disposed of, and the Brigade continued to advance to about —— where the Cavalry of the Enemy, being prepared to attack, the Brigade was formed in columns and then in squares. The interval between the 71st and 95th was larger than desirable, and when the Cavalry were just reaching the 71st Sir John Colborne brought down the 52nd to fill up the space, and [threw] in a most effective oblique fire on the Cavalry, which were in the act of attacking the 71st Regiment.

See Plan, p. 238.

Brigade in squares repulses a Cavalry attack.

After the Cavalry attacks had been disposed of, and subsequently when the Enemy's Infantry were again about attacking Hougoumont, the right of the Brigade was judged to be too near the enclosures of that place, and had it remained, would have been exposed to being taken in flank from thence. It was therefore, at the suggestion of Sir J. Colborne, retired, and again brought a little further back to about —— in order to be screened from the fire of the Enemy's Artillery by the fall of the slope.

Brigade retired so as to be under cover of the crest of the position.
A French Officer deserts, and gives information of the approaching attack of the Imperial Guard.

While in this position a French Officer deserted and came over to where the Brigade was, and gave information that the Imperial Guard was forming to make an attack on that part of the position.

It was not judged expedient to receive this attack, but to move forward the Brigade and assail the Enemy instead of waiting to be assailed, and orders to that effect were given.

The Brigade was at this time formed in line four deep —from right to left 71st, 52nd, 2nd 95th ; and the two Companies of the 3rd 95th on right of 71st.

The first encounter with the Imperial Guard was a very sharp tussle with its Tirailleurs, but this did not extend to our right further than the right of 52nd, and hardly to left of 71st.

When their Tirailleurs were disposed of, the 52nd were right shouldered forward by Sir J. Colborne, and the 71st conformed ; but it being considered that the interval between the right of 71st and the enclosures of Hougoumont left the right of the Brigade exposed, request was more than once made for troops from the other part of the Division to occupy this space and cover the flank of the 3rd Brigade, and at length Lieutenant-Colonel Halkett, with a part of his Hanoverian Militia Brigade was sent for this purpose, and as it came forward the 3rd Brigade advanced, the Imperial Guard was driven back, and the Brigade, continuing to advance, crossed the Genappe *chaussée,* and continued advancing in a direction nearly parallel to that *chaussée,* which was at some little distance on the right.

52nd right brought forward, so that their fire should bear upon flank of 2nd attacking Column. 71st conforming.

Some Hanoverians occupy space between right of Brigade and Hougoumont.

Imperial Guard is driven back; Brigade advances and crosses Genappe road. Moves on parallel to that road.

While advancing, the Duke of Wellington being with the Brigade, some Battalions of the Enemy were re-formed, and appeared inclined to stand. The Duke ordered them to be attacked, but it was suggested to his Grace that the Brigade, which from its rapid advance was somewhat loose in its formation, had better be halted and the files closed in. The halt was ordered accordingly, but after a few moments the Duke said, " They won't stand, better attack them," and the 3rd Brigade was accordingly again put in motion, and the Battalions of the Enemy withdrew, and fell into the mass of confusion which existed in our front.

Col. Hunter Blair.

These Battalions (Imperial Guards) were the last troops of the Enemy which had any appearance of order or formation.

COLONEL T. HUNTER BLAIR, C.B., UNATTD.
Major 91st Regiment, and Brigade-Major to Adam's Brigade.

No. 121.   *Leamington, Warwickshire, May 1st, 1835.*

. . . .

Waterloo

Since its receipt, I have again read with much attention the correspondence between Sir Hussey Vivian and Colonel Gawler on the " Crisis of Waterloo," and my first impression is thereby more confirmed, that essentially their opinions *now* nearly accord.

A subject so fully discussed leaves little room for addition.

Col. Gawler's account a faithful one generally, except as to share of 1st Guards, and 95th in repelling last attack of Imperial Guard.

Colonel Gawler having acknowledged the error into which he had fallen respecting the 71st Regiment, it appears to me that he has faithfully given the leading features of the position and movements of the Light Brigade, though I am not quite prepared to admit that the 1st Guards, and 2nd and 3rd 95th, may not be said to have co-operated in the repulse of the last attack of the Imperial Guard.

The French had partially gained the summit of our position.

My persuasion is that the summit of our position was partially gained by the Imperial Guard, and I recollect Sir John Colborne telling me immediately after the attack, that he had formed his left company *en potence*, refusing his flank in the apprehension of its being turned.

During total advance of Brigade, does not recollect seeing any Allied troops in front of it except retiring Cavalry.

During the diagonal movement of the Light Brigade, its attack on the Squares of the Old Guard, arrival at Belle Alliance after crossing the Genappe road, and final halt to allow the Prussians to pass through its ranks, I do not recollect ·to have seen in front of it any portion of the Allied Army, except the retiring small body of British and German Cavalry.

The 71st was certainly not the " Regiment in red." It crossed the road before reaching Belle Alliance, and I well remember an Officer of the Regiment chalking 71 on a number of Guns abandoned close to the north gable of the house.

After the repulse of the Squares of the Old Guard (I do not exactly recollect the spot) Sir Frederick Adam desired me to ride on the prolongation of our right in order to observe if any part of the Enemy seemed to threaten our right flank—then apparently quite unprotected. Having gone some distance, I met the Duke of Wellington moving at a quick pace, followed by one individual to whom I spoke. His answer was, *" Monsieur, je ne parle pas un seul mot d'Anglais."* I told him in French the order I had received. He replied, *" Le Duc lui-méme a été voir; il n'y a rien à craindre."* I rejoined the Brigade.

The above circumstance has always appeared to me and to those to whom I have related it, a very striking proof of the miraculous escape and providential care of that great man on this eventful day : his Staff, even Orderlies, almost all killed or wounded, the few that remained untouched carrying messages ; his only attendant a French Officer, attached to him by Louis XVIII.!!! If you wish to record it you are quite at liberty to use my name.

What a contrast to Napoleon, if what the Belgian Guide Da Costa told me when I revisited Waterloo in 1816 be true, that not a single casualty occurred amongst his numerous personal Staff.

.   .   .   .

And have, &c.,

THOS. HUNTER BLAIR.

FROM THE SAME.

Dunskey, Wigtonshire, November 29th, 1835.

.   .   /   .   .   .

I feel morally persuaded that the Light Brigade, more especially the 52nd and 71st, had been a considerable time in line four deep, before the attack was made.

I was in rear of the 52nd line in conversation with the late Sir Augustus Fraser, Horse Artillery, when the

Side notes:

After defeat of Squares of Old Guard, ordered to go and observe if right of Brigade was threatened.

Met the Duke followed by a Sardinian Officer, who told him the Duke had been to see himself, and that there was no danger.

Miraculous escapes of the Duke at Waterloo. Nearly all his Staff killed or wounded.

Napoleon's Staff untouched.

No. 122.

Waterloo.

The 52nd and 71st had been some time in line four deep before the French Guard attacked.

52ND REGIMENT.

A French
Officer, a
deserter, came
and gave
warning of
the attack by
the Imperial
Guard.

French Hussar Officer, a deserter, mentioned by Colonel Gawler, rode up to and joined us. He said we should be attacked by the French Guard within half-an-hour. Sir Augustus rode off to inform the Duke, then towards the left, desiring me to look to the deserter, whose information proved literally correct.

The French cannonade commenced before Sir Augustus' return. I sent the French Officer to the rear in charge of a Sergeant of the 52nd Regiment.

See No. 129,
p. 306.

Thinks that
the 71st could
not get into
line with the
52nd to share
in the attack
on the 2nd
Column of the
Imperial
Guard.

I agree with you in thinking that the advance Colonel Eeles refers to is the right shoulder movement into the position you have traced in a dotted line, and my impression also is that the 71st, though supporting the 52nd, could not complete that movement in time to enable them to share in the attack on the 2nd Column of the Imperial Guard. Major-General Sir Thomas Reynell, who commanded the 71st, might best elucidate the point.

The extract you give me from Colonel Eeles appears very faithful; he is quite right in conjecturing that in the advance Colonel Halkett's Brigade in column followed the Light Brigade, as did the other Hanoverians of the Division, accompanied by Sir Henry Clinton.

See preceding
letter. The
Officer attend-
ing the Duke
was Major
Count de
Sales, a Sar-
dinian Officer
attached to
his suite.

Lord Fitzroy Somerset mentioned to me in town last spring the mistake I had been led into in supposing that the Foreign Officer attending the Duke at the period I referred to was a Frenchman, he being a Sardinian.

I have, &c.,

THOS. HUNTER BLAIR.

THE 52ND REGIMENT—LIGHT INFANTRY.

LIEUT.-GENERAL LORD SEATON, G.C.B.

LIEUT.-COLONEL AND COLONEL SIR JOHN COLBORNE, K.C.B., 52ND REGIMENT.

No. 123.

Kitley, Greatupton [?], *February* 22nd, 1843.

I have been so fully occupied since the year 1815, that I have seldom had time or inclination to read any of the accounts of the Battle of Waterloo. Indeed, it has always been a most unpleasant task to refer to our past military operations, which are connected with many painful recollections.

I have cautiously abstained from giving opinions on controverted points that would draw me into discussions. I think, however, that it almost becomes my duty to give you every assistance in my power to enable you to compare the facts in my statement with the information which you have received from various sources, and to correct the errors which appear in the account you have forwarded to me.

We were all so intent in performing our own parts, that we are disposed to imagine that the Brigade or Corps with which we were engaged played a most distinguished part, and attribute more importance to the movements under our own immediate observation than they deserved. I am persuaded that none but mounted Officers can give a correct account of the Battle, and very few of those had an opportunity of seeing much beyond the limited space which they traversed.

I have, in great haste, from the impressions which I strongly retain at this moment, written down the principal facts which occurred under my observation, a kind of log-book from eleven o'clock to the close of the Action.

With respect to the troops that first entered Paris by the Bridge of Neuilly and the Bois de Boulogne—the Brigade of General Adam passed the bridge of Neuilly the night before the Duke took up his quarters in Paris, and halted at Neuilly, after having had a sharp discussion with the French Officer in command of the Squadrons of Cavalry at the bridge, who opposed our passage of the bridge in consequence of his having received no orders to give up his post.

The next morning Sir F. Adam's Brigade, unaccompanied by any other, marched by the Barrière de l'Etoile to the Champs-Elysées. The 52nd was posted near the Duke of Wellington's quarters. Several of the Garde de Corps of Louis XVIII. were compelled to take shelter

Adam's Brigade was the first to enter Paris.

behind the 52nd, before that Regiment had piled arms, in consequence of the insults they received from the National Guards, with which the Place Louis Quinze was filled. I return your paper. My log-book shall be forwarded to-morrow.

> I remain, &c.,
>
> SEATON.

Waterloo.   *Memoranda.*   *Kitley, February 24th, 1843.*

It was eleven o'clock when our Batteries (of twenty Guns, I believe), in position on the rising ground to *our* left of Hougoumont opened their fire on a Column advancing on Hougoumont.

First shot fired by Cleeves' Battery K.G.L. Its effect.

The French Commandant of the Première Légère mentioned to me, a few days after the Battle, that he was in the front of that Column, and that the first shot from our Guns killed and wounded three of his Regiment. At this time several shots reached the 52nd Regiment, then halted in column to the rear of the road leading to Merbe Braine, and the point of intersection of that road and the Nivelles road.

Desirous of seeing the commencement of the Action, I rode with Colonel Rowan to a commanding eminence. My attention was directed to the French Lancers, which showed themselves near the cross road leading to Braine-la-Leud, and cheering. After this cheer a large space of our position to the left of Hougoumont, appeared covered with our dispersed Cavalry, rapidly retiring. Two large masses of French Cavalry followed them in good order. They passed the Batteries of twenty Guns to which I have referred, which appeared abandoned, and had ceased to fire.

First charge of French Cavalry on right centre.

The 52nd and Brigade marched down into the valley to the left rear of Hougoumont. *See* Plan, p. 288.

I returned to the 52nd Regiment, which was on the march in column, and advancing towards the cross road that connects the high road from Genappe to Waterloo, and the road from Nivelles to Waterloo. The 52nd continued its march to the valley which separated the right central part of our position from the Enemy, and halted about five hundred yards in front of the cross road. I rode up the opposite ascent and observed two Guns pointed, and firing at our Column. I returned, and called out to Capt. Shedden, the Officer leading the Column, and desired him to tell me whether he could see these Guns. I formed two Squares on the appearance of the masses of Heavy Cavalry to our right, but nearer to the 71st Regiment than to the 52nd.

On the appearance of Cavalry, squares are formed. The 52nd, a strong regiment, forms two.

Several shells fell near the left angle of our more advanced Square, and the left side of it was grazed by a sharp fire. Lieutenant-Colonel Charles Rowan was anxious to take the command of the left Square in which Colonel Chalmers was, but on my acquainting him that I should superintend both the Squares he remained, at my request, with me. The front and right faces of this Square opened fire on the French Cuirassiers advancing towards us, and the French Cavalry halted and retired and appeared in disorder.

The Cavalry repulsed.

Colonel Hervey, one of the Duke of Wellington's Aides-de-Camp, brought an order from the Duke for the 52nd to retire up the hill. I mentioned to him that if the Duke had ordered us to retire with reference to our exposed position, that we were protected by the ground in front.

52nd ordered by the Duke to retire, if too exposed.

" Very well," he replied, " I will mention this."

However, soon after I had received this order I heard a great noise and clamour in the direction of Hougoumont, and observed the Nassau Regiments, I believe, running in disorder out of the wood; and supposing that Hougoumont would be abandoned and our flank would be exposed, I formed columns from squares, and wheeled into two lines, and this formation being completed, we faced about and retired in two lines through the Belgian Guns under the command of Colonel Gaeld [?], and as we were ascending the hill a French Colonel of the Cuirassiers galloped out of the French ranks, holloaing out " *Vive le Roi*," repeatedly, and rode up to me, addressed and said, " *Ce — Napoléon est là avec les Gardes. Voilà l'attaque qui se fait.*" This Officer remained with me for some time.

Fearing that Hougoumont would be abandoned, the 52nd retires.

A French deserter gives warning of the attack of the Imperial Guards.

The attacking Columns of the Imperial Guard moved along our left of Hougoumont, not by the Genappe road.—ED.

On approach of 2nd Column, orders his left Company to wheel to its left, and forms remaining Companies on it.

On our arriving near the cross road on the summit of the hill, near the Belgian Guns, I halted the 52nd. Many of our wounded were lying a few paces in our front. My anxious attention had been attracted to the dense Columns moving on the Genappe road towards the centre of our position, and observing their rapid advance I ordered our left hand Company to wheel to the left, and formed the remaining Companies on that Company. Colonel Charles Rowan assisted in completing this formation, with whom I had had some conversation on the intended movement, and on the necessity of menacing the flank of the French Columns.

52nd line thus nearly parallel with flank of French Column. A strong Company sent in front to skirmish.

This movement placed us nearly parallel with the moving Columns of the French Imperial Guards. I ordered a strong Company to extend in our front, and at this moment Sir F. Adam rode up, and asked me what I was going to do. I think I said, " to make that Column feel our fire." Sir F. Adam then ordered me to move on, and that the 71st should follow, and rode away towards the 71st.

Orders the skirmishers to advance and fire into the Column.

I instantly ordered the extended Company of the 52nd, about 100 men, under the command of Lieutenant Anderson, to advance as quickly as possible without any support except from the Battalion, and to fire into the French Column at any distance. Thus the 52nd formed in two lines of half Companies, the rear line at ten paces distance from the front—after giving three cheers, followed

The 52nd advances against the Column.

the extended Company, passed along the front of the Brigade of Guards in line, commanded by Sir John Byng, and about 500 [?] yards in front of them. If our line had been produced it would have formed an obtuse angle with this Brigade of Guards.

Column halts, wheels up its flank sections into a line facing 52nd, and opens a heavy fire.

The 2nd 95th was formed by

I observed that as soon as the French Columns were sharply attacked by our skirmishers, a considerable part of the Column halted and formed a line facing towards the 52nd, and opened a *very* sharp fire on the skirmishers and on the Battalion. The only skirmishers, I think, that were out on that day from *our* Brigade were those of the 52nd which I have mentioned, but I am certain that none fired but those of the 52nd. Three or four Companies of the 95th were formed on our left rather to the rear of our line; the remainder of the Brigade, the 71st, must have been at least six hundred yards to the rear when the 52nd commenced its movement towards the Imperial Guards; but I think I observed the 71st moving on, as well as the whole of Sir H. Clinton's Division, when we had advanced a few hundred paces.

I have no doubt that the fire on the flank of the French Column from the 52nd skirmishers, and the appearance of a general attack on its flank from Sir F. Adam's Brigade and Sir H. Clinton's Division generally, was the cause of the first check received, or halt made by the Imperial Guards. The 52nd suffered severely from the fire of the Enemy; the loss of skirmishers was severe, and the two Officers of the Company were wounded. The right wing of the 52nd lost nearly one hundred and fifty men during the advance; the Officer carrying the Regimental Colour was killed.

At this moment two or three Squadrons of the 23rd Dragoons appeared, directly in front of the line of the 52nd, approaching rapidly towards the line. The two Companies on the left halted and fired into them, supposing them to be the Enemy's Cavalry. My horse was wounded; I called out to the Adjutant to stop the fire, and whilst we were rectifying this mistake which had occurred, the only one that had occurred during the day, and which interrupted our march, the Duke of Wellington came to the rear of the left of our line near the two Companies which had fired. I said to his Grace, " It is our own Cavalry which has caused this firing." His Grace replied, " Never mind, *go* on, *go* on." We continued our advance, which soon brought us under the hill or ascent occupied by the Imperial Guards, and we found ourselves protected from their fire by the hill. Our line, from the badness of the ground and the interruption to which I have alluded, had thrown [the two right hand Companies into some

---

Marginal notes (right column):

the Duke on left, and in line with 52nd. 71st, on outer flank, was rapidly advancing, and perhaps 150 yards in right rear of 52nd; 600 yards would be in *rear of the Nivelles road!* —Ed. *See* General Plan, No. 2.

Has no doubt flank attack caused Column to halt.

Great loss sustained by 52nd from fire of Column.

During the advance, the two left Companies halt, and fire by mistake on retiring Squadron of 23rd Light Dragoons. *See* No. 48, p. 98.

Desired by the Duke to " go on."

Halts and re-forms under the hill where three Squares of the French Guard stand close to Genappe road.

See General
Plan, No. 3.

disorder, and I, suspecting the French Cavalry were not far from our right, called out to the Officers commanding Nos. 1 and 2 Companies to halt and bring up their Companies in good line, and whilst I was restraining the disorderly impetuosity of these Companies under great excitement, several Officers in front, Colonel Churchill and Colonel Chalmers, were cheering and waving their hats and caps in front.

The whole
Brigade is
formed in
line, and
advances
against the
Squares.

The Enemy
retires in
confusion.

At this time the 71st formed on our right flank, and I ordered the bugles to sound the advance, and the whole line charged up the hill; and on our arriving at the edge of the deep road, the opposite side of which the Imperial Guards had occupied, the 52nd fired, at least most of the Companies. We observed the Enemy in great confusion, some firing, others throwing away their packs and running to the rear.

The 52nd
crosses the
road,

And passes
eighty Guns
and carriages
abandoned.

The British
Cavalry were
in his right
front.—ED.
See General
Plan, No. 3.

Captain Cross called out that the French soldiers near us were going to surrender, but on their continuing to fire on us I ordered the 52nd Regiment to "pass the road," and the whole passed through the Guns and carriages, &c., and we formed Columns of Companies, our right resting on the road to Genappe. We moved on in column, and passed, I think, eighty Guns or carriages in about ten minutes after this new formation. No Cavalry whatever could be seen on our left, or to the left of the Genappe road, and I am sure that no British Cavalry were between us and the French for the last hour of the Battle. I think, therefore, that the attacks of our Cavalry at this time must have been made by the Cavalry which had passed in rear of the 52nd, and to the right of the Genappe road.

I observed smoke and firing towards Planchenoit, and to the right and left of the Genappe road. The 71st did not cross the Genappe road, but moved to the right, as well as part of Sir H. Clinton's Division.

The 52nd and
Prussians
meet.

At the junction of the Genappe road and the road leading, I believe, from Wavre to Nivelles, the skirmishers of the 52nd and the advance of the Prussians under General Bulow mixed. When we passed this point it was nearly dark. We halted a few hundred yards from it, and the whole of General Bulow's Corps passed our right on the road leading to Genappe.

The Duke of Wellington, on returning, I suppose, from Belle Alliance, passed the left of our Column and inquired for me, and left a message that we were to halt for the night. The Duke orders them to halt for the night.

Sir John Byng mentioned to me, at Paris, that he observed our movement in front of *his* Brigade, and that at this time his Brigade had no ammunition left. Lord Hill mentioned to me also that he was near the Brigade of Guards when he observed the 52nd moving across the plain, that some men of the British Guards were retiring, that he ordered them to advance, waving his hat to them.

I *think*, therefore, that *this* was the time when a portion of the Imperial Guards halted to fire on the 52nd, and that immediately after this halt the British Guards charged, and made their forward movement. It appears to me evident, if this statement be correct, the movement of the 52nd took place some time before any forward movement was made by the Guards.

.   .   .   .

I have been particular in stating many unimportant occurrences, because I am persuaded several absurd blunders and stories have originated from the movements of the 52nd, and General Adam's Brigade, having been misrepresented.

S.

LIEUT.-COLONEL G. GAWLER, K.H., UNATTACHED.
LIEUTENANT 52ND REGIMENT.

Derby, December 22nd, 1834.   No. 124.

.   .   .   .   .   .

Major-General Adam's Brigade, of which the 52nd Waterloo. formed a part, bivouacked on the night of the 17th–18th June nearly on the summit of a height between the

Nivelles Chaussée and *Merbe Braine,* 400 or 500 yards *East* of the latter village, A.

After daylight on the morning of the 18th June some Companies of the Brigade were sent to occupy Merbe Braine. The 52nd gave its right Company, to which I belonged. This Company was posted in the garden of a small country-house, of which the westernmost hedge was the limit, on that side, of the enclosures of Merbe Braine.

On the summit of the rise towards Braine-la-Leud two or three Battalion Columns were in sight, which proved to be Dutch or Belgic.

First Cannon-shot fired at 11.20 a.m.

While in this garden we heard the first cannon-shot of the Battle, fired in the direction of Hougoumont. An Officer near me pulled out his watch, and said it was "Twenty minutes past 11 o'clock." Soon after this, it might be about 12 o'clock, we were ordered to rejoin the Brigade. When we cleared the enclosures of the village, it was seen standing in open column in about the position B.

First positions of the Brigade.

The Brigade almost immediately advanced, the 52nd halted in close or quarter-distance columns of wings at about C. I feel much confidence as to the ground, as near that point its outline is remarkable. The crop about us was very low.

The first and greatest attack on Hougoumont was then going on, and we were evidently supporting what had now become the right wing of the Army in rear of Hougoumont. Cannon-shot fired at the troops in our front rolled over the hill behind which we were posted, and were (I believe) particularly annoying to the 2nd Battalion 95th. In consequence of this annoyance from the cannonade, the 52nd went over the rise to the ground D or *D, I think the former. From near this point the 51st Regiment was distinctly seen extended at E E.

Major Ross of that Regiment has since told me that the Company which he commanded occupied the point E on the *chaussée, covered by an abatis*. Major Ross told me

PLAN SHOWING
POSITIONS AND MOVEMENTS
OF ADAM'S INFANTRY BRIGADE

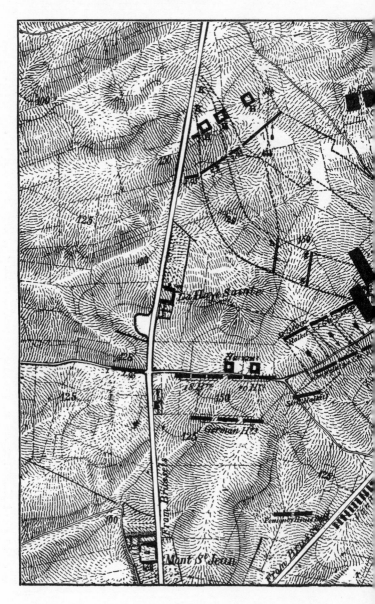

also that he did not *at any time* see any French soldiers to the westward of the *chaussée*. I do not know positively what became of the other Regiments of the Brigade during this interval, but *suppose* them to have remained at short distances from the 52nd. The crops about the spot D were very high.

I cannot speak with confidence to the precise time, but calculating from other occurrences of which the times are fixed, I think it must have been *after four o'clock* when the 52nd left the point D. It then proceeded in wing squares by the track *a a a* to F F on the exterior slope of the British position. Before it crossed the Nivelle *chaussée* Dutch Heavy Cavalry, wearing high feathers perpendicular to the top of their helmets, were seen retiring in confusion at *b b b*. The point at which the 52nd Squares crossed the first line of the Army, and near which it subsequently formed to receive the attack of the Imperial Guard, was occupied by Brunswickers in squares, front ranks kneeling.

Past 4 p.m. when the Brigade was moved down in the valley to the left rear of Hougoumont.

On crossing the summit the 2nd Battalion 95th was seen, as if taking up its ground, in square at F, annoyed by skirmishers from the great hollow of La Haye Sainte; and shortly after the 71st was visible in square at F, very near to the easternmost hedge of Hougoumont. The two Companies of the 3rd Battalion 95th with the 71st.

Adam's Brigade remained in this position F F F F, I think for *at least* an hour, until nearly six o'clock. During *the whole* of this time, no other Allied troops were seen *by us* in front of the position, unless *it might be* some Light Cavalry in rear of the north hedge of Hougoumont. On the French *position* scarcely any troops were visible. Their Artillery only certified that they were there. The great hollow about La Haye Sainte, however, was evidently occupied in force, from the boldness with which the French skirmishers pushed out of it, at times almost to the summit of the British position. From this hollow the Square of the 2nd 95th was, *I believe*, charged by Cavalry. I saw a large body of Cuirassiers move down the easternmost hedge of Hougoumont and charge the 71st. After

It remained in this position for at least an hour.

The Cuirassiers charge the 71st, and

then the right wing Square of the 52nd.

breaking upon its Square they rushed on in apparent infatuation upon the right wing of the 52nd, and received the fire of its front and right faces.

The 71st suffers much from the French cannonade.

In this position the 71st suffered very heavily and with admirable steadiness from the cannonade ; the 2nd Battalion 95th considerably, the 52nd but little, the difference of loss arising, I imagine, from the 71st being more advanced, and the 2nd 95th more elevated than the 52nd. The 52nd right wing Square was nearly in front of the Allied Field Battery, on which afterwards, when in line four deep, its right nearly rested.   .   .   .   .

About 6 p.m. the Brigade was retired behind the original position on the ridge, And formed a four-deep line.

At *about* six o'clock Adam's Brigade was ordered to retire behind the summit of the original position G G. On arriving there the 52nd at first formed quarter distance columns of wings and afterwards deployed into two lines, the left wing in rear, but closed up to one pace from the right wing. The other Regiments of the Brigade, I have every reason to believe, made precisely the same formation.

The order, I believe, was given by the Duke himself. At this time he passed unattended from the left to beyond our right and shortly after returned to beyond our left. In this position the 52nd *right* was under good cover—it was about forty paces *directly in rear* of the left of a Field Battery, which at intervals fired down the face of the hill.

.   .   .   .

The *left* of the 52nd was much more thrown back from the summit. *A low hedge ran across its front* at some distance from it. Individuals of Nos. 3 and 4 Companies remember this hedge distinctly as does the Adjutant, who was generally with Sir John Colborne in front of the *left* centre (see *U.S. Journal*, September, 1833, page 15). Sergeant Dolan of No. 4 Company, now a pensioner at Armagh, tore his leg so much in passing it that the Captain of his Company asked if he were wounded. I have good reason to believe that the 2nd Battalion 95th Regiment was near to our left, but, if anything, rather to its rear. The 71st Regiment was certainly *close to our right,* so close that, as I was very distinctly informed by an

Officer of the 3rd Battalion 95th, the two Companies of this Regiment had not room to deploy between us, but remained in column in rear of the 71st.

The last great attack of the French commenced about seven o'clock.   Judging from the information which I have received from others, and from my own recollections of the direction and duration of the musketry fire, *I think* that *about* the first *half-hour* was occupied in a direct attack of the Enemy, upon *the tongue of ground* which projects from the position, two or three hundred yards to the left of the position of the 52nd Regiment.

The last great attack of the French began about 7 p.m.

Before the attack commenced Sir P. Maitland's and Sir Colin Halkett's Brigades were advanced, upon *this very important tongue of ground,* to maintain it as long as possible from the possession of the Enemy.   This first part of the attack was made principally (I conclude) by the 1st French Corps.   The fighting was very close and desperate.   The British made a successful charge, but outflanked and overwhelmed by fresh Columns (perhaps the leading masses of the Guard) were compelled to retire rapidly.   Halkett's Brigade, which had suffered most severely, was moved by the Duke in person about 100 yards to the left and rear, and three Battalions of Brunswickers pushed forward to check the Enemy.

This refers to the repulse of the 1st attacking Column of the Imperial Guard, for an account of which *see* Maitland's Infantry Brigade.—ED.

The Brunswickers broke into great confusion, but were rallied by the Duke himself.   On the flanks of this attack the Enemy pushed forward swarms of skirmishers.   The 2nd 95th, and the 52nd threw out each a Company to check those in their front, but these Companies were immediately driven in by a charge of Cavalry from towards their left, and the 52nd came down to the "prepare for Cavalry."

The French Cavalry drive in the skirmishers of the 52nd and 2nd 95th.

Thus passed *the first half-hour* of the attack.   I have introduced in the above account of it very much that I know only from the testimony of others, because without it the following account of *the second half-hour* would be unconnected and somewhat unintelligible.

Sir P. Maitland's Brigade had by this time taken up a

line as much to the rear *at the least* as the left of the
52nd. I have no reasonable information as to what became
of the Brunswickers, or how the *immediate left* of the
Guards was then supported, but have *some* reason to
think that a part of Colonel Ompteda's Brigade was
there.

There was an interval of 10 to 12 minutes between the arrivals of the two attacking Columns.
—ED.

Without any *material* pause, the Enemy pushed on very
heavy masses composed *entirely* of the Guard, the *Moyenne*
leading rather on the Western side of the projecting
tongue of ground.

See General Plan, No. 2.

I cannot describe positively from my own observation
the formation of the Enemy, for, when the right of the
52nd subsequently crossed the summit, the smoke was
very dense ; but it has been confidently stated in the
Regiment that, as seen from *this* side, it was in two
Columns, in direct *échelon,* the left considerably to the
rear. It has also been stated that at first the opening
between the two Columns was distinctly visible. That the
flank of the Enemy was much longer than the front of
the 52nd Regiment seems to be established by the fact
(which I have verified from the Regimental Books) that
our loss of men *was as great* in the right Companies as in
the left.

The Brigade of Guns in front of the 52nd right, which
had fired incessantly during *the first half-hour,* was now
silenced by the intensity of the opposing musketry. The
extreme left of the Enemy's leading masses came nearly
in front of the extreme right of the Brigade of Guards,
and a desperate, and as I believe most *critical conflict* commenced at this point.

Not quite correctly described. The Duke, seeing Colborne's forward movement, pushed forward the 2nd 95th to conform to it.
—ED.

The Duke perceiving the almost overwhelming strength
of the Enemy in their *direct* attack rode in person to the
2nd 95th and ordered it to charge the flank of the Imperial
Column ; before, however, the 95th could obey the order,
Sir J. Colborne, who commanded the 52nd, either from
previous directions from the Duke, from catching his intention with regard to the 95th, or on his own responsibility in the excessive emergency of the moment, had given

the words, " Forward," and, after a very few paces, " Right shoulders forward " to his Regiment.

The right of the 52nd grazed the left Gun of the Battery in its front. The Captain of No. 1 Company (now Major Diggle) fell severely wounded close to its wheel.

So close was the left Company to the Imperial Column that it was compelled to wheel back on its right, while the rest of the Regiment came forward on their left. The Enemy was pressing on with shouts, which rose above the noise of the firing, and his fire was so intense that, with but half the ordinary length of front, *at least* 150 of the 52nd fell in less than four minutes. I almost think in less than three, for there was not the slightest check in the advance of the right flank below the average of the old wheeling time. Half the length of front, but *four* deep.—ED.

When the 52nd was nearly parallel to the Enemy's flank, Sir J. Colborne gave the word, " Charge, charge." It was answered from the Regiment by a loud steady cheer and a hurried dash to the front. In the next ten seconds the Imperial Guard, broken into the wildest confusion, and scarcely firing a shot to cover its retreat, was rushing towards the hollow road in their rear of La Haye Sainte, near to which, according to La Coste's account, Napoleon himself was then standing. The 52nd charge the French Column (and the 2nd 95th joins in the charge on the left of it. —ED.).

During the charge Sir J. Colborne was *in front* of the left centre, Lieut.-Colonel Chalmers with his cap on the point of his sword in front of the right centre, and Major-General Adam, who had galloped up from the 71st, in rear of the centre. Lieut.-Colonel Chas. Rowan fell on the left at about the same time that Captain Diggle was wounded on the right. The point at which the left of the 52nd crossed the original line of the left flank of the Imperial Guard *was at the highest point of the re-entering angle* formed by the projecting tongue of land, and the rise behind which the 52nd had been covered. I convinced myself of this fact the next morning by the manner in which the killed and wounded on both sides were lying.

Although there is reason to believe that the Enemy's second Corps was advanced to cover the left flank of his attack with its own left resting on the hedge of Hougoumont, yet no part of it came near enough to menace seriously the right flank of the 52nd Regiment during the whole of the forward movement and charge. This right flank appeared entirely clear of the enemy for at least 300 yards.

Adam's Brigade presses forward towards the Genappe road.

See No. 48, p. 98.

Three French Guns which enfiladed the 52nd at this point were driven off by the right section under Lieut. Gawler. —ED.

The 52nd continued pressing forward at a hurried pace, until its left was so near the hollow road in front of La Haye Sainte, that an Officer of the left Company *stepped out to see what the fugitives in it were doing.* In its course to this point the coming upon its front of a broken body of Dörnberg's Cavalry Brigade at *g*, and the throwing out of its right section to drive in some Guns by which it was enfiladed at about *h*, occurred, to the best of my recollection and judgment, as already described in my narrative of the " Crisis and Close, &c."

The 71st Regiment moved forward to protect the right flank of the 52nd Regiment as described in that narrative, I now think, however, *without firing.* The two Companies of the 3rd Battalion 95th formed line on the left flank of the 71st. The 2nd Battalion 95th followed up on the left flank of the 52nd, but, *I think,* did not get into line with it until it reached near to the hollow road, and then more as a body of skirmishers than as a line. This Battalion of the 95th suffered at some point in its advance a heavy loss. This *may* have been from the French occupying La Haye Sainte. Colonel Halkett's Hanoverian Brigade followed at some distance in support of the advance of Adam's Brigade, and some of the 1st Battalion 95th *may* have mixed with the 2nd 95th when passing La Haye Sainte. Besides these, I have *strong* reasons for

It was hardly so long before Vivian's Cavalry Brigade passed to the front. —ED.

believing *that no other portion of the Duke of Wellington's Army left the British position for a full quarter of an hour after the advance of the 52nd.*

Thus ended what may be considered as the *second half-hour* of the last great attack, at rather more than a

quarter past eight o'clock. The sun, I think, set before the
52nd reached near to the hollow road, twilight was sensibly
commencing when it subsequently crossed the *chaussée*.

For the movements and formations of the 52nd
Regiment during the subsequent pursuit I must refer you
to the narrative of the "Crisis and Close," with the
following corrections and additional notices.

The position in which Adam's Brigade found and attacked the three squares of the Old Guard covering the
retreat was at H H H, instead of being as inserted in the
Plan accompanying my printed narrative; and I have now
reason to think that, at this time, the two Companies of
the 3rd 95th were *between* the 71st and 52nd, and that a
considerable body of the 2nd 95th were to the left of the
52nd.

The whole
Brigade were
in one line.
—ED.
See General
Plan, No. 3.

I have some reason to think that the 71st formed a
two-deep line before this attack. The 52nd certainly continued four deep to the close of the day.

I very confidently believe that the 52nd crossed the
chaussée at K K, and the 71st very soon after it. I have
not traced the routes of the 52nd and 71st on the *East*
side of the *chaussée*, because I feel some doubts as to *the
depth of the sweep* which the two Regiments described. I
feel, however, *confident* that the Square of the Old Guard
threw off its knapsacks at about L, and that the 52nd
bivouacked for the night at M.

L is about
half-way be-
tween the last
houses of
Planchenoit
and the
Brussels road.
M is to the
left of, and
close to the
road, and to
the garden of
Rossomme.

On crossing the *chaussée*, the Prussian Artillery was
seen distinctly 700 or 800 yards towards the left, and in
passing to the east of La Belle Alliance some Prussian
cannon shot came over the heads of the 52nd, proving
that at this point the Prussians were still far to the left.
(See also Baron Müffling's "History of the Campaign,"
translated by Sir John Sinclair, page 35.)

[Omitted to be signed.]

The 71st Regiment—Light Infantry—Glasgow Highlanders.

MAJOR-GENERAL SIR THOMAS REYNELL, BART., K.C.B.

Lieut.-Colonel and Colonel T. Reynell, 71st Regiment.

No. 125.   *Avisford, Arundel, 15th November,* 1834.

Waterloo.

It was in line four deep. *See* Sir F. Adam, No. 120, p. 277. This was earlier in the day.—Ed.

You require to be informed of "the particular formation of the Regiment (about seven p.m.) when the French Imperial Guard, advancing to attack the right of the British forces. reached the crest of our position." The Regiment was at that time in square, as it had been, for the most part, during the time that the British Army acted upon the defensive, exposed to the Enemy's fire, and to repeated *visits* from his Cuirassiers. I do not say *attacks*, because these Cavalry Columns on no occasion attempted to penetrate our Square, limiting their approach to within ten or fifteen yards of the front face, when they would wheel about, receiving such fire as we could bring to bear upon them, and as they retired, *en passant*, that from the neighbouring Square. I do not recollect at any period of the Action to have seen any Infantry very near to us, still several Officers and men were killed and wounded by the fire of musketry.

On the night of the 17th, that previous to the battle, the 71st Regiment bivouacked in a fallow field on the extreme right, and, together with the other Regiments of Major-General Adam's Brigade, [was] placed *en potence* to the British line. From this position the Brigade moved, on the morning of the 18th, at the time that the Enemy's demonstrations left no doubt of his intention to attack the Allied Army, and formed, with the right thrown up and somewhat in advance, in two Columns each Regiment—probably with a view to deceive the Enemy by this multiplied array of Columns. Thus formed, they lay upon their arms in the rear of a rising ground, upon which, soon after, a Brigade of British Foot Artillery was posted, but which, attracting the Enemy's attention, brought down a heavy fire of shot and shell, very destructive in its consequences to our Columns lying in the rear.

See D. Col. Gawler's Plan, p. 288.

Our next movement was to the front, rather inclining to the left, to a position in rear of Hougoumont, where the Battalion, having united its wings, formed one Square.

See F Plan, p. 288.

. . . .

In this shape [four deep] we advanced, with our right flank so close to the hedge of the farm of Hougoumont, that several soldiers of the nearest Company were killed and wounded in passing. When all apprehension of further annoyance from the Enemy's Cavalry had ceased, we took advantage of the ground to display our full front by obliquing, in opposite directions, the two wings, and directed our march upon two Columns of French Infantry, which from the first had appeared at the bottom of the hill. These Columns did not wait our approach, but made off, and from the circumstance of our finding an immense quantity of arms lying against the walls of the houses in the village of Caillou [?Rossomme], I should incline to believe that they had broken without order and dispersed.

The advance of the Brigade ; 71st on 52nd right.

71st re-forms two deep.

The attack on the three French Squares near the Genappe road. *See* General Plan, No. 3.

After scouring Caillou, where we came in contact with the Prussian advance, we gave up the pursuit to them, and having retired a little to the right to a cornfield that had been cut, bivouacked there for the night.

. . . .

I have, &c.,

THOS. REYNELL,

Major-General.

MAJOR S. REED, HALF-PAY, 71ST REGIMENT.
CAPTAIN 71ST REGIMENT.

Douglas, 19th November, 1834.

No. 126.

. . . .

Waterloo.

At this distant period, and then acting as a Company Officer (commanding the right flank), I cannot be as correct as I could wish in tracing the movements of the 71st

Regiment, but as far as my memory allows me I have done so on your map.

As you particularly mention the hour of seven, I have marked our advance, bringing our right shoulders forward, leaving Hougoumont to our right. In this movement the *See* General Plan, No. 3. Regiment was formed four deep, supporting the 52nd in a charge on the Imperial Guard, who, I think, were either in square or column. I do not think they were in line.

The attack on the three French Squares. The two Regiments formed line, the 52nd still on the left. We here charged three Squares of the Guard, whom we broke and pursued, crossing the road leading to Genappe, when we brought left shoulders forward, the right of the 71st resting on La Belle Alliance. Of this I am more positive, as the Gun fired there by Captain Campbell, Aide-de-Camp to Sir Frederick Adam, was turned by some men of my own Company under the command of Lieut. Torriano. The French Squares having separated, the 52nd pursued what had been their right Square; the other two fell to our lot. They retreated by the right of Planchenoit, in front of which village we bivouacked for the night.

We were here passed by a body of Prussian Light Cavalry, their music playing *God Save the King*. The first and second Companies of the 71st were stationed in the village [? of Rossomme], where we found a park of seventy-two pieces of artillery which the Enemy had abandoned.

See Plan, p. 288. Our first position on breaking up from our bivouack on the morning of the 18th was in front [? rear] of Hougoumont, but at some distance. However, the French Artillery on the left of the Château were able to throw in a fire among us as we lay down under the slope of the hill, by which we suffered some loss, I think fifty men.

See Plan, p. 288. To gain our second position, which I have marked by squares, into which we were thrown constantly during the day, brought us on the plain in front [left rear] of Hougoumont. We were here constantly charged by the

French Cuirassiers, although we, I think, suffered no loss
from them. Yet we did from the fire of the Artillery.
We had two Officers and some [men] severely wounded in
this position. . . . . .

I remain, &c.,

S. REED,

Major, H.P., 71st Regiment.

THE 95TH RIFLES—2ND BATTALION.

CAPTAIN [?] T. R. BUDGEN.

CAPTAIN 95TH RIFLES.

London, December 17th [? 1834].　　No. 127.

. . . .

It was my duty the day after the Action to search　Waterloo.
for wounded, and to convey them into Brussels. In
passing over the Field I certainly endeavoured to ascertain the position the 2nd Battalion 95th Rifles occupied
before the final charge on the attacking French Columns.
I think your Plan gives a fairly correct representation　This Plan
of the position of our Brigade (General Adam's) ;　cannot be found.—ED.
although I think our formation was rather more in
advance of the road immediately previous to the Brigade
charging the French Columns, whose position is also,
I think, at that moment very correctly laid down.

My reason for thinking the Brigade was rather
more advanced at the time of charging, is that for several
hours previous, at intervals, the Brigade had been formed　This refers to the period when the
into squares of Battalions to resist the repeated charges　Brigade was
of the French Cavalry. I think the 2nd Battalion 95th　in the plain to
sustained and repulsed three several attacks about that　the left rear of Hougoumont.
time, and while in square I recollect seeing the French　*See* Plan,
Cavalry in possession of some Guns in our rear and　p. 288.—ED.
near the road.

I fully recollect also that a very short period (say　Line formed four deep
less than half an hour) before the last advance of the　before the last advance of
Enemy, our line was formed four deep, our formation　the Enemy.

having been previously two deep as usual. Immediately before the formation of four deep I think we retired a very short distance from the ground we had occupied while in square.

Just before the advance of the Battalion, the Duke rode along its front and spoke to the men, who cheered him.

After this last formation, and immediately before or during the right shoulder movement of the Brigade, the Duke of Wellington rode along our line. I conclude he himself directed the movement. It was the only moment I saw him during the day. He spoke to the men, they cheered him in return.

The French Columns halted on being taken in flank by the Brigade, And on its rushing forward they gave way without order or discipline.

I think the French Columns halted in consequence of our movement taking them in flank, and that the most effective fire of the Brigade was delivered at a less distance than fifty yards. After receiving it the French Column appeared to be in great confusion, and the Brigade rushing forward, they immediately gave way without retaining any order or discipline.

The 2nd 95th contributed to the result as much as any other part of the Brigade.

In this charge I am bound to say that the services of the 2nd Battalion Rifle Brigade, then 95th, were as conducive to the result as those of any other part of the Brigade, nor could it be otherwise, for from the moment of the charge no check took place, and the advance was at a most rapid pace.

This probably alludes to the Squadron of the 23rd Light Dragoons, which advanced *before* the French Column was attacked. —ED.

The Brigade attacks and drives off the three Squares close to the Genappe road. *See* General Plan, No. 3.

I have a full recollection that after the Enemy were broken and running away, the word was given to let the Cavalry through, and they passed through our line causing some confusion and breaks in it. After the Cavalry passed to the front the 2nd 95th continued to advance rapidly until it came on some bodies of the Enemy posted on some rising ground. A rush was made at them notwithstanding the disordered state of our line from the interruption of the Cavalry, and the dreadful miry state of the ground. These, I conceive must have been the rear Battalions of the Guard marked at D. The opposition they made was very ineffectual and slight. They were immediately driven off. The 2nd 95th certainly participated in this attack with the rest of the Brigade.

I do not think the position at D was quite so close to the high road, as I have no recollection of having passed a road with high banks at that time.

Because he crossed it *beyond* the high bank. —ED.

The 2nd 95th were not employed in skirmishing any part of the day, I am almost positive.

The Battalion, early in the day after crossing the Nivelles road, were much annoyed by a teasing cannonade, particularly while in square. No large bodies of Infantry of the Enemy passed very near it, but shortly previous to the charge it suffered considerably from musketry. I conclude the French Columns covered their advance by throwing out numerous skirmishers, as I do not think the fire from the head of the Column would have reached us, we being on its flank.

Thinks the last attack of the Imperial Guard was preceded by skirmishers.

. . . .

I have, &c.,

T. R. BUDGEN.

—— ALDRIDGE.
CORPORAL 2ND BATTALION, 95TH RIFLES.

December, 1834.   No. 128.

Statement by — Aldridge, late Corporal of the 2nd Battalion 95th Rifles, forwarded by Colonel Gawler, late 52nd Regiment.

Corporal Aldridge, 2nd Battalion 95th Rifle Corps, served in that Regiment twenty-two years, was in the Peninsular War and wounded at Salamanca; was at Waterloo. Discharged with a good character, of which " trustworthy " is one of the particulars. Has, besides, private testimonials from two Captains of the Regiment.

Corporal Aldridge gives the following particulars concerning the Action at Waterloo.

Waterloo.

This Battalion brigaded with the 52nd, 71st, and 3rd Battalion 95th; was in reserve during the first part of the Action, but suffered considerably, principally from Artillery. It afterwards moved up into the front line and relieved Brunswickers in squares.

Battalion in reserve at first, afterwards in front line, and subsequently

It formed square and moved to the front of the position. A Square of the 52nd was the nearest to it to the right.

Saw no friendly troops to the left; the French were in that direction, and annoyed his Battalion very much. French Cavalry charged close at them, and the left face of the Square suffered particularly from grape.

After some time retired behind the position, then one wing behind the other and so formed a four-deep line.

Aldridge then became the *left-hand man of the front rank.* Two or three hundred yards in front of the 2nd 95th was a by-road with something like a hollow about it. Nearly in front of Aldridge was the *right* of a Brigade of British Artillery. This Brigade was behind the by-road. Saw no Infantry to his left; saw the Hanoverians of *our* Division in line some distance to the rear.

The French came up in three Columns abreast of each other; they looked like quarter distance Columns. *Their left* was *obliquely to his left.* They rushed forward three times, and came *very* close to the Artillery. The Artillerymen *left their Guns*, except two or three who lay down under them. Saw the 52nd move forward to the right of the 2nd 95th and charge those Columns. *About* the same moment Lord Wellington rode up to the 95th and called out, " Who commands the 95th ? " Colonel Norcott and Major Wilkins had just been wounded, and at first no Officer answered. Then Lieut. Dixon, who commanded the second Company from the right, stepped forward. Lord Wellington said, " Order the 95th to charge." Lieut. Dixon then saw that Captain Logan, who commanded the right Company of the rear line, was in command, and gave the order to him. Captain Logan gave the word " Forward " to the Battalion. The Enemy gave way. One Artilleryman who was lying under the Guns jumped up with a match in his hand and let off two or three that were loaded. His comrades afterwards used to call him " Lord Waterloo." *The left of the* 95th passed *through the Guns.* The 95th did not lose a great many

Margin notes

moved in square down into the plain. *See* Plan, p. 288.

Much annoyed by fire of Enemy from direction of La Haye Sainte. Charged also by Cavalry.

Battalion retired behind the position, and forms four deep.

Aldridge became left-hand man of the Battalion.

A British Battery to his left front.

Attack of Imperial Guards.

Probably the skirmishers rushed forward.—ED.

Saw the 52nd charge the Columns.

About the same moment the 95th is ordered by the Duke to charge also.

Left of the 95th pass through the Guns.

men at this time. Joined immediately with the 52nd
pursuing the Enemy. Almost immediately after saw a small
body of English Light Dragoons *pass to his left* and go to
the front. Saw these Dragoons charge. Saw the French
Cavalry drive them towards the front of the 52nd. Very
soon after this a part of the 95th extended to skirmish.
The French were very thick to his left of a house. Is sure
it was *to his left* of the house. The 95th were in a *rye*
field—is sure it was a *rye* field. They lost more men here,
he thinks, than at any one other time in the day. They
then went on with the 52nd to attack some Squares of the
French rear guard. They were close to the great road.
He knows they were so, because he very soon afterwards
went down into the great road, and went straight on it
until the Battalion halted for the night. Just before they
halted they came to a village, through which they
skirmished; it was full of French Artillery. Halted at
the other end of the village on the right hand side of the
great road, near a large pond of water.

The 23rd
Light Drgns.
See No. 48,
p. 98.

D'Erlon's
troops to the
left of La
Haye Sainte.

Attack on the
three French
Squares near
Genappe road.

? Rossomme.

THE 95TH RIFLES—3RD BATTALION—TWO COMPANIES.

LIEUT.-COLONEL W. EELES, K.H., RIFLE BRIGADE.

CAPTAIN AND BREVET-MAJOR 95TH RIFLES.

Jersey, December 22nd, 1834.

In compliance with the request contained in your letter
of the 1st instant, I beg to say that the 3rd Battalion
95th Rifle Regiment formed part of the 3rd British
Brigade of Infantry at the Battle of Waterloo. That the
Brigade was formed during the early part of that day in
reserve; that the 52nd, 71st, and 2nd Battalion 95th,
while so formed, suffered I believe a good deal from round
shot. But the Companies of the 3rd Battalion 95th,
being posted in the enclosures on the right of the Brigade,
did not, until they advanced, lose a single man.

No. 129.

Waterloo.

Only *two Com-
panies* of the
3rd Battalion,
95th Rifles.
—ED.

Early in
the day
Brigade in
reserve, and
suffered con-
siderably
from|
French Artil-
lery fire,
except*
3rd Battalion
95th.

Later on the Brigade was advanced,

About the middle of the day, perhaps between one and two o'clock, but I cannot pretend to be accurate as to time, the Brigade advanced to the front. There was at this time a tremendous cannonade both from the English and French Batteries, and the smoke was so dense that I cannot venture any description of the appearance of the Field, except that I saw the English and French Cavalry opposed to each other.

And passed over the crest of the position, coming in contact with French Infantry (most probably a dense line of skirmishers. —ED.).

The Brigade continued to advance through the smoke until it passed beyond the crest of the British position; on the smoke clearing away, the 71st Regiment, with whom my Company of the 3rd Battalion 95th Regiment was then acting, found itself while in column very close to and in front of a large body of the Enemy's Infantry, formed in line, and dressed in grey great coats. The 71st immediately formed line, and I placed my Company of Rifles on the right of that Regiment. I can only here observe that the French and 71st were closer than I ever before saw any regular formed adverse bodies, and much nearer than troops usually engage. The French opened a very heavy fire on the 71st, who, nevertheless, completed their formation in the most regular and gallant style. I formed my Company on their right, and in line. During this operation the 71st and the Company of the 95th suffered severely, but imme-

The Enemy are repulsed, and retire unobserved in the smoke.

His Company dislodges a body of the French concealed in a hollow.

diately on being formed succeeded in repulsing the Enemy, who retired almost unobserved in the smoke. Finding, however, notwithstanding the retreat of the French, that many men, both in the 71st and the Company of the 95th, were still falling, I moved my Company forward, and found a considerable number of the Enemy in a dell in a rye field, from which place they were firing on the 71st.

The Company I commanded immediately attacked and drove them back to their position on the hill. While we were so employed I observed a large body of the Enemy's Cavalry advancing to attack us. We had just time to get

The 71st attacked by French Cavalry.

back and form in rear of the 71st Square, when the Enemy attacked that Regiment with much impetuosity and determination.

The charge was received with the utmost coolness and gallantry by the 71st.

The Cavalry were repulsed in this instance, and in all their other attacks, without occasioning the least loss or disorder to the Square of the 71st.   During one of these charges of the Enemy's Cuirassiers on the right angle of the front face of the 71st Square, I moved my Company from the rear to the right, in line with the rear face of the Square, and placing myself in front of it, kept every man from firing until the Cuirassiers approached within thirty or forty yards of the Square, when I fired a volley from my Company which had the effect, added to the fire of the 71st, of bringing so many horses and men at the same moment to the ground, that it became quite impossible for the Enemy to continue their charge.   I certainly believe that half of the Enemy were at the instant on the ground ; some few men and horses were killed, more wounded, but by far the greater part were thrown down over the dying and wounded.   These last after a short time began to get up and run back to their supports, some on horseback, but most of them dismounted.

I mention this merely to prove how perfectly impossible it is for Cavalry to arrive in sufficient force against Infantry, so as to be at all dangerous, if the Infantry will only be steady, and give their fire all at once.

After these various attacks of Cavalry had failed, everything remained for some time in a state of comparative quiet, and the Brigade remained in squares, with the 71st in square near the enclosure of Hougoumont, the 52nd in square of wings in the centre of the Brigade, and the six Companies of the 2nd Battalion of the 95th in square on the left of the 52nd.   In this manner the Brigade remained for a considerable time, much exposed to the fire of the Enemy's Batteries, and suffered considerably, particularly the 71st Regiment, with which Regiment my Company of the 3rd Battalion was formed, and, I believe, during this time, the late Colonel Fullerton's Company of the 3rd Battalion was acting with the 52nd Regiment.

Marginal notes:

These Cavalry attacks produce no effect.

His Company in right rear of the 71st Square pours in a destructive volley on the Cavalry.

For position of the Squares, *see* FFFF, Plan, p. 288.

About 6 p.m. the Brigade, suffering much from Artillery fire, is retired to the crest of the ridge.

As the Regiments of the 3rd Brigade were found to suffer from the Enemy's shot, while so exposed in the hollow, they moved back to the crest of the hill about six o'clock in the evening, or perhaps a little later. During the whole of this time, I mean from the time the French Cavalry ceased charging the Squares, I saw no French Infantry, but the crest of the hill of the Enemy's position was covered with a large body of Cavalry. During this time the Enemy was forming his Infantry for the last attack, called in your letter the "Crisis of the Battle." To meet this attack the 3rd Brigade was formed in line four deep in the manner I have marked on your Plan, which I return herewith.

The Enemy forms his Infantry for the last attack.
The Brigade in line four deep to meet it. *See* Plan, p. 288.

The 71st being on the right, the 52nd close on their left, and I believe the 2nd Battalion 95th on the left of the 52nd and close to the British position, the 3rd Battalion 95th being during this formation in reserve immediately behind the right of the 71st, where they were placed by Sir F. Adam.

See General Plan, No. 2.

The Brigade when so formed were on a height, or rather a little behind it, being brought considerably forward from the British line, so as to be able to bring their full front on the flank of the French advancing to the attack. In this order the Brigade waited for the advancing Enemy. I cannot myself, being at that moment behind the 71st, say what happened, except that after a violent cannonade from the British Guns, the 3rd Brigade opened a heavy fire and advanced on the line in which they had been placed.

The Brigade advances on the flank of the French Column,

The 3rd Battalion 95th Regiment moved on at the same time, and very shortly, as the 52nd and 71st opened out a little, was formed in line between these two Regiments. When the smoke cleared away a little I found that we were moving between both Armies, and driving some French before us in the greatest disorder. I was almost immediately ordered out to skirmish with my Company, and continued advancing in that manner until some English and German Dragoons, followed by some French, passed along the front of the Brigade. At the

And drives it away.

His Company ordered out to skirmish, and runs in on the

95TH RIFLES, 3RD BATT.

noise of the advancing horsemen, the Company of the 3rd Battalion, which was in front, ran in on the other Company, which was still between the 52nd and 71st. From that time it continued so to advance in that close and compact order, until the Brigade, still formed in line and four deep, came up to three Columns of the Old Imperial Guard, which they attacked, and defeated.

approach of the 23rd Lt. Dragoons. *See* No. 48, p. 98.

Joins in the attack on the three French Squares near the main road.

I believe there was at the time a Column of Colonel Halkett's Hanoverians in the rear of the 71st. I cannot positively assert that I saw them, but think I remember having done so, but I am sure that I saw Colonel Halkett himself ride forward round the right flank of the 71st and take a French Officer prisoner.

Saw Colonel Halkett take General Cambronne prisoner. *See* next letter.

I conclude, therefore, that his Brigade, or part of them, must have been near to the 3rd Brigade.

The Companies of the 3rd Battalion 95th were then again extended, and followed, as fast as they were able, accompanied by the 71st Regiment, still in line and four deep, the retiring French, until they came near some houses, which I believe to have been the farm of Rossomme. I then, having been for some time in command of the 3rd Battalion, thinking that the Enemy would make a stand, under cover of the houses, checked the advance of the Riflemen, and having drawn them close together, prepared to act in concert with the 71st Regiment. There was, however, no Enemy to attack. They had all gone off in the dusk of the evening, and the 71st and 3rd Battalion 95th bivouacked for the night on the right of the wood.

3rd 95th again extended, following the retiring French,

To the farm of Rossomme.

Probably the small wood on the opposite side of the road.—ED.

.   .   .   .

I have, &c.,

W. EELES,
Lieut.-Colonel Rifle Brigade.

GENERAL WILLIAM HALKETT, HANOVERIAN SERVICE.

LIEUT.-COLONEL COMMANDING A HANOVERIAN BRIGADE.

TO CAPTAIN L. BENNE, HANOVERIAN SERVICE.

No. 130.

Nienburg, December 20th, 1837.

DEAR SIR,—

Waterloo.

According to your wish I send you an account of the proceedings of the Osnabruck Battalion and of the capture of General Cambronne at the close of the battle of Waterloo, for Mr. Siborne's information.

When Adam's Brigade advanced, lost no time in following with the Osnabruck Battalion, taking it from the post of Hougoumont.

The moment General Adam's Brigade advanced I lost no time to follow with the Osnabruck Battalion (2nd Battalion, Duke of York), then on the left of Hougoumont, of which post I was in command, one of the Battalions of my Brigade occupying the wood and two others in the ditches in the rear, other troops occupying the enclosures, &c.

Sent his Brigade-Maj. for two more Battalions, but he was killed before delivering the message.

Got in line with Adam's Brigade.

During the advance I sent my Brigade Major, Captain v. Saffe, to bring up the two Battalions posted in rear of Hougoumont, but neither he nor the Battalions showed themselves. Next day I found that Captain Saffe was killed before having delivered the message. The Osnabruck Battalion soon got in line and on the right of Adam's Brigade. During the advance we were much annoyed by the Enemy's Artillery. The first Company of the Osnabruck Battalion broke into platoons, and supported by the sharpshooters of the Battalion, made a dash at the Artillery on our right and captured six Guns with their horses.

The Battalion captured six Guns with their horses.

Witnessed a successful charge of Cavalry on French Infantry.

Some hundred yards to our right were *some Troops* of Hussars (I believe the 10th). I rode up to them and got them to charge the head of a Column of Infantry, which was drawing to their left in rear of the French Guards. The charge succeeded admirably and the Column dispersed behind some enclosures, after which I saw no more of the Cavalry.

During our advance we were in constant contact with the French Guards, and I often called to them to surrender.

For some time I had my eye upon, as I supposed, the General Officer in command of the Guards (being in full uniform) trying to animate his men to stand.

After having received our fire with much effect, the Column left their General with two Officers behind, when I ordered the sharpshooters to dash on, and I made a gallop for the General. When about cutting him down he called out he would surrender, upon which he preceded me [to the rear], but I had not gone many paces before my horse got a shot through his body and fell to the ground. In a few seconds I got him on his legs again, and found my friend, Cambronne, had taken French leave in the direction from where he came. I instantly overtook him, laid hold of him by the aiguillette, and brought him in safety and gave him in charge to a sergeant of the Osnabruckers to deliver to the Duke; I could not spare an Officer for the purpose, many being wounded.

Capture of General Cambronne.

After this I kept in advance of Adam's Brigade; we soon pushed the two French Squares upon the mass of their Cavalry of all descriptions, who at one moment threatened us in a most *vociferous* manner. However, after receiving our fire they went off in all directions. About this time, Officers were flying in all directions, seemingly with orders from a superior. Some French Officers, prisoners, said it was Napoleon.

Got in advance of Adam's Brigade (*See* General Plan, No. 3), and drove on two French Squares.

We had the good fortune to take twelve or fourteen more Guns of the Guards, in full play on us. On our advance the sharpshooters, supported by a Company, were sent among a mass of Guns, and by their fire increased the confusion, made many prisoners, and cut the horses from the leading Guns. Next morning I found marked on these Guns 52nd, 71st, &c., for I had followed the Enemy on the Genappe road, where I met the Prussians, and moved on with them to some houses on the left of the road near Genappe, which houses I occupied during the night, the Battalion being much knocked up, and not seeing any red-coats in the rear.

The Battalion threatened by Cavalry, who made off on receiving its fire.

Captured twelve or fourteen more Guns.

Met the Prussians on the Genappe road, and advanced with them to near Genappe.

Soon after we halted, I sent the Major of the

Battalion with a Company into Genappe to see what was going on; at daylight I returned to the Field of Battle, sent the Guns and Horses taken to Brussels, collected my Brigade, and marched with them to Nivelles, when Lord Hill desired me to collect the Officers of the Brigade round him, on which occasion he paid them a handsome compliment.

I hope the above short account of what I recollect of the proceedings of the Osnabruck Battalion during the latter part of the ever-memorable Battle of Waterloo may prove of service to Mr. Siborne.

I remain, yours truly,

W. HALKETT.

P.S.—The Knapsacks in possession of the Hanoverian Troops were English, painted yellow. The Luneburg and Bremen Verden had green coats; the latter wore dark blue trousers.—W. H.

MITCHELL'S INFANTRY BRIGADE.

The 4th Infantry Brigade consisted of the 14th Regiment (3rd Battalion), the 23rd Royal Welsh Fusiliers, and the 51st Light Infantry, and was under the command of Lieut.-Colonel and Brevet-Colonel H. H. Mitchell of the latter Regiment.

At the commencement of the Battle of Waterloo the Brigade was posted as follows:—

Along the portion of the Avenue leading to Hougoumont from the Nivelles road, and next to the latter, was extended the Light Company of the 23rd. On its right was an *abatis* across that road, and a Company of the 51st was stationed close to it. Four more Companies of the 51st and the Light Company of the 14th

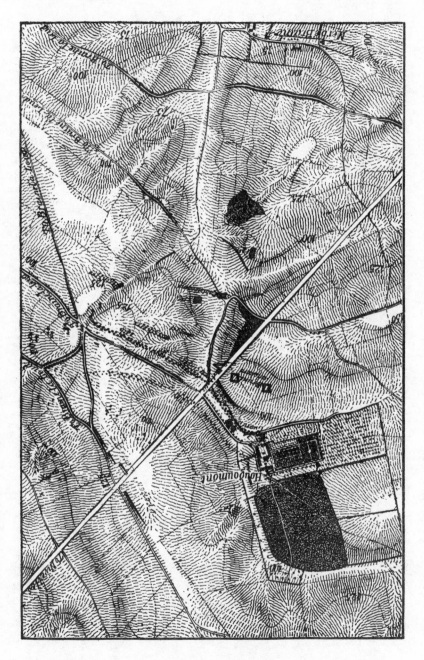

were extended along the hollow way in continuation of the Hougoumont Avenue, and the remainder of the 51st were in support about 200 yards to the rear. The 14th Regiment was posted still further to the rear as a Reserve to the Light Infantry of the Brigade, which was thus opposed to the extreme left of the French Line. These troops more or less occupied the same positions throughout the day.

The 23rd Regiment was stationed on the left of the Nivelles road, under the crest of the main ridge, and in rear of the 2nd Brigade of Guards.

The latter having been gradually moved down as reinforcements to Hougoumont, their ground was occupied by Brunswick troops, and the 23rd was advanced to an interval between the Brunswick Squares. Here it was suddenly ordered to prepare to receive Cavalry, instead of which the Chasseurs of the Guard appeared before it, whereupon the front face of the 23rd Square precipitately opened an ineffectual fire, but instantly recovering itself, the Regiment and the Brunswickers made good their defence.

The 23rd remained in square until the final advance, repelling several attacks of Cavalry. After one of these attacks, a body of Cuirassiers which had surrendered to the British Cavalry, breaking away from a weak escort, galloped down the Nivelles road in the endeavour to regain their own lines in that direction. They were fired upon by the 51st, and after suffering great loss, were for the most part taken prisoners by the Company at the *abatis*.

All the letters refer to Waterloo.

THE 23RD REGIMENT—ROYAL WELSH FUSILIERS.

MAJOR R. P. HOLMES, 23RD FUSILIERS.
LIEUTENANT 23RD FUSILIERS.

No. 131.   *Winchester, April 29th*, 1835.

.   .   .   .   .   .

To the best of my recollection the 23rd Fusiliers was
the only Regiment of the Division to which they were
attached absolutely engaged. Our Brigade was stationed
somewhere about Hal watching the road leading from
Lille to Brussels. The two Regiments brigaded with the
23rd—viz., 51st and 3rd Battalion 14th—remained during
the day in the second line, I think on the right of the road
leading to Nivelles.

During the night of the 17th June the 23rd bivouacked
in a rye-field near the village of Merbe Braine, but early
the following morning moved into the second line on the
left of the Nivelles road, in rear of a Battalion of Guards,
where the Regiment deployed into line and lay on the
ground, in consequence of the French having placed some
Guns on the Nivelles road which killed one of our Captains
and wounded some men.

Waterloo.
The 23rd was
first posted in
rear of the
2nd Brigade
of Guards.

The Guards
being moved
to Hougou-
mont, the 23rd
advanced in
square to their
position.

In conse-
quence of the
numerous at-
tacks of
Cavalry, re-
mained in
square all day.

The Guards in the front line having been withdrawn to
the support of Hougoumont, the 23rd formed square and
moved up into that line. In consequence of the numerous
attacks of Cavalry we remained in square the whole day.
I only recollect one attack of Infantry (in column) during
the day, which did not alter our formation. Some Regiment in our rear, I think the 71st, deployed into line and
advanced with the 23rd Square (a wing on each flank) some
distance down the slope of the hill. The Infantry having
given way a charge of Cavalry immediately followed. The
Regiment in line ran into square to our right, a little in
advance and nearer to the garden of Hougoumont.

Some of the
Cavalry at-
tempted to
retire by the

I believe the Cavalry that attacked these two Squares
were nearly annihilated. Having suffered much from the
Squares they attempted to retreat by the Nivelles road,

which was thickly lined with skirmishers, and the Officer who commanded the left company of the Regiment stationed on that road assured me at the time [that] scarcely a man succeeded in making his escape.

After this charge, finding that we were suffering both from the French Guns and the fire from the garden of Hougoumont, we again retired to our former position, where we remained until the attack on the centre by the French Guards, when we again advanced some short distance in square, then deployed and advanced in line ; but finding nothing to oppose us, we wheeled by Companies to the right and moved in column on the right of the Charleroi road to about,* where we bivouacked for the night, and on the following morning retraced our steps and rejoined the two other Regiments of the Brigade, and marched upon Cambray by the Nivelles road.

After the attack by the French Guards, deployed into line and joined in the General Advance.

* 300 yards short of La Belle Alliance. —ED.

.   .   .   .

Yours, &c.,

R. P. HOLMES,

Major 23rd Fusiliers.

THE 51ST REGIMENT—LIGHT INFANTRY.

COLONEL S. RICE.

MAJOR AND LIEUT.-COLONEL 51ST REGIMENT.

Leeds, December 6th, 1834.   No. 132.

.   .   .   .

The 51st Regiment was in the Corps of the Army immediately under Lord Hill—brigaded with the 14th and 23rd under the command of Colonel Mitchell, being a Light Corps, and standing at the head of the Column, upon its first formation at the crest of the position. Companies were in succession ordered in front, and occupied ground to the right of the Nivelles road, pretty nearly in a line with the Hougoumont farm. Lastly, the remaining Companies under my command descended and took possession of a favourable rising ground, covered with thick brushwood, and very defensible against any sudden attack of Cavalry. Here we remained posted, waiting orders.

Ordered by Lord Hill to hold his ground to the last, and to expect no support.

Late in the day, I forget the hour, an Aide-de-Camp from Lord Hill came down with an order to keep *this ground* to the *last*, as he was withdrawing his whole force to the left, and that I must not expect *any support*. Consequently I prepared myself to render as defensible as possible the post committed to my charge.

The 51st were in a manner separated from the rest of the Army, and took no part in the great movements.

Being so separated from the Army, you will perceive we bore no decided part in the Action, and were but holding ground during the great movements. The French had a line of Cavalry—vedettes—in our front, and to their rear at a considerable distance; I could perceive a body of Lancers, who no doubt were waiting some favourable moment to advance.

The French Cuirassiers endeavour to escape by the Nivelles road.

Situated as I was, I could see but little of what was going on to my left, except the charge of the French Cuirassiers on the left of Hougoumont farm, on the position. After [being] foiled in this attempt against the Squares, a considerable body passed down the Nivelles road, on which there was an *abatis*. I was so placed as to perceive this, and gave my parties in advance orders to fire, for, being so much in their rear, could not well distinguish friend from foe. The fire was successful, though some few miraculously cleared the *abatis*. I mention this merely to show our ground, [more] than anything else.

What I have offered I fear you will not consider very satisfactory, but you must bear in mind we were not connected during any part of the memorable day with any of the principal movements. In fact, I have considered my Regiment as a picket detached from the main body, throwing out skirmishers and supports, according to my own view, and in covering a certain space of ground.

.   .   .   .   .   .

I have been frequently questioned respecting the Battle of Waterloo and movements, and my reply has invariably been that I was so situated as to have but a partial view of the Field, and not engaged in the great conflict that was raging to my left. In fact, I may say that I was stationary throughout the day, and the only order I received was the one I have already mentioned.

. . . .

I beg, &c.,
S. RICE,
Colonel late 51st Regiment.

MAJOR J. ROSS, 51st REGIMENT.
CAPTAIN 51st REGIMENT.

Memorandum by Major Ross and Officers of 51st Regiment.

New Ross, County of Wexford, April 24th, 1835.

No. 133.

. . . .

On arriving at Waterloo from Grammont on June 17th, 1815, the 51st Light Infantry bivouacked during the night.

Waterloo.

On the morning of the 18th, the Brigade took up a position at about ten o'clock in rear of Hougoumont until the Enemy made their appearance on the rising ground of La Belle Alliance, when, on their Columns advancing, a Company of the Regiment was ordered to extend and cover the right of Hougoumont to meet the Enemy's skirmishers, who were moving forward at the head of their Columns.

From the undulating nature of the ground and the high standing corn, this Company (Captain Phelps') did not come in contact with the Enemy until within about seventy paces of each other, when a firing commenced. The Enemy's Cavalry were supporting their advance, but our Infantry at this time were not so supported. The Enemy retired slowly towards the enclosures of Hougoumont; their Columns were then halted upon the slope of the hill. About this period of the affair a small body of Light Cavalry came to support our skirmishers, and at the same time a Staff Officer arrived with a verbal order from Lord Hill to retire, and the Company retired in the usual way,

A Company of the 51st skirmished with the Enemy on the opposite rising ground

It was retired by order of Lord Hill.

skirmishing upon and near the Nivelles road, and halted on joining four Companies of the 51st under Major Keyt, and posted with their left on the road, and a few hundred yards to the right of Hougoumont supported by the remainder of the Regiment, which position the Regiment maintained during the day.

The Cuirassiers trying to retire by the Nivelles road.

At about two p.m., a small force of the Enemy's Cuirassiers that charged through our lines (and there surrendered) took an opportunity of breaking from a weak escort of Dragoons, and attempted to cut their way back by the Nivelles road, where a Company of the 51st Regiment was posted (Captain John Ross'). This Company was prepared to receive them in consequence of the supports and reserves of the 51st having fired at them *en passant*. They were commanded by an Officer who surrendered to Captain Ross, although he was closely pursued by some English Light Dragoons, to whom he would not again surrender, as he had formerly been their prisoner. There were twelve horses and eight Cuirassiers killed on this occasion, and the remainder, about sixty, were dismounted, taken, or dispersed. In this affair Captain Ross' Company had the advantage of an *abatis* across the road where it was posted.

FROM THE SAME.

No. 134.

Coventry, Warwickshire, August 16th, 1836.

Waterloo.
See Plan, p. 310.
Stations of the Brigade.

In the first instance I am not aware that a Company of the 14th Regiment was skirmishing along the broken bye-road or hollow way, as I only saw four Companies of the 51st there, and they had the good cover of this deep road and were posted so as to take advantage of it.

His own Company at the *abatis*.

One Company of the 51st (my own) was posted at the *abatis* on the high road, and the Light Company of the 23rd Fusiliers rested their right on the said *abatis*, their left communicating with the Guards that were lining the road from Hougoumont.

The other Companies of the 51st were placed as marked in your Plan.

. . . .

The approach to Hougoumont was, as previously stated, occupied by the Guards, their right resting on the Light Company of the 23rd Fusiliers, and this Company joined mine on the *abatis* in the manner represented in the Plan ; but all these troops had earlier in the day been further in advance, and they were recalled by an order from Lord Hill.

There were some straggling Brunswickers, who joined our ranks at this place, and a few of their old soldiers remained during the day with my Company, as they recollected me when serving with them in the 7th Division as Aide-de-Camp to Major-General De Bernewitz in the Peninsula.

Some Brunswick old soldiers join his Company.

I am not aware that there was any other Enemy's Infantry Column nearer than the one marked F, and I do not think that the Enemy's skirmishers at any time approached nearer than 60 yards.

This was the Column to the right of the wood of Hougoumont. *See* Plan, p. 310. —ED.

When the General Advance took place the ground in our front was vacated by the French Lancers, and all their troops were in retreat the moment it was ascertained that our Foreign Allies had arrived.

There were two Brunswick Squares during the day on the left of the road as marked by you B B, but I am not aware that there was *any large force* of Brunswickers on the right near the knoll, but there were certainly a few stragglers there.

See Plan, p. 310.

The 14th Regiment were as marked on the Plan, in rear of, and intended as a support to, the 51st.

Believe me, &c.,

JOHN ROSS.

HALKETT'S INFANTRY BRIGADE.

The 5th Infantry Brigade was composed of the 30th Regiment (2nd Batt.), the 33rd Regiment, the 69th Regiment (2nd Batt.), and the 73rd Regiment (2nd Batt.), and was under the command of Major-General Sir Colin Halkett, K.C.B., who was twice wounded at the Battle of Waterloo.

The Brigade reached Quatre Bras a little before 5 p.m. on the 16th June by the Nivelles road. It was at once moved up to the right between the *See* Plan of Bois de Bossu and the Charleroi road, in support Quatre Bras. of the Brunswickers, and of Pack's advanced Battalions. The latter having nearly expended all their ammunition, the 69th Regiment was pushed forward to their assistance.

Halkett, who had perceived the French Cavalry preparing to attack, sent word to the 69th to form square. They were in the act of doing so, when the Prince of Orange ordered them to form line, and the Cavalry approaching unseen, owing to the high-standing corn, suddenly charged the Regiment in this situation, completely rolled it up, and in the confusion captured one of its Colours.

The 30th Regiment, on the other hand, received the Cavalry in square, and repulsed them in such a manner as to call forth the commendations of Sir Thomas Picton.

When the Cavalry retired, the Square of the 33rd, which had been formed on rising ground, suffered so severely from the French Artillery fire, that it was found necessary to form it into line. The Regiment was advancing in that formation to

the support of some Brunswickers, when a report
was spread along the line that the French Cavalry
was in its rear, upon which it rushed into the wood
in disorder. Sir C. Halkett then came up, and,
seizing one of the Colours, made the Regiment
re-form upon it, and order was thus restored.

As the Guards gradually advanced through the
Bois de Bossu, Halkett's Brigade moved forward
up to the little rivulet, behind which it rested for
the night.

At Waterloo the Brigade was posted to the *See* General
left of Maitland's Guards, and thus formed the left Plan, No. 1.
portion of all the British Infantry on the right of
the Brussels Charleroi road.

Nearly the whole of the day it was formed in
squares to resist the repeated attacks of the French
Cavalry. Owing to the reduced state of the Regiments, the 30th and 73rd together formed one
Square, the 33rd and 69th another. The Light
Infantry of the Brigade was extended on the
exterior slope of the position during the intervals
between the Cavalry attacks.

In the evening, General Halkett being wounded
for the second time, the command of the Brigade
devolved upon Colonel Elphinstone, of the 33rd
Regiment.

When the British Guards advanced to drive back
the first attacking Column of the Imperial Guard,
the 33rd and 69th were pushed forward by Halkett
to cover their flank, which became exposed, as the
attack of the Imperial Guard was accompanied by a
corresponding advance of D'Erlon's Corps. Donzelot's Division of the latter moved forward in columns,

with Guns in the intervals, against Halkett's Brigade, and the troops on its left. The fire of some of these Guns on the Square of the 30th and 73rd was at one time so destructive, that it was thrown into some confusion, but the Enemy retiring at the moment, it was brought into order again.

The Brigade was then formed into line, and on the next and last advance of the French Infantry, received them with so well directed a volley, that after a little interval of musketry, they turned and fled.

The Brigade joined in the General Advance, and bivouacked for the night near La Belle Alliance.

Nos. 136, 137, 138, 141, 142, and 143 refer to Quatre Bras.

Nos. 136, 138, and 142 to the Retreat on the 17th June, and all the letters, except 137, 141, 142, and 143, to Waterloo.

LIEUT.-GENERAL SIR COLIN HALKETT, K.C.B., G.C.H.

MAJOR-GENERAL AND K.C.B., COMMANDING 5TH INFANTRY BRIGADE.

No. 135.

Waterloo.

Position of Brigade.

30th and 73rd formed in square. They repel charges of French Cavalry.

Also make a movement to retake La Haye, but fail.

33rd & 69th in double column in support,

93, *Sydney Place, Bath, November 5th, 1835.*

I have the honour to acknowledge the receipt of your letter of the 2nd, relative to the Battle of Waterloo, and in answer I beg to inform you that my Brigade was posted on the right of La Haye Sainte, and that the two Battalions, the 30th and 73rd Regiments, were formed in square, and that they were by the French Cavalry charged several times without effect. They also made a movement to the farmhouse when taken by the Enemy, but without effect and [with] considerable loss.

The remaining part of the Brigade (33rd and 69th Regiments) were in double column formed on the centre in support, but on the Enemy advancing upon the Guards, I moved them forward towards the position of the [French] Guards, and in their front, which had the good effect of arresting their progress; this movement created a heavy loss both of Officers and men.

and on approach of 1st attack of Imperial Guard are moved forward in support of the British Guards.

These are the *two only* subjects worth mentioning, excepting having sent out the Light Company of (I think) the 69th Regiment to skirmish with the Enemy, and having the Enemy on their flanks in La Haye Sainte, they were nearly annihilated. This was done by the *positive* order of the Prince of Orange, and seeing their unprotected state I recalled them.

The Prince of Orange orders a Light Company out to skirmish, with La Haye Sainte on its flank, so that it was nearly destroyed.

.   .   .   .

I remain, &c.,
COLIN HALKETT.

FROM THE SAME.

No. 136.

33, Gloucester Place, Portman Square, March 21st, 1837.

Quatre Bras.

I was the only General Officer with the Division in a field betwixt Quatre Bras and Nivelles. Unexpectedly I received an order to move on towards Quatre Bras, and on clearing the wood that ran down towards the Enemy's left, I received an order from Sir Thomas Picton to bring the left shoulders up of the leading Brigade, the *5th British* of the *3rd* Division (*the remainder to proceed towards the left,* of the *last*. I know nothing further of *their* transactions on that day). My order from Sir Thomas was to move through the wood, and if possible to fall upon the left of the French Army, and further to act as I thought most advantageous.

On arriving, ordered by Picton to move through the Bois de Bossu, and if possible to attack the French left.

See Plan of Quatre Bras.

In proceeding with the view to follow the directions I received, an A.D.C. of General Pack came up to me, stating that Pack's Brigade had expended nearly the whole of their ammunition, and that if I did not support him he would be obliged almost immediately to abandon the post he held, which was of great advantage to our position, &c. &c. Under these circumstances I directed the 69th

Pack, whose Brigade in front had nearly expended its ammunition, asks for support,
And the 69th is sent to him.

Regiment to proceed and form under cover of the farm-yard Pack occupied, and to communicate with the General, &c., and act according to his orders.   On my further

Halkett meets some Bruns-wickers retir-ing precipi-tately after having lost their Duke, and assists in restoring their order.
Considers he ought to remain in support of them.

advance to accomplish what I had been instructed to do, I found the Brunswick Corps, who had lost their Duke, retiring rather precipitately.   I immediately communicated with the Officer then commanding them (Olferman) and expressed my opinion as to the mode of their retrograde movement, and brought them up under cover in a ditch running nearly parallel to the line of the Enemy, and I considered it my duty to remain in support of the Bruns-wickers until further communication could be made with headquarters.

Having gal-loped to the front near Gemioncourt, sees the French Cav-alry preparing to advance.

In the meantime I, with one of my A.D.C.'s *galloped* to the *front* so as to clear the farm covered by wood which Pack occupied, and perceived a large Corps of Cavalry forming by detachments, moved forward under the appearance of going to water their horses.   I im-mediately, however, made my mind up as to their intention of moving forward almost immediately.   I had hardly returned to my Brigade when a heavy Artillery fire com-

Sent word to the 69th to prepare to receive them.

menced upon the road, and having sent Lieut. [? Kelsey] one of my A.D.C.'s to the 69th Regiment to inform them and Pack that I expected the Cavalry to advance, and I supposed the Guns indicated that intention, and that the 69th Regiment should, forthwith, prepare to receive Cavalry, I received an answer from the Commanding Officer of the 69th Regiment (Colonel Morice) that my order had been received and that he had attended to my

While form-ing square, the 69th were ordered by the Prince of Orange to form *line.*

instructions.   Unfortunately, in the act of forming square *an Officer high in rank* came up to the 69th Regiment, and asked what they were about.   The reply was the directions they received from me, on which he said [there was] no chance of the Cavalry appearing, and ordered them to

Upon which they were at-tacked by the Cavalry, who rode through them.

form column and to deploy into *line,* which of course was complied with, and during this very movement the Cavalry did attack, rode through the 69th Regiment, but situated *as they were,* the Enemy suffered a heavy loss.   On *our* side the same took place, and, most extraordinary, *one* of the *Colours* of the Regiment never appeared after the breaking up of the 69th Regiment by the charge. I can, I think, say *with truth* although the *Colour* was never seen or heard of, that it did *not* fall into the Enemy's hands, which of course is satisfactory.

This is an error. The Colour of the 69th was taken by Cuirassier Lami of the 8th Regiment. —ED.

I must relate an inquiry made by the Duke of Wellington through one of his Grace's A.D.C.'s, after my [illegible] instead of proceeding. My reply was what I have before related, and that I thought I could not leave the situation I was in until further support moved up. Another A.D.C. came up and desired me to effect what I was ordered if I could pass the wood. However, before I could put my Corps in motion the 1st A.D.C. returned with directions to follow up my views where I was, and to act accordingly. This answer relieved me from the duty I was first sent upon by Sir Thomas Picton, and there I remained and was partially engaged on two or three occasions.

When the Action ceased, I expected to be ordered to join my Division, instead of which, I think it was the Adjutant-General, Sir E. Barnes, came to me and wished to speak to me in private. From him I received the order to let my Brigade remain where they were, and employ them as I thought best, and that I was to command the advanced posts during the night, and that in the course of the night I should hear from Headquarters, &c. &c. I, of course, although more fatigued than ever I felt, naturally [was] flattered by the communication I had on the subject of myself, and in the course of the night Sir E. Barnes joined me and told me what had happened to the Prussian Army, and that his Grace directed I should retire before daybreak, and taking care that the Enemy did not observe our motions. Of course, everything to effect this was accordingly communicated along the advance line, and we retired, leaving fires, &c., as if we were in position, *without being pursued* by the *French*, and joined the Brigade on the march to the point I was directed [on] in good

On the close of the action, Halkett is ordered to command the outposts.

Hears of the Battle of Ligny, and receives the order to retire.

Retreat on 17th June.

A severe
march, owing
to the heavy
rain, and
being sent the
wrong way.

order.　And our march to Waterloo was a severe one, from having been led the wrong road by one of the Quartermaster General's Staff, and obliged to cross the country through water above the men's knees.

Fortunately having suspected something similar, I ordered back my Artillery, who got into the right road, otherwise I do not think I could have brought them with me on the 17th to Waterloo.　　.　　　.　　　.

Yours, &c.,
Colin Halkett.

FROM THE SAME.

No. 137.

Quatre Bras.

Calais, June 5th, 1839.

In answer to yours of the 28th May I do recollect a Battery of Artillery having made its appearance, but *where* I do *not* know, and it was so much in my rear that I paid no attention to it or its effects; and as to the retreat of my Brigade I must differ with you on that subject.

Retreat of
33rd into the
wood.

The only part that really did retreat was one Regiment (the 33rd), and which I was not all satisfied with.　The Regiment *with me,* or *near where I was,* did not make the least movement, only one wing thrown back.　The Brunswickers in my *front* took up my attention too much.　I must, however, do them the justice of saying that in this instance the French Cavalry had *no* effect upon them, nor did they move in any shape.

For explanation of this,
see No. 142,
p. 335.

The 33rd I rode to the moment I could absent myself from the front, and I recollect I had some difficulty in getting them to the order they ought to have remained in, and I took one of their Colours and advanced to the front with it, which I think had the desired effect, and soon got them into the order they ought *never* to have lost.　They then appeared steady and I left them.　At this period, however, the Cavalry were in, or had effected their, retreat, and I think they lost a great number of men and horses.

Yours, &c.,
Colin Halkett.

THE 30TH REGIMENT.

MAJOR J. PRATT, LATE 27TH REGIMENT.
LIEUTENANT 30TH REGIMENT.

London, March 23rd, 1835.   No. 138.

.   .   .   .

Having been wounded and obliged to leave the Field about six p.m., I am unable to give specific replies to your most important questions, which relate to a subsequent period, and I think you will readily agree with me that a young Subaltern Officer, such as I was at that period, harassed and fatigued after two days' previous marching, fighting, and starving (for by some mismanagement our Division was not provisioned), was not likely to take particular notice of the features of the ground over which he was moving, or to direct his observations much beyond the range of what was likely to affect himself and the few soldiers immediately about him.

.   .   .   .

But as you express a wish to be made acquainted with such details of these memorable events as came within my immediate observation, with a view to the compilation of a minute and correct explanatory narrative, I beg to refer you to the accompanying document, in which I have thrown together, in the shape of a journal, my recollection of the events in which I took part on the [16th,] 17th, and 18th June.

.   .   .   .   .   .

I have, &c.,

JOHN PRATT,
Major, late 27th Regt.

Recollections of the Battle of Waterloo—16th, 17th, and 18th June, 1815.

16th. The 3rd Division, after marching during part of Quatre Bras. the night of the 15th and the morning of the 16th, came into position at Quatre Bras between three and four p.m.,

30TH REGIMENT.

This is an error. The Brigade advanced to the right of the 5th Division. —ED.

and immediately took up the ground of the 5th Division (then retiring, and much crippled), and moved in advance. Was engaged until between nine and ten at night, when the Action terminated.

. . . .

The ground between it (Gemioncourt) and a wood on the right was occupied during the night by the advance posts of the British Brigade 3rd Division, the main body being concealed in the hollow ground in the rear.

17th. At daylight found ourselves in close contact with the Enemy's outposts, scarcely removed from each other by more than half musket shot.

. . . .

Retreat on the 17th.

At this time [9 a.m.] the 3rd was, I believe, the only Division of Infantry on the ground, the remainder of the Army having made a retrograde movement during the night, or early in the morning of the 17th. Between eleven and twelve a.m. received orders to withdraw, having as much address as possible not to attract the notice of the Enemy; passed the Hussar Brigade, which was formed half a league in the rear, and joined the Division *en route*.

About four p.m. the rain began to descend in torrents, and rendered the fallow fields almost impassable . . . and we filed into our position about half-past seven or eight o'clock.

. . . .

Waterloo.

18th. The appearance of the morning was most dismal and dreary . . . . .

Ordered to stand to their arms about 11 a.m.

About eleven a.m. the cry of "Stand to your arms" passed rapidly down the Line, and a general discharge or drawing of firelocks immediately took place, they being almost unserviceable from their previous use, and the heavy rain they were exposed to during the night. The line was ordered to retire a little to gain the interior slope of the position, and then formed into squares, two Regiments generally forming one square; thus in Sir Colin Halkett's Brigade the 30th and 73rd formed one, and the 33rd and

Brigade formed two Squares, 30th and 73rd one, 33rd and 69th the other.

69th the other square. These Regiments did not at that period average more than 450, or at the utmost 500 effective men each. After this formation the Squares lay down, and the crest of the position interposed between them and the Enemy. The Artillery was advanced in about the same proportion on the exterior slope, and the Light Troops of the Division moved to the front to cover and support it.

The Regiments did not average more than 500 men each. Squares lie down behind crest of position, Batteries in front.

This force consisted, to the best of my recollection, in the following details : Four British Light Companies formed into a Battalion under Lieutenant-Colonel Vigoureux, 30th Regiment; 1st and 2nd Light Battalions, K.G.L. They occupied the farmhouse and garden of La Haye Sainte—a Light Hanoverian Battalion and the Jägers von Kilmansegge (Rifles).

Light Troops of Division sent out in front in skirmishing order.

The orders delivered to me upon that occasion as Adjutant of the Light Battalion by Major-General Sir C. Halkett were to the following effect : "To cover and protect our Batteries. To establish ourselves at all times as much in advance as might be compatible with prudence. To preserve considerable intervals between our extended files for greater security from the fire of the Enemy's Batteries. To show obstinate resistance against Infantry of the same description, but to attempt no formation or offer useless opposition to charges of Cavalry, but to retire in time upon the Squares in our rear, moving in a direct line without any reference to Regiments or Nations. When the charge was repulsed, to resume our ground."

Orders issued to the Light Infantry of the Brigade by Sir C. Halkett.

. . . .

About mid-day, rather before twelve, the first shot was fired . . . It was the first report that reached my ears that morning, and was directed against masses of Infantry moving on Hougoumont. The Enemy's Artillery did not reply for some time, but we could see them distinctly taking up their position immediately in our front.

. . . .

The Enemy's Artillery had now opened a tremendous fire along the entire extent of the left centre of the

The Enemy's Artillery open

a heavy fire, chiefly on our Batteries.

position, but chiefly directed against our Batteries. Several large shells also fell with precision in the midst of us, but the ground being very soft, generally buried themselves deep, and did not do as much mischief as under other circumstances might have been the case.

The Light Troops advance to the foot of the hill.

Driven back by a charge of Cavalry.

The Light Troops crept down the hill to nearly its foot. Did not at first encounter any Infantry, but were driven back by a charge of Cavalry. Took refuge in the Squares, and when the charge was repulsed immediately occupied former position.　　.　　.　　.　　.　　.

The fire of the Enemy's Artillery became now very galling, exposed as we were to it, and almost all the Artillery horses had already fallen under it.

.　　.　　.　　.　　.　　.

These charges repeated. In the intervals the skirmishers are opposed by skirmishers.

In the interval we experienced more than one charge of Cavalry, and the Light Infantry, in their occasional advances, now encountered the same description of force, usually engaging and sustaining a desultory fire near the foot of the respective positions.

.　　.　　.　　.　　.

The Enemy's Batteries, too, had gained considerably in advance, and the Light Troops were now invariably assailed by grape as well as musketry, when they showed themselves at the foot of the position, endeavouring to offer a

The Enemy's Infantry establishes itself well in advance, preparing for the final attack.

feeble resistance to the encroachments of the Enemy's Infantry, now establishing itself well in advance, and evidently preparing for the final attack.

.　　.　　.　　.　　.

Throughout the whole day, and during my frequent advances and retreats, I only once, or at most twice, entered my own Square, the line on which I had to direct myself usually leading me on a German or Hanoverian Square.

Such was the nature of the struggle that took place, during the greater portion of the day, on that part of the position situated between La Haye Sainte and Hougoumont, and which is, I believe, usually denominated the " left centre."

Towards the close of the day I found myself for the last time near the bottom of our slope with the few Light Troops that were remaining. The firing on the left had slackened or ceased, and the Enemy's position in our immediate front was being covered with Infantry. Their Artillery also had taken up a position much in advance, and was firing, chiefly grape, amongst the scattered Light Troops, which were gradually retiring before the overwhelming force opposed to them.

La Haye Sainte being in possession of the Enemy, our left was necessarily much thrown back, so as to place us nearly in *échelon* with the crest of the position. It was at this period that I was wounded, and, of course, I ceased to be an eye-witness of what took place afterwards.

> After La Haye Sainte was taken by the Enemy, the left of the line of skirmishers is much thrown back.
>
> Is wounded before last attack of the French.

. . . .

J. P.

MAJOR E. MACREADY, 30TH REGIMENT.

LIEUTENANT [?] 30TH REGIMENT.

3, *Stratford Place, April 23rd*, 1846.　No. 139.

. . . .

I enclose you a letter I have by me (which you can keep), written 1836, to Gawler, but never sent, as after it was done, my disinclination to come forward as a controversialist induced me to keep it back and leave the matter alone. . . . . .

Always, &c.,
EDWARD MACREADY.

TO LIEUT.-COL. GAWLER, UNATTACHED.

Kandy, Ceylon, November 30th, 1836.

SIR,—Although a stranger to you, I can readily believe　Waterloo. that I need not apologise for troubling you with a few observations on certain points whereon, in your letter inserted in the last July number of the *United Service Journal,* you express yourself desirous of information.

.　　.　　.　　.　　.　　.

They were sent by the Duke to fill up a gap in the line on the left of Halkett's Brigade.

A heavy Column of Brunswickers came up to our left (30th and 73rd Regiments) in the evening of June 18th. A remark upon them in my Journal states that "they fell back at first bodily, but were rallied and afterwards stood their ground." If I am not deceived, Captain Hughes, 1st West India Regiment (then a Lieutenant of the 30th, and, if I may be permitted to say so, a *most* gallant officer), received a wound while assisting to rally them. But I do not think that these Brunswickers were *engaged* with the Guard. I saw no troops of the Guard to the French right of that Column which advanced on us (30th and 73rd), and which, though it came over the hill in beautiful order, was an inconceivable short time before us, turning and flying to a man at the single volley we fired, and the hurrah that followed it. Having expected great things from them, we were astonished at their conduct, and we young soldiers almost fancied there was some "ruse" in it. The men I spoke to as they lay wounded were all of the "Moyenne Garde."

Repulse of a French Column by 30th and 73rd.

The attacking Column of the Guard advanced against the British Guards, who were right of 33rd and 69th, who were again right of 30th and 73rd. Therefore, this portion of "Moyenne Garde" must have been combined with Donzelot's Division, which attacked Halkett's left. —ED.
See General Plan, No. 2.

By the way, it may lead to misconception if I do not mention that by some arrangement, of which I know nothing, the contiguous Columns and subsequent Squares of the 30th and 73rd Regiments were to the *left* of those formed by the 33rd and 69th Regiments.

"That there was a great giving way near this point about this period *is* certain" enough. But I believe you must consider what follows to a certain extent as private, for I should be loth to offend any of my old friends by causing a public allusion to an awkward circumstance, of which I really know nothing but its alarming consequences.

Perilous confusion into which the 30th and 73rd were thrown.

Late in the day the French had brought up two Guns on the crest of our position, which fired grape into our Square (30th and 73rd) with very deadly effect. Some one in authority must have thought that the bank of a hedge which ran a very short distance in our rear would afford us some cover, and in an evil moment we received the commands to face about and march down to it.

You may readily conceive that fire would not slacken on a body effecting such a movement; but though suffering sadly, and disordered by our poor wounded fellows clinging to their comrades thinking they were being abandoned, our little Square retained its formation, and we had all but reached the hedge, when a body of men (British) rushed in amongst us, turned us altogether into a mere mob, and created a scene of frightful confusion. Fortunately the Enemy took no advantage of it.

Nothing could be more gratifying than the conduct of our people at this disastrous period. While men and Officers were jammed together and carried along by the pressure from without, many of the latter, some cursing, others literally crying with rage and shame, were seizing the soldiers and calling on them to halt, while these admirable fellows, good-humouredly laughing at their excitement, were struggling to get out of the *mêlée,* or exclaiming " By G—d, I'll stop, Sir, but I'm off my legs." *Gratifying conduct of the men.*

I know nothing that remedied this terrible disorder but a shout which some one raised, and in which all joining the mass halted as if by word of command. An Officer was immediately desired by Major Chambers (who fell some minutes later) to take such men as he could get in addition to the Light Company, then reduced to fourteen rank and file, and to push up the hill as far as he dare to cover the re-formation. This was effected without difficulty, and all afterwards went right. *And re-establishment of order.*

The falling back in Halkett's Brigade, and of the Brunswick Column occurred very near together, and I can readily conceive this to have been the period to which the French *"Témoin Oculaire"* alludes to when he speaks of Battalions being seen *" en débandade"* on our height.

Of these facts, therefore, I feel that I can assure you, —1st. That a heavy Column of Brunswickers was on the immediate left of the 30th and 73rd Regiments in the

Genl. Alava
was Spanish
Commissioner
to the British
Army.—ED.

evening of the 18th June, and that General Alava's and
the "other testimony" are reconcilable and true. 2nd.
That a body of German Legion Cavalry passed to the front
by the right of the 30th Regiment at the very finish (we
did not advance beyond the crest of our own ridge); and
3rd, that the unaccountable movement I have mentioned,

The disorder
was nearly
fatal to the
remains of
Halkett's
Brigade.

with its accompaniments, was as near as possible being
fatal to the remains of Halkett's Brigade at a most eventful
period of the day.

Believe, &c.,

EWD. MACREADY,

Captain 30th Regt.

THE 33RD REGIMENT.

COLONEL W. K. ELPHINSTONE, 33RD REGIMENT.
LIEUT.-COLONEL 33RD REGIMENT.

No. 140.

Enfield, November 28th, 1834.

. . . .

Waterloo.

33rd had been
in advance on
left of Brussels
road during
night of 17th.
Next morning
was moved
along cross
road to posi-
tion of Brigade
on left of
Guards.

33rd and 69th
form one
square.

About
7 o'clock
Brigade
formed in line
four deep.

Final attack
of the French.

I beg to inform you that the 33rd Regiment, after
being withdrawn from the left of the road near La Haye
Sainte, where it was placed in advance on the night of the
17th, moved along a cross road or lane behind that farm,
and was formed in square with the 69th Regiment at some
distance to the right, and in rear of La Haye Sainte, in
échelon to the Square of the 30th and 73rd Regiments,
which were further in advance. Between four and five
o'clock the two Regiments moved forward, and soon after
formed line with the 30th and 73rd. The Brigade (5th)
then advanced to the top of the hill on rising ground, and
about seven o'clock, when the Enemy's final attack was
made, was formed four deep, on the immediate left of the
1st Guards.

At this time Columns of French Infantry were advancing, with Guns between the heads of the Columns.

These, when within a short distance of our position, halted and soon after gave way.

The 5th Brigade, which had suffered much during the Action and at Quatre Bras, was not ordered forward. It was afterwards moved a little in advance and remained on the ground during the night .   .   .   .

I have, &c.,

W. K. ELPHINSTONE.

LIEUT.-COLONEL J. M. HARTY, 33RD REGIMENT.

CAPTAIN 33RD REGIMENT.

140, *Leeson Street, December 22nd,* 1842.

No. 141.

Quatre Bras.

On my return home yesterday I received your note respecting the movements of the 33rd Regiment at Quatre Bras, and feel sorry that it is not in my power to give any authentic information respecting them, inasmuch as being Captain of the Light Company of the Regiment which formed part of the Flank Battalion, I was absent from my own Corps during the day.

Detached from his Regiment with th Light Infantry of the Brigade.

The Flank Battalion consisted of the Light Companies of the Brigade under the command of Lieutenant-Colonel Vigoureux of the 30th Regiment, and we were under him, acting in the vicinity of, and in connection with, his own Regiment commanded by Lieutenant-Colonel Hamilton, so much so that we (the Battalion) formed square with that Corps when charged by French Lancers, on which occasion the firm conduct of the Square called forth the unqualified approbation of the late Sir Thomas Picton, who was an eye-witness, and galloped up ; and, calling for the commanding officer, told Colonel Hamilton that he would report their gallant conduct to the Duke.

The latter forms square with the 30th Regiment.

Picton tells the Commanding Officer of the 30th that he will report the gallant conduct of the Square to the Duke.

.   .   .   .   .   .

Believe, &c.,

J. M. HARTY.

F. H. PATTISON, ESQ.

LIEUTENANT 33rd REGIMENT.

TO HIS BROTHER, J. PATTISON, ESQ.

No. 142. *Dalmain, December 6th, 1842.*

MY DEAR JOHN,—I think the best way I possibly can answer Captain Siborne's query about the 33rd Regiment is by giving him a short sketch of what came under my notice at the Battle of Quatre Bras. In doing so it must be recollected that I took no notes, and that since then twenty-seven years have elapsed, and therefore my statement is dependent entirely upon memory, may not be absolutely right in every particular, but will be found substantially correct.

As far as I remember, I think it must have been between four and five o'clock in the evening that Sir Colin Halkett's Brigade advanced to that spot which is intersected by four roads, and from which fact the Battle derives its name, being Quatre Bras, or four arms. At this period the Scotch Division under Sir Thomas Picton was actively engaged a little in advance on the great road which leads to Charleroi. Immediately on getting there, orders were given for the Brigade to move forward to the right, and support the right of Picton's Division.

A movement agreeably to this order took place, each Regiment advancing in open column of Companies, preserving their respective distances, so as to deploy into line when necessary. The ground through which we had to advance was much undulated, and in full crop of rye, which in that rich and luxuriant country grows excessively high, and on this account obstructed observation.

As we advanced, the leading Company of our Regiment reached a prominent part of the field and observed the French Cavalry advancing to the charge. Orders were then given to form square to receive the Enemy. The Enemy, perceiving we were prepared for them, instead of advancing, made a movement to the left, broke in upon

Marginal notes: Quatre Bras. See Plan. | Halkett's Brigade arrived between 4 and 5 p.m. | Ordered to move round the Bois de Bossu to the right, and support the right of Picton's Division, which was advanced towards Gemioncourt. | Cavalry being perceived, the 33rd formed square.

the open Columns of the 69th Regiment, which, being on a low part of the field, had not observed them. The havoc that then took place was very great, and one of their Colours, I think the Regimental Colour, was carried off in triumph.

All this took place with amazing rapidity and despatch, and the 33rd was not left long to contemplate objects with indifference. As I have already observed, we were made aware of the approach of the Cavalry, and that by the Grenadier Company, it having reached rising ground, and having formed square upon that Company, the whole Regiment were placed as a beacon in presence of the Enemy. Immediately a park of Artillery was opened at point blank distance upon our Column. The destruction consequent upon this was fearful. At this time Captain Hay, having moved from the head of his Company to encourage the face of the Square fronting the Enemy, was cut in two by a cannon ball, and poor Arthur Gore's brains were scattered upon my shako and face.

It was soon found necessary to deliver the Regiment from this untoward situation, which was done by deploying into line in an angular position. Upon getting into this new position, we were supported on the right by a Regiment of Brunswick Cavalry, which behaved with great intrepidity. In advance, near the corner of the wood, a Regiment or Brigade of Brunswick Infantry were fiercely engaged.

At this time the 33rd moved towards them; but upon getting near the wood, a report being spread that the Cavalry were in the rear, the Regiment entered it and dispersed. It was at this time that Colonel Parkinson was wounded. He, with Captain Knight, Lieutenant Thane, and myself, went into the wood near the same place. Captain Knight formed the men near us, and advanced some distance towards the place where we thought the Enemy were; but soon being at a loss to know where we were going in the wood, we retrograded, and came out of it upon one of the intersecting roads, as already alluded to.

Upon getting there we found a Brigade of the Guards, which were immediately advanced.

The report of Sir Colin Halkett having seized one of our Colours and re-formed the Regiment may be true, and upon reflecting, a vague impression of that kind fleets over my mind; but as the party with which I was connected, consisting of the above-mentioned Officers and about fifty or sixty men, found the Regiment upon returning formed on the outside of the wood, if such a circumstance took place, none of us saw it.

By this time, the Guards having advanced and forced the Enemy from the field, no other active movement took place with Sir Colin Halkett's Brigade that evening, but we, with the rest of the Army, slept on the Field of Battle all night.

The retreat. Early on the morning of the 17th the Brigade, being under arms, was ordered to move from its position, and from the direction it took we were all of the opinion that an attack was to be made upon the right wing of the French, which rested upon a wood on a hill a considerable distance from our left.

Our conjectures, however, were fallacious, and I believe our apparent advance towards the Enemy was intended as a feint to deceive them, as we no sooner crossed the road, which was contended for by Picton's Division the previous evening, and had got between the wood and the Enemy so as to intercept from their view our movements, than we entered into a bye-road and retreated.

We continued to retreat without any pause until we reached the well-known town of Genappe, where the Brigade halted to get refreshment, no provision having been given out since it left the cantonments before daybreak on the 16th. However, from the cowardice of the Commissariat—whose duty it was to make provision for the troops, but who, in a panic, fled—no refreshment could be obtained there, except what was got by the men individually here and there.

After halting a considerable time the retreat was con-

tinued, and we were soon aware, from constant firing of
Light Troops and field pieces, that the Enemy pursued.
At this time everything appeared extremely disheartening,
and the very elements of nature seemed to be frowning
upon and contending with us. A dark, fearful looking
cloud arose above the direction of the Enemy, and approaching us, poured down such torrents of rain, and discharged
such vivid lightning, accompanied with such tremendous
peals of thunder, that, though long in a tropical climate,
I never beheld or heard the like before.

The great
thunderstorm.

The Army still continued to retreat, until it arrived at
the place destined for its position. It was here that I saw
Sir Thomas Picton for the first and last time, who ordered
the 33rd to act as an advanced picket, and which bivouacked that night in a field to the left of the great road of
our position.

33rd ordered
by Picton on
outpost duty
to the left of
the Brussels
road.

Yours, &c.,

F. H. PATTISON.

THE 69TH REGIMENT.

CAPTAIN B. PIGOT, LATE 69TH REGIMENT.
LIEUTENANT 69TH REGIMENT.

Mansfield, Notts, July 7th, 1844. No. 143.

. . . .

If I had known you would have received any information, I should have been happy to have given it to you
regarding the affair of the 16th June, being wounded
in it.

Quatre Bras

I was wounded at the same time with Major Lindsay;
he commanded No. 1, I commanded No. 2. Poor man,
the loss sustained by the Grenadier, Nos. 1 and 2, Companies was greatly attributable to him, halting those
Companies, making them face to right about, in open
Column, and commence firing upon the Cuirassiers. But
for that we should have got into square, as it was those
Companies [that] were really cut down. Poor man, to

Wounded at
the same time
with Major
Lindsay, to
whom he at-
tributes the
Regiment not
getting into
square on the
approach of
the French
Cavalry.

the day of his death he regretted having done so, but at the time he did it for the best.

Officers killed on 16th and 18th June.

On the 16th Lieut. Wightwick, my subaltern, was killed, on the 18th Colonel Morice, Captains Curzon, Hobhouse, and Blackwood were also killed, making five Officers. You say one Officer killed at Quatre Bras, and three at Waterloo, which should be four on the 18th.

I remain, &c.,
BROOKE PIGOT,
Captain 69th Regiment. Retired Full Pay.

LIEUTENANT H. ANDERSON, 75TH REGIMENT.
LIEUTENANT 69TH REGIMENT.

No. 144.

Thexford, November 18th, 1835.

Waterloo.
At the time of the advance of the Imperial Guard, the 69th and 33rd formed one square.

Our formation on the advance of the Imperial Guard (about 7 p.m.) was in square, the 33rd Regiment forming a portion of it. I was wounded at the moment the Guard gained the crest of our position, and remained for some time insensible to passing events.

I do not remember seeing the Brunswickers near us at that period of the action, but I recollect *perfectly* having seen, a short time previous to the advance of the Guard, some Foreign Corps in rear of our left, having shakos covered with white.

Never heard of a published account of the British Line being forced. Never heard it alluded to, and does not believe it.

I never was aware till I read your letter that there was any published account of our Line having been forced at *any* period of the Battle, and though I have often fought the Battle o'er again with my old companions in arms, I never heard the circumstance alluded to, nor do I believe it ever occurred. If it had, I must have heard it from my brother Officers who had the good fortune to see the Enemy retreat. I believe I may say *run*.

I have, &c.,
H. ANDERSON,
Lieutenant 75th.

THE 73RD REGIMENT.

LIEUT.-COLONEL DAWSON KELLY, C.B.

MAJOR 73RD REGIMENT, AND ASSISTANT QUARTER-MASTER GENERAL.

Armagh, November 26th, 1834. No. 145.

. . . . . .

I beg to say that I should have been most happy in affording you the detailed information you desire relative to the operations of the 73rd Regiment during the Battle of Waterloo, but being on the Staff of the Quarter-Master General's Department, at that period, I had not an opportunity (except in occasionally passing by) of witnessing the various formation of squares and changes of position, which the frequent attacks both of Cavalry and Infantry, upon that particular point, throughout the day, occasioned to the 5th Brigade.

Waterloo.

Was on the Quarter-Master General's Staff.

It was, however, upon the advance of a body of Cavalry early in the day, that the Duke of Wellington with his Staff were obliged to take shelter in a Square formed by the 73rd and 30th Regiments. It was also at the crisis which you more particularly allude to, I should say about half-past six, when passing with the Duke and other Officers of the Staff in the rear of the 5th Brigade there appeared to be some little confusion, when the Duke, without directing himself particularly to any person, said, " See what's wrong there."

The Duke and his Staff take shelter in the Square of the 30th and 73rd.

The Duke seeing some confusion in the Brigade, orders it to be seen to.

I rode up to the Brigade, and while addressing myself to Sir Colin Halkett, he at the instant received a wound in the face, the ball passing through his mouth, and he was consequently obliged to retire to the rear. Colonel Elphinstone, commanding the 33rd Regiment, then ran up and asked if I had any orders. I replied none beyond inquiring into the cause of the confusion ; he stated that they were much pressed, and the men exhausted. Colonel

Sir C. Halkett wounded (the second time), and obliged to leave the field.

Col. Harris of the 73rd being severely wounded, the command devolves on Col. Elphinstone of the 33rd.

Recommends to him how to prepare for a fresh attack.

Two Sergeants of the 73rd report to Major Kelly that all their Officers are killed or wounded.

He therefore takes command of the Regiment.

The *last* attack of Donzelot's Division. —ED.

After one well-directed volley into them, and a short interval of musketry, they flee.

The Brigade joins the General Advance.

Harris of the 73rd had been severely wounded, and the command of the Brigade had devolved upon him, and he added, " What is to be done? What would you do? "

At this period the attacking Column was again retiring, and having observed that the different Battalions of the Brigade had got intermixed from the frequent formation of squares, I advised Colonel Elphinstone to order both Officers and men to resume their respective stations, to form as extended a front as possible, directing them to cover themselves as well as they could by lying down, to renew, or check their flints, and to fresh prime, so as to meet the next attack with the best means left us. This he instantly directed, and I should mention here that while in conversation with Colonel E., one or two sergeants of the 73rd came up and told me they had no one to command them, the Officers all being killed or wounded.

I therefore considered it my duty to remain with them, and upon my saying so, they cheered and instantly returned to their several posts. Thus situated we remained for a short time inactive, when the *last attacking Column* made its appearance through the fog and smoke, which throughout the day lay thick on the ground. Their advance was as usual with the French, very noisy and evidently reluctant, the Officers being in advance some yards cheering their men on. They however kept up a confused and running fire, which we did not reply to until they reached nearly on a level with us, when a well-directed volley put them into confusion which they did not appear to recover, but after a short interval of musketry on both sides, they turned about to a man and fled.

Whether any of our troops (as Colonel Gawler states in his " Crisis ") had assailed them in flank or rear it was impossible to know from the confusion of the moment, but after a very short period the order came down the Line from the right to advance, which we obeyed as soon as the Brigade was formed, and continued until beyond La Belle

Alliance, when we were ordered to halt, and remained on
the ground throughout the night, the Prussians having
taken our place in pursuit of the Enemy.

I have, &c.,

DAWSON KELLY,

Lieutenant-Colonel.

FROM THE SAME.

Armagh, October 14th, 1835.   No. 146.

.   .   .   .

I think I mentioned to you in my former letter the Waterloo
cause of my having joined the 5th Brigade at the period of
Sir C. Halkett's being wounded, together with Colonel
Elphinstone's exertions in taking the command.

With respect to your present inquiry, it is fully within The last
my memory that the fog and smoke lay so heavy upon the French
ground that we could only ascertain the approach of the attack.
Enemy by the noise and clashing of arms which the French
usually make in their advance to attack, and it has often
occurred to me from the above circumstance (the heavy
fog), that the accuracy and the particulars with which the
Crisis has been so frequently and *so minutely* discussed,
must have had a good deal of fancy in the narrative.

You are aware that the Guards were stationed considerably to the right of the 5th Brigade. I can therefore
only say that when the *last* attacking Column emerged from
the smoke in *our front* the French Officers were in the
front cheering on their men, but whether they were of the
Imperial Guard, or of D'Erlon's Corps we had no oppor- It was Donze-
tunity of judging. I should rather think the latter, for lot's Division
after some firing between us the Enemy retreated without Corps which
any *very apparent* cause. I presume it might have been attacked the
about this time that some of our troops had got to the rear *See* marginal
or flank of the Enemy, which caused their sudden retreat; note, p. 330.
but as I have already said, from the heaviness of the —ED.
atmosphere we *could see but* little of what was going on in
our front. There was certainly no appearance of Cavalry

73RD REGIMENT.

The 73rd lost 21 Officers killed and wounded out of 25.

at this period, but when the order came from the right to advance, the 5th Brigade moved straight forward without encountering either friend or foe until near La Belle Alliance, when they were ordered to halt and remained during the night. The 73rd Regiment had twenty-one Officers killed and wounded out of twenty-five in the field, and as I presume you are in possession of the Returns you will perceive a proportionate number of the Battalion.

Death of Col. Sir Wm. Delancey, K.C.B., Deputy Quar.-Master Genl. (not mentioned in former letter).

Death of Lieut.-Col. Canning, A.D.C. to the Duke.

I believe in my former letter I mentioned the circumstance of poor Colonel Delancey's death. It was shortly after we had halted as above on the field that one of the men came to me to say that an Aide-de-Camp of the Duke of Wellington was wounded and lying near, when, upon going with him, I found Colonel Canning in the greatest possible agony. He had received a musket shot in the centre of the abdomen, and, although perfectly collected, he could hardly articulate from pain. We raised him, however, to a sitting position by placing knapsacks round him, but a few minutes terminated his existence.

. . . .

I remain, &c.,

DAWSON KELLY.

MAJOR J. GARLAND, HALF-PAY.

CAPTAIN 73RD REGIMENT.

No. 147.
Waterloo.

Dorchester, Dorset, December 4th, 1834.

On my return from Weymouth I found your letter of the 6th ult., and which I shall reply to with as much accuracy as the long period which has elapsed since the Battle will allow me, as well as my having been very severely wounded about the time you put your first query, "7 p.m."

Wounded about 7 p.m.

The 30th and 73rd in one square nearly all day, and repeatedly

I recollect we had been in square composed of the 30th and 73rd Regiments nearly all the Action and were repeatedly charged by the Cuirassiers during the day and about half-past six or seven o'clock the Duke of

Wellington rode up and asked who commanded the Square. I replied Colonel, now Lord, Harris, who happened at that moment not to be so near his Grace as myself. He then desired me to tell Colonel Harris to form line, but should we be attacked by the Cuirassiers to re-form square. I delivered these orders to Colonel Harris and we formed line, and in the act of forming line I received my wound.

charged by French Cavalry.

The Duke gives orders to the Square to form line, but if attacked by Cavalry to re-form square.

. . . .

During the early part of the day, before we formed square, we were in column of quarter distance under a hill out of sight of the Enemy, with the Household Brigade and Heavy Cavalry in our rear in a bottom, and, *to the best of my recollection*, Hougoumont on our right and La Haye Sainte on our left. During the time we were in square we were kept continually on the alert by the repeated charges of Cuirassiers, so that the Enemy nearest us all day were Cavalry; but as I was wounded just as we were about to change our position, I cannot speak of what was in front of the 73rd as the Regiment advanced.

Position of Brigade early in the day.

I have, &c.,

JOHN GARLAND,

Major, Half-pay.

KEMPT'S INFANTRY BRIGADE.

The 8th* Infantry Brigade was composed of the 28th and 32nd Regiments, the 79th Regiment, Cameron Highlanders, and the 1st Battalion of the 95th Rifles. It was under the command of Major General Sir James Kempt, K.C.B., and formed part of the 5th Division commanded by Lieutenant-General Sir Thomas Picton, G.C.B.

The Division arrived at Quatre Bras about a

---

* The 6th and 7th British Brigades of the Army in Belgium were not at Waterloo.

See Plan of
Quatre Bras,
No. 1.

quarter to three p.m. on the 16th June, and was at once posted along the Namur road, Kempt's Brigade being on the left of the line.

The 28th Regiment was soon marched down to occupy the Farm of Gemioncourt, but it was already in the possession of the Enemy, and the 28th rejoined the Brigade. The 95th Rifles were similarly detached to endeavour to occupy the village of Piermont, but that was also strongly held by the French. The Battalion, however, in conjunction with some of the Allied Troops, successfully resisted all the efforts of the French during the day to turn the left flank of the Army by the Namur road.

The skirmishers of the Division were thrown out in front, and after suffering severely for some time from the French cannonade, it was ordered to advance against the Infantry in front of the road.

Kempt's Brigade charged, and drove the Enemy down the hill to the fences at the bottom, and was then recalled.

The 28th, together with the 1st Royals, were afterwards marched in column to the relief of the 42nd and 44th Regiments, which were very hardly pressed by the French Cavalry near Gemioncourt. At the last moment the 28th and Royals suddenly formed a single square in a position so as to combine a flanking fire with that of the 42nd and 44th, and although constantly assailed, it always beat off the Cavalry. The 32nd and 79th were also formed in flanking squares, and sustained repeated attacks of the Cavalry with similar results.

See General
Plan, No. 1.

At Waterloo the Brigade was posted on the

right of Picton's Division, and was drawn up a little in rear of the Wavre road, with its right resting on the Brussels or main road, the 95th occupying the sandpit further down the main road, the knoll on the left of the sandpit, and the hedge-row in rear of both, with some advanced Companies. This hedgerow furnished the materials for forming an *abatis* on the main road below.

At the time of D'Erlon's first attack on the Division, the other Regiments of the Brigade were formed in line about fifty yards in rear of the hedge along the Wavre road, 32nd on the right, 28th on *See* Plan, p. 38. the left, and 79th in the centre, their Light Companies being extended in advance of the position.

The Column which attacked this Brigade was diverted by the fire of the 95th more to its right, so as to lead it on to the left of the 79th and right of the 28th. The advanced Companies of the 95th on being outflanked by the Column, retired on their reserves, as did also the Light Infantry of the Brigade on their respective Regiments.

The Column arrived within forty yards of the Wavre road, when it halted and began to deploy to its right. At this favourable instant Picton ordered the Brigade to fire a volley into it and charge. Having delivered its fire, and after a momentary confusion in getting through the hedge, it re-formed and dashed at the Column.

At this moment Picton was killed by a musket ball, which struck him on the right temple.

The Enemy fled in confusion down the slope, followed by the Brigade, which, however, was soon recalled. In advancing, the left wing of the 28th became engaged with a separate Column, into which it fired at the moment the Column was being charged by the Royal Dragoons, which Regiment it followed down the hill, and assisted in securing a great number of prisoners.

The 95th, on returning from the charge, resumed their advanced positions as before held. These positions, however, they were obliged to abandon on the capture of La Haye Sainte by the French, who immediately occupied them, and from thence, as well as from their advanced parties on the right of the main road, kept up an unremitting and most destructive fire on Kempt's Brigade and other troops, which was vigorously replied to, notwithstanding the exposed position of the latter.

This continued until the repulse of the Imperial Guard, upon which the French in and near La Haye Sainte hastily retreated, and the Brigade joined in the General Advance.

Nos. 153 and 156 refer to the march on Quatre Bras.

Nos. 149, 153, and 156 to Quatre Bras.

No. 156 to the retreat on the 17th June, and

All the letters, except Nos. 149, 153, and 156, to Waterloo.

GENERAL SIR JAMES KEMPT, G.C.B., G.C.H.

MAJOR-GENERAL AND K.C.B.

TO SIR HUSSEY VIVIAN.

No. 148.　　　　　　　　　　　　　　　　*No date.*

Waterloo.

MY DEAR VIVIAN,—　　　.　　　.　　　.　　　.

On the death of Picton, commanded all the troops

My Brigade consisted of the 28th, 32nd, 79th, and 1st Battalion 95th Regiments, and on poor Picton's fall (in the *first* attack that the Enemy made) the command of the 5th Division, with the 6th that had just come up to our support, and all the troops, in short, on the *left* of the Great Brussels road, devolved upon me throughout the day.

On the 18th, the 95th Regiment was in front of the other Regiments of my Brigade, occupying a knoll and some broken ground as Light Troops, and in a line with a considerable Corps of Belgian and Nassau Infantry. All these retired as the head of the Enemy's mass of Infantry approached them, at which critical moment, and just as the French Infantry were gaining the road and hedgerow which runs all along the crest of the position, I met it at the charge with the 28th, 32nd, and 79th Regiments in line, and completely repulsed the Enemy's Column, driving it in a state of the greatest confusion down the slope of the position.

This was *completely effected*, and I was in the act of restraining the men from the pursuit (having no support whatever), when General Ponsonby's Brigade of Cavalry charged a *separate Column* that had come up to our left where Pack's Brigade was stationed. The Enemy made three different attempts to carry the position immediately on the left of the road where my Brigade was posted, and were invariably repulsed in the same manner. *Not one single Cavalry soldier* co-operated *with this Brigade* throughout the day.

I have thus, my dear Vivian, briefly mentioned to you what took place on the right of the 5th Division, as you wished it. .   .   .   .   .   .

Ever, &c.,

James Kempt.

28TH REGIMENT.

THE 28TH REGIMENT.

COLONEL R. LLEWELLYN.

MAJOR 28TH REGIMENT.

No. 149.   *Felsham Lodge, Leatherhead, 16th March,* 1837.

Quatre Bras.

I have already thought the Battle of Quatre Bras one of the most splendid achievements of the war, reflecting the greatest credit on the British troops engaged, sustaining and repelling one of the most determined attacks (of all arms) [that], in my little experience, I can remember, and had it not been so closely followed by the very decisive and important, but all-absorbing Victory of Waterloo, perhaps the gallant exploits and unexampled bravery that marked that day would, under other circumstances, have excited even more admiration than was actually associated with it.

The corn was so high that it was nearly impossible to see beyond the ranks.

The French Cavalry used to plant a flag in front of the Square as a mark to charge on.

The rye in the field was so high, that to see anything beyond our own ranks was almost impossible. The Enemy, even, in attacking our Squares, were obliged to make a daring person desperately ride forward to plant a flag, as a mark, at the very point of our bayonets. On this they charged, but were invariably repulsed.

It fell to the lot of the 28th to bear a leading share in this Action, and I may say they lost there none of their former reputation.

They were frequently hardly pressed, but never lost their discipline and their self-possession.

When hardly pressed, Picton exclaimed, " 28th, remember Egypt ! "

Once, when threatened on two flanks by what Sir Thomas Picton imagined an overwhelming force, he exclaimed, " 28th, remember Egypt." They cheered and gallantly beat back their assailants, and eventually stoo on their position.

I remain, &c.,

R. LLEWELLYN.

APTAIN J. W. SHELTON, HALF-PAY, 28TH REGT.

LIEUTENANT 28TH REGIMENT.

Rossmore House, Ballingarry, September 29th, 1839.   No. 150.

About half past one o'clock the Enemy's Column, which believe to have consisted of four Battalions, advanced nearly in front of the 79th, but rather to its left, and to the direct right of the 28th. Kempt's Brigade was then moved up to the hedge, gave a very steady volley into the Enemy's Column, and charged (after having crossed the hedge) while the Enemy, who were in great confusion, attempted a deployment to their right, but which they were unable to complete, and got into great irregular bodies. *Waterloo. D'Erlon's 1st attack on Picton's Division. One Column directed on left of 79th and right of 28th. Brigade gave a volley into it, crossed the hedge and charged, throwing it into confusion.*

It was at this moment that the Heavy Brigade came up, when the 28th wheeled by sub-divisions to its right and made way for the Dragoons, who passed through the intervals; but as the latter came up in most regular order, there was in some cases not room for a Troop to pass through, and I perfectly recollect a Squadron of the Royals inclining considerably to its left to clear our left wing, which, after crossing the hedge, became separated from the right, and some way down the slope encountered a Column of the Enemy on its own left; but whether this was a reserve Column or a portion of the Division which was beaten at the hedge and re-formed again, I am unable distinctly to say. My impression is that it was some of the beaten Column, as the Dragoons passed on to engage a large reserve Column which was coming on, but still lower down the hill, leaving the left wing of the 28th *closely* engaged with the Column in its own immediate [front]. *Royal Dragoons came up and passed through intervals made for them by 28th. A Squadron inclined left to clear left wing, 28th. The latter separated from right wing, and encountered a separate small Column. Royals passed on, and charged a large reserve Column, and broke it.*

The Column which was charged by the Royals was broken, and the greater part of both taken prisoners. *Greater part of both Columns taken prisoners.*

I do not recollect that the Dragoons charged the Column (it was a small one, apparently of not more than two Battalions) which the left wing of the 28th encountered after its separation from the right wing, but I distinctly saw them charge the heavy Reserve Column and break it.

The greater number of the French threw down their arms when broken by the Cavalry.

The *left wing* of the 28th followed the Royal Dragoons some distance down the slope of the hill after their successful charge, and assisted in securing about 1,000 prisoners, whom they guarded to the rear of the hedge, and rejoined the right wing, which they found already formed about eighty paces to the rear of the hedge.

Lieutenants Clarke and Gilbert were seriously (the former mortally) wounded, after crossing the hedge. Captain Kelly and myself were not wounded until *late* in the evening, so that I never quitted my Company for a moment, and had ample opportunity of observing all the movements which took place.

The greater number of the French upon being charged by Royals, threw down their arms.

Left wing of 28th followed Royals down the hill, and assisted in securing about 1,000 prisoners.

Officers of the 28th wounded.

Believe, &c.,

JOHN WILLINGTON SHELTON,
H.P. 28th Regt.

CAPTAIN W. F. B. MOUNSTEVEN.

ENSIGN 28TH REGIMENT.

TO MAJOR RIACH, 79TH HIGHLANDERS.

No. 151.

Manchester, August 19th, 1839.

Waterloo.

D'Erlon's first attack on Picton's division.

French Column attempted to deploy.

28th poured in a volley, sprang over the hedge and charged.

Column fled.

The two wings

MY DEAR RIACH,— .

The 28th was lying a short distance behind the hedge when the Enemy's Columns were put in motion. When they had advanced pretty near, we were moved up to the hedge, and on our reaching it found a French Column attempting to deploy at probably thirty or forty yards on the other side. We then poured in our fire, sprung over the fence, and charged. The Enemy ran before we could close with them, and, of course, in great confusion.

In advancing in pursuit of them the wings of the Regiment separated, and I, carrying the King's Colour, went on with the right wing. When we had proceeded a little way we perceived through the smoke another body of troops in column immediately in our front, which we mistook for some Corps of the Allies, and many of the Officers (I amongst the rest) cried out to the men, " Don't fire, they are Belgians."

of 28th separated in the advance.

.   .   .   .   .   .

This caused a momentary check of the wing, when we quickly discovered our mistake by the Enemy making off with all speed in the direction of the French position.

Which also retreated speedily.

Immediately after this, when all the force that was originally opposed to the 28th had been driven back in confusion, the Regiment was ordered to halt and re-form, and almost at the same instant, as well as I can recollect, I saw a Regiment of Dragoons charge a Column or Square—for which it was I really cannot tell—and instantly break it.

Immediately after this saw a Regiment of Dragoons charge a Column and break it.

I well remember the intense anxiety we felt when we saw some of the gallant, but over-rash fellows, without stopping to form again, ride on headlong at what appeared to me an immensely strong Corps of support in perfect order, but which I do not see marked down in the Plan. On this Column they, of course, made no impression, but suffered some loss, although as far as I could see, a fire was opened upon them from only a small portion of it.

Some of the Dragoons rushed without order on a Corps in support, and suffered for it.

The charge on the Square which was broken took place some distance in our front, but a little to the left, from which it is evident Sir William Ponsonby's Brigade must have passed our flanks whilst we had been too busy for me to observe them, and probably the Officer of the Royal Dragoons might have seen our wings disunited as he passed, and fancied it had been caused by the attack of the French instead of the pursuit of them. However, as to " the right wing being wheeled by sections to the left, &c.," I can assure you nothing half so regular came within my notice.

This Plan means a sketch drawn by Capt. Siborne, in accordance with information previously received, and sent to Capt. M. for verification.—ED.

In the sketch annexed the French Column is not only represented as having pierced the 28th, but as having also crossed the hedge. This positively never took place in our

See above remark.

32ND REGIMENT.

The Enemy
did not cross
the hedge in
front of the
28th.

part of the position ; but, on the contrary, the Enemy was routed on his own side of the hedge, in the manner I have mentioned. On this point I am perfectly certain, for I well recollect looking over the hedge the moment before we charged, and admiring the gallant manner the French Officers led out their Companies in deploying.

Believe, &c.,

WM. F. B. MOUNSTEVEN.

THE 32ND REGIMENT.

LIEUT.-COLONEL F. CALVERT, HALF-PAY.

MAJOR 32ND REGIMENT.

No. 152.

Hunsdon House, Ware, April 19th, 1835.

Waterloo.

I must proceed as well as I can in answering your Queries, which I have numbered in the order they appear in your letter.

At 7 p.m.
32nd was
posted behind
Wavre road,
with its
right on
Brussels road.

1st. The 32nd Regiment was in line on the crest of the hill behind the hedge which was at right angles from the road leading from Brussels to Charleroi, nearly opposite to the farmhouse of La Haye Sainte.

Enemy
advanced to
final attack on
either side of
Brussels road.

2nd. The Enemy descended from their position in columns along the aforesaid road, and on each side of it.

Position of
the Regiment
in the morn-
ing.

The 32nd Regiment was in Sir James Kempt's Brigade and in the Division of Sir Thomas Picton. It suffered severely in the Action of the 16th at Les Quatre Bras, and on the morning of the Battle of Waterloo was posted with its right on the road from Brussels to Charleroi, extending along the hedge mentioned in my reply to the first query. The remainder of the Brigade was to its left. with the exception of the Rifle Corps, which, with a Belgian Battalion, covered the front as skirmishers.

From about half-past twelve p.m., the Brigade had to sustain repeated attacks (in one of which Sir T. Picton was killed) from, I believe, the entire first Corps of the French Army. At about three o'clock Sir John Lambert's Brigade (27th, 4th, and 40th) arrived. The 32nd was then formed in support, still keeping the ridge, from which it never was allowed to move.

D'Erlon's repeated attacks on Picton's Division.

Shortly afterwards it was formed in square, though not menaced by Cavalry, following the example of the rest of the Army to the right and left of the road. At about five o'clock the Duke of Wellington rode up and ordered the Regiment to deploy. Later in the evening (the 27th having nearly lost all its men) it advanced again towards the hedge until it joined the rest of the Army in its final charge.

Formed in square, though not menaced by Cavalry. Ordered by the Duke to deploy. Later in the evening advanced to the hedge. Joined in the final Advance.

.   .   .   .

I have, &c.,
F. CALVERT,
Lieut.-Col. H.P.

FROM THE SAME.

United Service Club, March 11th, 1837. No. 153.

.   .   .   .

The Regiment marched from Brussels early on the morning of the 16th of June, and halted for a couple of hours near the village of Waterloo. It then resumed its march, and arrived at Quatre Bras about two o'clock.

Quatre Bras.

Arrived from Brussels about 2 o'clock.

It was moved immediately along the Namur *chaussée* until it came to the point which I have marked on the map, where it formed line awaiting the approach of the Enemy, who were descending in column from the opposite hill.

Took up a position on Namur road. See Plan of Quatre Bras, No. 1.

When this attacking force had crossed both hedges lining the meadow in the bottom, and had commenced ascending our position, the 32nd Regiment poured in upon it a heavy fire succeeded by a charge. This the Enemy did not wait to receive, but retired with precipitation, and

French attacked in column. 32nd poured in a heavy fire and charged. Enemy retired precipitately.

32nd halted, and retired to original position.

getting entangled in the hedges on returning to their position must have suffered considerable loss. We halted and re-formed at the first hedge, when Sir Thomas Picton desired the Regiment to retire to its original position.

79th went on still further, but soon recalled.

The 79th Regiment on our left, carried on by its ardour, went on much further, crossed the meadow, and even ventured to assail the Enemy's position. They were, however, soon recalled.

Similar attacks renewed, and repulsed in the same way. 32nd took up ground for the night near Charleroi road.

Attacks similar to the above were renewed several times during the evening, and always with similar results. After the Action was concluded our ground was occupied by some German troops, when we moved to our right, and took up our ground for the night near the high road between Quatre Bras and Charleroi.

On the following day we were the last Infantry that left the ground, and retired about eleven o'clock a.m. followed by the Cavalry, which had arrived during the night.

·   ·   ·   ·   ·   ·

I have, &c.,
F. CALVERT,
Colonel Unattached, late of 32nd Regt.

CAPTAIN R. T. BELCHER, HALF-PAY.

LIEUTENANT 32ND REGIMENT.

No. 154.

Waterloo.

Memorandum.

Bandon, February 27th, 1843.

32nd on right of Kempt's Brigade.

The 32nd Regiment formed the right of Sir James Kempt's Brigade, the 95th, which on the line of march usually formed the right, being detached skirmishing. The Regiment was formed into six divisions in consequence of its reduced numbers, having suffered severely at Quatre Bras. I commanded the left centre division.

Reduced to six divisions.

D'Erlon's attack on Picton, when Brigade

In the second [? first] attack of the French Infantry on the left centre of the line, the Brigade advanced in line to charge. Immediately on passing the narrow road which ran along our front, the Ensign carrying the Regimental Colour was severely wounded. I took the Colour from him until another Ensign could be called.

Almost instantly after, the Brigade still advancing, and the French Infantry getting into disorder and beginning to retreat, a mounted [French] Officer had his horse shot under him. When he extricated himself we were close on him. I had the Colour on my left arm and was slightly in advance of the division.

He suddenly fronted me and seized the staff, I still retaining a grasp of the silk (the Colours were nearly new).

At the same moment he attempted to draw his sabre, but had not accomplished it when the Covering Colour-Sergeant, named Switzer, thrust his pike into his breast, and the right rank and file of the division, named Lacy, fired into him. He fell dead at my feet.

Brevet-Major Toole, commanding the right centre division at the moment, called out " Save the brave fellow; " but it was too late.

ROBERT T. BELCHER.

79TH REGIMENT—CAMERON HIGHLANDERS.

CAPTAIN K. J. LESLIE, H.P., 60TH RIFLES.
LIEUTENANT 79TH HIGHLANDERS.

Wilton, Cork.

. . . .

No. 155.

The 79th were on the left of the 4th [5th] Division flanked by Hanoverian troops drawn up in line with Artillery in front at the north side of the lane, where there was a hedge as marked in your plan, the Light Company to which I belonged being extended in the lane and in front, together with other Light Companies of the Division, to cover the Artillery, which was advanced to bear upon the Enemy in their attack. This was our general position during the day. The constant fire prevented me from remarking as much of the movements as I otherwise could have done.

Side notes: advanced to charge. Ensign Birtwhistle carrying 32nd Regimental Colour severely wounded. Colour taken by Lieutenant Belcher. Gallant attempt of a French Officer to seize it. The Officer is killed. Waterloo. Kempt's Brigade was on the right of the 5th Division, and the 79th were in the centre of the Brigade. —ED. *See* Plan, p. 38.

79TH HIGHLANDERS.

D'Erlon's first attack on Picton.

The 79th charge the Enemy and put them to flight.

? Netherlands Artillery.— ED.

Gallant conduct of one of the Greys.

The final advance of the French checked by the vicinity of the Prussians.

Only three Officers of the 79th came out of action with it.

The principal attack upon our Division was that in which the French advanced in column, flanked by Cavalry, almost to the Guns. Our charge, supported by the gallant Scotch Greys, &c., was conducted with great steadiness, and soon put the Enemy to flight, who continued firing over their shoulders.

Nothing could exceed the conduct of the Brunswick Artillery upon this occasion. They were in front of our Light Company and never left the Guns, but cheered at every well-directed shot. The French loss, particularly that of the Guards, was excessive, from the well-directed fire of our Artillery.

During this attack I observed one of the Scotch Greys, who either broke or lost his sword in an attack with one of the Cuirassiers, obliged to retreat along the line, pursued by his assailant, and when enabled to gain some distance from him, secure a sword and return to the attack, cutting down his pursuer. During this we were in square, after the charge, to resist the Cavalry, after which we resumed our position.

This attack was late in the day, and we had not long regained our position when, at the period to which you allude, the Enemy in front of us seemed moving forward a fresh Column for a simultaneous attack to that on the right of our Line. This was checked by the appearance of the Prussians breaking from the wood on the left of our position.

.   .   .   .

Half of our loss was on the 16th at Quatre Bras. I had the good fortune to make one of three Officers who marched with the Regiment out of action on 18th.

I have, &c.,

KEVAN J. LESLIE,
Capt. H.P., 60th Regt.

MAJOR A. FORBES, 79TH HIGHLANDERS.

LIEUTENANT 79TH HIGHLANDERS.

Paisley, May 3rd, 1837. No. 156.

. . . .

I now enclose a short detail of the movements of the 79th on the 16th and 17th of June, which I hope may be useful to you.

. . . .

I have, &c.,

ALEX. FORBES,

Major 79th Regiment.

16th June, 1815.

At ten o'clock on the night of the 15th June the troops at Brussels received orders to hold themselves in readiness to march at a moment's notice. About twelve o'clock the bugles were sounding throughout the town for the troops to assemble, rations were issued for three days, and the Division began its march about four o'clock on the following morning on the road leading to Charleroi.

March to Quatre Bras

Soon after the Division halted in the Forêt de Soignies, near the village of Waterloo, three leagues from Brussels, the Duke of Wellington, accompanied by some of his Staff, was observed passing to the front. The soldiers began to cook provisions, and an idea pretty generally prevailed that we should return to Brussels, from a supposed probability of wrong information regarding the Enemy's force, or that his intention had been frustrated by the Prussian and Belgian Armies of observation. Before the cooking was completed orders were received for the Division instantly to resume its march.

We now for the first time distinctly heard cannonading in front, and as we proceeded on our march, under an excess of heat and dust through Genappe to Quatre Bras, we met on the road a wounded Belgian soldier. Quatre Bras is a farm or hamlet, seven leagues from Brussels, consisting of a few scattered houses, deriving its name from the intersection here (nearly at right angles) of the Brussels road by that leading from Nivelles to Namur.

Arrival at
Quatre Bras.

The Column (left in front) halted in the road and piled arms in the then order of march for about a quarter of an hour.   From a rising ground at the head of the Column, adjoining the above houses, we had a full view of the Enemy, who appeared obliquely to our left at the distance of about half a mile, in movement to his front.

The
cannonade at
Ligny heard.

A brisk and extended line of cannonading was at the same time perceived in the direction of the Prussian Army on the left.   A Battalion of Belgians was observed at some

Quatre Bras.

See Plan of
Quatre Bras,
No. 1.

distance in our front, which had begun to exchange a few shots with the Enemy, and to retire slowly on his nearer approach.   In support of this Battalion the Companies of the Rifle Brigade attached to the Division were sent out.

The Brigade
takes up a
position along
the Namur
road on the
left of the
Army.

The 8th and 9th British Brigades then broke off to their left, lining the Namur road, the banks of which were here on either side considerably elevated.   The 79th Regiment formed the extreme left of the British Army, and the 92nd Regiment the right of the two Brigades in question, being posted immediately in front of Quatre Bras.

The Enemy
advanced to
attack, and
the Light
Companies of
the Brigade,
and a further
portion of the
79th, are
thrown out.

Our ground had scarcely been thus occupied when the Enemy's advance appeared.   The Light Companies of the 8th Brigade, to which were added the 8th Company and marksmen of the 79th Regiment, were immediately thrown out, when the Action commenced.   This movement was ordered by the Duke of Wellington in person, who was here present with his Staff.   It was then a quarter to three

In an hour's
time the
Brigade ad-
vances and
charges the
Enemy, who
retire.

o'clock.   These troops maintained their situation for an hour against the constantly increasing numbers of the Enemy, who had by this time displayed a force which rendered it necessary for the Brigade (28th, 32nd, and 79th Regiments) to charge.

But fresh
Columns come
on, and the
Brigade is

His advanced troops were compelled to retire.   But to them succeeded fresh Columns of Infantry, with whom the Action was renewed.   About this time many casualties were caused by the augmented fire of the Enemy and our exposed situation. The Brigade was ordered to retire some distance towards its former position on the road, where it could with more advantage meet the Enemy's approach, a movement which was performed with regularity. In the meantime the right of the Division was warmly engaged.

The Royals, 28th, and 42nd Regiments were repeatedly charged by the Enemy's Cuirassiers, who were constantly repulsed. To a body of these the 92nd Regiment opposed a destructive fire, and against a Column of Infantry made a gallant and successful charge.

The 79th Regiment had received orders to form in column on the road, and to act as circumstances might require. Being afterwards threatened by Cavalry, it formed and moved forward in square, but without being attacked. In short every Regiment, from the sudden and peculiar nature of the attack, seemed to act independently for its own immediate defence, a measure rendered still more necessary by the Enemy's superiority in Cavalry, and the Regiments being now posted, not at prescribed intervals of alignment, but conformably to the exigency of the moment, by which each of them was exposed to be separately assailed.

The Enemy's Column suffered much from the well-directed fire of some field-pieces which had by this time been brought up, and which greatly aided in checking his further advance.

He had now failed in every attack, and it growing dark, the troops of the Division began to occupy their bivouac for the night on a space of ground in *advance* of the *Namur road* and of our original position, within the angle formed by the same road and that leading from Brussels to Charleroi. At 9 o'clock all firing ceased, and the 79th bivouacked in front of their original position.

During the several engagements of *this day* the 79th lost 1 Staff and 28 rank and file killed; 3 Field Officers, 6 Captains, 7 Subalterns, 10 Sergeants, and 248 rank and file wounded.

79TH HIGHLANDERS.

17th June.

At daylight on the 17th we were in full expectation of a renewal of the attack; but a few shots only were fired by the pickets. A retreat was ordered at 1 o'clock on the Brussels road, and with a view to deceive the Enemy during this operation, the Light Companies of the 8th Brigade were drawn out at some distance in front.

The Retreat on Waterloo.

The Army continued to retire under an excessive hot sun, covered by our Artillery and Cavalry, till we had passed Genappe, when it began to rain heavily. The Division now halted for about half an hour, and a marauder was punished. About dusk we filed off the road to our right at the farm of La Haye Sainte, halting in cornfields under cover of a rising ground, which next day served as a good position.

The thunder-storm.

The Brigade takes up its position at Waterloo.

From the summit of this ground, and previous to entering our bivouac, a few shots were discharged by the Artillery of the Division on the heads of the Enemy's Columns as they were seen lining the opposite height; the remainder of the Army occupied the continuation of the ridge to our right (as we fronted the Enemy) across the Brussels road, the Cavalry of the Army formed in rear of Mont-St.-Jean. The Artillery of the Division (in advance of which were strong pickets) remained posted in our front. The left of the Division extended towards Ohain, its right resting on the Brussels road.

The Artillery of the Division fires a few rounds at the Enemy.

The ground occupied by the remainder of the Army.

A. CRUIKSHANK, ESQ.

IN THE RANKS OF 79TH HIGHLANDERS.

No. 157.

Manchester, September, 1839.

It will afford me very great pleasure indeed should any of the circumstances hereafter detailed be found useful to you in furtherance of your great work, but having been in the ranks at Waterloo, and of course sufficiently occupied in attending to orders, &c., I fear that such information as it is in my power to give must be consi.lered very limited. I shall now, however, proceed, according to the best of my recollection, to describe what took place.

When the 79th were deploying into line at the commencement of the Action (they having been previously in column) the Light Company, to which I then belonged, were ordered out and extended. On our reaching the hedge (or nearly so), where the Guns (I think Rogers's Brigade) were stationed, we passed through the Belgian Infantry, who were retiring, and pushed down the slope in front of the hedge into the valley, where we were for some time engaged with the French skirmishers; but a strong Column of the Enemy appearing on the top of the opposite ridge immediately in our front, and a second Column was at that moment seen advancing along the valley to our left, which must have come in contact with the 28th Regiment, we were consequently obliged to retire, and joined the Regiment on its reaching the hedge, when a tremendous conflict ensued between our Line and the opposing Columns, which, it has been said, pushed themselves so far forward as to reach the hedge; but I can positively assert that the French did not reach that point, if I except indeed some few of their sharpshooters which came up the hill with the Light Infantry, but were quickly driven back.

At the beginning of the Battle the Light Company was thrown out skirmishing into the valley.

Withdrawn on D'Erlon's Columns approaching.

Conflict with the Columns.

At this time I saw, but certainly very imperfectly, a forward movement of the French Cavalry on our right, and some of the Cuirassiers had actually reached the point of the hedge on the main road (and the scene was altogether extraordinary), but they were charged I think from the right of the road, at, or about the same time that our Brigade charged down the slope, and completely routed the Enemy's Columns, when the Cavalry came up, and completed what had been so gloriously begun, by gallantly charging the flying Infantry and making a great number of prisoners.

The French Cuirassiers charged by the 2nd Life Guards.

After Kempt's Brigade had driven the French Columns down the slope, Ponsonby's Cavalry came up and completed their rout, taking many prisoners.

At the time the Dragoons passed the line to charge the Enemy's Columns as above, the 79th were in the act of

Dragoons
passed, the
79th were
re-forming.

re-forming on the French side of the hedge, but not in any
unusual degree of disorder. I did not observe the Artillery
move from their position, but they might have done so
unknown to me. They did fire over our heads while
skirmishing in the valley. The Rocket Brigade were
stationed I think considerably to our left.

The 79th
formed square,
but were not
attacked by
Cavalry.

Perhaps this
was later in
the day.—ED.

The 79th Highlanders did form square on the slope in
front of the hedge to resist Cavalry, but which did not
however come near us, and whether it was exactly at this
period of the action I cannot now call to my memory.

. . . .

Believe, &c.,

A. CRUIKSHANK.

THE 95TH RIFLES—1ST BATTALION.

LIEUT.-GENERAL SIR ANDREW F. BARNARD, G.C.B., G.C.H.

LIEUT.-COLONEL AND BREV.-COLONEL, AND K.C.B., 1ST BATTALION
95TH RIFLES.

No. 158.
Waterloo.

46, Wilton Crescent, November 20th, 1834.

Having received a wound which disabled me, and
being obliged in consequence to quit the field at about
three o'clock in the day on the 18th June, 1815, I could
not venture to return the plan which you forwarded until
I met with an Officer who could give me exact information
on the subject, which I have acquired from Captain
Kincaid, who was on that occasion Adjutant of the 1st
Battalion of the Rifle Brigade.

The Battalion
at 7 p.m.

The fire of the Battalion was principally directed at
the Corps of the Enemy, immediately on the opposite side
of the Brussels road and above La Haye Sainte, the other
Corps of the 5th Division and some of General Lambert's
being occupied in keeping down the fire of those in
front, and on the ground which rises abruptly with the
remains of a hedgerow of trees upon it, which was the

advance of the 95th in the morning. The 27th were formed in square at a very short distance in the rear of the 5th Division, and suffered very much from the Enemy's fire.

.   .   .   .

I remain, &c.,
A. F. BARNARD.

(*Postscript.*)—In the morning the 1st Battalion were formed in the same ground as now represented in the plan, but with two Companies on the abrupt ground in front, with the hedgerow, part of which was cut down, and an *abatis* formed across the road half way up the hill from La Haye Sainte, and one Company under Colonel Leach being posted in the gravel pit.

Position of the Battalion in the morning. *See* Plan, p. 38.

When the Enemy made their first attack, this Company was soon obliged to join the others, and although they maintained their ground sufficiently to change the direction of the Enemy's Column, they were obliged eventually to retire as it passed their left flank, and to join the Companies at the hedge, to which the Enemy approached so close that there could not have been above two yards, if so much, between their front rank and that of the Corps opposed.

D'Erlon's first attack.
The Company in the gravel pit outflanked, and obliged to join those at the hedgerow

A fire ensued, which was very heavy, but of short duration, as they began to move off as soon as it was possible for such a mass to effect it (N.B., Sir Thomas Picton was killed at this moment), and the charge of General Ponsonby's Brigade, which took place on our left, completed their rout.

After a heavy fire of short duration, the Enemy retired.
Picton killed.
Charge of Ponsonby's Cavalry.

Our formation was the same subsequently, and as the Enemy advanced afterwards with more caution, and captured La Haye Sainte, our advanced Companies maintained their ground longer, but the fire from the Enemy's sharpshooters caused us some loss, and, amongst the rest, I was wounded, and cannot pretend to give any further account of the movements of the Corps further than what is stated previously; but I believe the advanced Companies were very shortly afterwards obliged to abandon their ground and

After the capture of La Haye Sainte by the French, the advanced Companies suffered some loss.
Sir A. Barnard wounded.
The advanced

95TH RIFLES, 1ST BATT.

Companies
obliged to
abandon their
ground, which
was occupied
by the
French.

Attack of 2nd
Life Guards
on the
Cuirassiers.

join the Battalion, and the French occupied it during the remainder of the Action.

I ought to mention that at the moment of the repulse of the French in the morning, the French Cuirassiers had advanced so far on the opposite side of the Brussels road as to be in our rear, but at the same moment were charged so gallantly by one of the Regiments of Life Guards that they gave way in great confusion, and having got into the road carried away the *abatis* by the rear, though it impeded their progress sufficiently to enable the Life Guards to cut down a good many of them.

LIEUT.-COLONEL J. LEACH, C.B.

CAPTAIN AND BREV.-MAJOR 95TH RIFLES.

No. 159.   *Memorandum.*   *No date.*

Waterloo.

Sent to occupy
the sandpit
close to main
road with two
Companies.
See General
Plan, No. 1.

Remainder of
the Rifles at
the hedgerow
on the summit
behind.

D'Erlon's 1st
attack.

The two
Companies
driven in,

And subse-
quently the
whole Bat-
talion, which
falls back on
the 32nd.

See Plan, p. 38.

The Rifles and
32nd fire a
volley and

Previous to the attack on the 5th Division, I was sent in command of two Companies of Riflemen to occupy an excavation (from which sand had been dug) *close* to the Genappe road and on its *left*. This was at the base of the hillock, on the summit of which the remainder of the 95th Rifle Corps was posted to support the two advanced Companies.

The fierce onset of the French with overwhelming numbers forced back my two Companies on the main body of the 95th Regiment, and this hillock was also instantly assailed in such a manner as to render it impossible for one weak Battalion, consisting only of six Companies, to stem the torrent for any length of time. We were consequently constrained to fall back on the 32nd Regiment, which was in line near the thorn hedge which runs from the Genappe road to the *left*, and along the front of Picton's Division.

We were closely pressed and hotly engaged during the retrograde movement, and very soon after reaching the spot where the 32nd was in position, a volley and a charge of bayonets caused the French to recoil in disorder and with a heavy loss; and it was at this moment of fire, smoke, and excitement that the Heavy Cavalry of the Army suddenly appeared amongst us, and instantly charged that Infantry which the fire and charge of bayonets from Picton's Division had previously shattered and broken.

charge, driving the French before them.

The Heavy Cavalry charge the retreating French Infantry.

.   .   .   .

FROM THE SAME.

Worthing, Sussex, November 22nd, 1840.

No. 160.

.   .   .   .

Previous to the second grand attack on our Division, I was detached with two Companies of the 95th Riflemen as before, to occupy the excavation near the road, from whence gravel had been dug, the remaining four Companies of our Battalion occupying the knoll above it.

Waterloo.

Detached with two Companies as before.

The great effort of the French appeared to be to carry the farmhouse of La Haye Sainte, and this they were enabled to do (in spite of the obstinate and gallant defence of the occupants) in consequence of the ammunition of the Germans being expended, and there being no mode of supplying them with more.

D'Erlon's 2nd attack and capture of La Haye Sainte.

This, however unavoidable, was highly disastrous to the troops of Picton and Lambert, for the French instantly filled the house with swarms of sharpshooters, whose deadly fire precluded the possibility of our holding the knoll and the ground immediately about it, and they established also a strong and numerous line of Infantry, extending along the front of Kempt's Brigade.

Serious conse quences to Picton's and Lambert's Troops.

The 95th retire to the hedge of the Wavre road, and the French occupy the knoll and ridge in front of it.

Those Frenchmen, however, *knelt down*, and exposed only their heads and shoulders to our fire, and in this manner the contest was carried on between them and us until the General Advance of the whole of the Duke of Wellington's Army against the French position immediately after the total defeat of the Imperial Guards.

See General Plan, No. 2.

From the time that La Haye Sainte fell into the hands of the French until the moment of the General Advance of our Army, the mode of attack and defence was remarkable for its *sameness*. But I speak merely of what took place immediately about *our* part of the position.

From the loss of La Haye Sainte to the General Advance, a close and continued contest of musketry fire.

It consisted of one uninterrupted fire of musketry (the distance between the hostile lines I imagine to have been rather more than one hundred yards) between Kempt's and some of Lambert's Regiments posted along the thorn hedge, and the French Infantry lining the knoll and the crest of the hill near it. Several times the French Officers

The French Officers try to induce their men to charge, but without result

made desperate attempts to induce their men to charge Kempt's line, and I saw more than once parties of the French in our front spring up from their *kneeling position* and advance some yards towards the thorn hedge, headed by their Officers with vehement gestures, but our fire was so very hot and deadly that they almost instantly ran back behind the crest of the hill, always leaving a great many killed or disabled behind them.

During this musketry contest, which I firmly believe was the closest and most protracted almost ever witnessed,

Apprehensions of the French advancing along the main road and turning Kempt's right.

some apprehension was entertained that the French would endeavour to force their way along the *chaussée*, and attack the *rear* of the troops lining the thorn hedge, and on a report of the kind being made to me by one of our Officers, coupled with a suggestion that a part of the 95th Riflemen should be *concentrated* on the *extreme right*, so as to fire

But these were groundless, on account of the position of the 27th Regiment.

into the road, my reply was, " The 27th Regiment is in square in our rear, having one of its faces looking directly into the road, and that Regiment must protect our rear, for the French are gathering so fast and thick in our *front* that we cannot spare a single man to detach to the right."

I merely mention this to show in what manner we were employed at this period of the day. I concluded also that the Regiments of Infantry, which were in reserve behind us, and (I believe) some Cavalry not far off, would have instantly attacked any French force which might have menaced the rear of Kempt's Brigade by the *chaussée*.

Only a few minutes before

A very short time (a few minutes only I think) before Picton's Division joined in the General Advance against the

French position, the French suddenly evacuated the farm-house of La Haye Sainte and the ground near it, and retreated in haste; and this, I conclude, was in consequence of the total repulse of the Imperial Guards, and the forward movement of a part of the Duke of Wellington's right wing.

the General Advance the French evacuate La Haye Sainte and ground near it.

.   .   .   .

Believe me, &c.,
J. LEACH.

CAPTAIN J. KINCAID, LATE RIFLE BRIGADE.
LIEUTENANT AND ADJUTANT 1ST BATTALION 95TH RIFLES.

Bridewell Hospital, London, May 2nd, 1839.   No. 161.

.   .   .   .

On the first attack of D'Erlon's Corps at Waterloo.

Waterloo. D'Erlon's first attack.

The Reserve of our Battalion was not *in* the Wavre road, but immediately behind the second hedge, with our right literally resting on the Namur [Genappe] road within two or three yards of the brink of its steep bank. The front hedge was a very imperfect one, showing merely a bush here and there.

The Reserve of the Rifles was behind the hedgerow in front of the Wavre road.

See Plan, p. 38.

I had been in the early part of the Action in advance with our Companies on the knoll, and cannot speak to the precise position of Kempt's Brigade, nor whether any space was left between the right of the 32nd Regiment and the Namur [Genappe] road for our Reserve to fall back into. All I remember is that his line seemed to stand about fifty yards from the hedge.

Kempt's line about fifty yards in rear of the hedge of the Wavre road.

My recollections of that interesting moment are as follows :—

We had held the knoll longer than prudence warranted with the Enemy already round both flanks, and we were consequently obliged to make the best use of our heels to get into the position. I had just dashed my horse through a gap in the hedge (I was Adjutant) when I observed our Reserve beginning to retire. Our two Field Officers had

The knoll on the left of the sandpit.

Companies in front obliged to retire to reserve behind the hedgerow been wounded the instant before, and the next in command at the moment, believing it to be intended that he should give his place to the skirmishers and join the line, he had just put them in motion for that purpose, but knowing the mistake, Sir Jas. Kempt having previously informed me that he would advance with his line to join us as soon as necessary, I called a halt, and we formed them to receive the attack where they then stood, about ten yards from the hedge. Sir James Kempt at the same moment advanced his Brigade. They did not come quite up to the same line with us, but I think delivered their fire about twenty yards from the hedge. I cannot say whether any part of his line overlapped our rear, but it will serve to simplify conflicting opinions, to say that we only held a front of three Companies (the skirmishers having doubled in rear of the Reserve, there was no time for anything else), so that even if the 32nd did overlap our Battalion about two-thirds of that Regiment must still have been engaged. Our Battalion continued the charge as far as the knoll, but I do not think the Regiment on our left crossed the Wavre road, for although there were a few straggling red coats among us, I do not remember seeing any formed body near.

I should have thought that the Enemy's left Column could not have gone so much to their right as you have drawn it, and that they must have brought up about the right of the 79th from the direction I saw them taking, when some yards on our side of the knoll, but as the hedge afterwards hid them from my sight they probably edged more away.

When we first took possession of the knoll, before the Battle began, there was almost a hedge of bushes and underwood, with a tall tree in the centre, lining the abrupt face of it on our side. We cut down most of the bushes to form an *abatis* across the road, and our two Medical Officers took post behind the tree as the most secure place for their operations. The tree was a naked one with a bushy top. One of the first of the Enemy's

Side notes:

The Battalion beginning to retire by mistake to the Brigade position, he corrects it.

The Brigade advances, and the whole throw their fire into the Column, and charge.

The Battalion charges as far as the knoll.

The hedgerow with a tall tree, whose top a French round shot causes to fall on the Medical Officers of the Battalion.

round shot struck it about two-thirds up, bringing the whole of the bushy part down on their devoted heads and nearly smothering them among the branches.

. . . .

I am, &c.,
F. KINCAID,
Late Capt. 1st Rifle Brigade.

PACK'S INFANTRY BRIGADE.

The 9th Infantry Brigade consisted of the 1st Regiment Royal Scots, 3rd Battalion, the 42nd Regiment, Royal Highlanders, the 44th Regiment, 2nd Battalion, and the 92nd Regiment, Highlanders. It was commanded by Major-General Sir Denis Pack, K.C.B., and belonged also to Sir Thomas Picton's Division.

On the arrival of the Division at Quatre Bras, Pack's Brigade was posted along the Namur road, with its right adjacent to the houses of Quatre Bras. *See* Plan of Quatre Bras, No. 1.

When the Division advanced against the Enemy, as stated on page 344, the 92nd Highlanders were ordered to continue to line the portion of the road next to Quatre Bras. The 42nd Highlanders and 44th Regiment moved forward across the cornfields in front of the road to within a very short distance of Gemioncourt, and to the left of the Charleroi road.

Here they were suddenly and unexpectedly attacked by a portion of the French Cavalry which were pursuing the Brunswick Hussars along the *chaussée*, and so closely as to be mistaken by the two Regiments for Allies. The 42nd nearly succeeded in forming square, but the two Companies of the rear face had not time to complete it, and a body of Lancers penetrated with them into the Square. Although they caused some loss, particularly in Officers, the Lancers were quickly hemmed inside the Square, and either bayoneted or taken prisoners.

The attack on the 44th was still more unexpected. The Lancers advanced against the rear of that Regiment still in *line*, whereupon the rear rank was faced about, and it gave the Cavalry such a volley, that they fled in confusion.

Meanwhile, the remainder of the Cavalry which pursued the Hussars came under the fire of the 92nd, which obliged it to take to a precipitate flight.

The 42nd and 44th, in their advanced and exposed positions, became the objects of repeated assaults by the French Cavalry, and of a heavy cannonade during the intervals of these attacks, but, though with greatly diminished numbers, they successfully repelled the former. At length Sir Thomas Picton brought up the 1st Royals and 28th to their relief, as described in page 344. Later on the ammunition of Pack's advanced Regiments became so much exhausted that he was compelled to apply to Halkett's Brigade for assistance. *See* No. 136, page 321.

The 92nd, still on the Namur road, next repelled a considerable body of Cuirassiers which advanced along the Charleroi *chaussée*, and afterwards two Columns of Infantry, which moved against them from the Bois de Bossu, charging them and driving them some distance along the skirts of the wood.

At Waterloo the Brigade was posted some distance to the left of Kempt's Brigade, at first about two hundred yards in rear of the Wavre road in the following order: 1st Royals on the right, 42nd, 92nd, and 44th on the left. *See* General Plan, No. 1.

When D'Erlon first advanced against Picton, the Brigade, excepting the 44th, was lining the Wavre road, and the right French Column was directed against it, principally against the 92nd. The Column pushed on in such a bold and determined manner as to cross the hedge of the road and throw the Highlanders into some temporary confusion. Here the French began to reply to the fire of the latter, which, however, was now most destructive, and the Brigade received the order to charge. *See* Plan, p. 38.

At this moment the Scots Greys came up, and, passing through and mingling with the 92nd, charged the Column, both Regiments mutually cheering and shouting, "Scotland for ever!" The Highlanders joined in the charge, and assisted in the capture of great numbers of prisoners.

After D'Erlon's attack had been repulsed, Pack's Brigade was closed to the right on Kempt, so as to fill up the gap made by the retreat of the Dutch-Belgians.

Towards evening the Brigade was moved still further to the right, and placed in reserve to Kempt's and Lambert's Brigades, with the exception of the 1st Royals, who were in the front with the latter, and lining the Wavre road.

The Brigade subsequently joined in the General Advance.

No. 169 refers to the march on Quatre Bras.

Nos. 163, 164, 165, 166, 167, and 169 to Quatre Bras.

No. 169 to the retreat on 17th June, and

Nos. 162, 163, 164, and 168 to Waterloo.

The 1st Regiment—Royal Scots—3rd Battalion.

LIEUT.-COLONEL R. MACDONALD, LATE 35th REGIMENT.

Captain and Brevet-Major 1st Royals.

No. 162.   *Southsea House, near Portsmouth, December 29th,* 1838.

I have the honour to address you on the subject of your "Guide to the Model of the Battle of Waterloo" at a quarter past 7 p.m.

Waterloo.   At the Battle of Waterloo I was Captain and Brev.-Major in the 3rd Battalion Royal Scots. I was present with it on the 16th, 17th, and on the 18th, until nearly the close of the Action—perhaps eight o'clock in the evening, when I fell wounded and was carried off the field.

Succeeded to the command on Lieut.-Col. Campbell being wounded.

Lieut.-Colonel Campbell, Major in the Regiment, commanded the Battalion, and upon his being wounded, between twelve o'clock and two p.m., or thereabouts, I succeeded to the command, and retained that command until carried off the field. I regret to observe that by No. 41 of "The Guide" the 3rd Battalion is erroneously placed, for on the 18th, after the morning, it was never in contiguous column with the 42nd; it was moved from the left to the position it occupied the whole of that afternoon, having no troops in its front but the French, a position more in advance than is stated in No. 41, where the Royals suffered severely from a little rising ground, rather in its

After the morning the Royals were not in contiguous columns with the 42nd.

They occupied a position more in advance than shown in the

1ST ROYALS.

front and on its right, where Lieut.-Colonel Campbell was Model, and suffered severely from the fire of the French troops on the high ground in front of the Wavre road. Wounded late in the evening.

wounded, where I succeeded to him, and where I remained with the Battalion until carried off the field wounded, late in the evening.

Having served in the Royals from early of the year 1803 until 1823, seen much service with the Regiment, and obtained the Brevet rank of Major for services at St. Sebastian in the 3rd Battalion, I naturally am warmly interested in my old Corps, and I feel very desirous that it should be placed, in your extremely ingenious and handsome Model of the Battle of Waterloo, in the position it occupied on that memorable day.

The returns of killed and wounded will show how severely the 3rd Battalion Royal Scots suffered in that Battle.

I have, &c.,
R. MACDONALD,
Lieut.-Colonel, late of 35th Regiment.

FROM THE SAME.

Southsea House, near Portsmouth, February 14th, 1839.   No. 163.

Quatre Bras.

At or about three o'clock p.m. on the 16th, upon Picton's Division arriving at the top of the hill just above Quatre Bras, where it halted for a short time, the 3rd Battalion Royal Scots was moved away from Pack's Brigade to the left of the high road, and formed in column at quarter distance; moved down a slope to the cross road, and there formed in line under the immediate direction of Sir Thomas Picton and Sir James Kempt. The French were then coming on in force, and the Royals were ordered to advance and attack. They did so, suffering severely both in Officers and men killed and wounded, but succeeded in completely repulsing and driving back the Enemy through several fields of very high corn.

See Plans of Quatre Bras. The Royals moved from the Brigade down to the Namur road and formed in line.

Advance and attack the French successfully, but suffer severely.

After this it was again formed in column, quarter distance, and joined the 28th Regiment also in column,

Joined the 28th in

column, and moved forward against a body of Cavalry. The two Regiments form one square and beat off the Cavalry.

Royals form line again. At dusk rejoin the Brigade.

moved forward to the front and right towards a large body of French Cavalry, accompanied by Sir Thomas Picton and Sir James Kempt. Halted and formed in square (the Royals and 28th), having these two General Officers in its centre; this Square was charged several times, but no impression was made on it, and the Enemy were repulsed with great loss. We then formed line, and remained until nearly dark, when we were ordered to retire and rejoin our Brigade. In so doing we passed through the troops, Cavalry and Infantry, who had come up in the interval. Sir Thomas Picton passed the greater part, if not the whole, of the night (16th) in the field, within a few yards of the Royal Scots.

On the 17th the Battalion is praised by Sir J. Kempt for its gallant conduct the previous day.

On the 17th Sir James Kempt called together the remaining Officers of the 3rd Battalion, and was pleased to express to them his high approbation of their gallantry and conduct, and of that of the men, in the Action of the previous day. But except retiring with the rest of the Division to the position of Waterloo, our rear being protected by the Cavalry, we had no more to do on that day.

Waterloo.

D'Erlon's 1st attack.

Respecting the grand attack of the 18th on Picton's Division when that General was killed, I am of opinion (but I did not refer to my watch) that it took place at an earlier hour than about two o'clock. The 3rd Battalion was in close column, and I, being Captain of the Light Infantry Company, was with it at my post in the rear, the Column being right in front, therefore could not distinctly see whether the Regiment was at all covered in its front; but I believe it was the Royal Dragoons and the Scotch Greys who passed us (I think) by the left of our Column to charge the French Infantry, which they did most gallantly, and on their return, with a large number of prisoners, we cheered them.

D'Erlon's 2nd attack.

After this the Royal Scots were moved forward to the hedge you mention, ordered to form line and lie down. The Enemy came on in a most gallant manner, extended in skirmishing order, spreading on our front and right. Sir Denis Pack, addressing me, said, " Do you think you can

hit those fellows from here ? " I replied, " No, but more
to the right I think they could." The Light Company
were then ordered out to skirmish (*see* N.B.). They were
soon called in, the Battalion formed into open column, and
moved to its right, under a heavy fire of cannon, to the
position I mentioned to you in my letter of December 29th.

I do not know where the other Regiments of Pack's
Brigade were moved, but a considerable time afterwards,
seeing Sir Denis Pack approach, I, being in command, at
the request of the Officers, and seeing we were so much
reduced, went to him to ask our being relieved for a short
time, but he gave me no answer. Upon looking round I
saw the 42nd in column considerably in our rear in
reserve. I recognised them by their bonnets and red
feathers, but the other Regiments near or with them I
could not.

The Battalion suffered severely.

About the time we discerned the Prussians coming on
from the left, part of the 92nd Highlanders came up to our
right; the 28th were then on our immediate left.

I beg to call your attention to the returns of killed
and wounded on the 16th and 18th. I doubt if any
Infantry Regiment there suffered more severely than the
3rd Battalion Royal Scots.

I have, &c.,

R. MACDONALD,

Lieut.-Colonel, late 35th Regiment.

N.B.—My only remaining Subaltern—the other two
having been wounded on the 16th—lost an arm close to me,
the Lieut. Lane who died Barrack Master of Clonmel.

THE 42ND REGIMENT—ROYAL HIGHLANDERS.

COLONEL J. CAMPBELL, C.B.

CAPTAIN AND BREV.-MAJOR 42ND HIGHLANDERS.

TO MAJOR-GENERAL SIR GUY CAMPBELL, BART.

No. 164.   *Liverpool, March 15th, 1838.*

MY DEAR GUY, ...

Quatre Bras. See Plan.

When the 42nd first halted on the road from Brussels, :· was close to some houses on the left. We moved forward, and soon after turned off to the left and formed line, facing

42nd in cornfield in front of the Namur road.

as I have marked on the Plan. I think we were under the rising ground, which I suppose must have been the cornfield with some houses on our right; soon after we were attacked by the Cavalry. We formed square and had some

Formed square when attacked by Cavalry. Retired in square followed by the Cavalry.

fighting. After we retired in square, still followed by the Cavalry, we halted close to a large farmhouse with a wall round it, and were ordered to lay down. The Artillery were immediately behind on a rising ground, and were firing over us. It was Sir John Elly who told us to lay down.

Formed line again and advanced, he thinks.

We formed line, and, I think, advanced, and remained at ordered arms. Many Officers were standing together.

Loss of Officers.

Two [were] mortally wounded, and others slightly. You may recollect Gordon, he was shot through the head and lived till next morning. At that time I don't recollect the Regiments near to us. You say the 92nd were in our rear on the road when we were in the cornfield; in that case, we must have fronted different from what I now suppose. As to the position of the Enemy, they appeared in different Columns with an advance of skirmishers. I don't particularly recollect the white house.

Waterloo.

In close column of Regiments.

When we retired on the 17th and took up our position at Waterloo on the 18th, we were in close column of Regiments. We moved direct to the right, column at half or quarter distance, and returned to the same ground. This movement I

Column moved twice

think we repeated twice, and were under the fire of the

French Artillery the whole time. Towards evening we formed three or four deep and advanced. The Prussian Cavalry passing through the intervals, perhaps more than a section thrown back, we were not particular as to the exact pivot men, any number according to circumstances. On the 16th, after dark, the French occasionally fired some Guns.   .   .   .   .   .   .

Yours affectionately,

J. CAMPBELL.

SERGEANT ALEXANDER McEWEEN,
42ND HIGHLANDERS.

Memorandum.   *No date.*

No. 165.

Quatre Bras.

The 42nd were not a quarter of an hour in the field before they were charged by the Lancers. They must have been at the time a little in advance of the Namur road, expecting the remainder of the Brigade to form upon them. The 44th moved up to the left instead of the right of the 42nd, its proper place. A few skirmishers were out in front. Lancers appeared approaching quietly as if reconnoitring.

42nd immediately charged by the French Lancers.

They were in advance of the Namur road, and to the left of the Charleroi road.

Sergeant McEween said to his commanding Officer, " Those are French Lancers." The latter replied, " No, they belong to the Prince of Orange ! " Sergeant McEween said he was sure they were the 3rd French Lancers, whom he had formerly seen when a prisoner of war. Proposed to fire at them to see what notice they would take of the shot. He fired, and they immediately advanced against the 42nd. The skirmishers ran in with the cry, " Square, Square, French Cavalry ! "

He recognised the Lancers as the 3rd French, fired at them, and they immediately attacked.

The Lancers overtook two Companies in the act of completing the Square. Several of the 42nd were cut off, but a portion of the Lancers became hemmed inside the Square by the remainder of those two Companies, and were instantly bayoneted.

The Brigade formed line and advanced. The 79th skirmishing down by the ditch and hedges in front of the

The Square was not completely formed, and some Lancers got inside, and were bayoneted.

Brigade advanced.

Heavy fire from French skirmishers, and cannonade from their heights.

French position. A great fire from the close skirmishers, and cannonade from the French heights. Retired on perceiving the French Cavalry, and formed squares.

Retired and formed square on perceiving their Cavalry.

Effect of 42nd fire on French Cavalry.

Alternate forming of line and square.

The French Cavalry wore blue *cloaks*. The 42nd observed that the only effect produced on them by their fire was to make the French Dragoons reel back a little in their saddles. A cry was raised, "They are in armour. Fire at their horses!" There was constant repetition by each Regiment of deployment into line and re-formation of square. Sergeant McEween was wounded down at the ditch.

THE 44TH REGIMENT—2ND BATTALION.

COLONEL G. O'MALLEY, C.B., 88TH REGIMENT.

MAJOR AND BREV.-LIEUT.-COLONEL 44TH REGIMENT.

No. 166.

Quatre Bras.

Portsmouth, May 10th, 1837.

.　　.　　.　　.　　.　　.　　.

The charge of the French Lancers upon the rear of the 42nd and 44th.

The Lancers were not recognised as French, except by the old soldiers who fired on them.

When their fire was stopped, the Lancers charged the rear of the line, and through the centre.

See next letter.

One Lancer made a dash at the Colours,

I have the most full and perfect recollection of the charge made at Quatre Bras by the French Lancers upon the rear of the 42nd and 44th Regiments soon after they got clear out of the tall rye and were in line. These Lancers passed on our right flank in pursuit of the Brunswickers, so close that they actually were considered as of the same body, though some of the old soldiers of the 42nd and 44th appeared to know better, as they opened a sort of oblique fire upon them, to check which every possible effort was made by desire of Sir Denis Pack, and when the soldiers were so influenced by Officers, &c., that their fire ceased, these brave French Lancers wheeled short round, and to the astonishment of Sir Denis Pack and myself, they were close in our rear immediately, and through our centre, cutting down several men, as described by Lieut. Riddock, before there was a conviction on the minds of any but the old soldiers who first fired upon them that they were French. One very dashing fellow charged at the Colours, wounding Ensign Christie, who carried one of them, with the lance in the exact manner described by Lieut. R., when Ensign Christie in the most cool and praiseworthy manner dropped the flag to save it, part of which the Lancer actually tore off and possessed himself of, when he was killed, as my recollections serve me, by bayonets of the 44th, with which he was in a manner taken from his horse by the brave men, instead of having been shot as Lieut. R. states. Indeed he might have been shot as well as bayoneted in the manner I describe.

wounding Ensign Christie, who carried one of them, and dropped it to save it. The Lancer tore off a portion of it, but was bayoneted and killed.

The gallantry of this particular Lancer, the gallantry and coolness of the French Lancers altogether, and the great bravery and steadiness of the soldiers of the 42nd and 44th Regiments, both of which Corps at the time were all strangers to me, made such an impression on my mind as never has been, nor never can be, removed. I have to this hour in my possession the part of the flag which the Lancer tore off when he wounded Mr. Christie.

The gallantry of the French Lancers, and also of the 42nd and 44th.

You say " It is not clear from what Lieut. Riddock says whether the Regiment was in line or in column when charged by the Lancers." I am quite certain both 42nd and 44th were in line when charged as described. I have a full recollection of the want of ammunition for a long time, as stated by Lieut. R., and of the great and distressing loss experienced by the 42nd and 44th in consequence thereof. I also know that the 44th had very considerable loss in Officers and men as well as the 42nd, and that both Corps acted together as one Regiment for most part of the day under the immediate command of Sir Denis Pack.

The 42nd and 44th were in line when they were charged. Loss from want of ammunition.

Both Corps acted as one Regiment, under Sir Denis Pack.

.   .   .   .

Believe, &c.,
GEO. O'MALLEY.

LIEUTENANT A. RIDDOCK, HALF-PAY, 44TH REGIMENT.

LIEUTENANT 44TH REGIMENT.

No. 167.   *Kirktown of Deskford, Banffshire, April 11th, 1837.*

. . . .

Quatre Bras.

At this time several Squadrons of French Lancers had got through between the Squares of the right Brigade, and having no reserve to support us, they advanced in regular order at full canter in our rear. We from their appearance supposed them to be Belgians, from their uniform, and having been but a short time in the Action, were still keeping the French Army at bay with the bayonet, when the 2nd Battalion 44th Regiment were attacked in the rear by the Lancers, who were slaughtering our supernumeraries and our rear rank men. This was a critical moment, you may be sure, but with the usual cool and characteristic bravery of the 2nd Battalion 44th Regiment, the rear rank faced right about and repulsed them with great loss. So well directed was the fire that few escaped from our rear.

One of these old grey-headed devils dashed through our centre, sending his lance in at the left eye of the Senior Ensign, James Christie, down through his face until it went through his tongue and under the jaw, [the Lancer] expecting to carry off the Colours. But no, he (Ensign Christie) dashed the Colour down and fell above them [? it]. The fellow was shot a few yards in front of the Regiment.

Immediately after this the Regiment retired, and the other Regiments of the Brigade, about 50 or 60 paces, leaving two Companies, or as many men under the command of an Officer as would cover the front of the Regiment, keeping up a constant fire on the French advanced lines. By this time (four o'clock) our Regiment was reduced to a mere skeleton, having lost in killed and wounded about 16 Officers, and upwards of 200 men.

Margin notes:

The French Cavalry in rear of the 44th mistaken for Belgians.

The 44th in line attacked in the rear by the Lancers.

The rear rank faces about and fires into them, so that few escaped. One Lancer mortally wounds Ensign Christie, and tries to take the Colour from him. The latter throws the Colour to the ground, and falls on it. The Lancer is shot.

It became my duty to command the party in advance (the Regiment and Brigade being in squares), not thirty yards from the French, and I continued in that position until my ammunition was totally exhausted; the French picking my men off as fast as they could load and fire, and our ammunition being intercepted by the frequent and daring charges of the French Cavalry, round and round, and in the rear of our little Squares. I deemed it proper to call the attention of the General, Sir Denis Pack, to the awkward situation my men and I were in; his orders were to close my men to the centre and join my Regiment.

I did so in so far, but ere this time a number of Squadrons of French Cuirassiers and Lancers were sweeping the field in the rear, round and round every Square, showing no mercy, dashing at and sticking the helpless wounded Officers and men that unfortunately lay without the protection of the Square. I could compare them to nothing but a swarm of bees.

At this time I and my men were cut off from the Regiment. I instantly formed four deep and charged bayonets, the rear rank with ported arms, and fought my way through the French Cavalry until I reached the south side of the Square of my Regiment. But so hot and hard pressed was the Regiment on all sides, that I could obtain no admittance, and my ammunition being gone, as before mentioned, we had no other alternative than [to] lie down close to the Square, and crave their friendly protection.

The loss of the French Cavalry at this time, was very great, in proportion to the [loss of] the British Infantry.

. . . .

We were by this time so much reduced in numbers that the 44th could only form into four small Companies, which were now commanded by that brave and meritorious Officer, Lieut.-Colonel O'Malley, now in command of the 88th Regiment. The different Regiments of the Division, although reduced to mere skeletons, kept possession of the ground the French occupied at the commencement of the possession of the ground occupied by the French in the morning.

Action the whole of the afternoon, never giving [way] one inch, although repeatedly charged with Infantry and Cavalry.

Last attack of Cavalry about 6 p.m.

About six o'clock we again sustained a dreadful contest with a host of Cavalry that threatened total destruction, so much so that Sir Denis Pack rode up to the bayonets of the 44th with his hat in his hand waving to cease firing, when Col. O'Malley called out to us, "You are as brave as lions; attend to my orders, and we shall yet repulse them." His orders were attended to, and the firing increased with double vigour, with such effect that no penetration could be effected by the French Cavalry on any point of the British Square.

Lieut.-Col. O'Malley had only joined the Regiment a few days before.—ED.

Great loss of the French Cavalry.

The loss the French Cavalry sustained in this contest was immense; several hundreds of men and horses covered the ground all around us. This was the last charge made by the French Cavalry on the 5th Division for the afternoon, but [it] was succeeded by a hot and destructive fire of musketry and artillery until past eight o'clock p.m.

I have, &c.,

ALEX. RIDDOCK.

THE 92ND REGIMENT—HIGHLANDERS.

MAJOR R. WINCHESTER, 92ND HIGHLANDERS.
LIEUTENANT 92ND HIGHLANDERS.

No. 168.

Fort George, November 24th, 1834.

Waterloo.

Their numbers were about 3,000.—ED.

At the commencement of the Action a Corps of Belgians of from 8,000 to 10,000 men were formed in line in front of the 5th Division, but soon after they were attacked and their skirmishers driven in on their line, the whole of them retired through the 5th Division, and were seen no more during the Action. After this the Enemy made several severe attacks on the 5th Division. About two or three o'clock in the afternoon a Column between 3,000 to 4,000 men advanced to the hedge at the roadside which leads from the main road near La Haye Sainte beyond the left of our position.   Previous to this the 92nd had been lying down under cover of the position when they were immediately ordered to stand to their arms, Major-General Sir Denis Pack calling out at the same time, "92nd, everything has given way on your right and left and you must charge this Column," upon which he ordered four deep to be formed and closed in to the centre. The Regiment, which was then within about 20 yards of the Column, fired a volley into them. The Enemy on reaching the hedge at the side of the road had ordered arms, and were in the act of shouldering them when they received the volley from the 92nd.

D'Erlon's 1st attack on Picton. *See* Plan, p. 38.

Another writer puts it—"92nd, everything has given way in *your front*"— that is, the Belgians had retired.—ED.

The Scots Greys came up at this moment, and doubling round our flanks and through our centre where openings were made for them, both Regiments charged together, calling out "Scotland for ever," and the Scots Greys actually walked over this Column, and in less than three minutes it was totally destroyed, 2,000, besides killed and wounded, of them having been made prisoners, and two of their Eagles captured. The grass field in which the Enemy was formed, which was only an instant before as green and smooth as the 15 acres in Phœnix Park, was in a few minutes covered with killed and wounded, knapsacks and their contents, arms, accoutrements, &c., literally strewed all over, that to avoid stepping on either one or the other was quite impossible ; in fact one could hardly believe, had he not witnessed it, that such complete destruction could have been effected in so short a time.

Charge of the Scots Greys. Enthusiasm of the two Regiments, which charge together.

Appearance of the ground after the charge.

Some of the French soldiers who were lying wounded were calling out "*Vive l'Empereur,*" and others firing their muskets at our men who had advanced past them in pursuit of the flying Enemy.

The Regiment was then recalled and formed on its former ground. Soon afterwards the Enemy commenced

92nd recalled to their former ground.

D'Erlon's
2nd attack.

a cannonade and an attack with his Infantry and Light Troops supported by his Cavalry along our whole line, which continued with little intermission until about the time he made his last great effort near La Haye Sainte, during the greater part of which time the 92nd was formed in square.

92nd moved about 7 p.m. towards the main road.

When the Imperial Guards were advancing at seven o'clock p.m. to attack the left centre near La Haye Sainte, the 92nd Highlanders, who were then near the extreme left of the line, were ordered up to the left of the main road near La Haye Sainte.　They moved in column at quarter distance, and when about half-way between the

A shell falls in the midst of the Column on the march. How its destructive effects were evaded.

left and the road, a shell fell in the midst of the Column. The Companies in rear of it faced about and doubled to the rear until it had burst, then faced about again, and doubled up to their .proper distances from the leading divisions without any word of command having been given.

On arriving at the left of the road, found the troops there engaged in driving the Enemy from the crest of the position which he had gained.

Just as we arrived at the left of the road, our troops were in the act of charging the Enemy and driving them from the crest of our position, which he had gained a short time before.　The rush upon the Enemy was so great that it forced them, together with some of our Guns, from which they had previously driven our gunners, into a sandpit on the left of the road near La Haye Sainte.　Upon this the Enemy retired in great confusion, lining the opposite side of the sandpit, the hedge, and the farm of La Haye Sainte with his skirmishers.

The firing of the Prussians heard.

Lieutenant Winchester wounded and obliged to quit the field.

About this time the fire of the Prussians informed us of their advance from the wood upon the Enemy near Planchenoit.　Soon after this I was wounded and obliged to quit the field.

I have, &c.,

ROBERT WINCHESTER,

Major 92nd Highlanders.

FROM THE SAME.

3, *Upper Dean Terrace, Edinburgh, March 2nd,* 1837.   No. 169.

Agreeably to my promise, I send you a sketch of the position of the troops at Quatre Bras on June 16th, 1815, and a memorandum of the operations of the 92nd Highlanders on that day and the one following.

. . . .

Believe, &c.,
ROBERT WINCHESTER.

Memorandum of the march of the 92nd Highlanders from Brussels to Quatre Bras on June 16th, 1815, and their operations on that day and the day following.

Edinburgh, February 27th, 1837.

The troops in Brussels got under arms between nine and ten o'clock on the evening of June 15th, 1815, and remained upon their private parades until a little before daybreak, when the 5th Division assembled in the park, where several days' biscuit was served out to the troops, and about sunrise they proceeded upon the road which passes through the Forest of Soignies, and were halted upon the skirts of it opposite to the village of Waterloo. While we remained there the Duke of Wellington passed on his way to Marshal Blücher's headquarters at Ligny. *16th June.*

March to Quatre Bras.

During a halt at Waterloo the Duke passes on his way to see Blücher.

Soon after the men had done their cooking and had got their breakfasts the Division moved on Quatre Bras, where it arrived between two and three o'clock in the afternoon. About the time the leading Regiments arrived at Quatre Bras, the Enemy were driving in the Duke of Brunswick's Corps and some Belgians who had been pushed on as far as the village of Frasne, the Enemy at the same time endeavouring to turn their left flank. Our Division in consequence, and without halting, was ordered immediately to deploy to their left to repel this attack, and were at the instant engaged with the Enemy in the wheatfields. *Quatre Bras.*

Arrived between 2 and 3 p.m.

Picton's Division was immediately deployed to the left of Quatre Bras,

92ND HIGHLANDERS.
and engaged
with the
Enemy.

See Plan of
Quatre Bras.

The Duke
ordered the
92nd to form
line on the
Namur road,
with its right
on the
Quatre Bras
houses.

In conse-
quence of the
French
cannonade,
the Duke
ordered the
92nd to lie
down in the
ditch of the
road, and did
the same with
his Staff.

The
Cuirassiers
charge the
92nd still in
line. The
Duke gives
the order when
to fire.

Great loss of
the Cavalry,
which faced
about and
galloped off.

The French
Cavalry
charge again,
with a similar
result.

Incident of a
French Officer
trying to es-
cape by the
rear of the
92nd. The
Duke directs

Somehow or other, the 92nd was the last Regiment of the Division which reached Quatre Bras, and consequently must have been out of its natural order in Brigade; but why it happened to be so I cannot explain, but I have heard it said that it was ordered by the express desire of the Duke of Wellington to take up its station at Quatre Bras. The Division marched on this place left in front.

On the arrival of the 92nd at Quatre Bras, Lord Wellington then desired Colonel Cameron to form line upon the road, with his right resting on the houses at Quatre Bras. His Grace took his station on foot, with his Staff, at the left of the Regiment. By this time the whole of the rest of our troops were warmly engaged with the Enemy. They then opened a cannonade on his Grace, his Staff, and the 92nd from several Guns posted upon the heights at the side of the road leading to Charleroi. The Duke ordered the Regiment to lie down under cover in the ditch, which was in our front at the edge of the road, which he and his Staff did also close to our left.

The French Cuirassiers soon after this, under cover of their Guns, came charging up the fields in front of the Regiment, *which still remained in line.* Lord Wellington, who was by this time in rear of the centre of the Regiment, said, " 92nd, don't fire until I tell you," and when they came within twenty or thirty paces of us, his Grace gave the order to fire, which killed and wounded an immense number of men and horses, on which they immediately faced about and galloped off.

Shortly afterwards they formed again, and, accompanied by a body of Light Dragoons, charged up again in our front. They were all allowed to come within about the same distance as before, when we fired as formerly, and the same result was effected, causing great loss to them in killed and wounded. At this time a French Officer of Light Dragoons, thinking his men were still following him, got too far to be able to retire by the way he had advanced, galloped down the road in the rear of our Regiment. The Duke of Wellington observing him, called out, " Damn it,

92nd, will you allow that fellow to escape?" Some of the men turned immediately round, fired, killed his horse, and a musket ball at the same time passed through each foot of the gallant young Officer. I was afterwards billeted with him in the same house at Brussels for six months, and then went with him to Paris, where I received much kind attention from him—Monsieur Burgoine—and his family.

The Regiment was soon again charged by two other Columns of Cavalry, supported by two Columns of Infantry. We fired on the Cavalry when they came within the usual distance, and dispersed them with great loss. The Duke then said, "Now 92nd, you must charge these two Columns of Infantry." We instantly leaped over the ditch, headed by Sir Edward Barnes and other Officers of the Duke's Staff, and Colonel Cameron. We drove them in an instant behind some houses and garden walls, where they ran for shelter, from which we also speedily drove them. Here Colonel Cameron received his mortal wound, on which he lost the power of managing his horse. The animal turned round and galloped with all his speed along the road until he reached Quatre Bras, where Colonel Cameron's groom was standing with his led horse. The horse then suddenly stopping, pitched the Colonel on his head on the road.

Following them across the Charleroi road, we continued to drive them before us for a considerable distance along the skirts of the wood situated to the right of Quatre Bras, and in the angle of the roads which led to Nivelles and Charleroi. During our advance the Enemy kept upon us a heavy cannonade, but when we had got as far as the elbow of the wood, we retired into it. As the Enemy was making a disposition to charge us with Cavalry, we maintained our position there until we were relieved by the Guards in the evening. We were then ordered to retire through the wood, and form behind the houses at Quatre Bras, where we remained all night, and cooked our provisions in the cuirasses which had belonged to the French Cuirassiers whom we had killed only a few hours before.

Great losses
of the 92nd.

In these operations the 92nd lost four Officers killed,
Colonel Cameron and another Officer mortally wounded, and
upwards of one-half of the rest of the Corps killed and
wounded. Sir Thomas Picton, to whose Division we
belonged, on returning to the rear in the evening after the
Action was over, not knowing then that we had been
engaged till he saw the remains of the Regiment, when he
inquired what this was, he was told it was the 92nd, on
which he asked, " Where is the rest of the Regiment? "
Brevet Lieut.-Colonel Mitchell being wounded soon after
Colonel Cameron was, the command of the Regiment
devolved on Major Donald McDonald, which he held
during the remainder of the Action, and on the two days
following.

Previous reports in
Brussels as to
Napoleon's
Cavalry.

Lieut. Winchester found
cuirasses
pierced by
musket balls
through both
breast and
back plates, as
well as the
man's body.

During this night, the 16th, and the following morning, the Duke of Wellington's Army was concentrated at
Quatre Bras. Previous to our advance it was reported in
Brussels that Napoleon had equipped a body of horsemen
in armour impervious to musketry, and would consequently
break all our Squares of Infantry. But so far from this
being the case, I observed on going over the Field of Battle
on the morning of the 17th, that our musket balls had not
only gone through the front plate, but the man's body and
also the plate of armoury behind.

17th June.
Blücher's supposed position
at Sombref
found to be
occupied by
the Enemy.

Apprehensions in the
Duke's Army.

Ascertained
that Napoleon
was moving
troops on the
Allied left.

I understood, after Blücher had been defeated at Ligny
on June 16th, that it was so arranged that he was to take
up a position at Sombref, where he would have been in
communication with the left of the Duke of Wellington's
Army. But on the morning of the 17th, when the Duke
sent a patrol of Cavalry to communicate there with
Blücher, it was found to be occupied by the Enemy, and no
one then in our Army had the most distant idea what had
become of Blücher and his Army. At this unexpected
intelligence the greatest consternation pervaded the whole
of the Duke's Army. About this time it was ascertained
that Napoleon was moving several large bodies of troops to
our right [? left].

After the Duke had heard that Blücher was not to be

found at Sombref, I saw his Grace with the Prussian or Austrian Envoy, I forget which, who was attached to his Grace's Headquarters, with his hands in his pantaloon pockets, pacing quickly backward and forward, now and then suddenly stopping, talking to the Envoy very loud and with much animation.

Between seven and eight o'clock on the morning [of the] 17th, the Duke had received intelligence that Blücher was retiring with his Army on Wavre, on hearing which his Grace immediately put his Infantry in motion to take up a new position upon the heights near Waterloo, and in front of the village of Mont-St.-Jean. The 92nd formed the rear guard to the Infantry, the Cavalry of Lord Uxbridge covering the movements of the whole.

Intelligence being received of Blücher's retreat on Wavre, the Army is ordered to retire.

Retreat on the position of Waterloo.

On the arrival of the 92nd near the house of La Belle Alliance, we were relieved by a Corps of Foreign troops, I believe they were the Duke of Nassau's. Before we reached our place in position, the Enemy were on the heights at La Belle Alliance cannonading us, and his Cavalry and Infantry were then engaged with our advanced troops. Shortly after this the pickets were posted, and the firing ceased on both sides. This must have been between six and seven o'clock in the evening.

ROBERT WINCHESTER,
Major 92nd Highlanders.

LAMBERT'S INFANTRY BRIGADE.

The 10th Infantry Brigade consisted of the 4th Regiment, King's Own, the 27th Regiment, Inniskillings, and the 40th Regiment. It was under the command of Major-General Sir John Lambert, K.C.B.

The Brigade arrived at Waterloo on the morning of the 18th June, by forced marches from Ghent, and was placed in reserve in rear of the farm of Mont-St.-Jean, and when Ponsonby's Cavalry advanced to charge D'Erlon's Columns, it was moved forward and placed on the left of the Brussels road, in rear and in support of Picton's Division.

About three in the afternoon it was brought up to the front line, and stationed with Kempt's Brigade in rear of the Wavre road, and to the left of the Brussels *chaussée*. Upon the capture of La Haye Sainte by the French, and their consequent occupation of the knoll and high ground in front of the Wavre road, and the advanced position of their troops on the other side of the *chaussée*, the Brigade, like Kempt's, became exposed to a most destructive fire.

See General Plan, No. 2.

Previous to the attack of the Imperial Guards on the British right centre, the 4th Regiment was (with the 95th) extended along the front edge of the Wavre road, commencing from the *chaussée*, and the 40th (with the remainder of Kempt's Brigade) was deployed behind the embanked hedge on the rear side of that road.

The 27th was posted in square in the angle formed by the two roads, having one face parallel with, and close to the *chaussée*, for the purpose of throwing a flank fire on the French Troops, should they succeed in advancing further on the opposite side of it, as appeared very probable, or of pouring a close fire into any Column endeavouring to penetrate the position by the high road itself.

The French crowd of skirmishers on the other side of the *chaussée*, seeing this formation of the 27th, opened such a close and deadly fire on the

Regiment, that in a few minutes it lost more than half its numbers. On the defeat of the Imperial Guards, the French were speedily driven, and hastily retreated, from their positions in and near La Haye Sainte, which was taken possession of by Lambert's Brigade together with the 1st Royals.

All the letters refer to Waterloo.

LIEUT.-GENERAL SIR JOHN LAMBERT, G.C.B.

MAJOR-GENERAL AND K.C.B., COMMANDING 10TH INFANTRY BRIGADE.

3, Harley Street, December 18th, 1834.　　No. 170.

. . . .

The 6th Division, agreeable to the General Order dated Brussels, May 21, 1815, was composed of the 10th British Brigade and the 4th Hanoverian Brigade, with the 7th British Brigade of Artillery. The 10th Brigade was laying at Ghent, and did not receive orders to move until the 17th, and various unavoidable circumstances prevented its arrival at the village of Waterloo until ten o'clock on the morning of the 18th, when it received orders to take up its position at Mont-St.-Jean. *The Brigade arrived at Waterloo at 10 a.m. on the 18th.*

Posted at first at Mont-St.-Jean in reserve.

After the Enemy had been repulsed in its first attempt on the British line, about twelve o'clock, the Brigade was ordered into its position in the line which I have marked on the Plan. The formation of the Brigade about the period you name (viz., seven o'clock p.m.) was the right Regiment (27th) in square and the other Regiments in line, and the Hanoverian Brigade, which had fallen back about one hundred yards, in squares of Regiments (4). *After D'Erlon's 1st [? 2nd] attack was moved up to the position.*

At 7 p.m. the Brigade was in line, except the 27th in square on the right.

The great effort of the Enemy in his last attack was on the right of the road leading from Brussels to Genappe. They advanced upon the left in line, but never came up to the crest of the position, as they had done in two previous attacks. When they commenced retiring on the right, an *See General Plan, No. 2.*

When the Imperial

Guard attacked on the right, D'Erlon did not advance so far as in the two previous attacks.

Brigade joined in the General Advance.

This was an artificial mound about sixty yards in front of the hollow way on the other side of the main road.—ED.

See Note, p. 396.

order arrived for the whole Line to advance. They were driven out of the farm of La Haye Sainte by the 6th Division, and the line was not halted until it reached the Belle Alliance, where it took its position for the night.

Regarding the nature of the ground, it was all arable, very deep from the heavy rain that had fallen during the preceding night. On looking at the plan, I would observe that the road to Wavre from the Brussels road is a *sunken* road, *i.e.*, with high banks and a hedge on either side, and also the high road from Brussels to Genappe, in the position, had high banks; and likewise, after the Enemy got possession of the Haye Sainte, they kept constantly sending small detachments to a mound close to the intersection of the Brussels road to Genappe, which forced the Hanoverian Brigade of the 6th Division to fall back, and which would have allowed the Enemy to advance if it had not been for the Square of the 27th Regiment, as its position will point out. This mound should appear, it strikes me, as it was so important in that part of the line, and so honourable and fatal to the 27th Regiment, which kept its formation and lost more men and Officers than any Regiment during the day, and would otherwise have afforded an opportunity to the Enemy to have made an impression in a very serious part of the Line.

I remain, &c.,

JOHN LAMBERT,

Lieut.-General.

FROM THE SAME.

No. 171.　　　　　　　　　　2, *Harley Street, April 2nd*, 1836.

.　　.　　.　　.　　.　　.　　.

The 10th Brigade did not move to the front until after the first attack on our left had commenced; therefore I cannot speak to the movements of Sir Wm. Ponsonby's Brigade, or Sir Thomas Picton's Division, excepting that on my Brigade coming up, we found the Division already engaged with the Enemy, the bayonets nearly touching.

D'Erlon's 2nd attack.

After the Enemy had been driven back in this attack the 10th Brigade remained in front, and the 32nd was placed in reserve. The object of the 27th Regiment (where I chiefly was) being in square was that its right resting on the high road to Genappe, to show a front parallel to the road, and offer a flank fire, should the Enemy advance on the other side of this road. Regarding the Belgians I can say nothing. Object of the 27th being in square.

When the General Advance was ordered, at half-past seven, I do not recollect that the Enemy made any stand at the Haye Sainte; all that could get away retired, leaving it full of wounded, and many prisoners were made there. At the General Advance the Enemy made no stand at La Haye Sainte.

. . . .

I remain, &c.,

JOHN LAMBERT, L.G.

THE 4TH REGIMENT—KING'S OWN.

MAJOR J. BROWNE, UNATTACHED.

LIEUTENANT 4TH REGIMENT.

Barnes, Surrey, April 21st, 1835.   No. 172.

. . . .

As for the gallant Regiment to which I had the honour to belong, it marched into its position, *band playing* and Colours flying, about half-past eight o'clock in the morning of the 18th. I was a Lieutenant in it at the time, though my Company was antedated to January. I was twice wounded, though rather slightly, during the early part of the day. Waterloo. The 4th marched into position, band playing and Colours flying. Twice slightly wounded early in the day.

About the period of the Battle selected for representation on your Model, I received a severe wound in the head, and remained on the field 19 hours, supposed to have been killed. At the time I was shot (by Col. Brooke's letter to my mother) we were marching forward to charge the Enemy. The 4th, 27th, and 40th Regiments were in the same Brigade under the command of Sir J. Lambert. At 7 p.m. severely wounded in the head as the Regiment was marching to charge the Enemy.

4TH REGIMENT.

The 4th the only Regiment present which had returned from the American War; very weak in consequence.

The 4th Regiment being the only Regiment of the American Army which was in the Field, it had very few Officers or men, no Field Officer (as Colonel Brooke commanded the Brigade), only two Captains, one of whom commanded the Regiment.   .   .   .

I also fancy that Regimental Officers, and more particularly Company Officers, have little time or opportunity of knowing anything beyond their own Division or Brigade, and that the smoke, the bustle, which I fear is almost inseparable to Regiments when close to the Enemy, and more particularly the attention which is required from the Company Officers to their men, intercepts all possibility of their giving any correct account of the battles in which they may be engaged.

.   .   .   .

I have, &c.,
J. BROWNE,
Major Unattached.

MAJOR C. LEVINGE.

LIEUTENANT 4TH REGIMENT.

No. 173.

Edinburgh, April 26th, 1835.

Major Levinge presents his compliments to Mr. Siborne, and would have answered his letter of the 24th February had he been able to give any information of consequence, but as the 4th Regiment only arrived on the ground of Waterloo just before the Action commenced, and early next morning continued their march, he had but little opportunity of observing much of the ground, which was much trodden down before their arrival.

Waterloo.

4th extended for best part of day with 95th along Wavre road. Early in the day charged to the hedgerow.

The 4th Regiment was extended the principal part of the day with 1st Battalion Rifles along the narrow road near La Haye Sainte. Early in the Action they charged to the hedge over the grand pit, but soon were ordered to retire to the road.

THE 27TH REGIMENT—INNISKILLINGS.

CAPTAIN E. W. DREWE, 95TH REGIMENT.

LIEUTENANT 27TH REGIMENT.

Memorandum.   *No date.* No. 174.

It appears to me that there is some confusion of the No. of the Brigade in which the 27th was with that of the Division. The 4th, 27th, and 40th Regiments formed the 1st Brigade of the 5th [? 6th] Division, which was being formed for Sir Lowry Cole. This Brigade was the only part of the American Army that had joined the force under the Duke, and had been quartered at Ghent as guard on Louis XVIII. Sir John Lambert commanded it.

At a late hour on the night of the 15th June we Waterloo. received a sudden route, and by forced marches reached the forest side of the village of Waterloo about six o'clock on the morning of the 18th June. Were occupied some time in clearing the road of provision carts containing bread, forage, and spirits that had been left on the road by the peasantry taking their animals from the carts, and concealing themselves in the wood.

After this very essential job was completed the Brigade moved towards the front, passing the village and review of the Duke, who stood in a balcony on the left side of it, going towards the Field of Battle. When we had passed the village we were directed to proceed towards the left of the Army, but had not gone far in this direction until we were countermanded and desired to occupy the ground in In the morn-rear, that is the village side of Mont-St.-Jean, as a reserve ing the of column of Companies. In this order arms were piled, stationed in and the men lay down, and many of them continued to reserve near sleep until a short time past three o'clock p.m. This Jean. position was taken up about eleven o'clock a.m., and immediately the Battle began on the right towards Hougoumont, and gradually extended towards the left, apparently

extremely hot in the centre on each side of the road leading towards La Haye Sainte and about the Wavre road
that crossed to the left.

Our men continued as before described quite unconscious
and apparently careless of the part they were shortly about
to take. Several of them were wounded by a few
straggling shot that passed from the Enemy over or
through our advanced lines, and a few killed.

About quarter past 3 p.m. it was ordered up into the front line.

At about quarter past three o'clock the welcome and
anxiously sought for tidings to advance reached us,
when every man grasped his firelock and moved forward
with a decided, firm, and confident step, passing close to
and by the left of Mont-St.-Jean, crossing the short valley,
and proceeded to ascend the gradual rising ground on the
left of the Brussels road and close to the cross road leading
towards Wavre. On reaching this station we formed
columns of Companies at quarter distance left flank to the
Enemy—the 4th Regiment on the right, the 40th on the
left, and both considerably in rear of the 27th, which
accounts for the few casualties in those Corps, comparatively
speaking, with the 27th, as they were in a great measure
covered by the rising ground in front, whilst the 27th was
exposed from being on the highest ground to all that
came.

The 27th in front, the 4th and 40th in rear.

The 27th most exposed from being on higher ground.

Received his third wound previous to the General Advance.

I had received my third wound about a quarter before
seven o'clock, and was then carried from the field, and just
previous to the formation of the line to meet the advancing
French Guards, who I believe were advancing in columns
of Brigades and Corps; but not having seen these manœuvres
I don't like to speak from hearsay.

E. W. DREWE.

NOTE.—Out of a total strength of 698, the 27th had two Officers killed,
and thirteen wounded, 103 N.C.O.'s and men killed, and 360 wounded, or
a total loss of 478.—ED.

FROM THE SAME (MAJOR).

Valetta House, July 23rd, 1842.   No. 175.

Lambert's Brigade, consisting of the 4th, 27th, and 40th, did not reach the front line until nearly four o'clock. It was in reserve from the commencement of the Battle, namely about quarter past eleven a.m. until three p.m., when it was called to the front, passing the rear of the farm house.

Waterloo. Lambert's Brigade in reserve from the commencement of the Battle till 3 p.m.

When we reached the prominent part of the ground, on the left of the road leading from the village towards La Belle Alliance, the 95th Regiment, I believe four Companies, occupied a small fence considerably in front, having a few unconnected trees (thorns) in it. We, the 27th, being in the centre of the Brigade, occupying the highest part of the ground close to the road, as we were considerably in advance of either the 4th or 40th. The other two Corps being in a great degree concealed by rising ground from the destructive fire to which my Regiment was exposed, whilst in square and at times in columns of Companies at quarter distance.

On Brigade coming to the front, 27th occupied highest ground close to road, and in advance of 4th and 40th, which were less exposed.

The attacks to which you alluded were made previous to the advance of Lambert's Brigade, and the greatest portion of the Enemy's Column were made prisoners from a feint having been made in our line; the part of the Column not taken did move in the direction of Kempt's Brigade, but they were at no time charged by Lambert's Brigade from the reasons I have already given, we being distant spectators of the Battle until three p.m.

27th much exposed in either square or quarter distance column. D'Erlon's 1st attack previous to advance of Lambert's Brigade.

I feel a degree of diffidence in speaking so decidedly in contradiction to the deceased Officer's letter of the 4th mentioned in your note; I, however, do so from personal observation and recollections, which are as vivid to me at the present moment as they were on the 18th June.   I am, &c.,

EDWD. WARD DREWE.

THE 40TH REGIMENT.

LIEUT.-COL. F. BROWNE, HALF-PAY, RIFLE, BRIGADE.

MAJOR 40TH REGIMENT.

No. 176.   *Winchelsea, May 6th,* 1835.

Waterloo.

At the moment when the French Imperial Guards advanced to attack the British position, the 40th Regiment, which had previously, and mostly throughout the day, been in square against Cavalry, were formed in line, and thus quickly advanced to the brow of the hill, where there was a low and somewhat broken down hedge, short of which we halted and over which we fired. There were a few large trees here and there along the hedge, particularly on our side of it, the branches of which were much cut and lopt by cannon shot; but of what description the trees were I cannot now recollect.

The 40th Regiment was lining the hedge of the Wavre road.

A column of Alix' Division, D'Erlon's Corps.

A heavy Column of French Infantry was advancing; at the moment I observed them they were rather in front of the farmhouse of La Haye Sainte, by, I believe, the left of it, as we faced the house; they having then crossed the road. The divisions of the Column appeared to me to be at about quarter distances.

La Haye Sainte was to the right front of the 40th.

The 40th was formed rather *facing* the house, the latter being a *little* to the right of the Regiment, but more in front of us. There were several other similar Columns advancing at the same time upon different points of our position, both to the right and left of the house; and much Cavalry were congregating or re-forming in the, or more properly speaking, that part of the Enemy's position which artists would term the middle distance. In the extreme distance was the Observatory (the key of the French position).

To the right of the house and near it, was a bank or small hill, which was occupied by the head of a French Column halted, but not very regularly formed. I think they had been driven back from their attempt to ascend the hill, partly by our fire, and partly by that of the troops on our right; but the cloud of smoke in which we were almost constantly enveloped prevented me from discovering their object in remaining there thus exposed, which they did in the most dauntless and daring manner; as fast as they fell their places were supplied with fresh troops, until the General Advance of the British, when they retired. Whilst we were in this situation, boxes of ammunition were placed at intervals along our rear, from about fifty to one hundred paces from us, so that the men could help themselves when they required it.

During the action, there was a Highland Brigade very much reduced (I think the 42nd and 97th—[92nd], and another regiment, which I cannot recollect) moved up, I believe from the left, and formed in close columns or solid squares upon our left, but something to the rear of us; after we had finally advanced to the hedge, as I have mentioned, I did not observe which flank they had again moved upon, but in looking to our rear for a moment I observed that they were gone.

Our Brigade, under Sir John Lambert, consisted of the 4th, 27th, and 40th Regiments (observe, that the 27th under Col. Hare consisted of seven Companies only, viz., the Light, and six Battalion; the Grenadiers, and the two other Battalion Companies had not arrived), the 4th properly on the right, the 27th on the left, and the 40th in the centre. But we had changed our ground so often throughout the day, that we could not always observe the same order; the 27th being sometimes on our right, and the 4th on the left; the 40th also occasionally to the right or left of the Brigade whilst in close columns or squares, but when in line always in our proper places. There were also some Belgian troops (particularly Cavalry with yellow jackets) in our neighbourhood, and in the rear of our flanks.

Advance of the Prussians.

The Prussian army had appeared, about an hour previous to our final advance to the hedge, debouching from the wood some considerable distance to the left of our position, but nearer to that of the French; and were rapidly advancing along the plain, having previously attacked, and were then in the act of turning the Enemy's right. This, I presume, was the occasion of the confusion, which was at that time so manifest in the Enemy's lines, and amongst several of his Divisions, and which the Duke of Wellington so promptly took advantage of.

I have, &c.,

FIELDING BROWNE,

Lieut.-Col. H.P., Rifle Brigade.

COLONEL S. STRETTON, HALF-PAY.

CAPTAIN AND BREV.-MAJOR 40TH REGIMENT.

No. 177.   *Lenton Priory, Notts, February 7th,* 1837.

Replies to Lieutenant Siborne's inquiries on the subject of the Battle of Waterloo, by Colonel Stretton, then Brevet-Major 40th Regiment, in charge of the left wing of that Corps.

Waterloo.

40th commanded by Major Heyland, who was killed, twelve other Officers and 180 men killed and wounded.

The Regiment went into action on the morning of the 18th June, about 720 rank and file, commanded by Major Heyland; their loss on that day was—Major Heyland, killed, twelve other Officers and 180 men killed and wounded.

Formation of the Enemy at 7 p.m.

Double line of skirmishers on the knoll and high ground in front of the Wavre road.

The formation of the Enemy's force immediately in our front was a double line of tirailleurs, supported by a heavy Column of Infantry; the former had possession of a rising ground on the opposite side of the road to the farm of La Haye Sainte, who, whilst laying down, appeared to select their objects with great precision. It appeared to me that this force formed the French line which, supported as above, charged our front that evening, as some of them were bayoneted *close* to our front rank.

The field, immediately about the 40th, was thickly scattered with horses and men of the French Cavalry, who repeatedly charged our Squares (without making any impression), and who, passing and returning between the Squares of the 40th, 27th, and 4th Regiments, suffered severely from the fire of each.

On the left of the 40th at the commencement of the Action, were a Rocket Brigade, and one of Artillery; the tumbril of the latter was blown up by a shell from the Enemy, and both were silenced before the close of the Action, by the numerous Artillery of the French.

The formation of the 40th at the period when the French Imperial Guards advanced to attack the right of the British force was in line, having previously repulsed the Enemy's Cavalry in Square.

The 40th was in line at the last attack of the French.

When the British line moved forward, the 40th drove the Tirailleurs from the rising ground in its front, and occupied it; at the same time the 27th, with Grenadiers of the 40th, took possession of the farm of La Haye Sainte, in which they made prisoners of a General Officer and a party of the Enemy.

The 40th drove the skirmishers from their front and occupied the high ground.

The 27th, with the Grenadiers of the 40th, took possession of La Haye Sainte.

Towards the evening, whilst the Regiment was in open column, a round shot from the Enemy took off the head of a Captain (Fisher) near me, and striking his Company on the left flank, put *hors de combat* more than twenty-five men. This was the most destructive shot I ever witnessed during a long period of service.

Destructive effects of a round shot.

The 4th Regiment was upon the left of the 40th, the 27th upon its right, part of the right wing of the latter was upon the main road.

. . . .

S. STRETTON,
Colonel H.P., late Major 40th Regt.

MAJOR P. BISHOP, UNATTACHED.

CAPTAIN 40TH REGIMENT.

No. 178.

Waterloo.

The 40th in
the General
Advance.

The Duke
cheered by the
Regiment.

Leamington Spa, April 30th, 1835.

I think about seven o'clock on the evening of the 18th, the 40th Regiment had formed into line, after having just charged the Enemy, in which we lost several Officers and men, and amongst them Major Heyland (our then Commanding Officer). The Duke of Wellington came up to us at the moment, and we gave him three hearty cheers. I was, from circumstances, in command of the Regiment at the time.

We were in Sir John Lambert's Brigade, and Sir Lowry Cole's Division, and upon the right of the road leading from Brussels to Genappe, and nearly in line with Hougoumont.

I am, &c.,

P. BISHOP,

Major, Unattached, late 40th Regt.

LA HAYE SAINTE.

The two following Letters are from Major Græme, a Scotch officer, who was a Lieutenant in the King's German Legion, and took part in the gallant defence of La Haye Sainte. No. 180, however, contains only a short extract from the original Letter.

The buildings of this Farm were so disposed as to form three sides of a square. On the north (or British) side was the Farm-house itself, with a portion of the Stabling; on the west side the remainder of the Stables and Cow-houses; and on the south (or French) side a large Barn.

A brick wall, extending along the great road,

united the north and south Buildings, and completed the quadrangle. About the centre of this wall was the lean-to called the "piggery." The Orchard was at the south, and the Kitchen Garden at the north end of the Buildings.

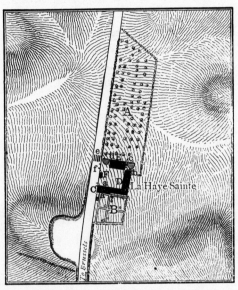

A, Orchard; *B*, Kitchen Garden; *C*, Dwelling-house; *D*, Stables; *E*, Barn; *F* 'Piggery'; *a a*, Passage through house; *b*, Gate of Stables; *c*, Door of Barn *d*, Pond; *e*, Abatis; *f*, Great Gate in Wall.

A large gate opened, nearly opposite the end of the barn, through the boundary wall on to the road, as did also a doorway close to the end of the dwelling-house. There was another gate in the end of the Stables, and a large door in the nearest end of the barn, both opening out into the fields. There was a passage right through the dwelling-house, leading from the farmyard into the kitchen garden. An *abatis* had been formed across the high road at the south end of the boundary wall.

The great barn door had been broken up for firewood the previous evening, and means for putting the Buildings in a proper state of defence were utterly wanting. The post was held by Major Baring with six Companies of the 2nd Light Battalion of the King's German Legion, of which he placed three in the orchard, two in the buildings, and one in the garden.

At the time of D'Erlon's first advance on Picton's Division, one Brigade was moved to attack La Haye Sainte. The Companies in the orchard retired before superior forces into the barn. The garden in rear of the house was also surrounded by the Enemy, and the Company stationed in it retired into the buildings, which were successfully defended against the assaults of the French, who retired on the repulse of D'Erlon's attack, and that of the Cavalry combined with it.

The post was now reinforced by two more Companies, and the defence was limited to that of the buildings and garden, the orchard being abandoned.

After some time it was again furiously attacked by the French, who made the greatest efforts to push through by the open door of the barn, but the fire of the Germans was so destructive that the French left seventeen dead on the spot.

Meantime, the ammunition of the defenders was becoming very much exhausted, and Major Baring sent repeated messages for a fresh supply, but he only obtained reinforcements.

The Enemy again attacked with the same determination as before, and finding they could not effect an entrance into the barn, set fire to it. The only means of extinguishing the flames were by taking water with the men's camp kettles from the pond, but in doing so the Germans were much exposed and suffered great loss. They succeeded, however, in putting out the fire, and the French once more withdrew.

Towards evening the ammunition of the defenders began to fail utterly. The Enemy again advanced to the attack, in two Columns. They again set fire to the barn, and the flames were extinguished as before. Major Baring now sent to the rear urgently requesting a supply of ammunition, failing which he must necessarily abandon his post.

The French forced their way through the gate into the stables, but the door from thence into the yard being barricaded, few could enter at a time, and were instantly bayoneted. They now climbed on to the roof of the stables, from whence they picked off the Germans, who, from want of cartridges, were at their mercy.

Major Baring then gave the order to retire through the passage in the dwelling-house into the garden, and ultimately to the main position.

MAJOR G. D. GRÆME, K.H., HANOVERIAN SERVICE.

Lieutenant 2nd Light Battalion K.G.L.

No. 179.   *Inchbrakie, Crieff, December 6th,* 1842.

I fear my memory does not serve me so as to give you any material information on the subject, but I have endeavoured to the best of my power to answer your queries.

Believe, &c.,

George Drumd. Græme.

La Haye Sainte.

At time of D'Erlon's first attack no French Cavalry on left of the farm.

First stationed behind *abatis*, afterwards on roof of piggery.

French attacked Picton with thick line of skirmishers in front of Columns.

Defenders of the farm fired on them as they advanced.

In retreating, French near La Haye Sainte were followed by 2nd Life Guards pursuing some Cuirassiers.

None passed through *abatis*.

Ground literally covered with

In the first attack I perceived *no* French Cavalry on the British left of the farm of La Haye Sainte. I was favourably situated, and think I must have seen them had there been any, being placed with a section of our Rifles behind the *abatis* across the high road a little in front of the great gate of the farm, afterwards with about a dozen men on the top of the "*piggery?*" (there was a calf in it!)

The [French] Infantry came down in heavy columns with a line of skirmishers as thick almost as an advancing line of our troops. When close upon us we entered the farm, and closed the gates, and poured a constant fire on their Columns as they passed us, and even until they were up on the crest of the British position, when they were repulsed and broken by the British line, and repassed us like a flock of sheep, followed by the Life Guards, who came down the hollow road or sandpits, pursuing some French Cuirassiers (who, I presume, had been separated from their Regiment in the rear or to the right of our farm). A party of our men sallied out and pursued in the crowd a considerable way up towards Belle Alliance. None passed *through* our *abatis*, as we afterwards returned, and I placed my men behind it as before.

The ground was literally covered with French killed and wounded, even to the astonishment of my oldest soldiers, who said they had never witnessed such a sight. The French wounded were calling out "*Vive l'Empereur,"* and I saw a poor fellow, lying with both his legs shattered, trying to destroy himself with his own sword, which I ordered my servant to take from him.

French killed and wounded.

At this moment a curious circumstance occurred. Both Armies were quiet in their positions, and the Artillery had ceased firing, when we perceived a single French Cuirassier riding down the *chaussée* towards us. As he approached he waved with his sword, so that I said he must be a deserter, and would not allow my men to fire. He rode close up to the *abatis*, and raising himself in his stirrups as looking tó see what was behind it, then wheeled round his horse, and galloped back to the French position, and in the hurry I believe the gallant fellow luckily escaped our shots which were sent after him.

Exploit of a single Cuirassier.

The French came down obliquely towards the farm in the first attack, over the fields as well as down the high road. A large Column was all day in the rear [? front] of the farm, and trying to get possession of the barn, the door of which was open towards our right. They never tried to escalade, and we kept them off the great gate by firing from the piggery (where I was placed most of the day), although the *abatis* served them for cover, unfortunately.

The Frerch trying to get possession of the Barn.

They never tried to escalade the boundary wall.

I saw no *Sapeurs*. We had no loopholes excepting three great apertures, which we made with difficulty when we were told in the morning that we were to defend the farm. Our Pioneers had been sent to Hougoumont the evening before. We had no scaffolding, nor means of making any, having burnt the carts, &c. Our loopholes, if they may be thus termed, were on a level with the road on the outside, and later in the day the Enemy got possession of the one near the pond, and fired in upon us. This they also did during the first attack on the roadside.

He saw no French Sappers.

There was no scaffolding, only a few big holes instead of loopholes in wall. These holes on a level with road, and from one of them the French fired on parties carrying water from pond.

. . . .

I may add that the barn was filled with straw, and it was a fortunate circumstance that it was all carried off by the different troops during the night, the French

repeatedly having tried during the attack to set it on fire.
Lieut. Carey, in spite of the Enemy's fire, went out, and
with his men, poured water on the flames.

FROM THE SAME.

No. 180.   *Inchbrakie, Crieff, December 6th,* 1842.

Mrs. Græme encloses a letter giving an account of the
Battle of Waterloo, written by her husband with his left
hand, then being at the age of eighteen; which may be
interesting, as written at the moment; but which she
requests may be carefully and speedily returned, as to her
it is of considerable value.

La Haye
Sainte.

The retreat of
the defenders
through the
passage in the
house.

Ensign Frank
saves Lieut.
Græme from
being shot by
a French
soldier.

Ensign Frank
wounded and
concealed
under a bed
during time
French were
in possession.

Another
account says
that two men
took refuge in
the same
room, and
were shot by
the French,
saying, "*Pas
de pardon à ces
coquins verds.*"
—Ed.

Lieut. Græme
taken prisoner,

Extract.   *June,* 1815.

We had all to pass through a narrow passage. We
wanted to halt the men and make one more charge, but
it was impossible; the fellows were firing down the
passage. An Officer of our Company called to me, "Take
care," but I was too busy stopping the men, and answered,
"Never mind, let the blackguard fire." He was about
five yards off, and levelling his piece just at me, when
this Officer stabbed him in the mouth and out through
his neck; he fell immediately.

But now they flocked in; this Officer got two shots,
and ran into a room, where he lay behind a bed all the
time they had possession of the house; sometimes the
room was full of them, and some wounded soldiers of
ours who lay there and cried out "pardon" were shot,
the monsters saying, "Take that for the fine defence you
have made."

An Officer and four men came first in; the Officer got
me by the collar, and said to his men, "*C'est ce coquin.*"
Immediately the fellows had their bayonets down, and
made a dead stick at me, which I parried off with my
sword, the Officer always running about and then coming
to me again and shaking me by the collar; but they all

MAJOR GRÆME

looked so frightened and pale as ashes, I thought, "You shan't keep me," and I bolted off through the lobby; they fired two shots after me, and cried out *"Coquin,"* but did not follow me.

but escapes and rejoins his Battalion,

I rejoined the remnant of the Regiment, when we were immediately charged by Cuirassiers. All the Army was formed in squares. We hastily got our men into a hollow, and peppered them so, I believe they found the cuirass not thick enough for rifles.

Which beats off the Cuirassiers by firing from the hollow way.

.   .   .   .

(Was wounded soon afterwards in right arm.)

Wounded later in right arm.

THE END.

INDEX.

───◆───